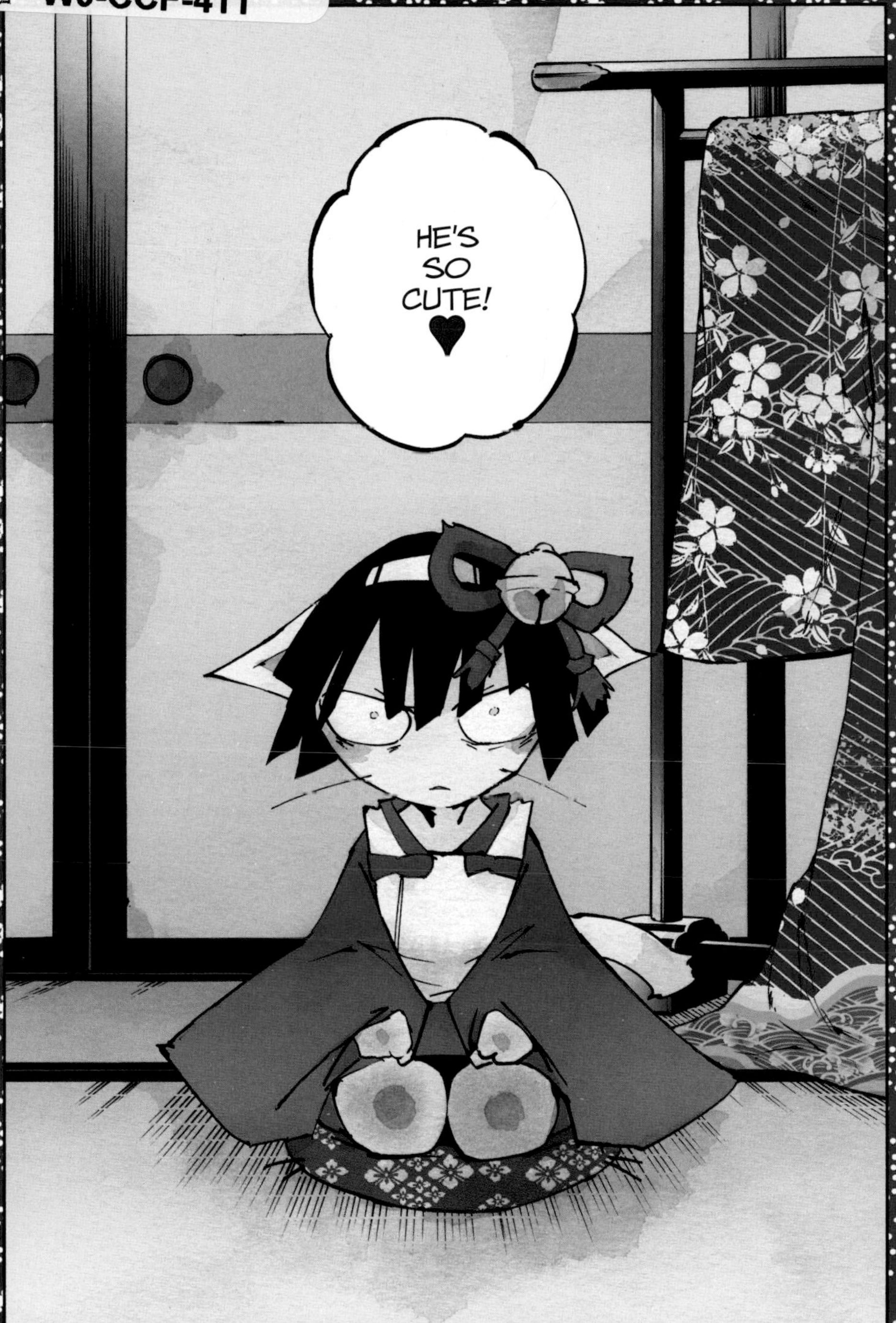
HE'S SO CUTE! ♥

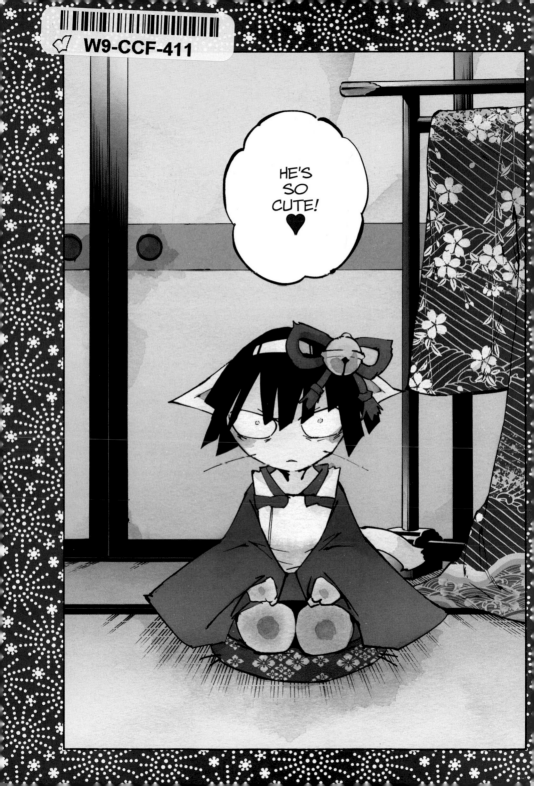

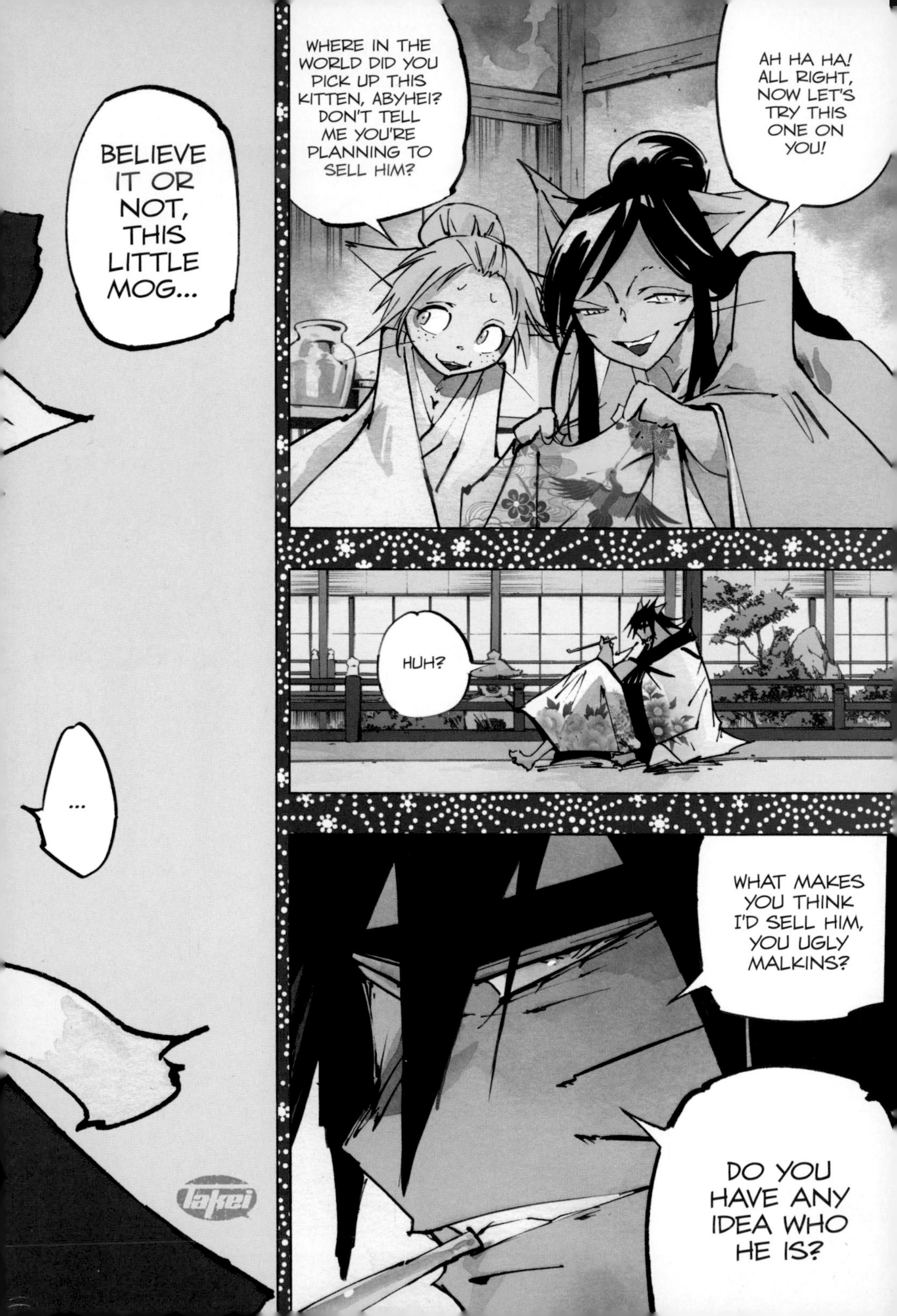
AH HA HA! ALL RIGHT, NOW LET'S TRY THIS ONE ON YOU!
WHERE IN THE WORLD DID YOU PICK UP THIS KITTEN, ABYHEI? DON'T TELL ME YOU'RE PLANNING TO SELL HIM?
HUH?
WHAT MAKES YOU THINK I'D SELL HIM, YOU UGLY MALKINS?
DO YOU HAVE ANY IDEA WHO HE IS?
BELIEVE IT OR NOT, THIS LITTLE MOG...
...

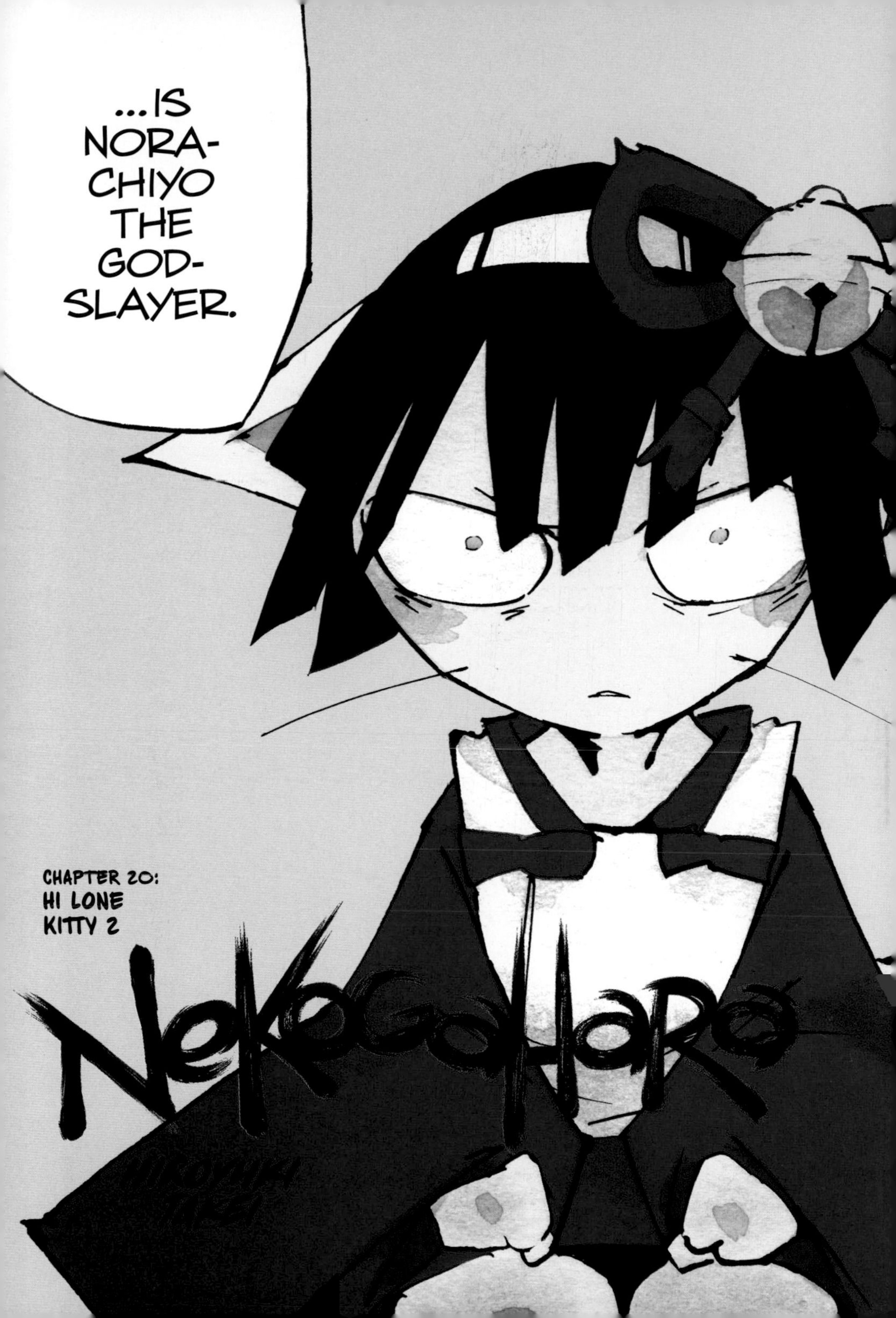
...IS NORA-CHIYO THE GOD-SLAYER.
CHAPTER 20: HI LONE KITTY 2
NEKOGAHARA

NEKOGAHARA VOLUME FOUR CONTENTS

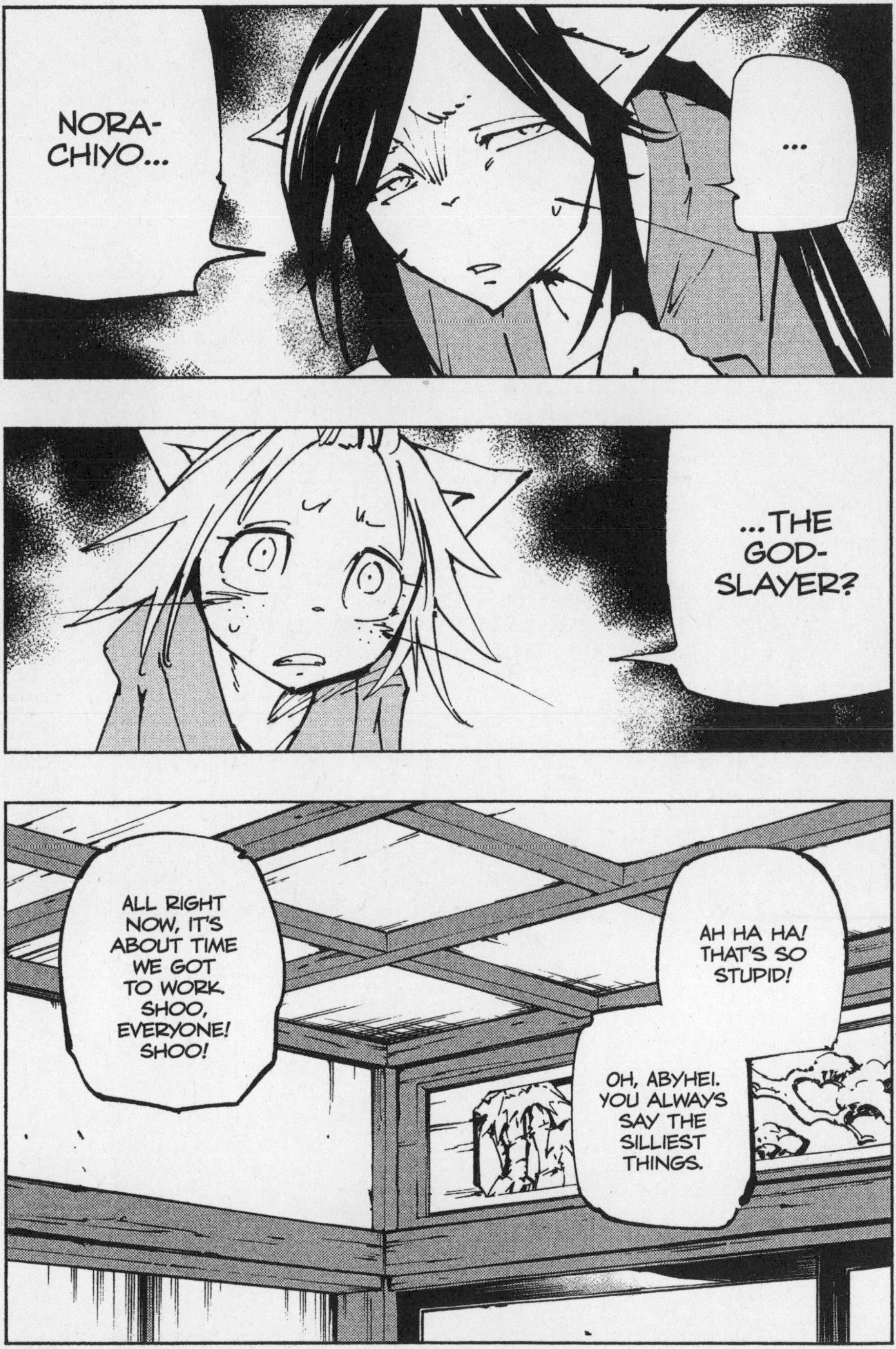
...
NORA-CHIYO...
...THE GOD-SLAYER?
AH HA HA! THAT'S SO STUPID!
OH, ABYHEI. YOU ALWAYS SAY THE SILLIEST THINGS.
ALL RIGHT NOW, IT'S ABOUT TIME WE GOT TO WORK. SHOO, EVERYONE! SHOO!

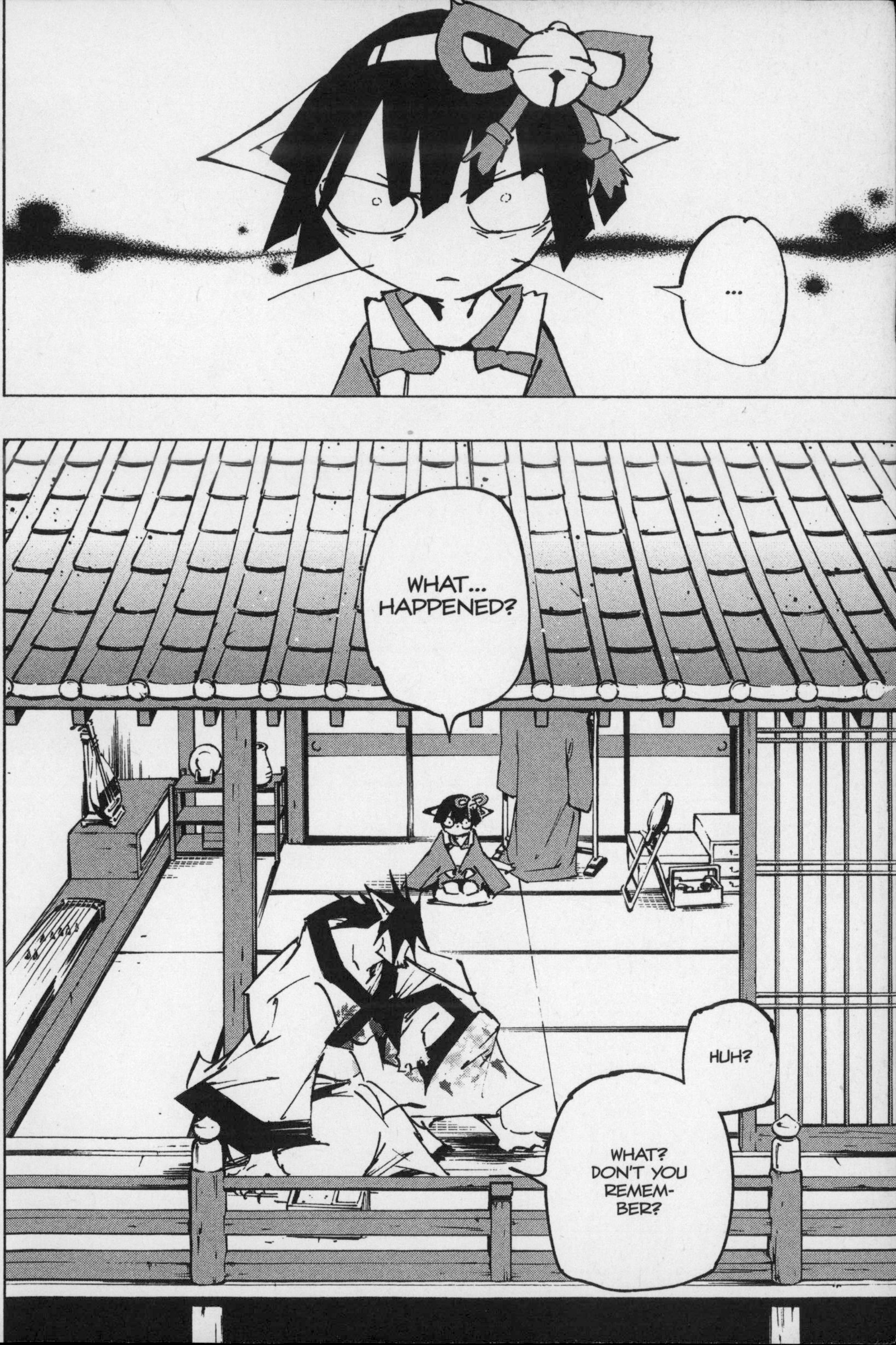
...
WHAT... HAPPENED?
HUH?
WHAT? DON'T YOU REMEMBER?

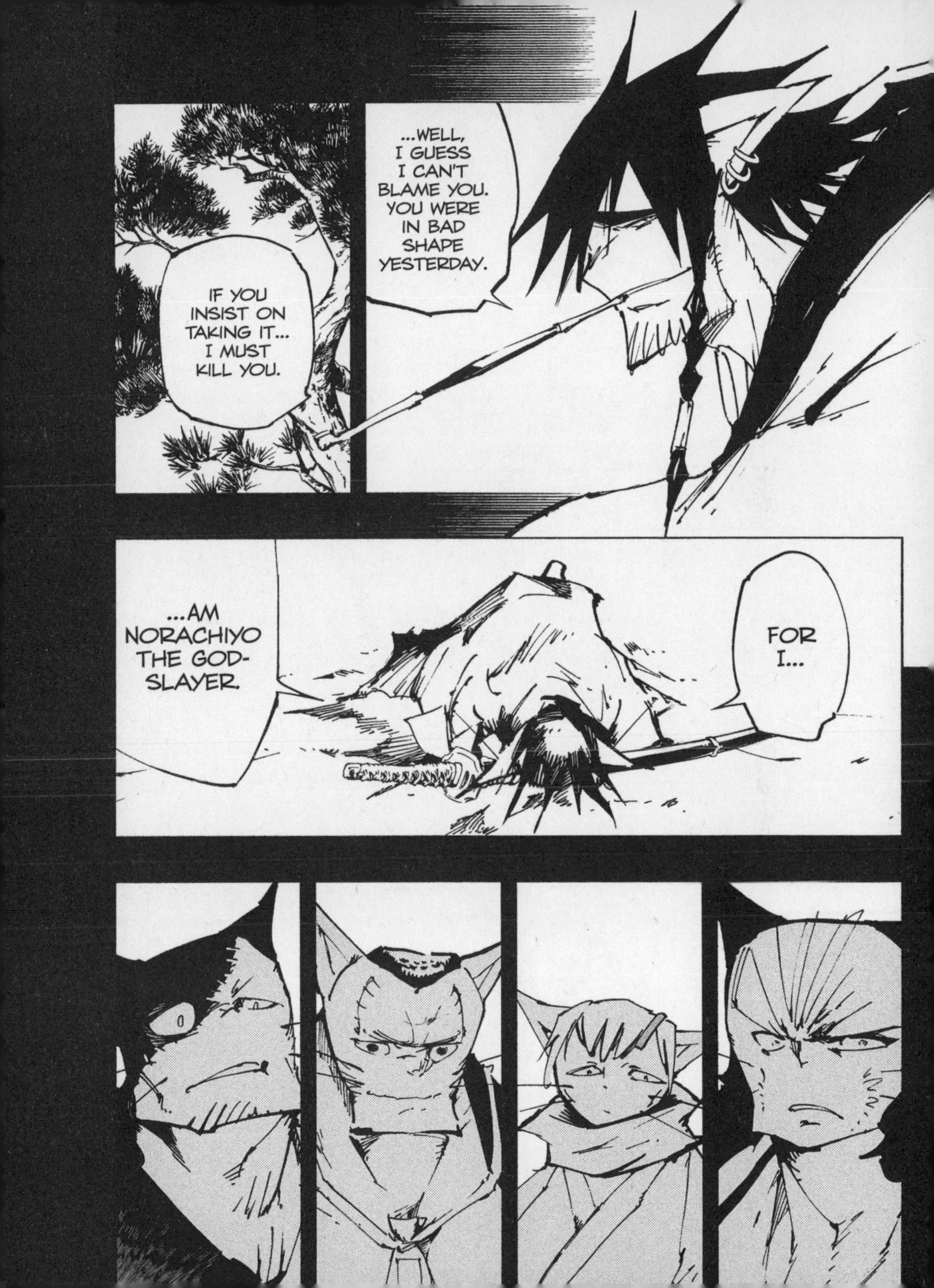
...WELL, I GUESS I CAN'T BLAME YOU. YOU WERE IN BAD SHAPE YESTERDAY.
IF YOU INSIST ON TAKING IT... I MUST KILL YOU.
FOR I...
...AM NORACHIYO THE GOD-SLAYER.

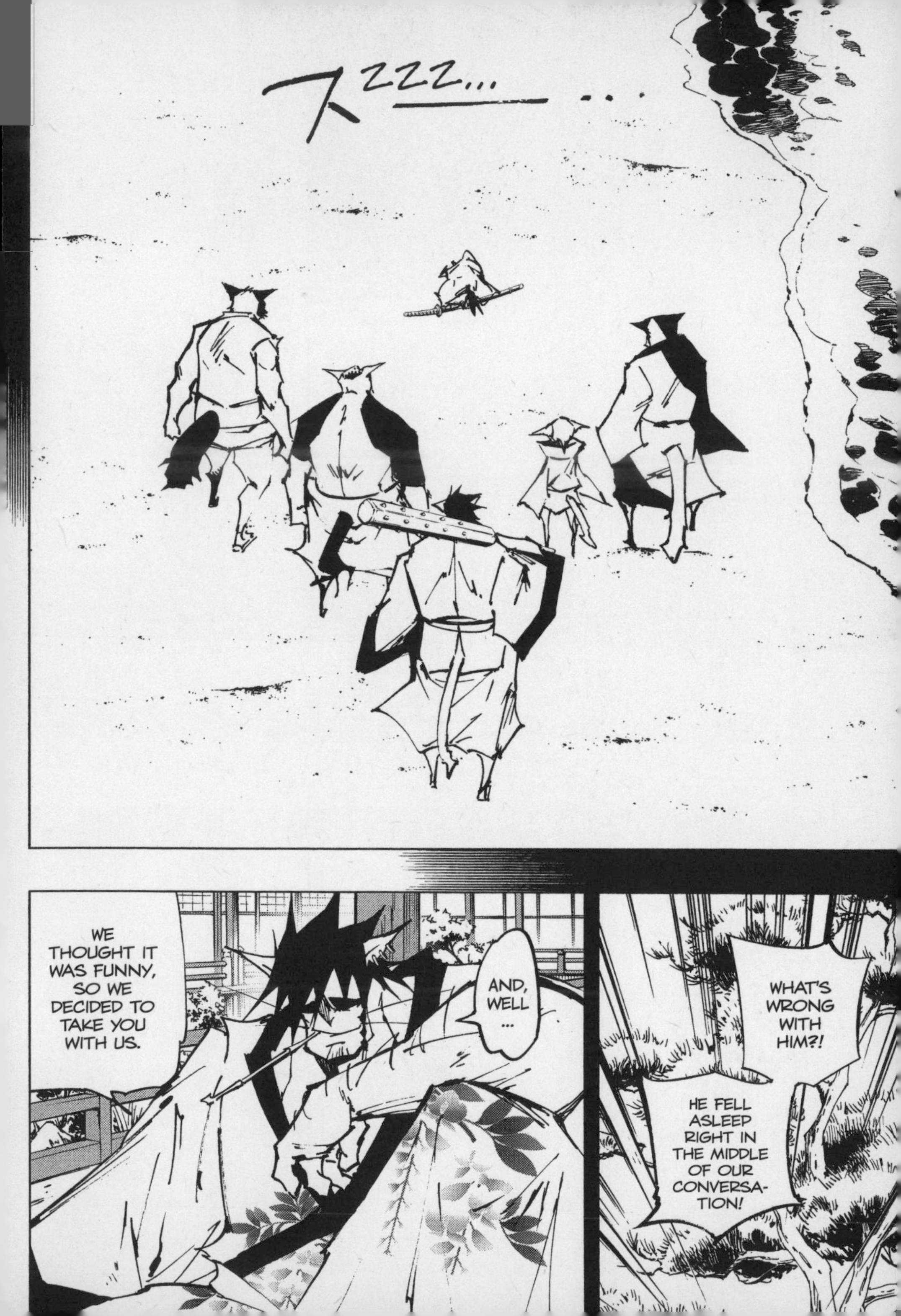
Zzzz...
...
WHAT'S WRONG WITH HIM?!
HE FELL ASLEEP RIGHT IN THE MIDDLE OF OUR CONVERSATION!
AND, WELL ...
WE THOUGHT IT WAS FUNNY, SO WE DECIDED TO TAKE YOU WITH US.

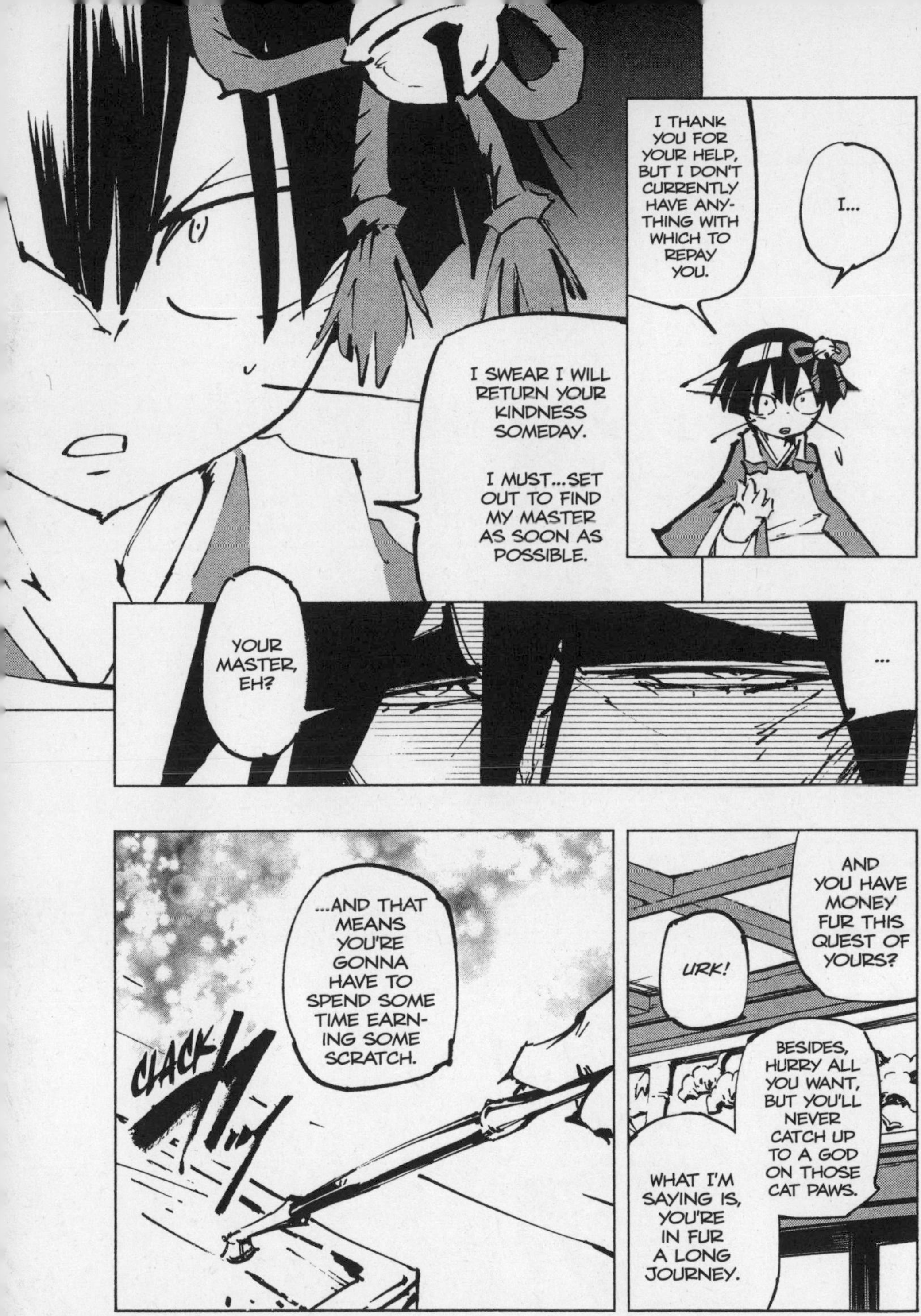
I...
I THANK YOU FOR YOUR HELP, BUT I DON'T CURRENTLY HAVE ANYTHING WITH WHICH TO REPAY YOU.
I SWEAR I WILL RETURN YOUR KINDNESS SOMEDAY.
I MUST...SET OUT TO FIND MY MASTER AS SOON AS POSSIBLE.
...
YOUR MASTER, EH?
AND YOU HAVE MONEY FUR THIS QUEST OF YOURS?
URK!
BESIDES, HURRY ALL YOU WANT, BUT YOU'LL NEVER CATCH UP TO A GOD ON THOSE CAT PAWS.
WHAT I'M SAYING IS, YOU'RE IN FUR A LONG JOURNEY.
...AND THAT MEANS YOU'RE GONNA HAVE TO SPEND SOME TIME EARNING SOME SCRATCH.
CLACK

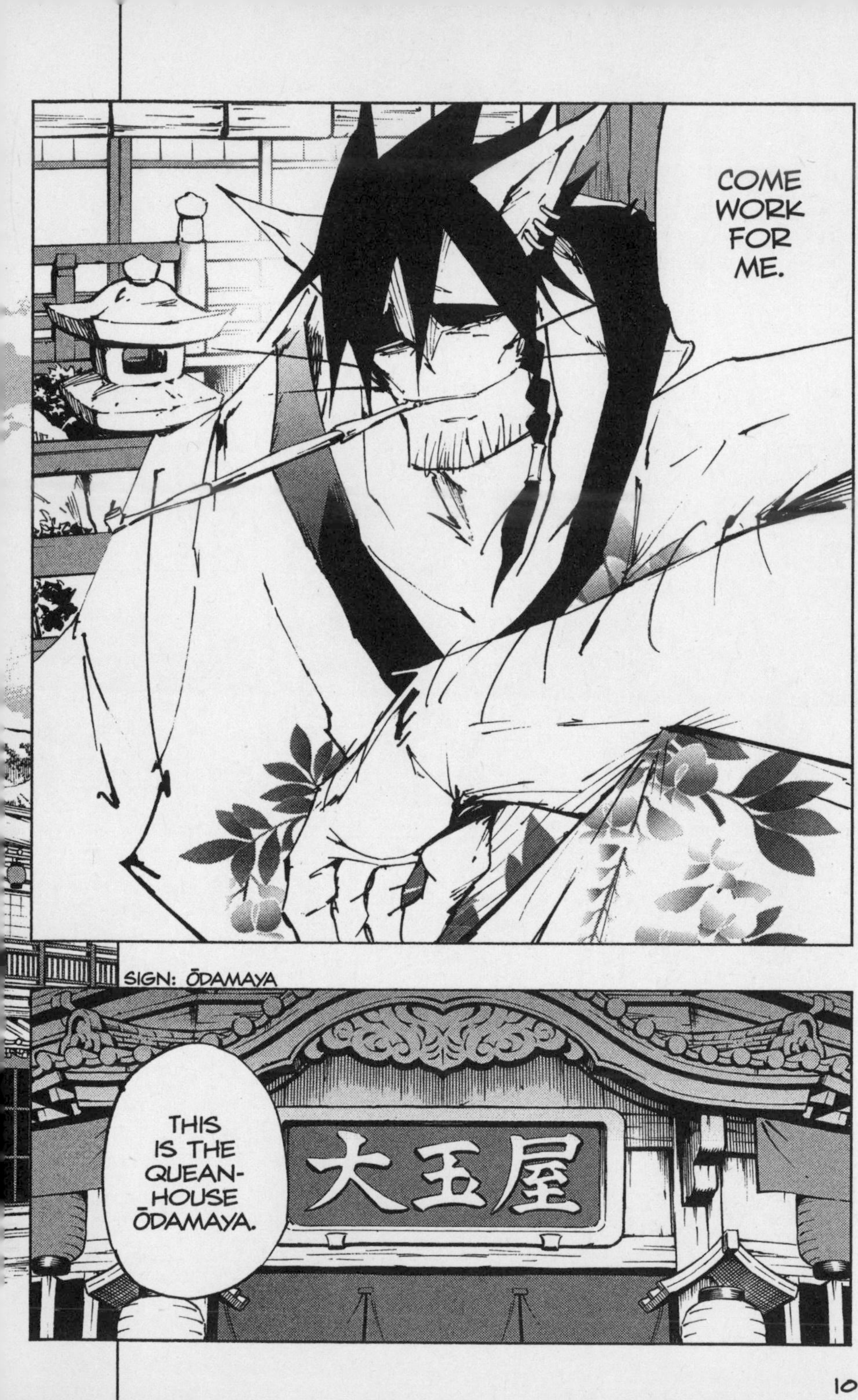
COME WORK FOR ME.
SIGN: ŌDAMAYA
大玉屋
THIS IS THE QUEAN-HOUSE ŌDAMAYA.

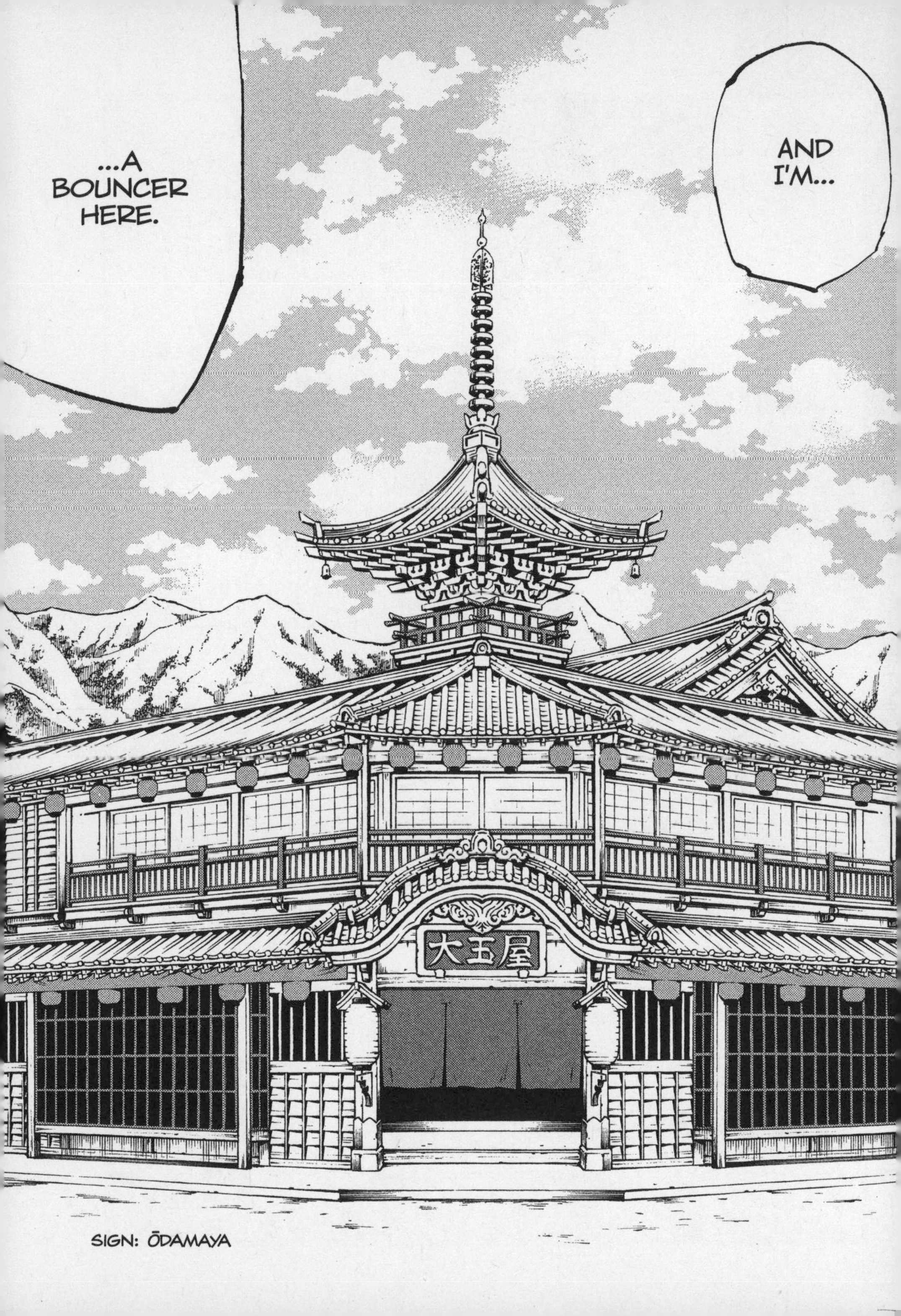
AND I'M...
...A BOUNCER HERE.
大玉屋
SIGN: ŌDAMAYA

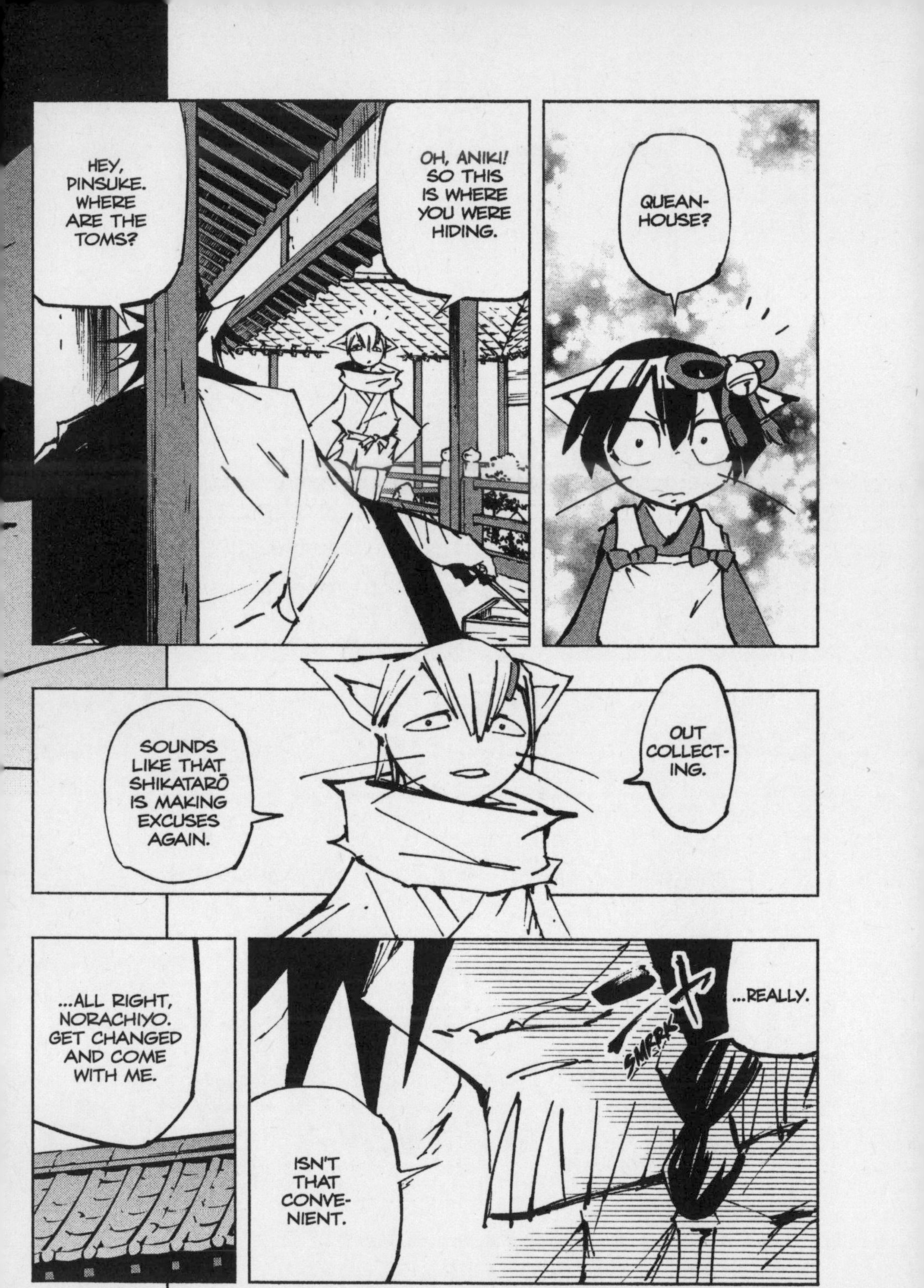
QUEAN-HOUSE?
OH, ANIKI! SO THIS IS WHERE YOU WERE HIDING.
HEY, PINSUKE. WHERE ARE THE TOMS?
OUT COLLECTING.
SOUNDS LIKE THAT SHIKATARŌ IS MAKING EXCUSES AGAIN.
...REALLY.
SMRRK
ISN'T THAT CONVENIENT.
...ALL RIGHT, NORACHIYO. GET CHANGED AND COME WITH ME.

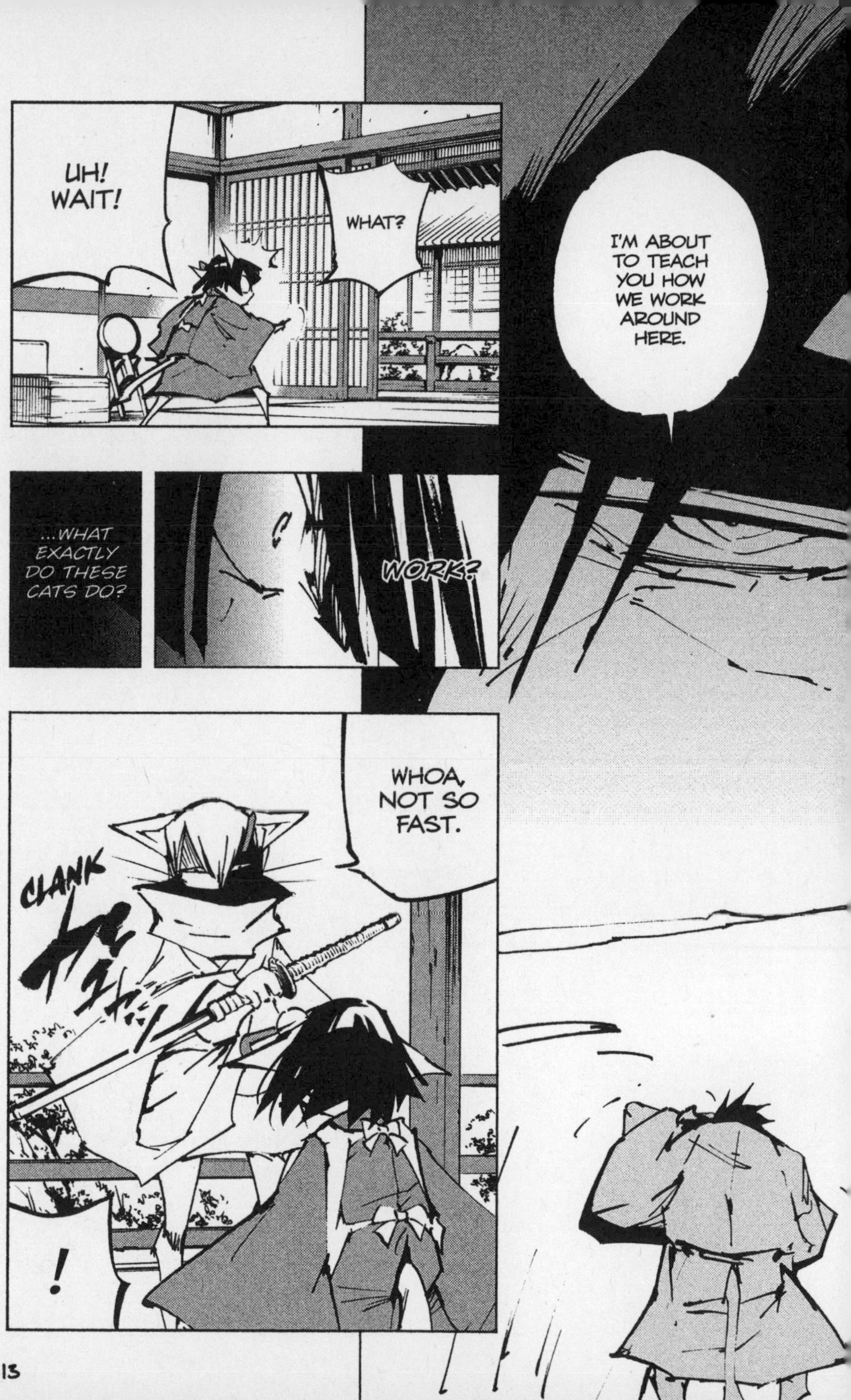
I'M ABOUT TO TEACH YOU HOW WE WORK AROUND HERE.
UH! WAIT!
WHAT?
WORK?
...WHAT EXACTLY DO THESE CATS DO?
WHOA, NOT SO FAST.
CLANK
!

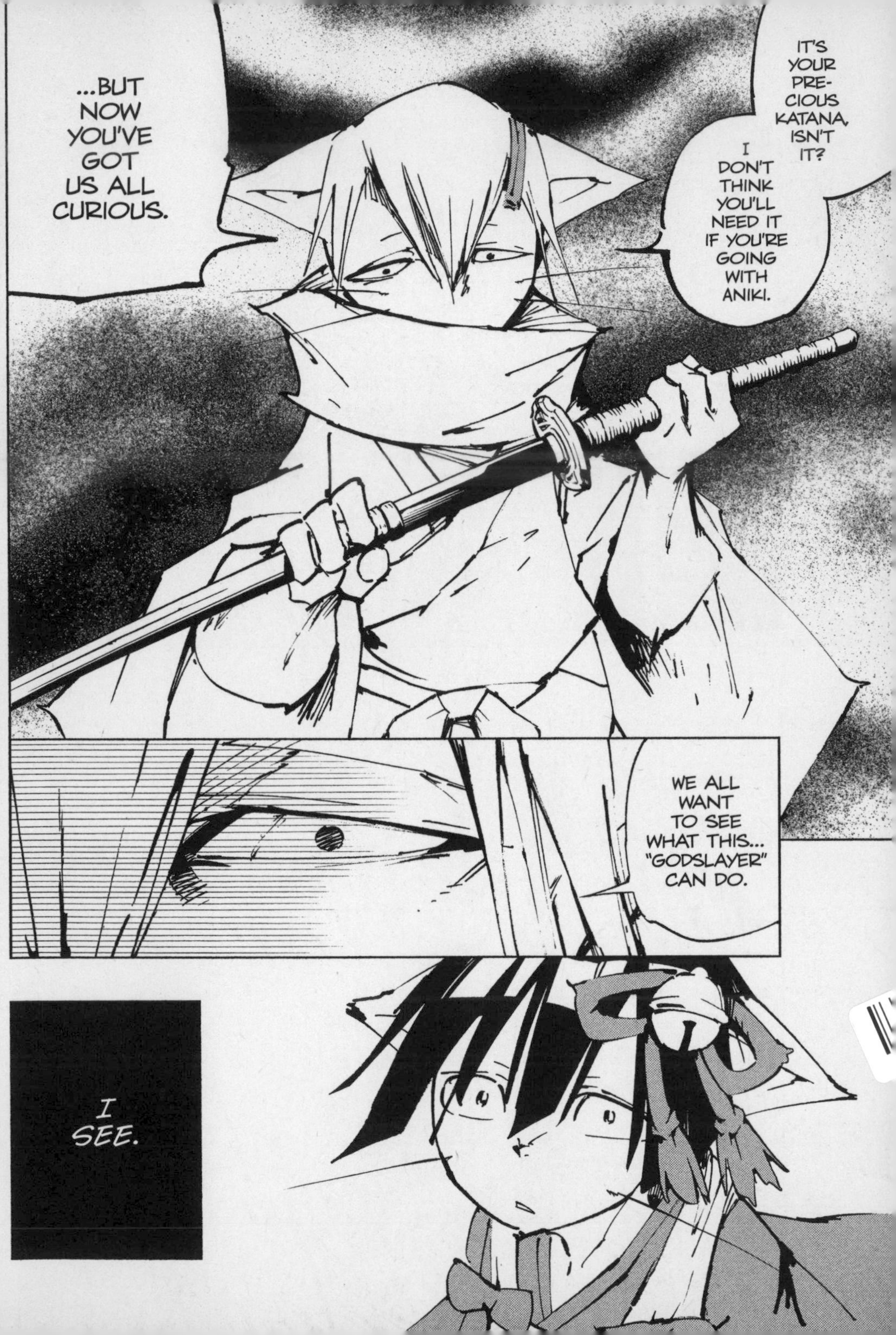
IT'S YOUR PRECIOUS KATANA, ISN'T IT?
I DON'T THINK YOU'LL NEED IT IF YOU'RE GOING WITH ANIKI.
...BUT NOW YOU'VE GOT US ALL CURIOUS.
WE ALL WANT TO SEE WHAT THIS... "GODSLAYER" CAN DO.
I SEE.

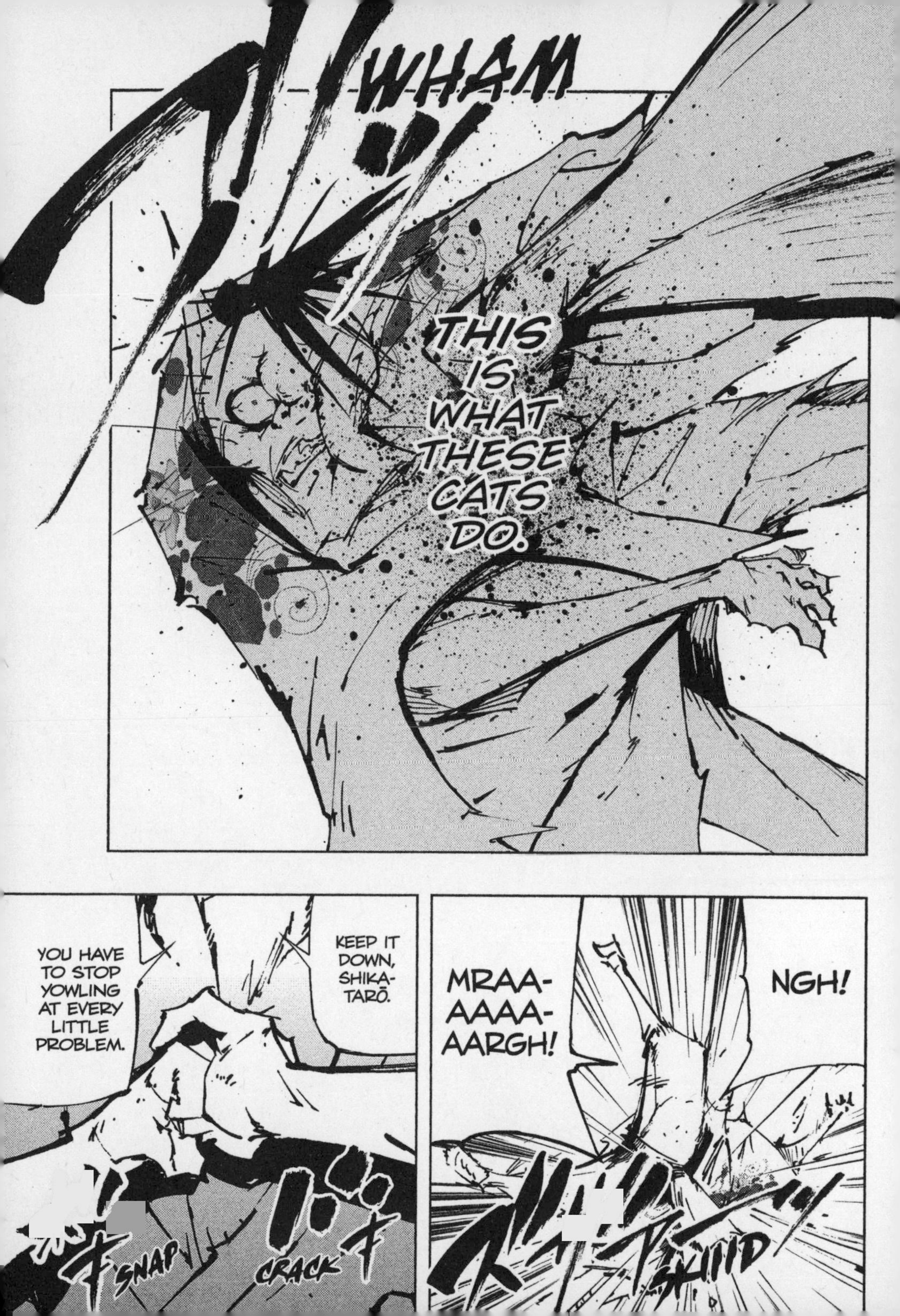
WHAM
THIS IS WHAT THESE CATS DO.
NGH!
MRAA-AAAA-AARGH!
SKIIID
KEEP IT DOWN, SHIKA-TARŌ.
YOU HAVE TO STOP YOWLING AT EVERY LITTLE PROBLEM.
CRACK
SNAP

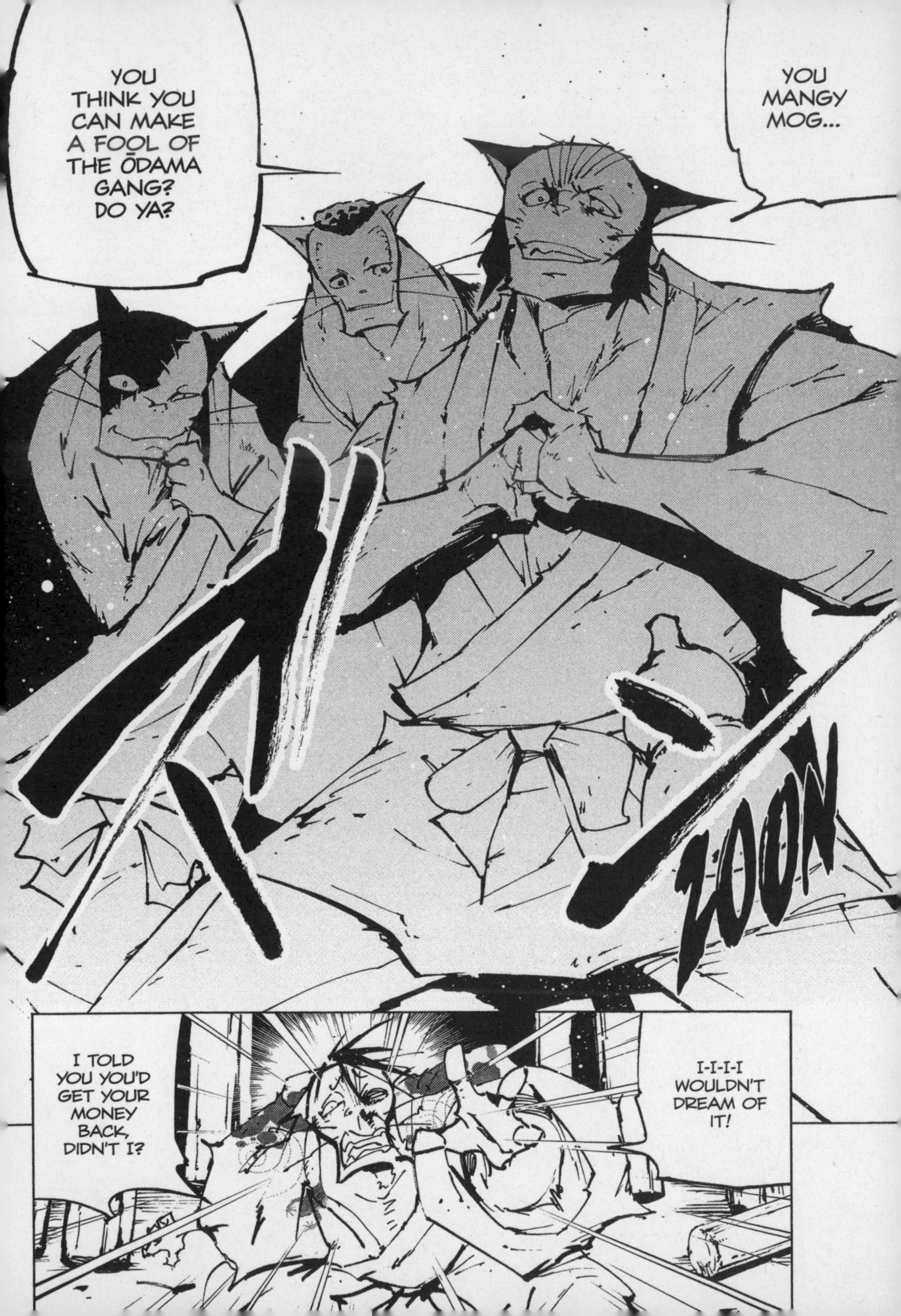
YOU MANGY MOG...
YOU THINK YOU CAN MAKE A FOOL OF THE ŌDAMA GANG? DO YA?
ZOON
I-I-I-I WOULDN'T DREAM OF IT!
I TOLD YOU YOU'D GET YOUR MONEY BACK, DIDN'T I?

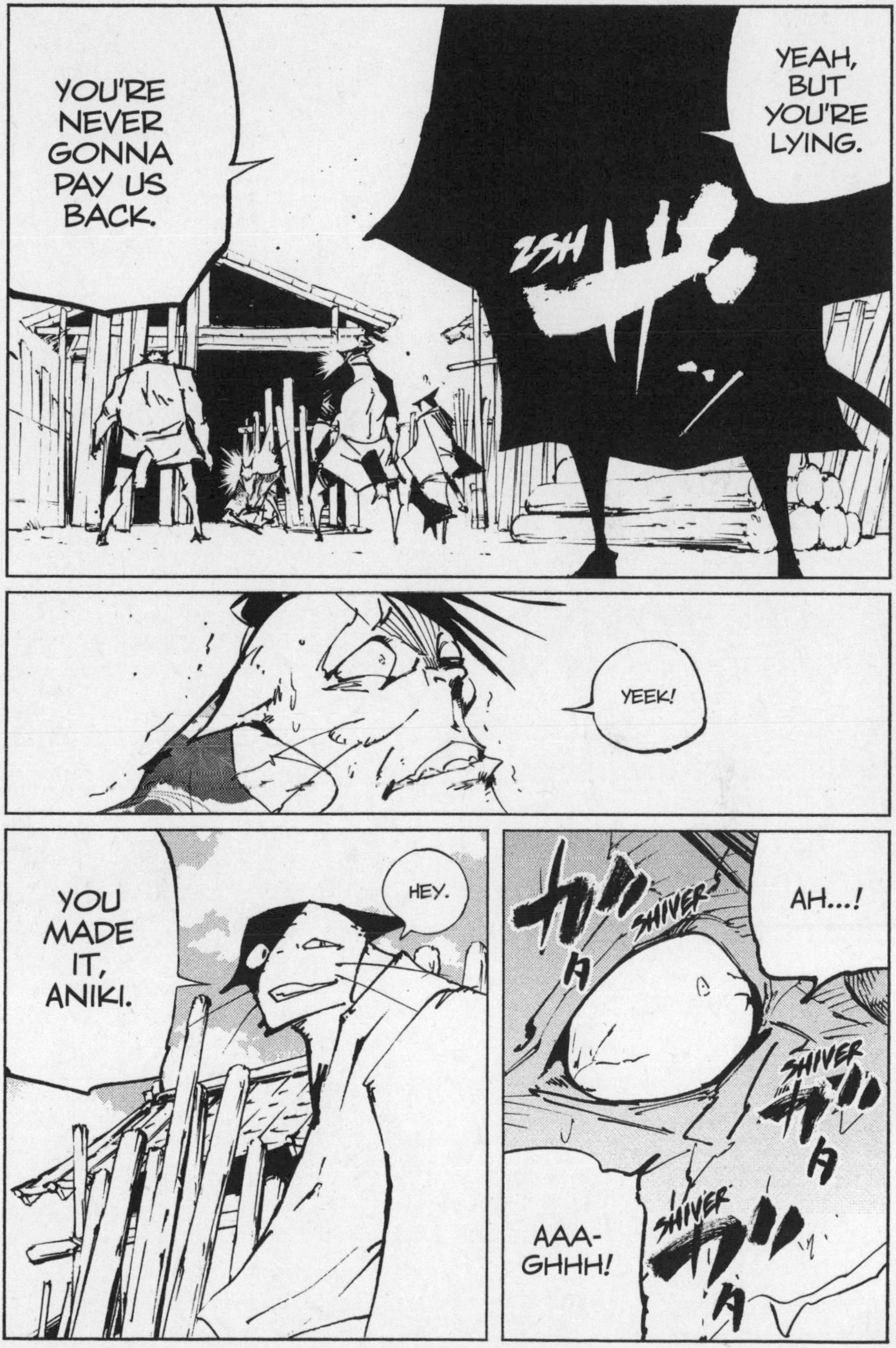
YEAH, BUT YOU'RE LYING.
ZSH
YOU'RE NEVER GONNA PAY US BACK.
YEEK!
AH...!
SHIVER
SHIVER
SHIVER
AAA-GHHH!
HEY.
YOU MADE IT, ANIKI.

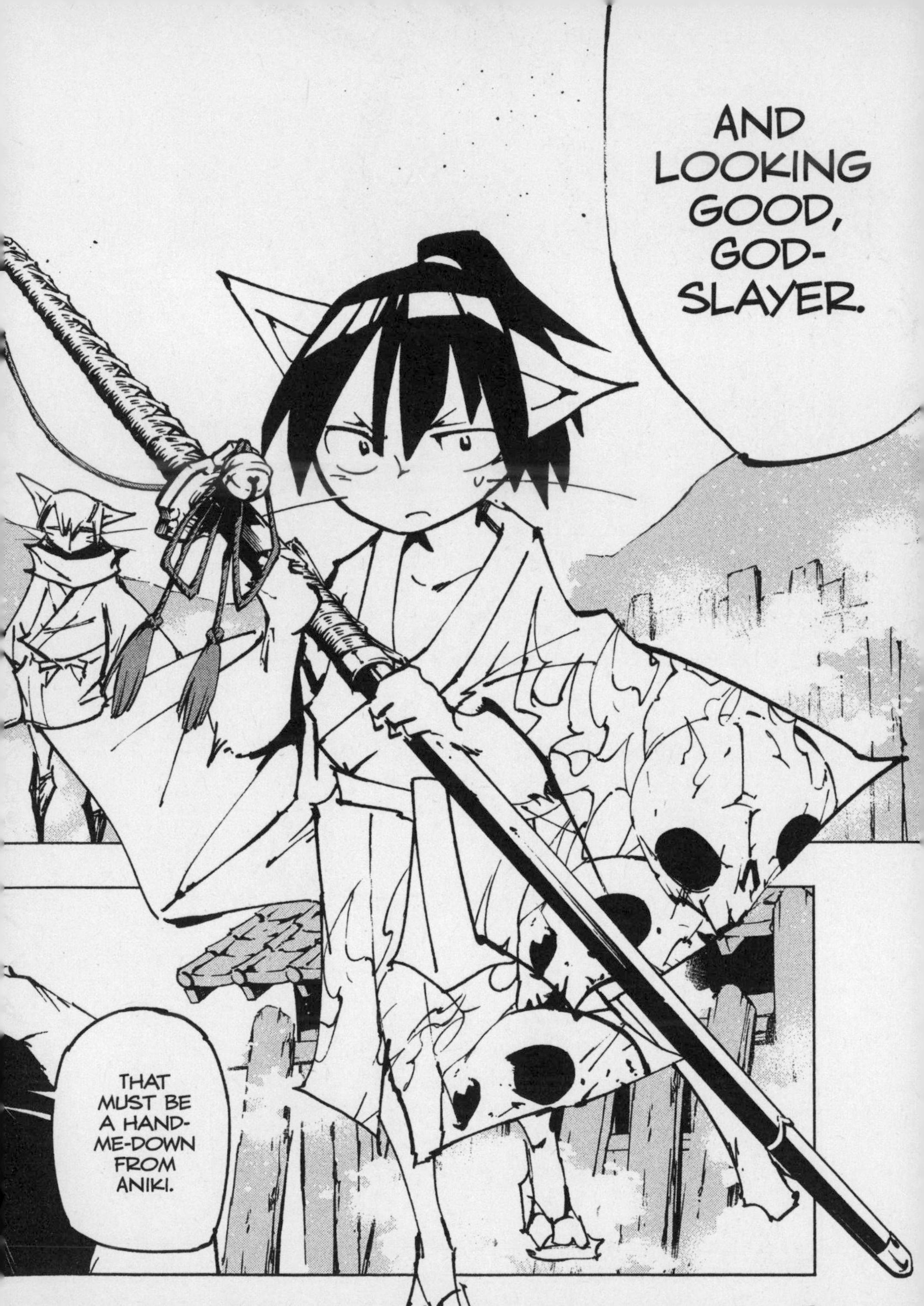
AND LOOKING GOOD, GOD-SLAYER.
THAT MUST BE A HAND-ME-DOWN FROM ANIKI.

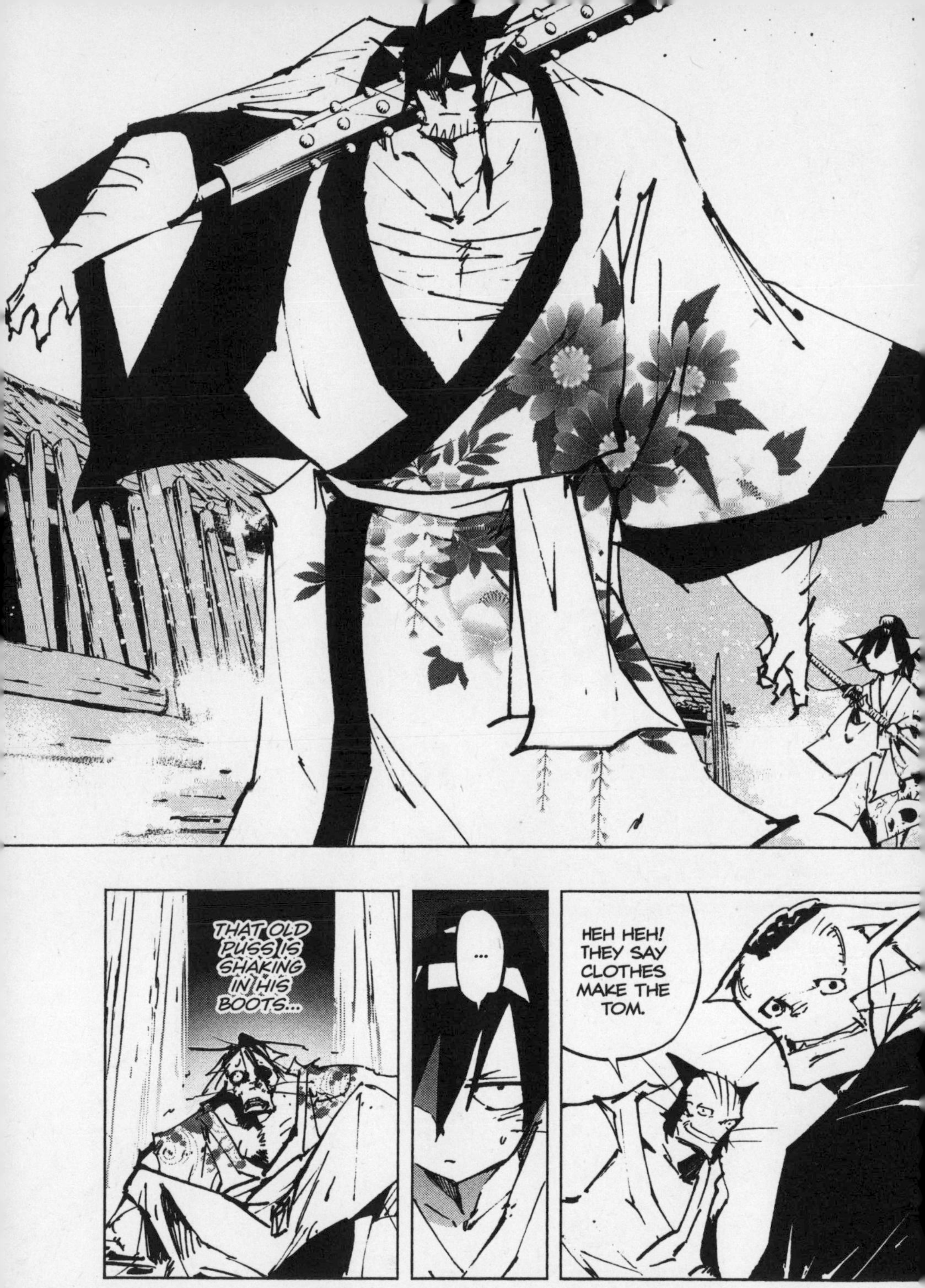
HEH HEH! THEY SAY CLOTHES MAKE THE TOM.
...
THAT OLD PUSS IS SHAKING IN HIS BOOTS...

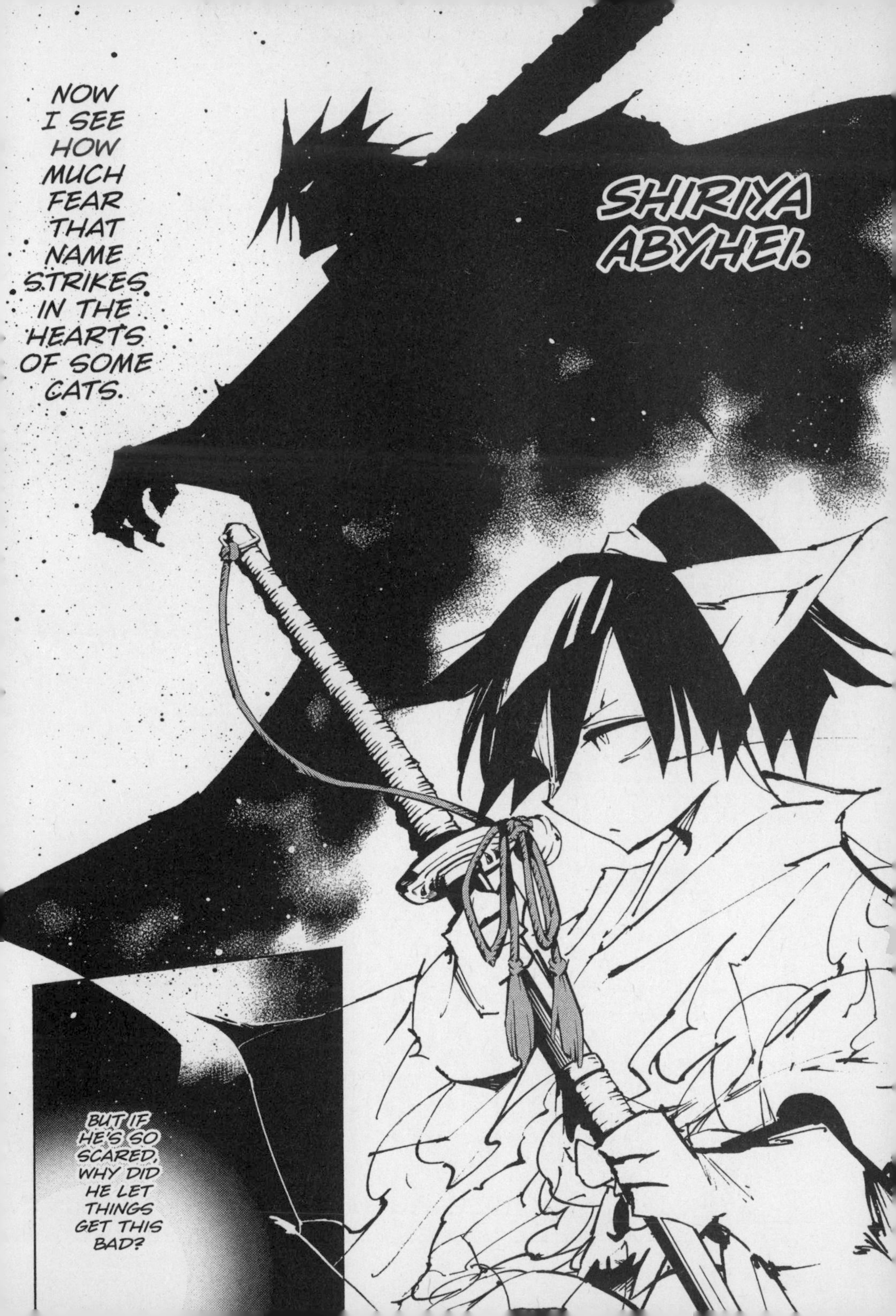
SHIRIYA ABYHEI.
NOW I SEE HOW MUCH FEAR THAT NAME STRIKES IN THE HEARTS OF SOME CATS.
BUT IF HE'S SO SCARED, WHY DID HE LET THINGS GET THIS BAD?

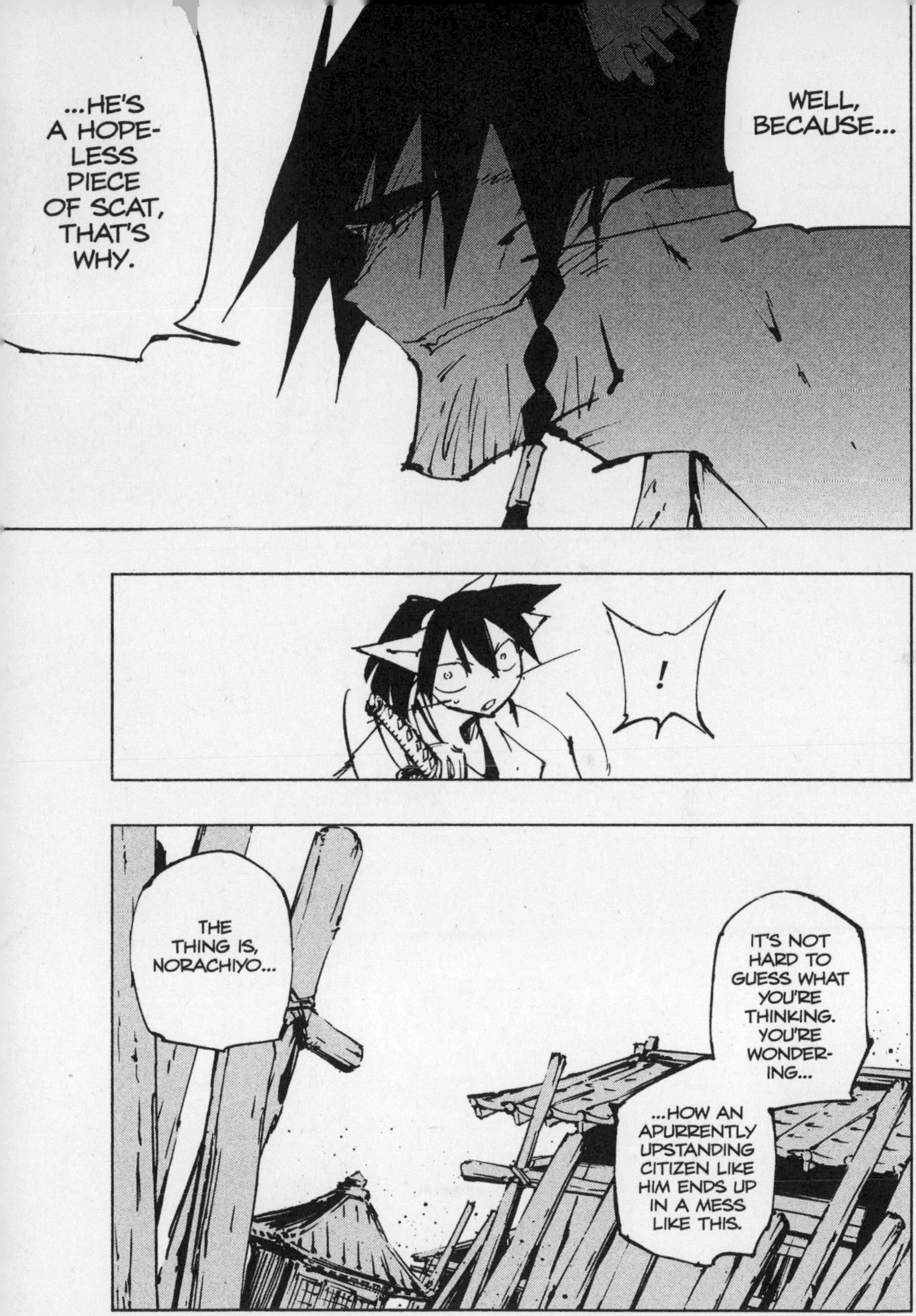
WELL, BECAUSE...
...HE'S A HOPE-LESS PIECE OF SCAT, THAT'S WHY.
!
THE THING IS, NORACHIYO...
IT'S NOT HARD TO GUESS WHAT YOU'RE THINKING. YOU'RE WONDER-ING...
...HOW AN APURRENTLY UPSTANDING CITIZEN LIKE HIM ENDS UP IN A MESS LIKE THIS.

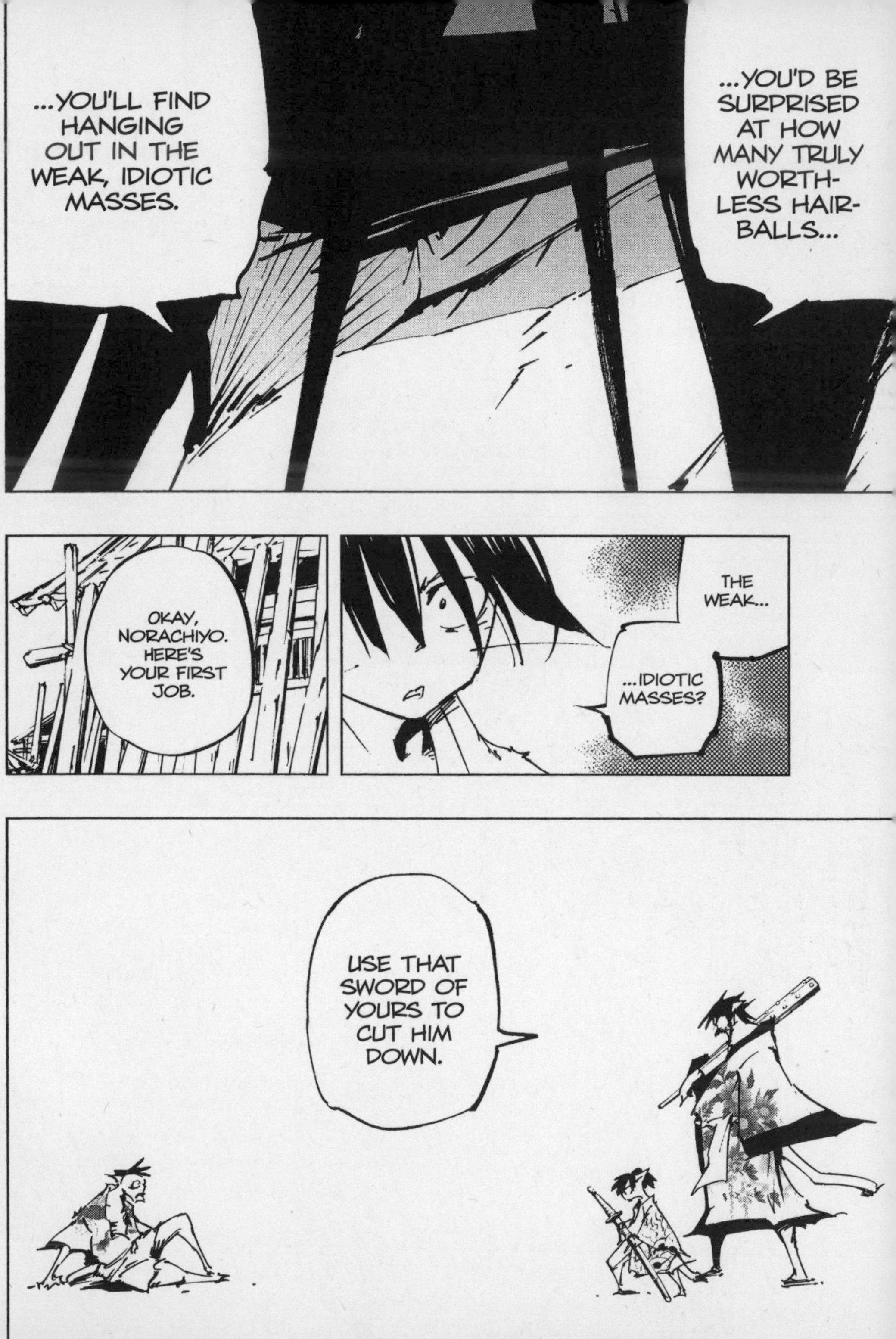
...YOU'D BE SURPRISED AT HOW MANY TRULY WORTH-LESS HAIR-BALLS...
...YOU'LL FIND HANGING OUT IN THE WEAK, IDIOTIC MASSES.
THE WEAK...
...IDIOTIC MASSES?
OKAY, NORACHIYO. HERE'S YOUR FIRST JOB.
USE THAT SWORD OF YOURS TO CUT HIM DOWN.

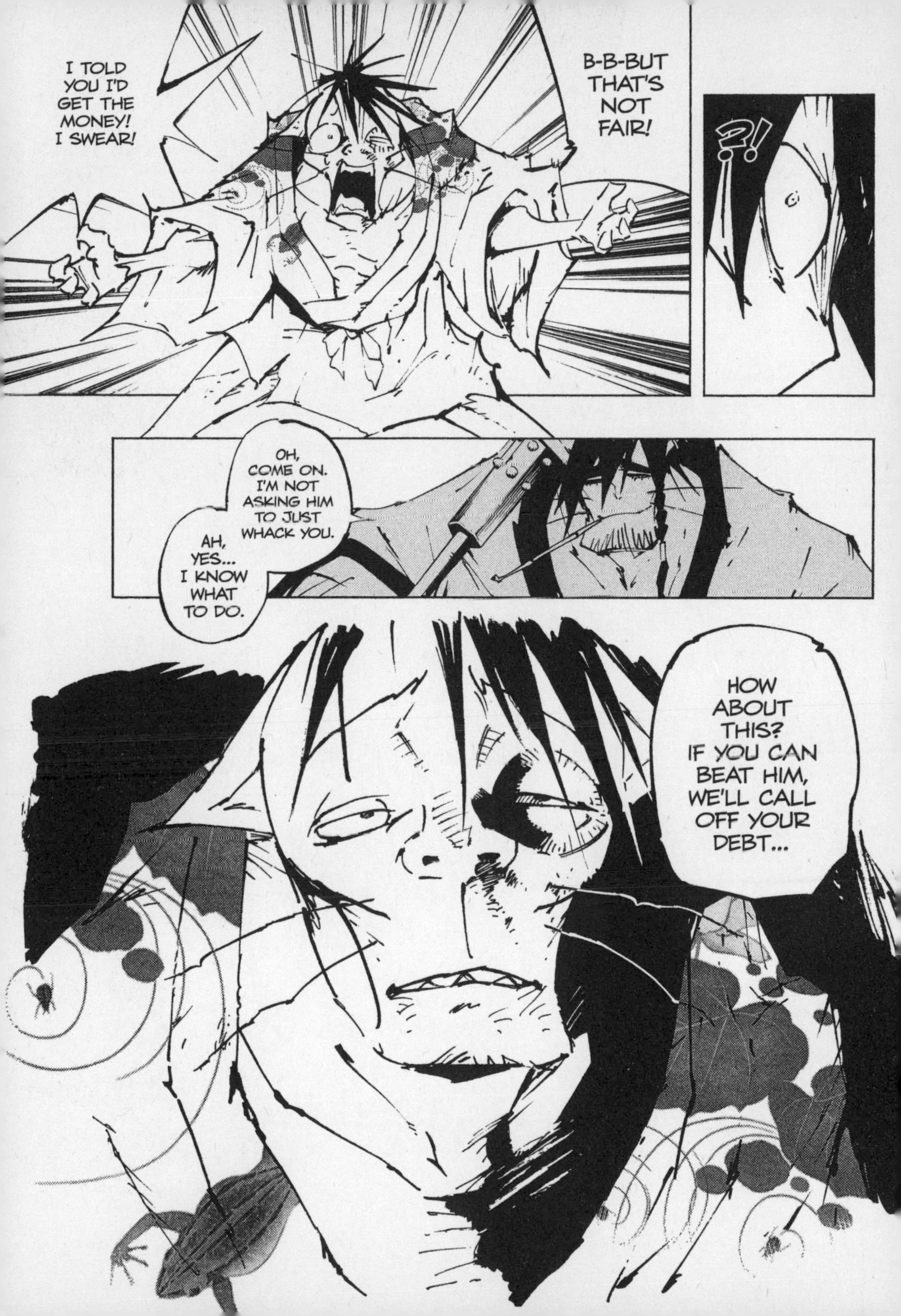
?!
B-B-BUT THAT'S NOT FAIR!
I TOLD YOU I'D GET THE MONEY! I SWEAR!
OH, COME ON. I'M NOT ASKING HIM TO JUST WHACK YOU.
AH, YES... I KNOW WHAT TO DO.
HOW ABOUT THIS? IF YOU CAN BEAT HIM, WE'LL CALL OFF YOUR DEBT...

猫ヶ原

ネコガハラ

NeKoGaHaRa

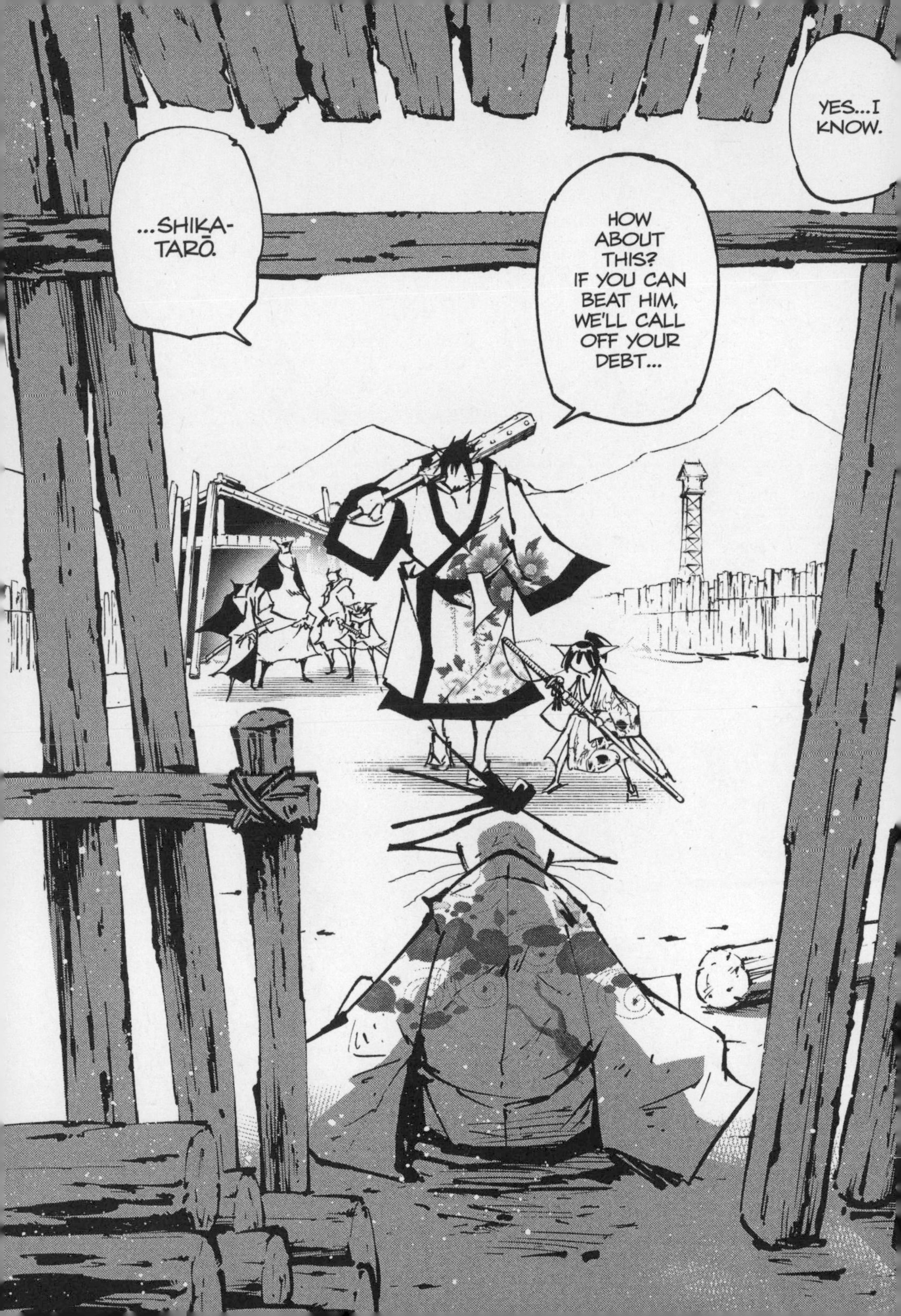
YES...I KNOW.
HOW ABOUT THIS? IF YOU CAN BEAT HIM, WE'LL CALL OFF YOUR DEBT...
...SHIKA-TARŌ.

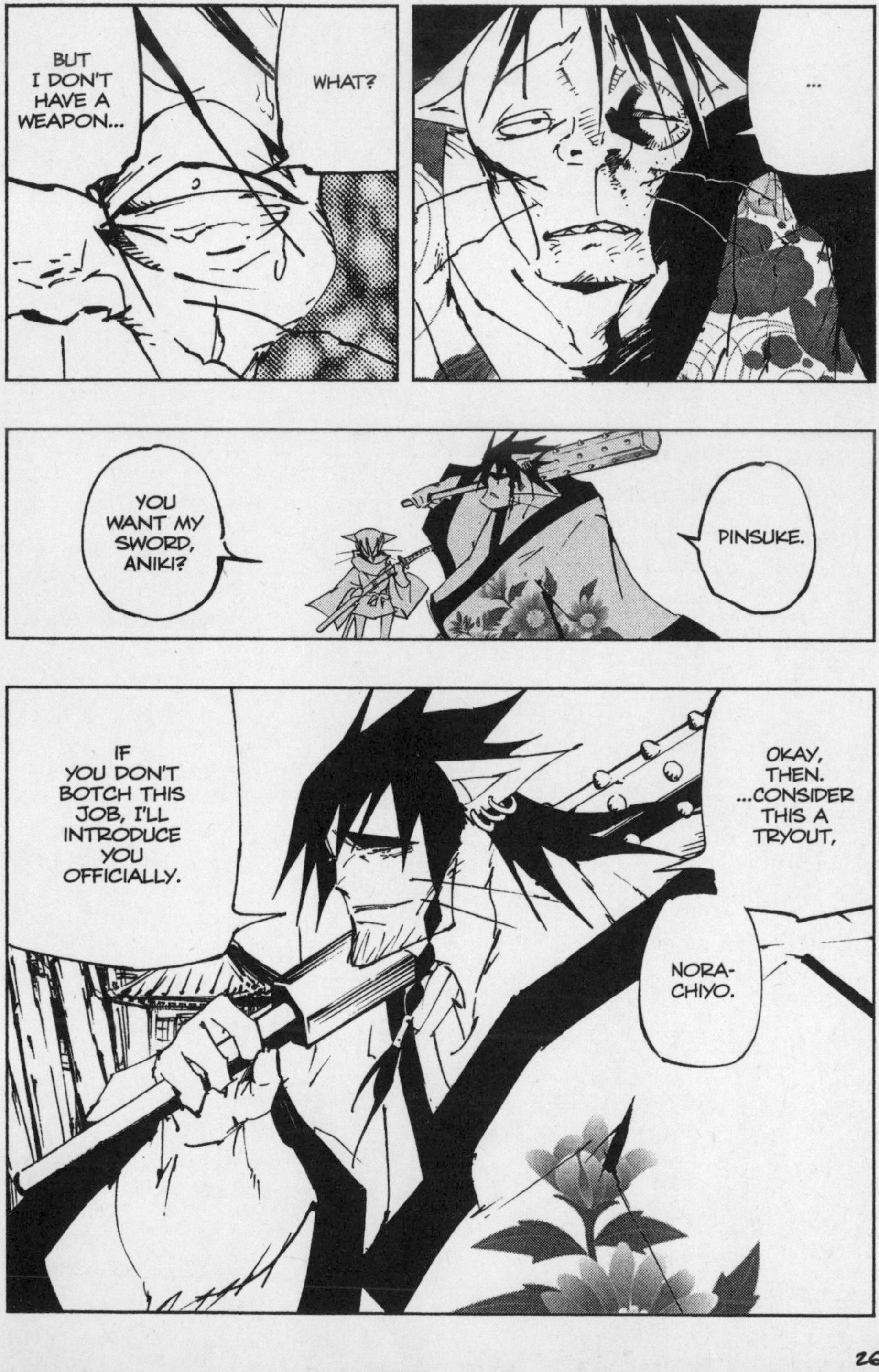
...
WHAT?
BUT I DON'T HAVE A WEAPON...
PINSUKE.
YOU WANT MY SWORD, ANIKI?
OKAY, THEN. ...CONSIDER THIS A TRYOUT,
NORA-CHIYO.
IF YOU DON'T BOTCH THIS JOB, I'LL INTRODUCE YOU OFFICIALLY.

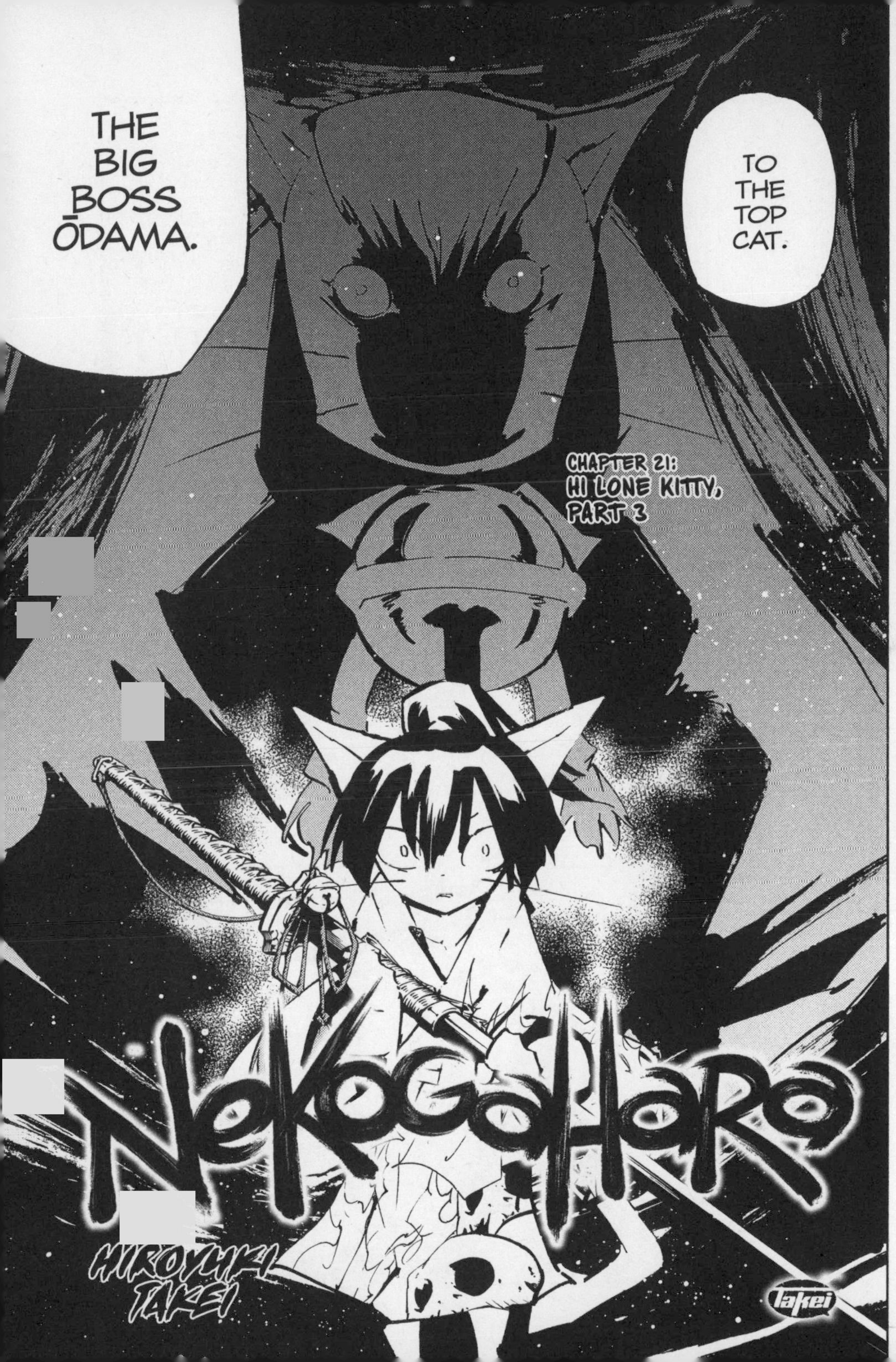
TO THE TOP CAT.
THE BIG BOSS ŌDAMA.
CHAPTER 21: HI LONE KITTY, PART 3
NEKOGAHARA
HIROYUKI TAKEI
Takei

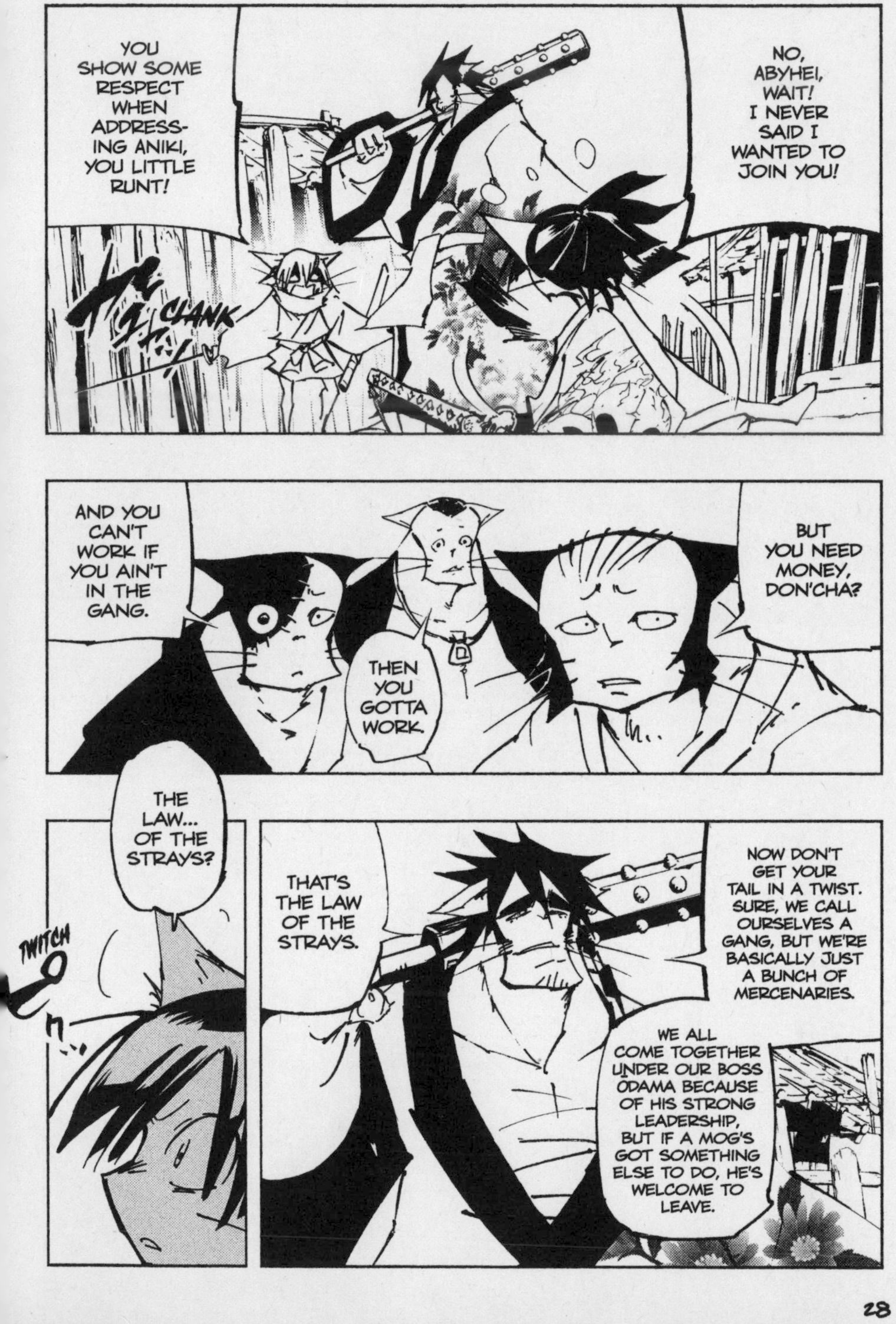
NO, ABYHEI, WAIT! I NEVER SAID I WANTED TO JOIN YOU!
YOU SHOW SOME RESPECT WHEN ADDRESSING ANIKI, YOU LITTLE RUNT!
CLANK
BUT YOU NEED MONEY, DON'CHA?
THEN YOU GOTTA WORK.
AND YOU CAN'T WORK IF YOU AIN'T IN THE GANG.
NOW DON'T GET YOUR TAIL IN A TWIST. SURE, WE CALL OURSELVES A GANG, BUT WE'RE BASICALLY JUST A BUNCH OF MERCENARIES.
WE ALL COME TOGETHER UNDER OUR BOSS ODAMA BECAUSE OF HIS STRONG LEADERSHIP, BUT IF A MOG'S GOT SOMETHING ELSE TO DO, HE'S WELCOME TO LEAVE.
THAT'S THE LAW OF THE STRAYS.
THE LAW... OF THE STRAYS?
TWITCH

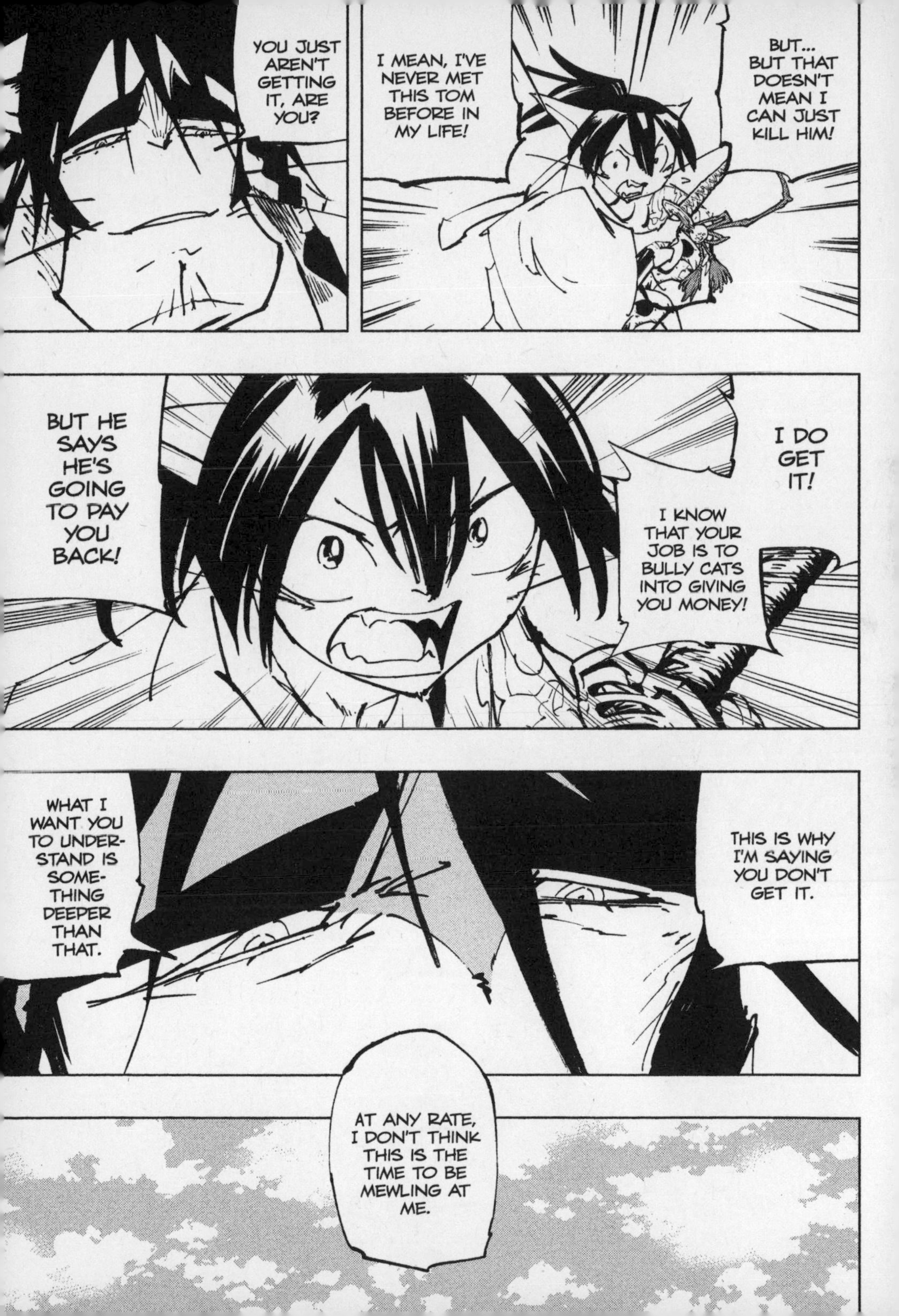
BUT... BUT THAT DOESN'T MEAN I CAN JUST KILL HIM!
I MEAN, I'VE NEVER MET THIS TOM BEFORE IN MY LIFE!
YOU JUST AREN'T GETTING IT, ARE YOU?
I DO GET IT!
I KNOW THAT YOUR JOB IS TO BULLY CATS INTO GIVING YOU MONEY!
BUT HE SAYS HE'S GOING TO PAY YOU BACK!
THIS IS WHY I'M SAYING YOU DON'T GET IT.
WHAT I WANT YOU TO UNDER-STAND IS SOME-THING DEEPER THAN THAT.
AT ANY RATE, I DON'T THINK THIS IS THE TIME TO BE MEWLING AT ME.

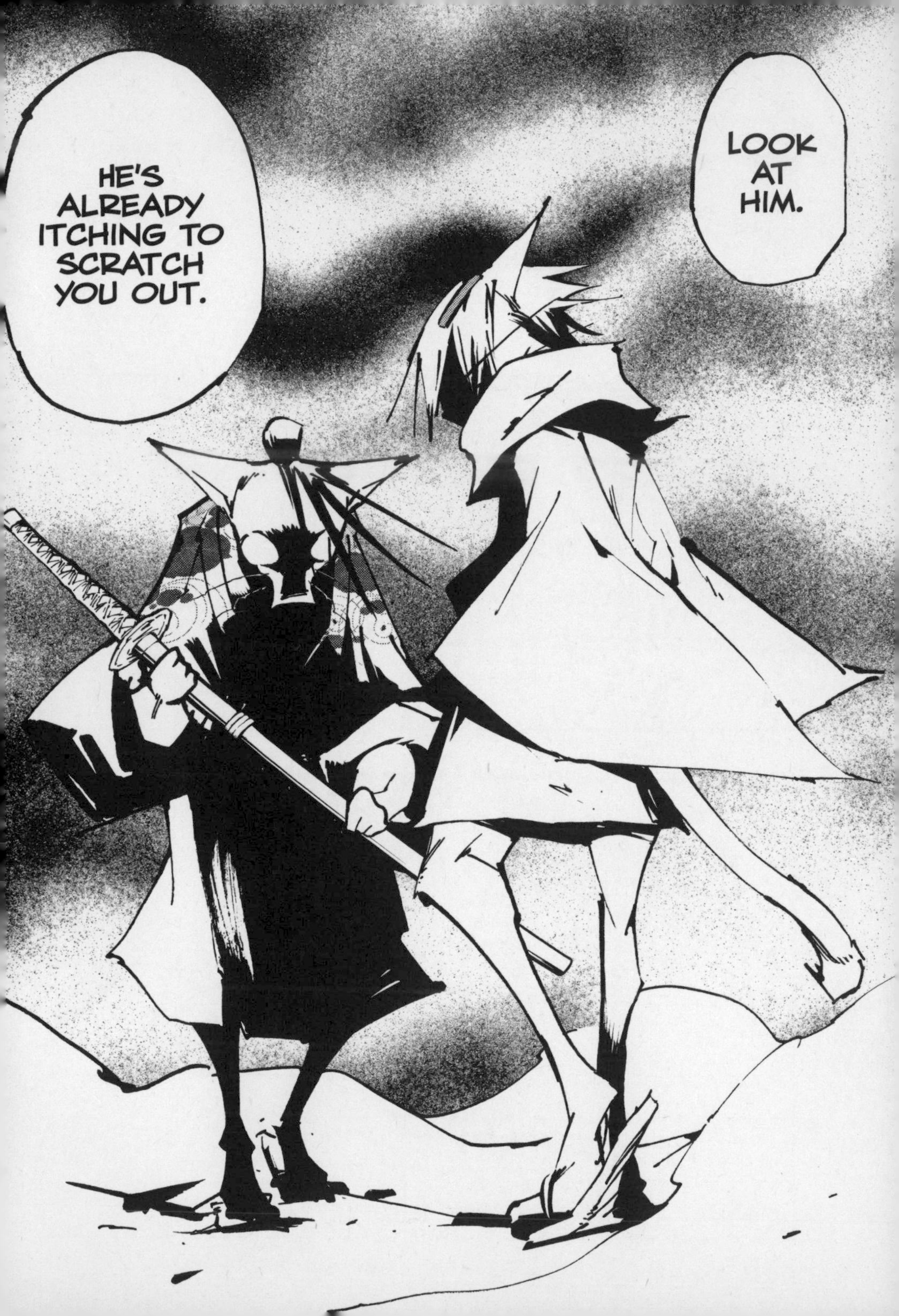
LOOK AT HIM.
HE'S ALREADY ITCHING TO SCRATCH YOU OUT.

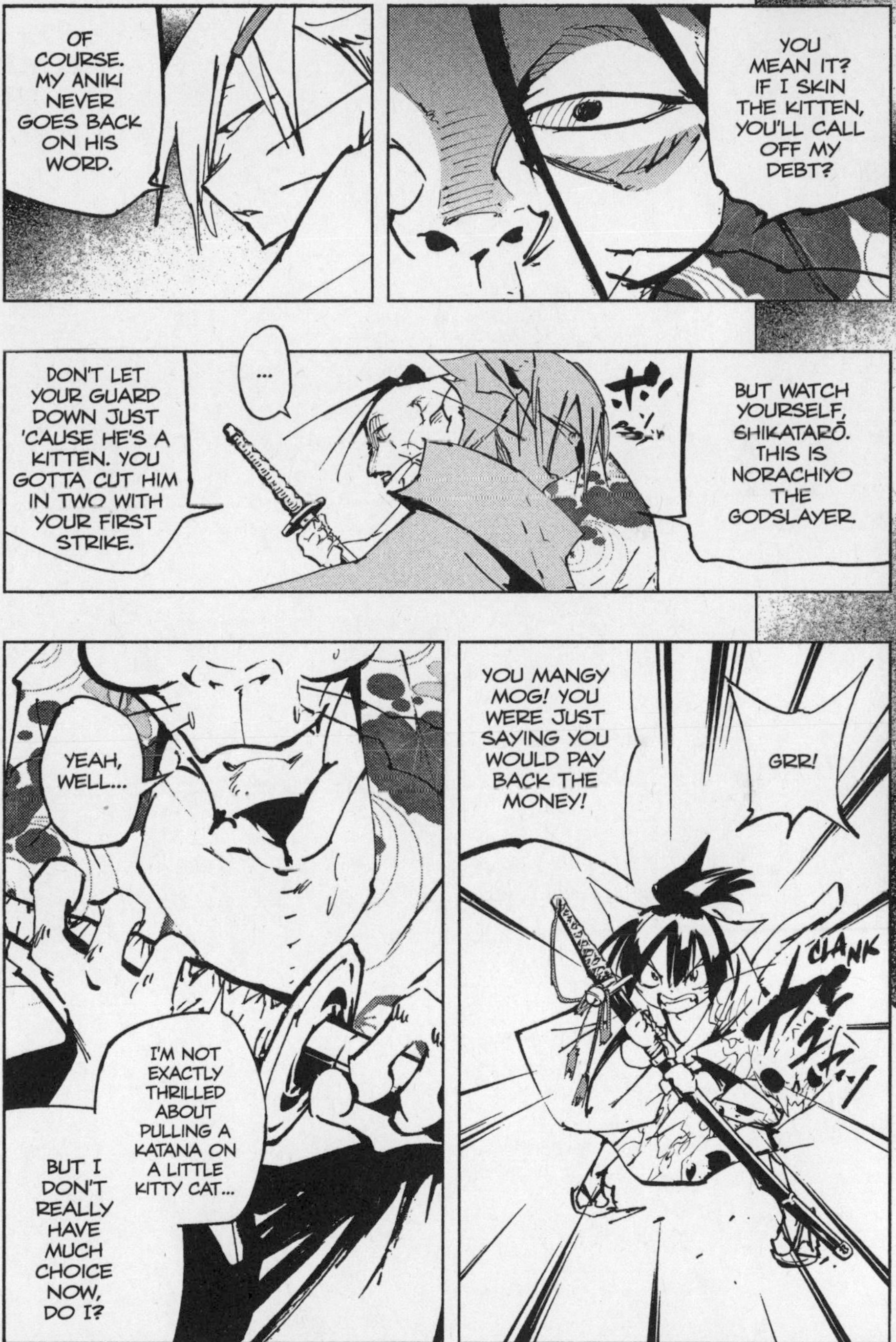
YOU MEAN IT? IF I SKIN THE KITTEN, YOU'LL CALL OFF MY DEBT?
OF COURSE. MY ANIKI NEVER GOES BACK ON HIS WORD.
BUT WATCH YOURSELF, SHIKATARŌ. THIS IS NORACHIYO THE GODSLAYER.
...
DON'T LET YOUR GUARD DOWN JUST 'CAUSE HE'S A KITTEN. YOU GOTTA CUT HIM IN TWO WITH YOUR FIRST STRIKE.
YOU MANGY MOG! YOU WERE JUST SAYING YOU WOULD PAY BACK THE MONEY!
GRR!
CLANK
YEAH, WELL...
I'M NOT EXACTLY THRILLED ABOUT PULLING A KATANA ON A LITTLE KITTY CAT...
BUT I DON'T REALLY HAVE MUCH CHOICE NOW, DO I?

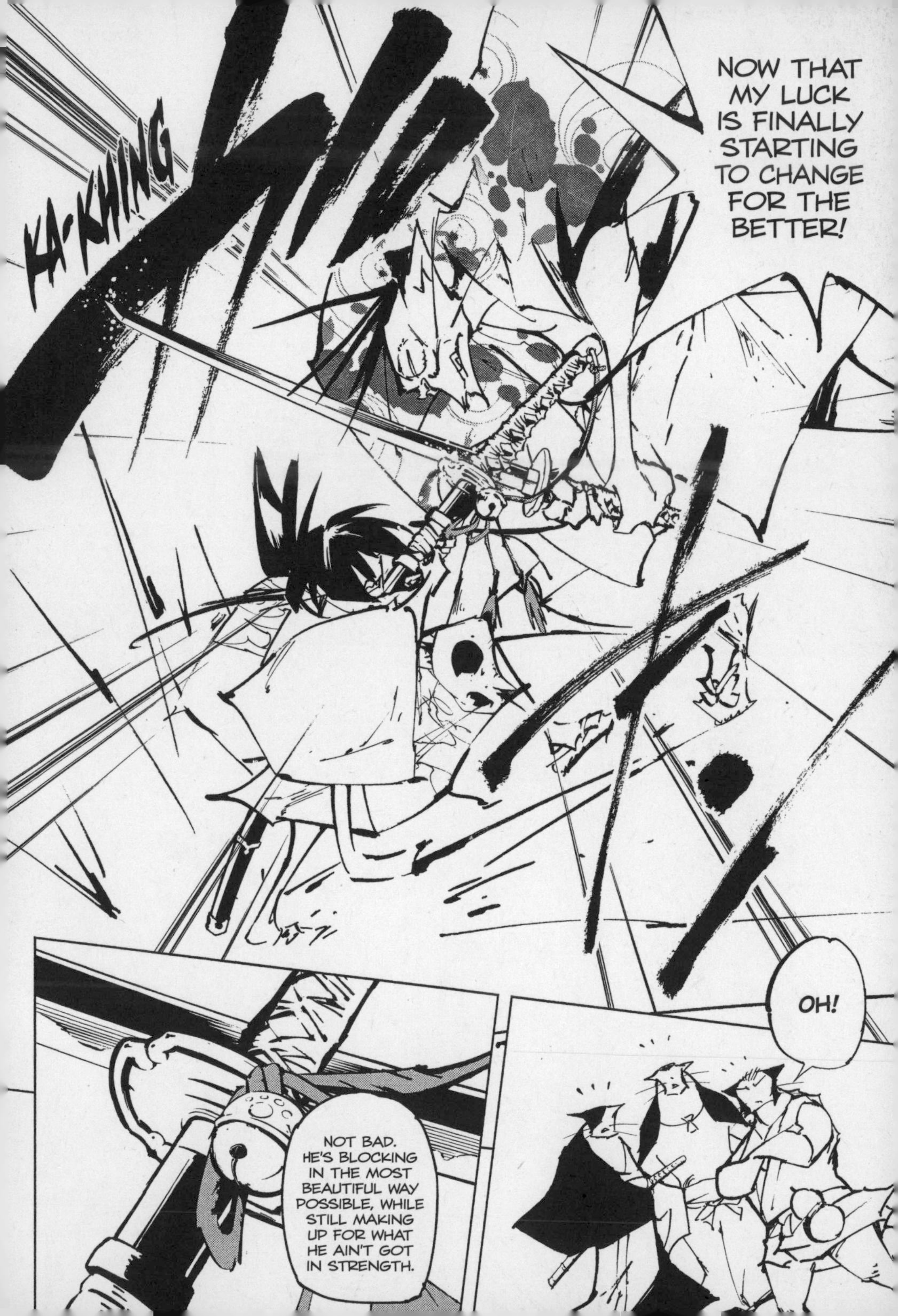
NOW THAT MY LUCK IS FINALLY STARTING TO CHANGE FOR THE BETTER!
KA-KHING
OH!
NOT BAD. HE'S BLOCKING IN THE MOST BEAUTIFUL WAY POSSIBLE, WHILE STILL MAKING UP FOR WHAT HE AIN'T GOT IN STRENGTH.

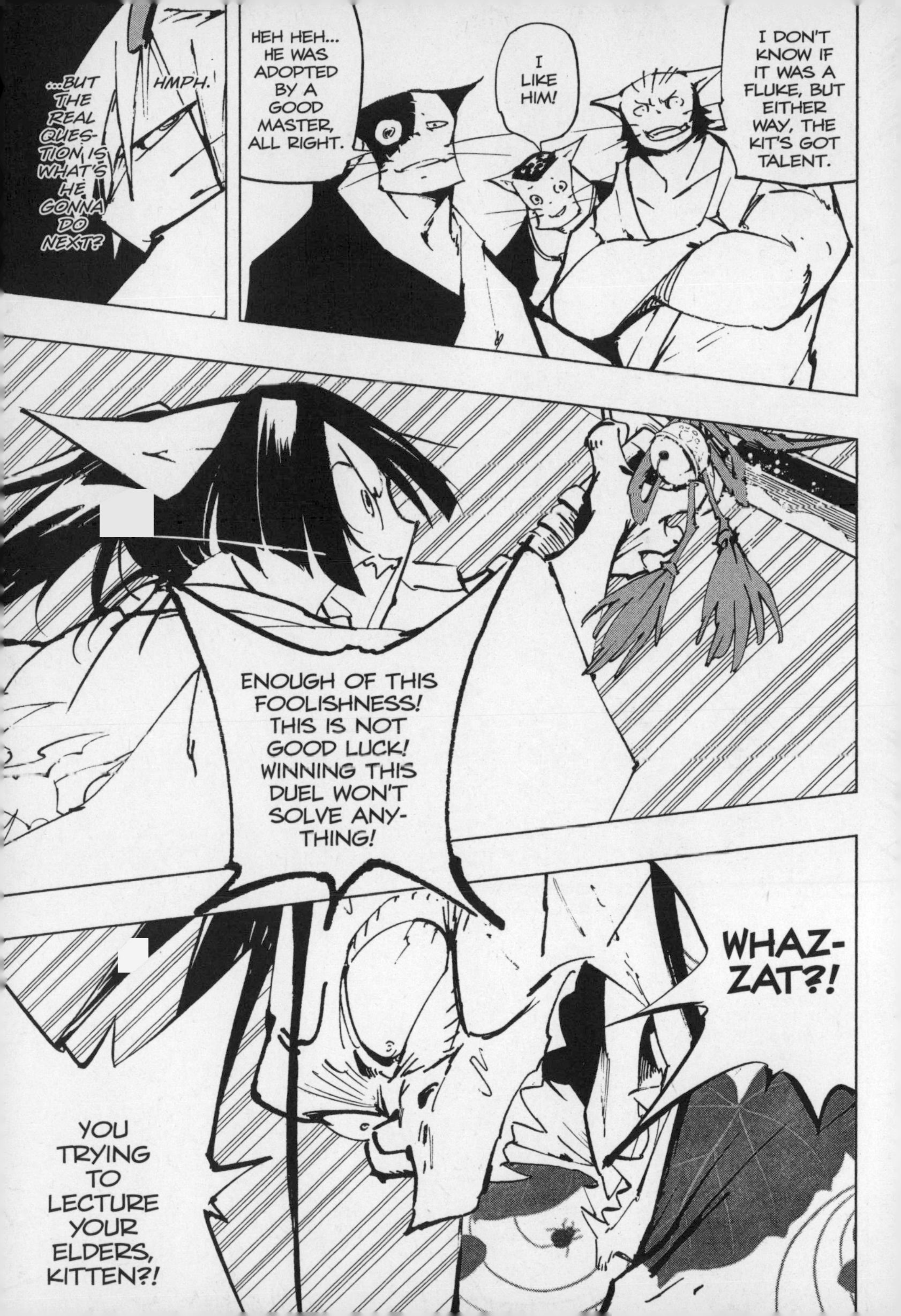
I DON'T KNOW IF IT WAS A FLUKE, BUT EITHER WAY, THE KIT'S GOT TALENT.
I LIKE HIM!
HEH HEH... HE WAS ADOPTED BY A GOOD MASTER, ALL RIGHT.
HMPH.
...BUT THE REAL QUES-TION IS WHAT'S HE GONNA DO NEXT?
ENOUGH OF THIS FOOLISHNESS! THIS IS NOT GOOD LUCK! WINNING THIS DUEL WON'T SOLVE ANY-THING!
WHAZ-ZAT?!
YOU TRYING TO LECTURE YOUR ELDERS, KITTEN?!

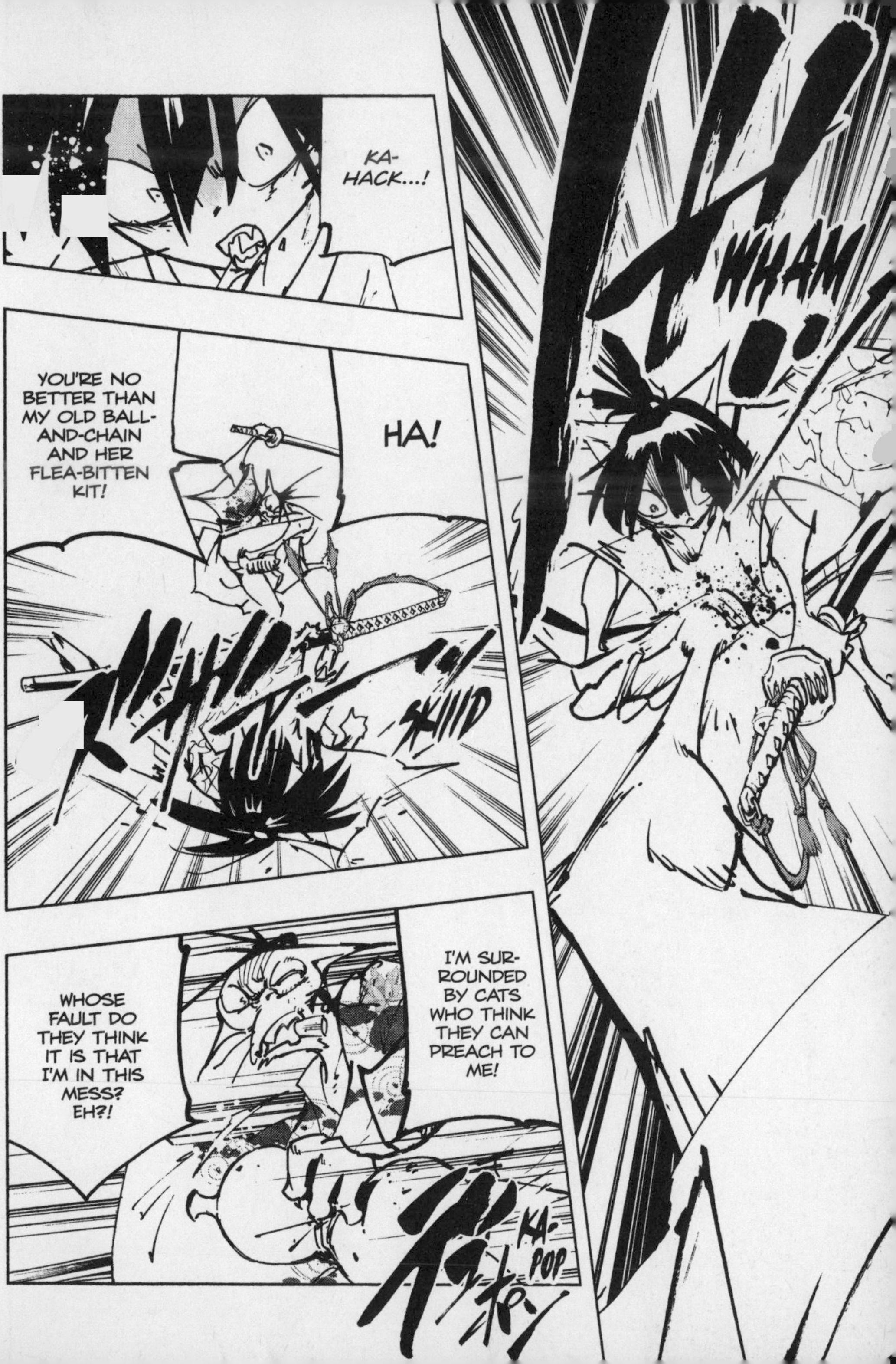
WHAM
KA-HACK...!
YOU'RE NO BETTER THAN MY OLD BALL-AND-CHAIN AND HER FLEA-BITTEN KIT!
HA!
SKIIID
I'M SURROUNDED BY CATS WHO THINK THEY CAN PREACH TO ME!
WHOSE FAULT DO THEY THINK IT IS THAT I'M IN THIS MESS? EH?!
KA-POP

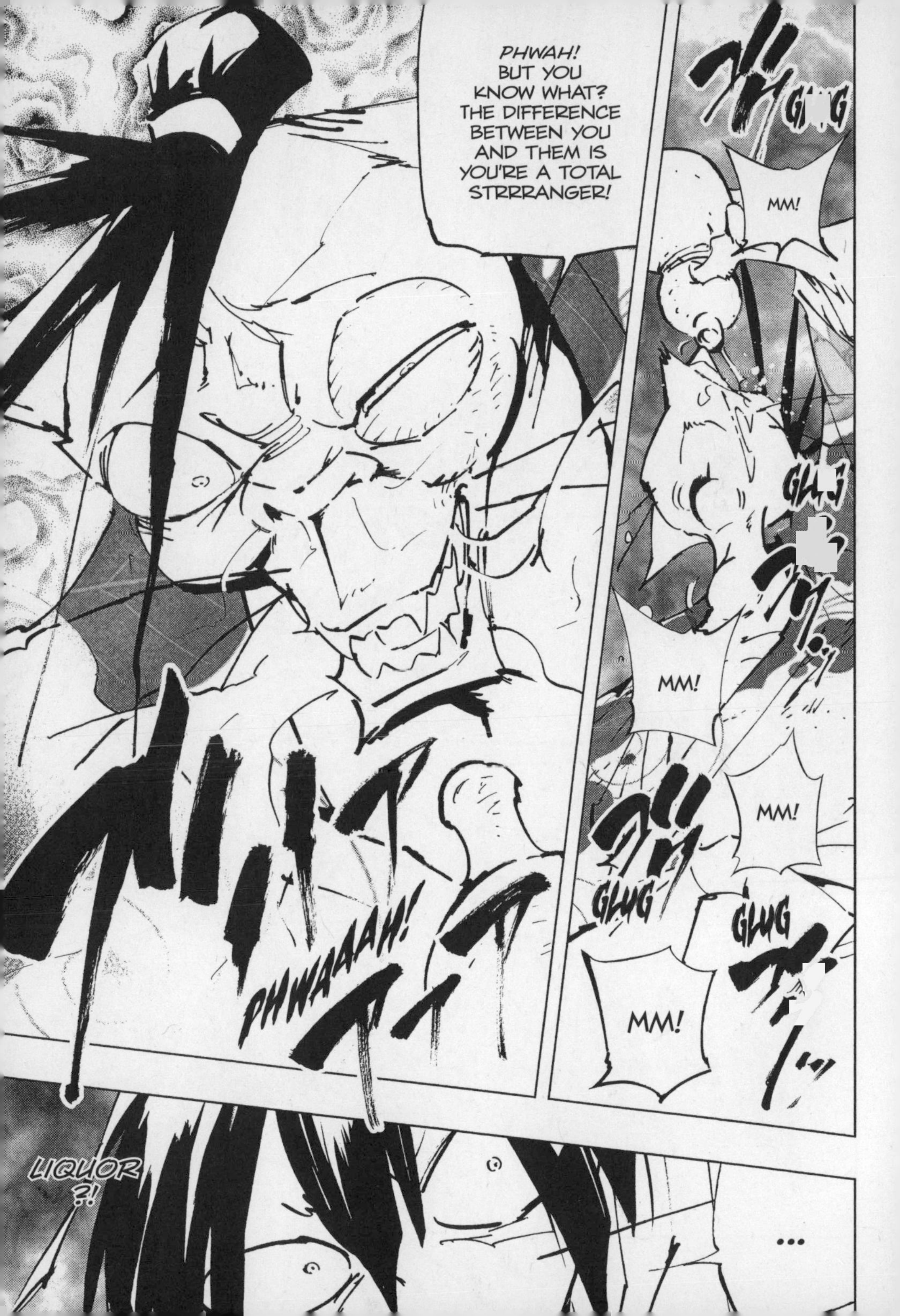
MM!
MM!
MM!
GLUG
GLUG
MM!
PHWAH!
BUT YOU KNOW WHAT? THE DIFFERENCE BETWEEN YOU AND THEM IS YOU'RE A TOTAL STRRRANGER!
PHWAAAH!
...
LIQUOR?!

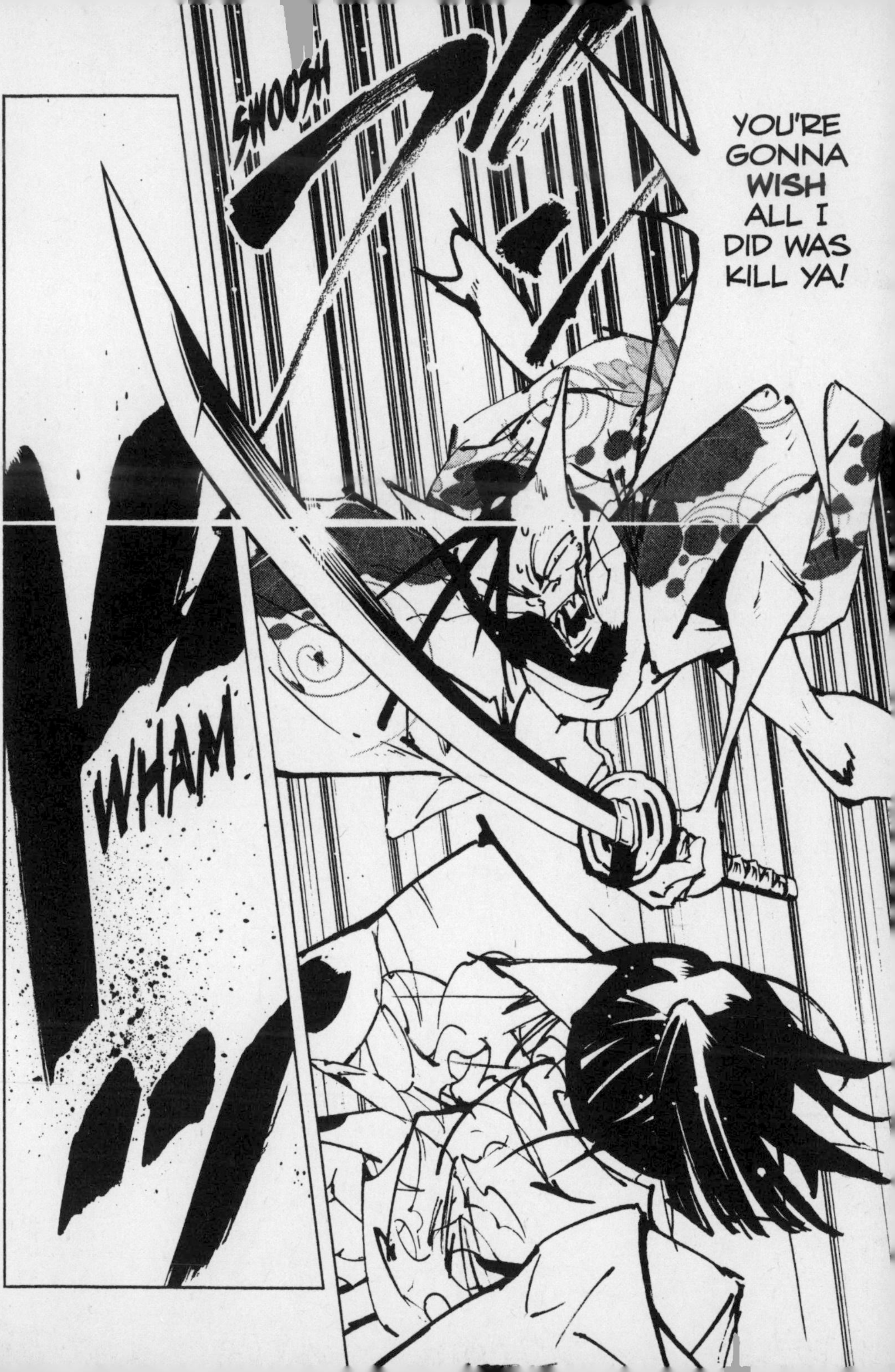

YOU'RE GONNA WISH ALL I DID WAS KILL YA!
SWOOSH
WHAM

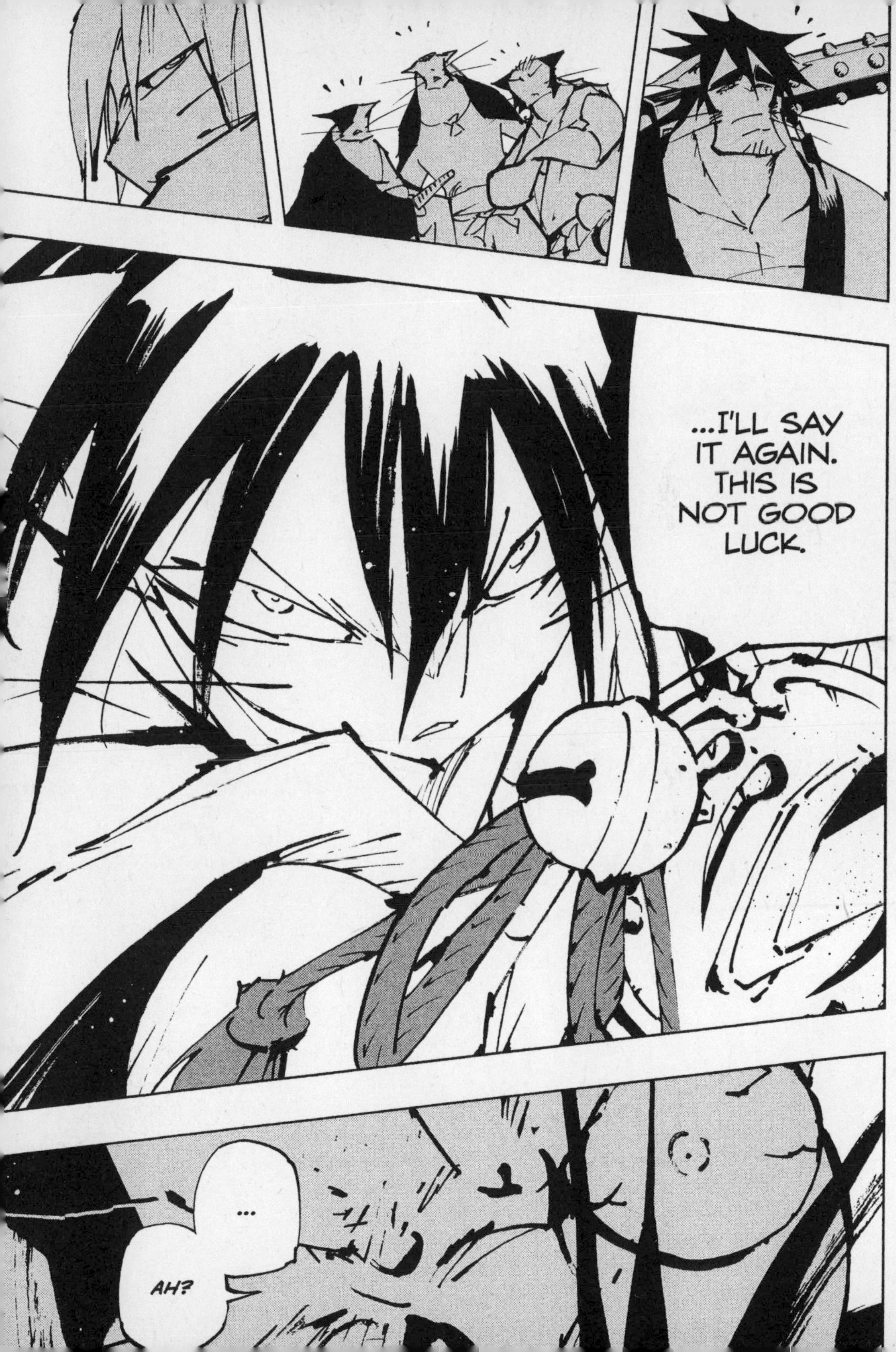
...I'LL SAY IT AGAIN. THIS IS NOT GOOD LUCK.
...
AH?

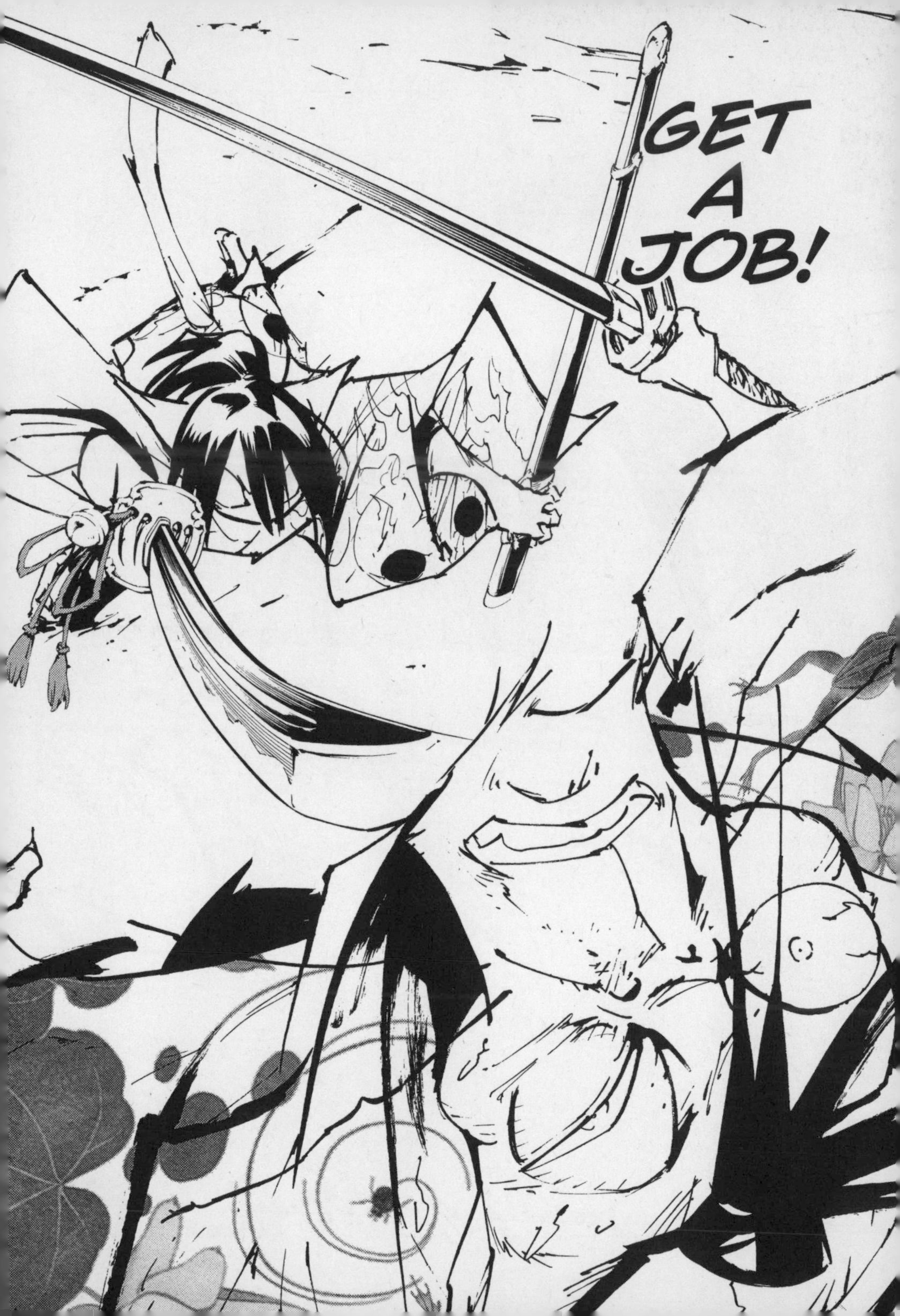
GET A JOB!

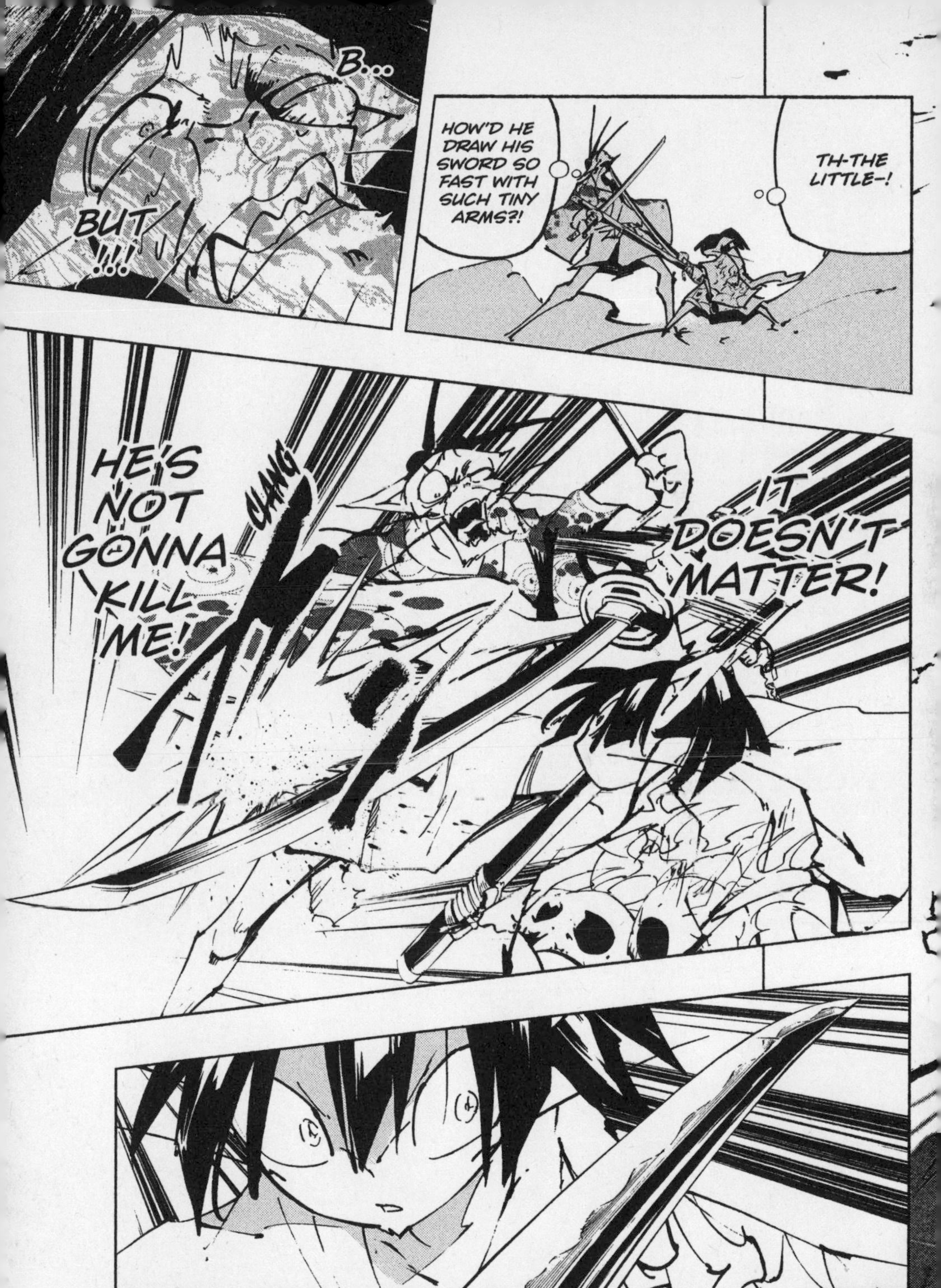
TH-THE LITTLE-!
HOW'D HE DRAW HIS SWORD SO FAST WITH SUCH TINY ARMS?!
B...
BUT!!!
IT DOESN'T MATTER!
CLANG
HE'S NOT GONNA KILL ME!

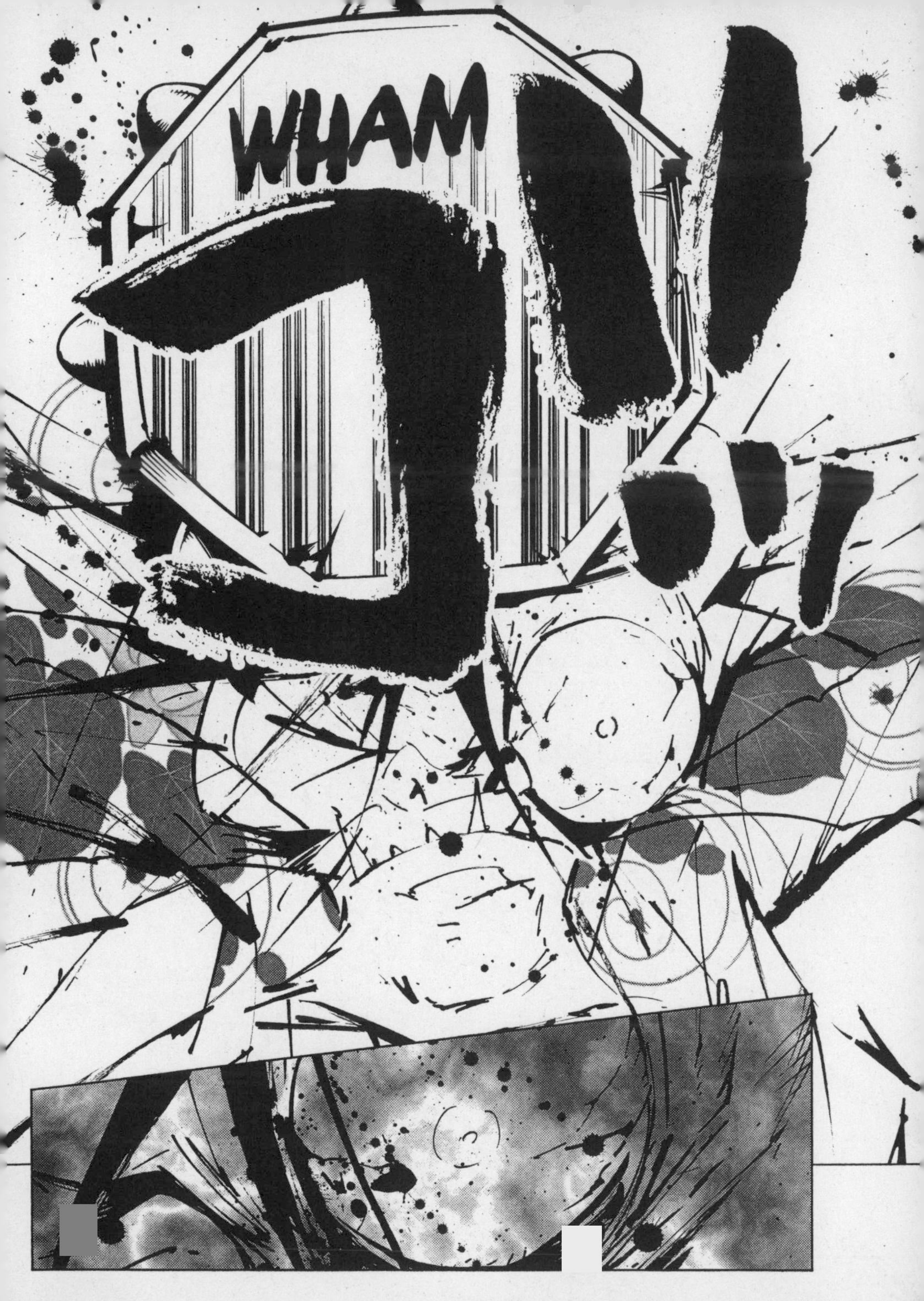
WHAM

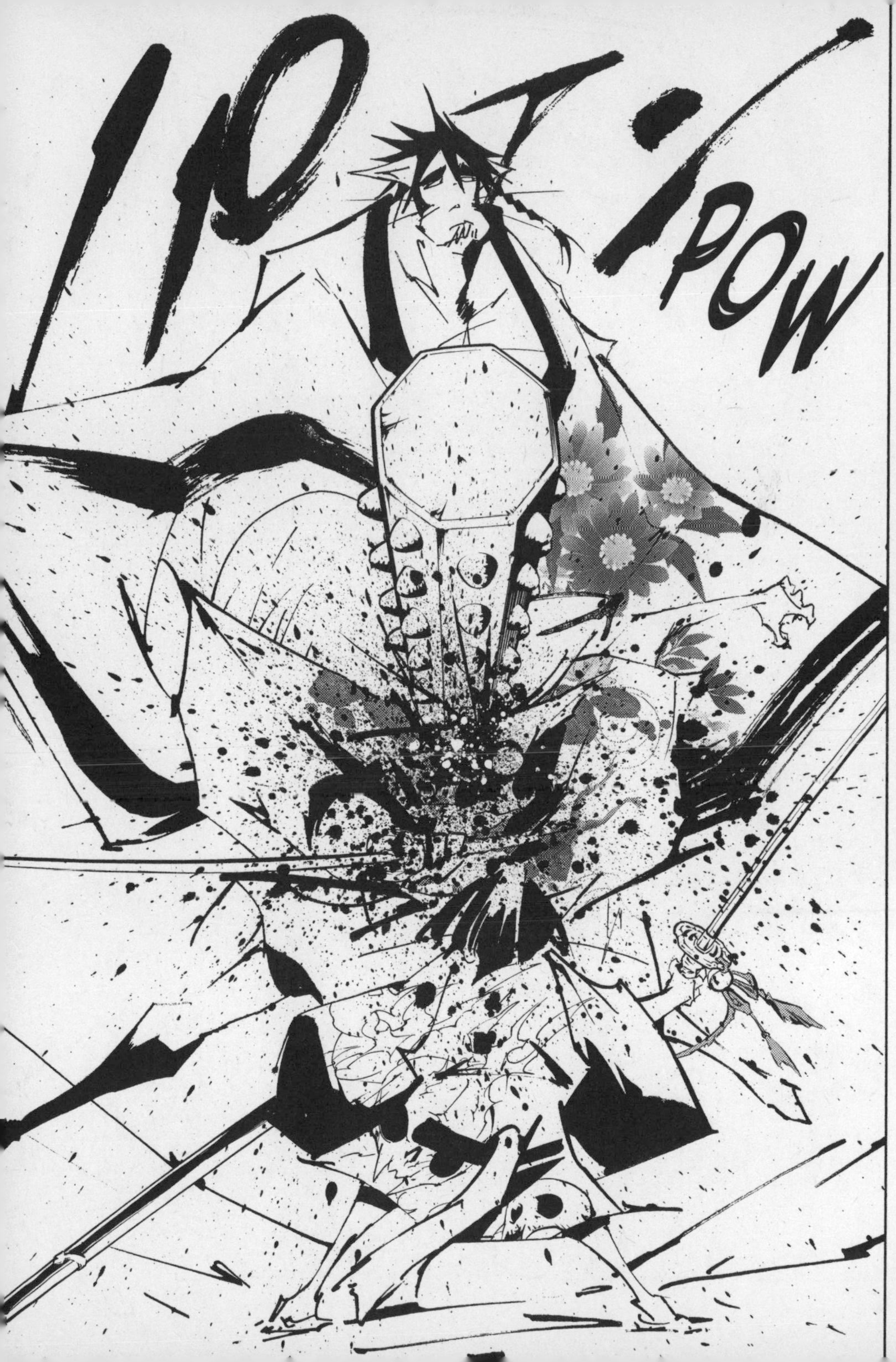
POW

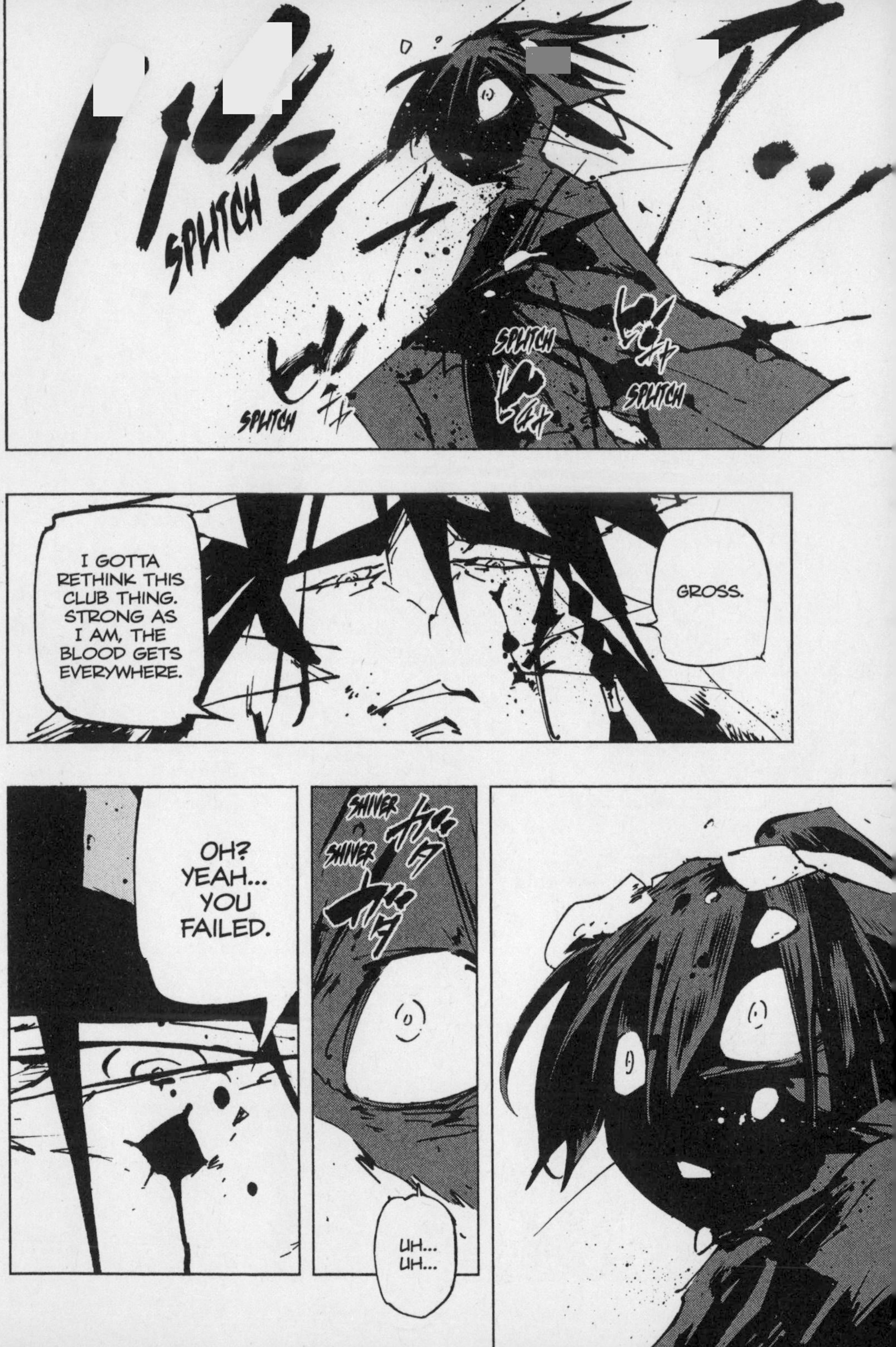
SPLITCH
SPLITCH
SPLITCH
SPLITCH
GROSS.
I GOTTA RETHINK THIS CLUB THING. STRONG AS I AM, THE BLOOD GETS EVERYWHERE.
SHIVER SHIVER
UH... UH...
OH? YEAH... YOU FAILED.

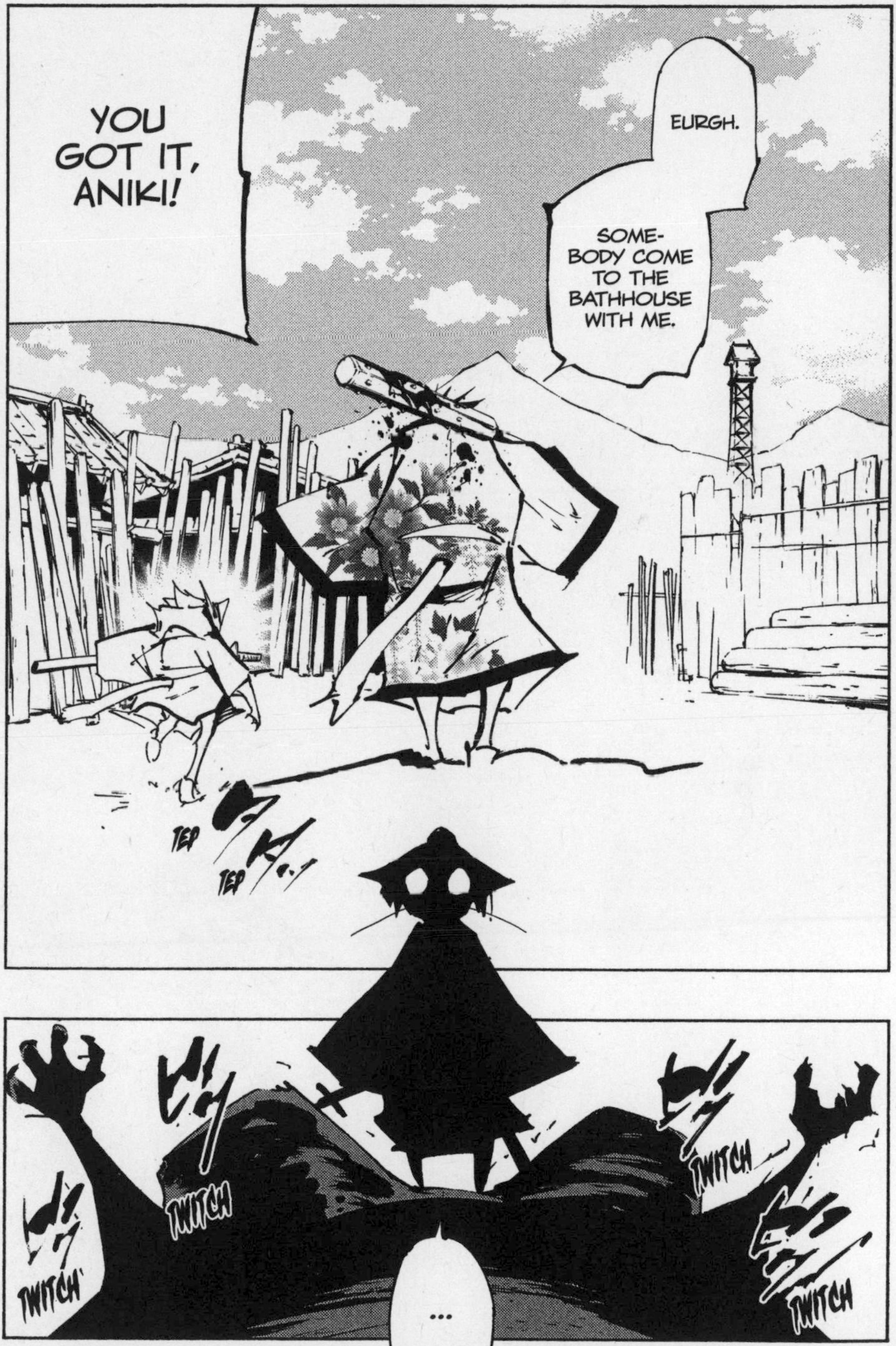
EURGH.
SOME-BODY COME TO THE BATHHOUSE WITH ME.
YOU GOT IT, ANIKI!
TEP
TEP
TWITCH
TWITCH
TWITCH
TWITCH
...

猫ヶ原

NeKoGaHaRa

ネコガハラ

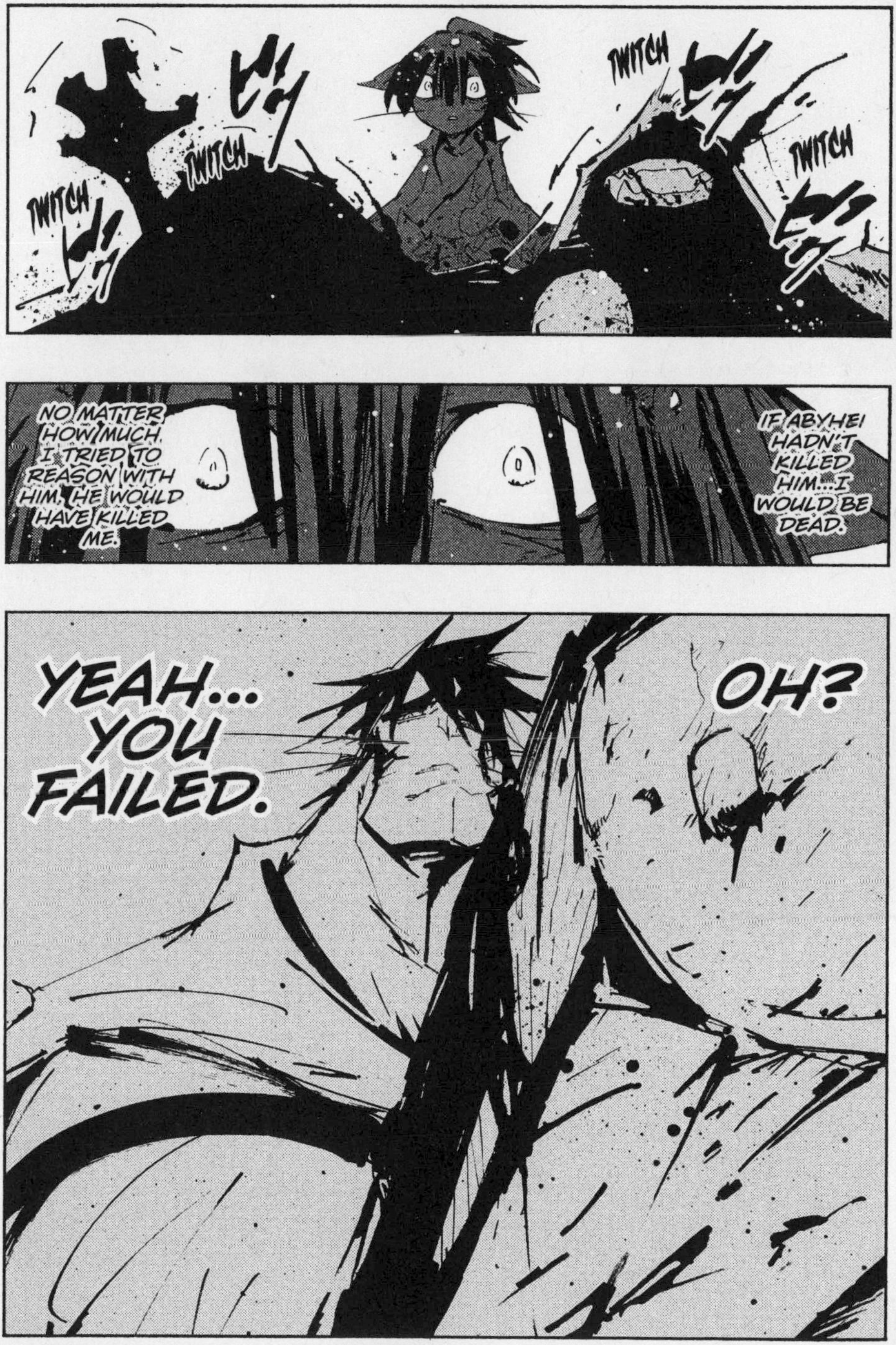
TWITCH
TWITCH
TWITCH
TWITCH
IF ABYHEI HADN'T KILLED HIM...I WOULD BE DEAD.
NO MATTER HOW MUCH I TRIED TO REASON WITH HIM, HE WOULD HAVE KILLED ME.
OH?
YEAH... YOU FAILED.

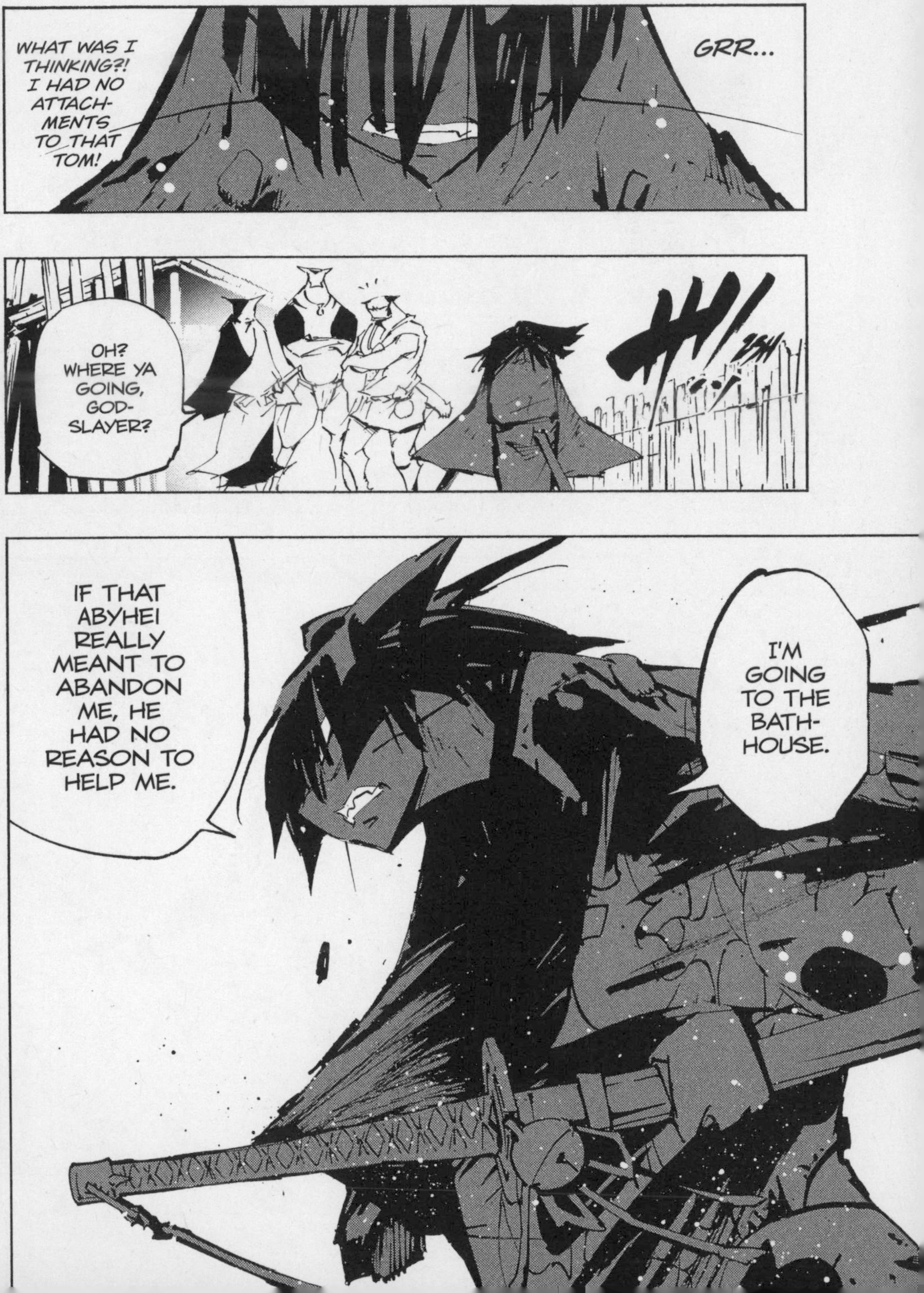
GRR...
WHAT WAS I THINKING?! I HAD NO ATTACHMENTS TO THAT TOM!
OH? WHERE YA GOING, GOD-SLAYER?
I'M GOING TO THE BATHHOUSE.
IF THAT ABYHEI REALLY MEANT TO ABANDON ME, HE HAD NO REASON TO HELP ME.

NEKOGAHARA

HIROYUKI TAKEI

CHAPTER 22:
HI LONE KITTY,
PART 4

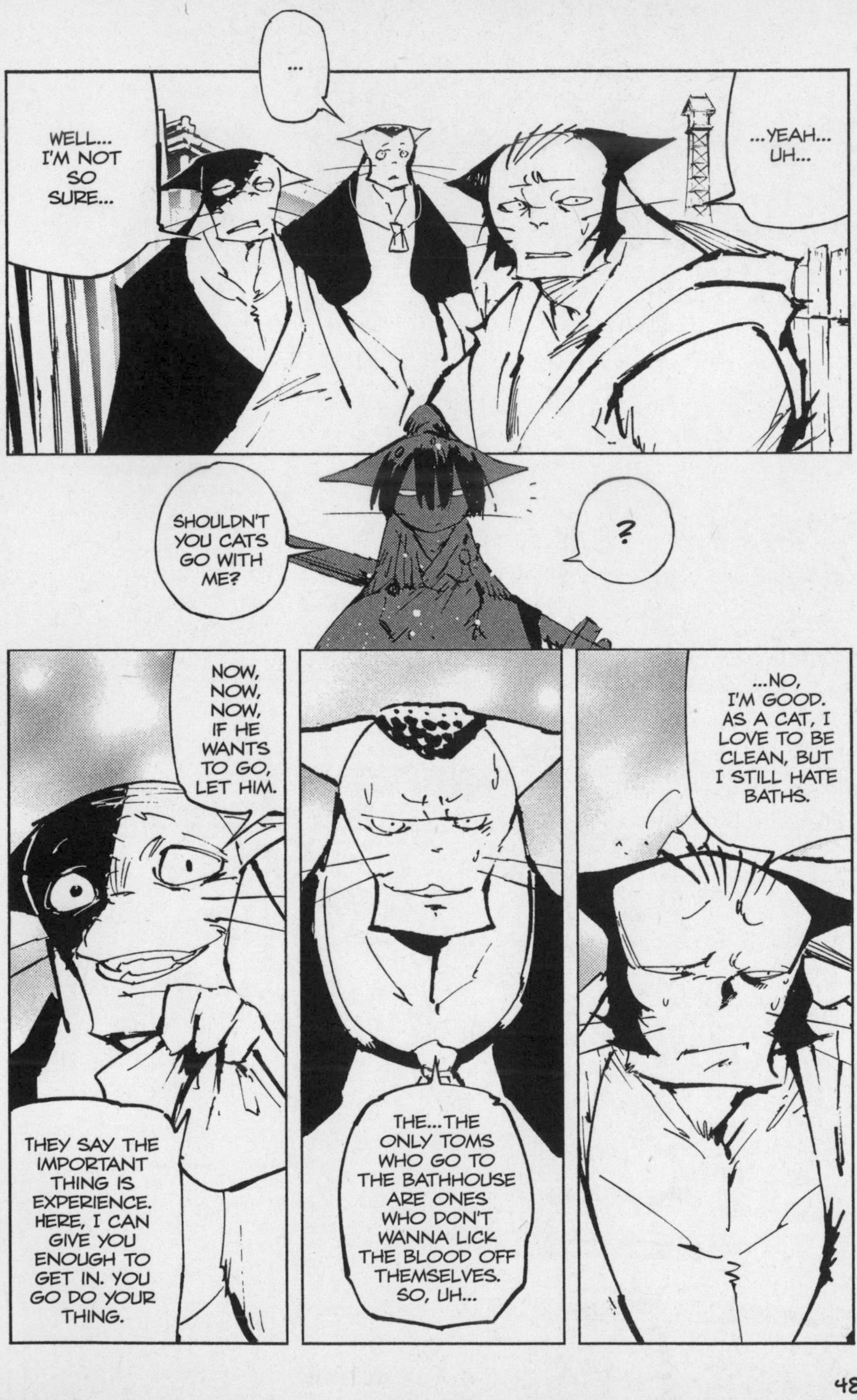
...YEAH... UH...
...
WELL... I'M NOT SO SURE...
?
SHOULDN'T YOU CATS GO WITH ME?
...NO, I'M GOOD. AS A CAT, I LOVE TO BE CLEAN, BUT I STILL HATE BATHS.
THE...THE ONLY TOMS WHO GO TO THE BATHHOUSE ARE ONES WHO DON'T WANNA LICK THE BLOOD OFF THEMSELVES. SO, UH...
NOW, NOW, NOW, IF HE WANTS TO GO, LET HIM.
THEY SAY THE IMPORTANT THING IS EXPERIENCE. HERE, I CAN GIVE YOU ENOUGH TO GET IN. YOU GO DO YOUR THING.

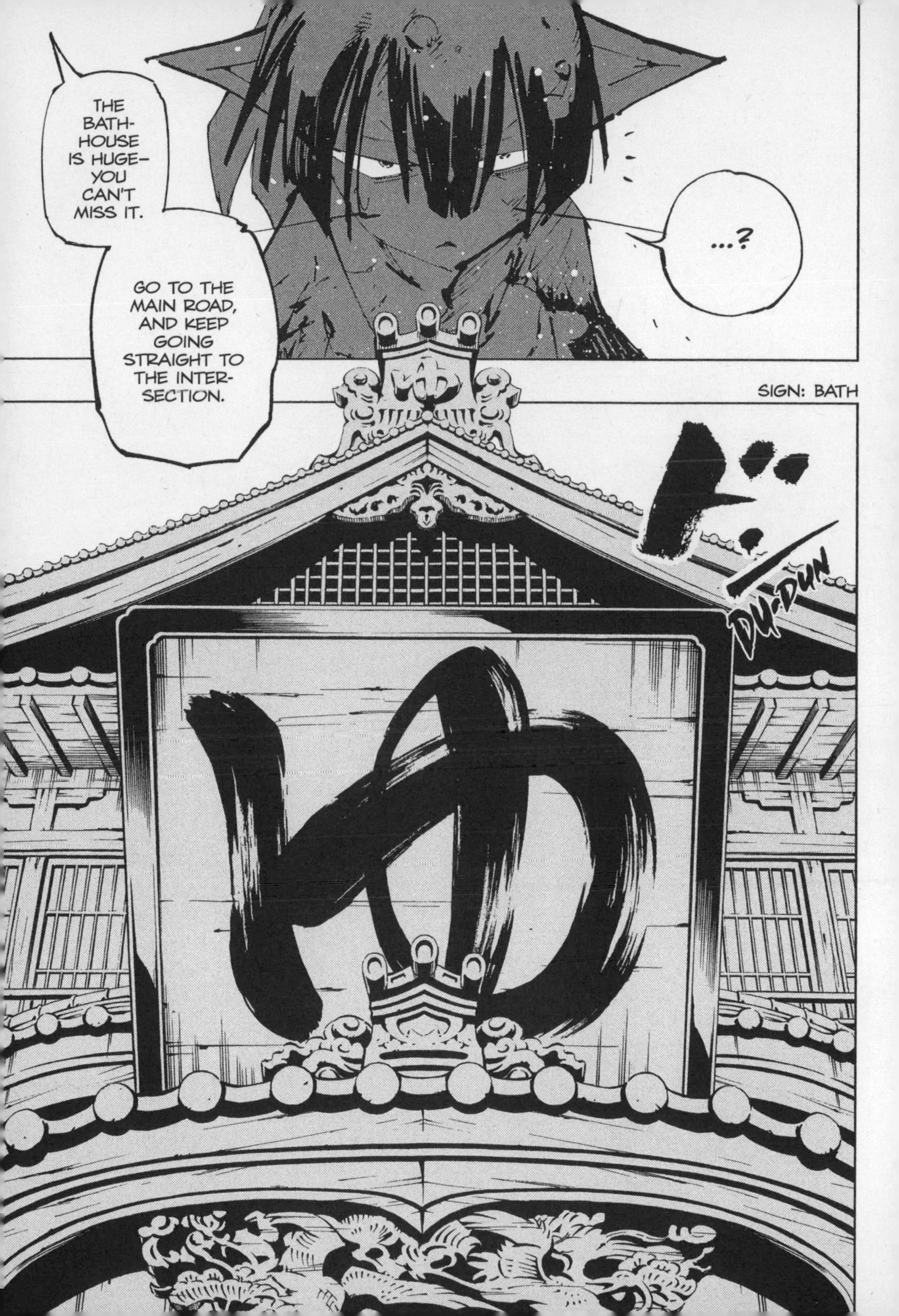
THE BATH-HOUSE IS HUGE–YOU CAN'T MISS IT.
...?
GO TO THE MAIN ROAD, AND KEEP GOING STRAIGHT TO THE INTER-SECTION.
SIGN: BATH
DU-DUN

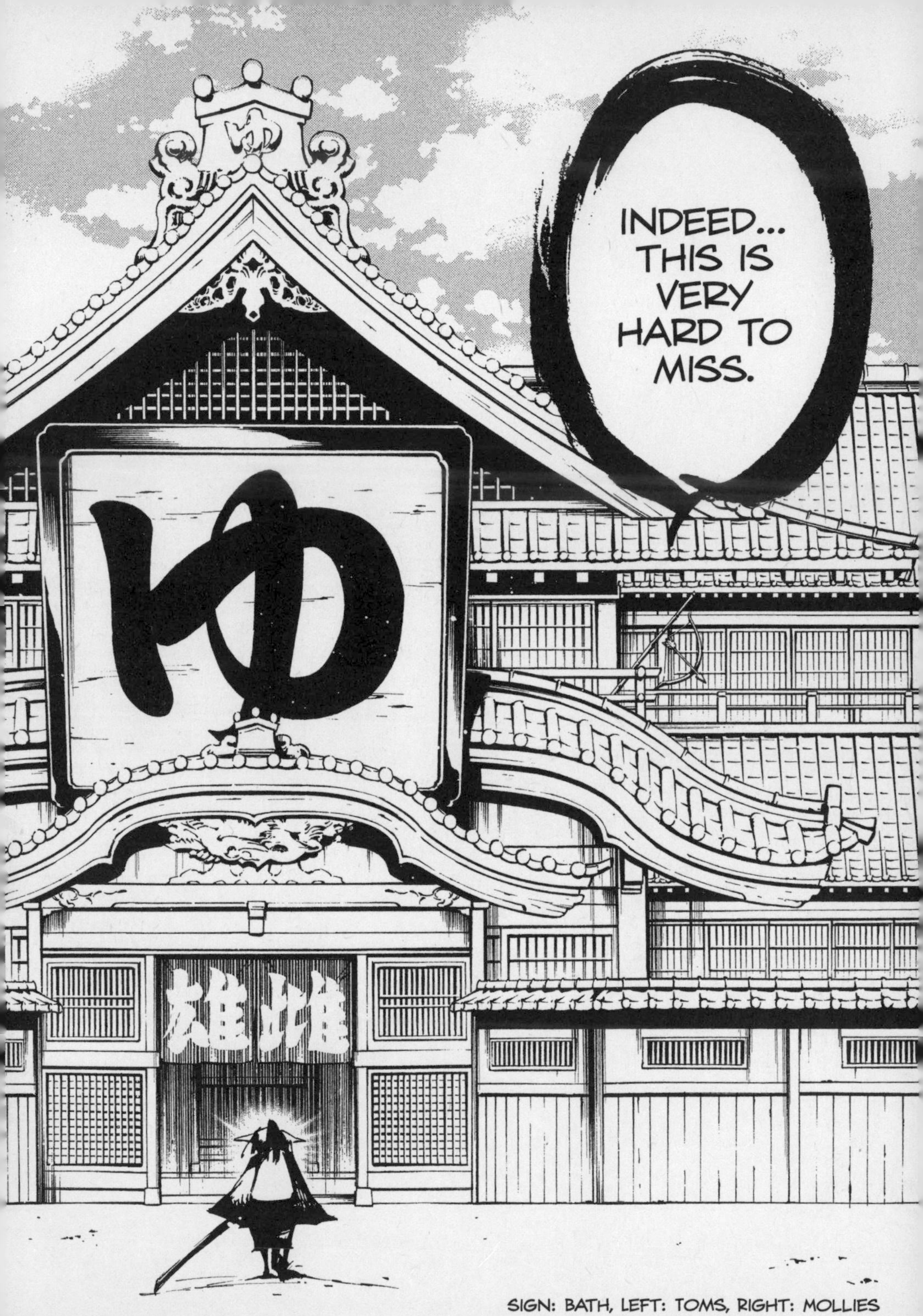
INDEED... THIS IS VERY HARD TO MISS.
ゆ
雄 雌

SIGN: BATH, LEFT: TOMS, RIGHT: MOLLIES

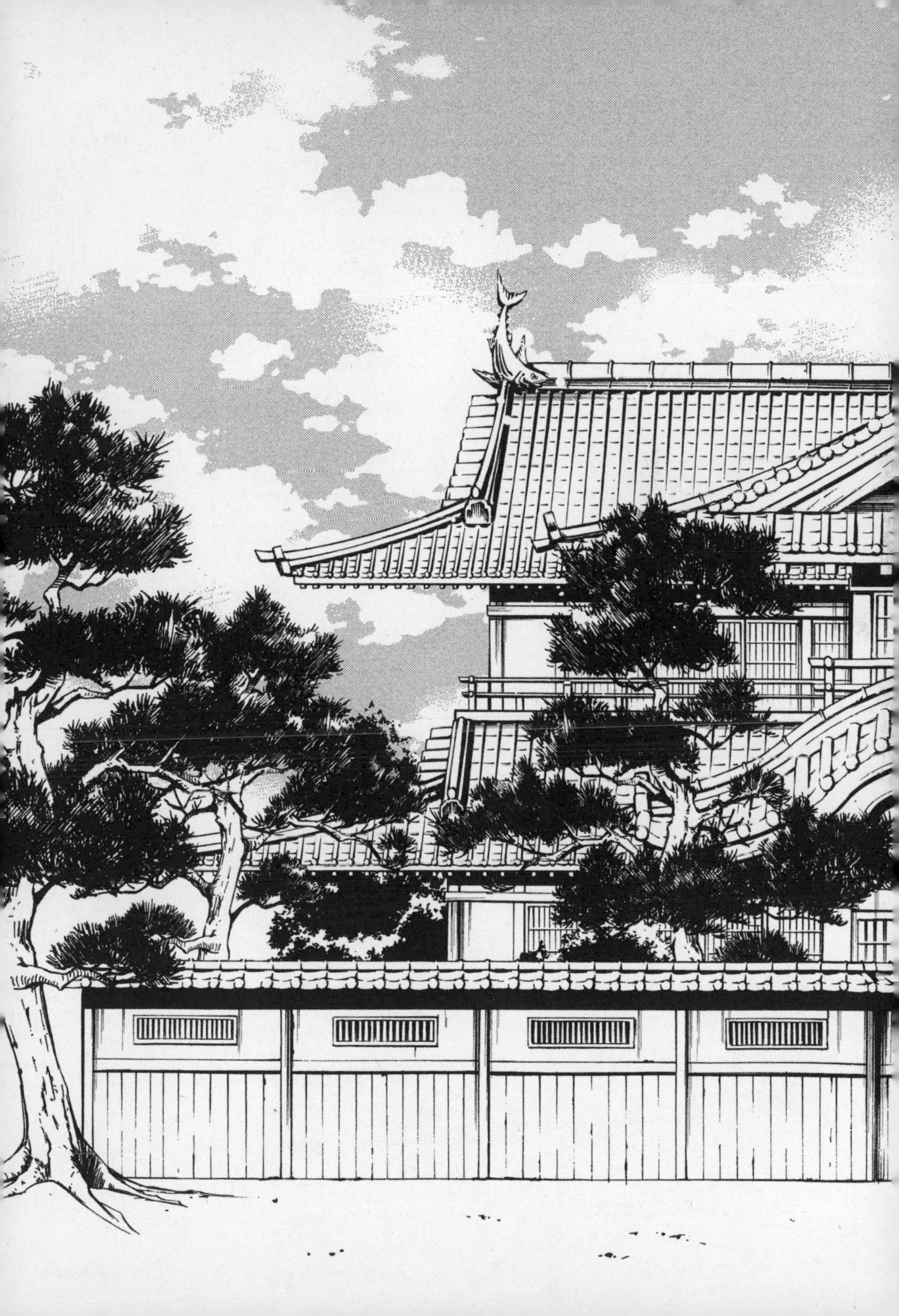

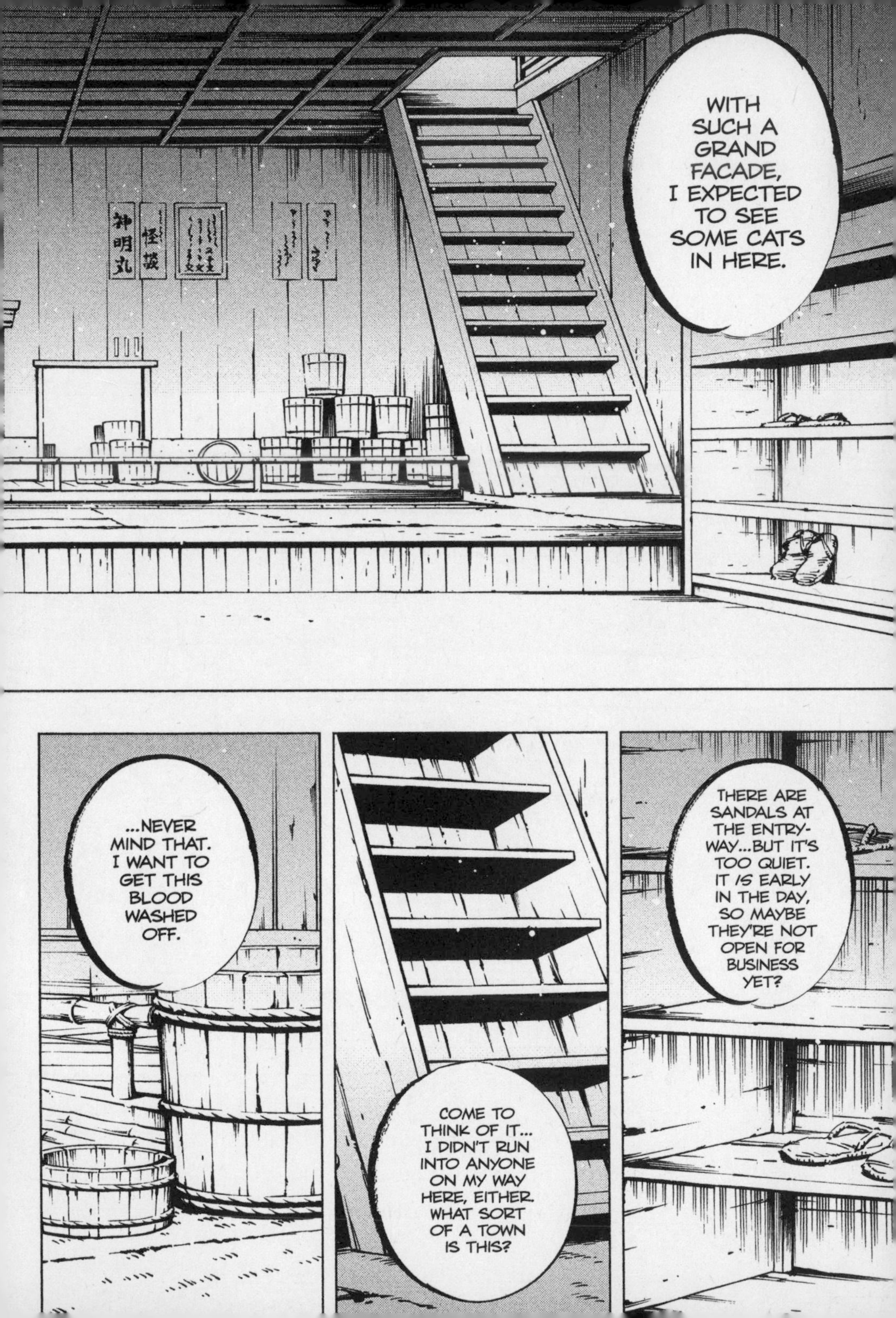
WITH SUCH A GRAND FACADE, I EXPECTED TO SEE SOME CATS IN HERE.
THERE ARE SANDALS AT THE ENTRYWAY...BUT IT'S TOO QUIET. IT *IS* EARLY IN THE DAY, SO MAYBE THEY'RE NOT OPEN FOR BUSINESS YET?
COME TO THINK OF IT... I DIDN'T RUN INTO ANYONE ON MY WAY HERE, EITHER. WHAT SORT OF A TOWN IS THIS?
...NEVER MIND THAT. I WANT TO GET THIS BLOOD WASHED OFF.

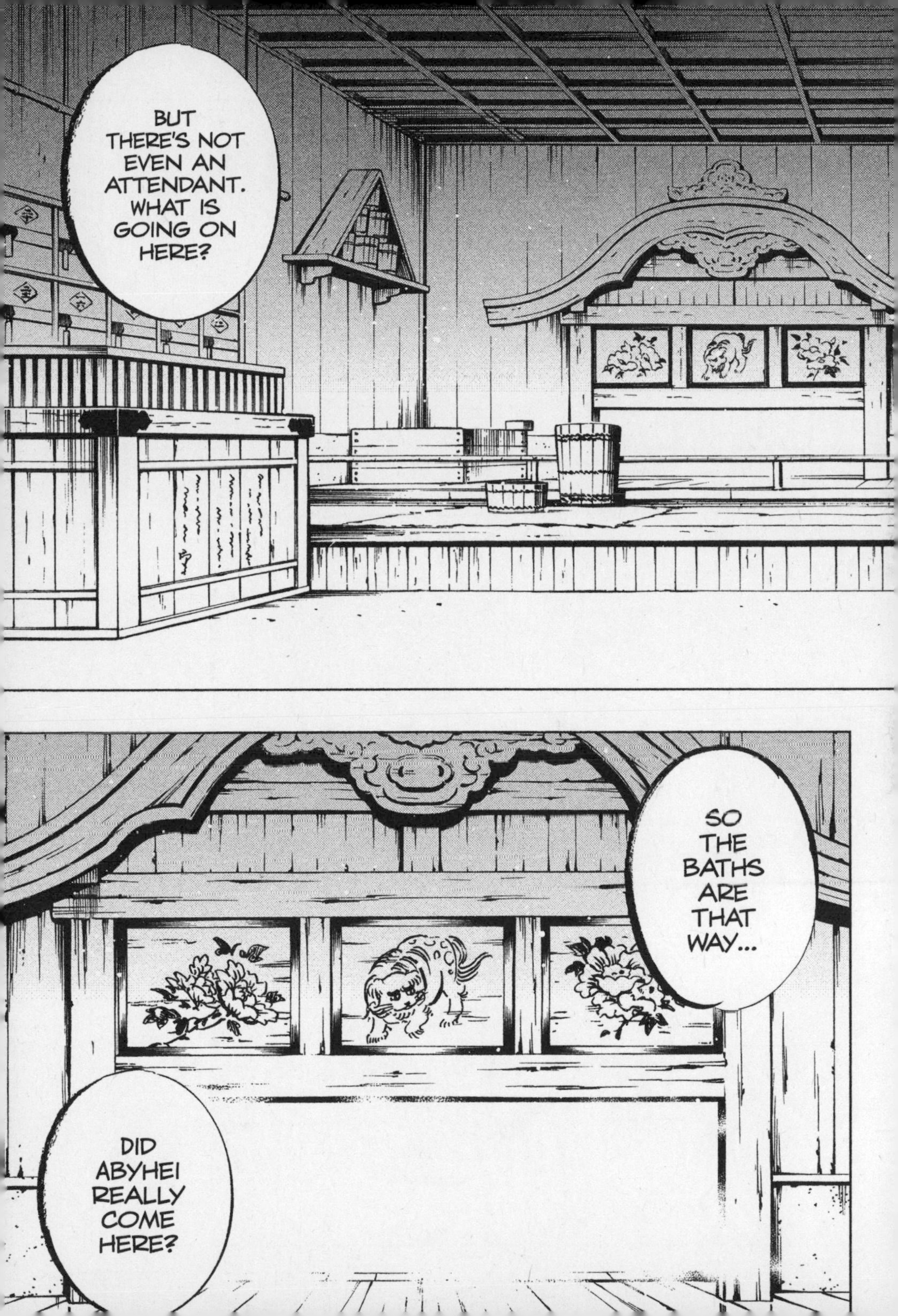
BUT THERE'S NOT EVEN AN ATTENDANT. WHAT IS GOING ON HERE?
SO THE BATHS ARE THAT WAY...
DID ABYHEI REALLY COME HERE?

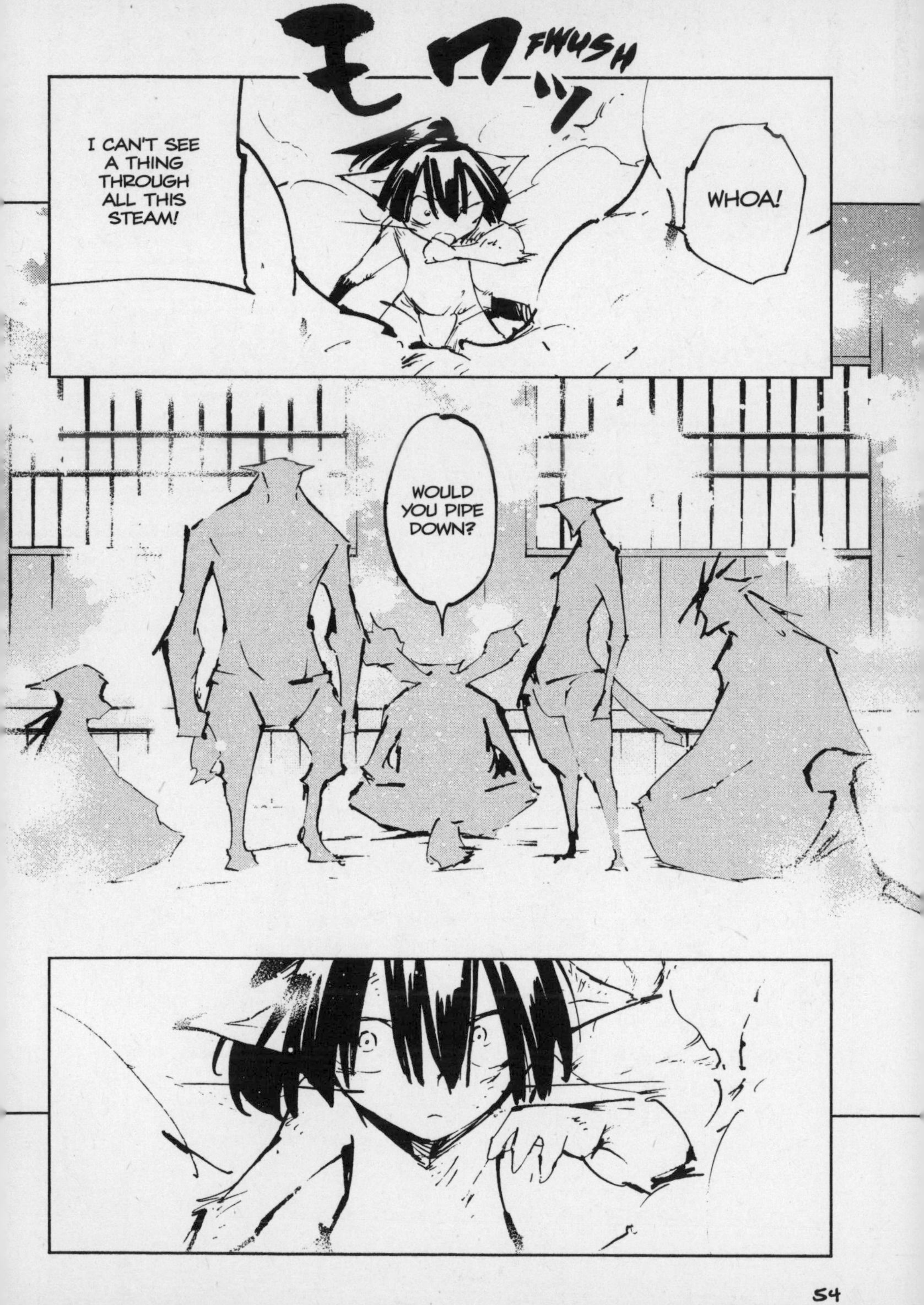
モワッ
FWUSH
WHOA!
I CAN'T SEE A THING THROUGH ALL THIS STEAM!
WOULD YOU PIPE DOWN?

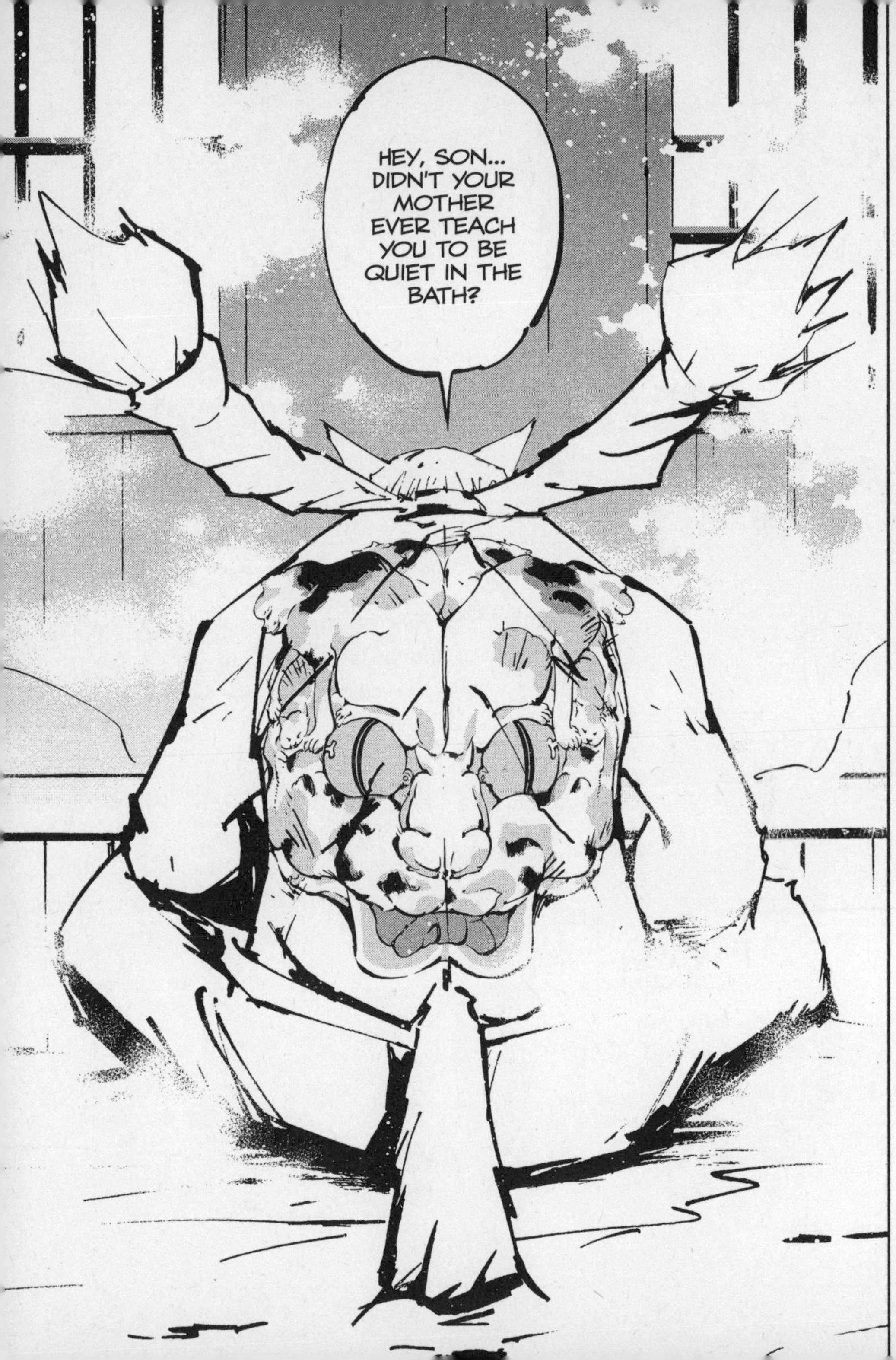
HEY, SON... DIDN'T YOUR MOTHER EVER TEACH YOU TO BE QUIET IN THE BATH?

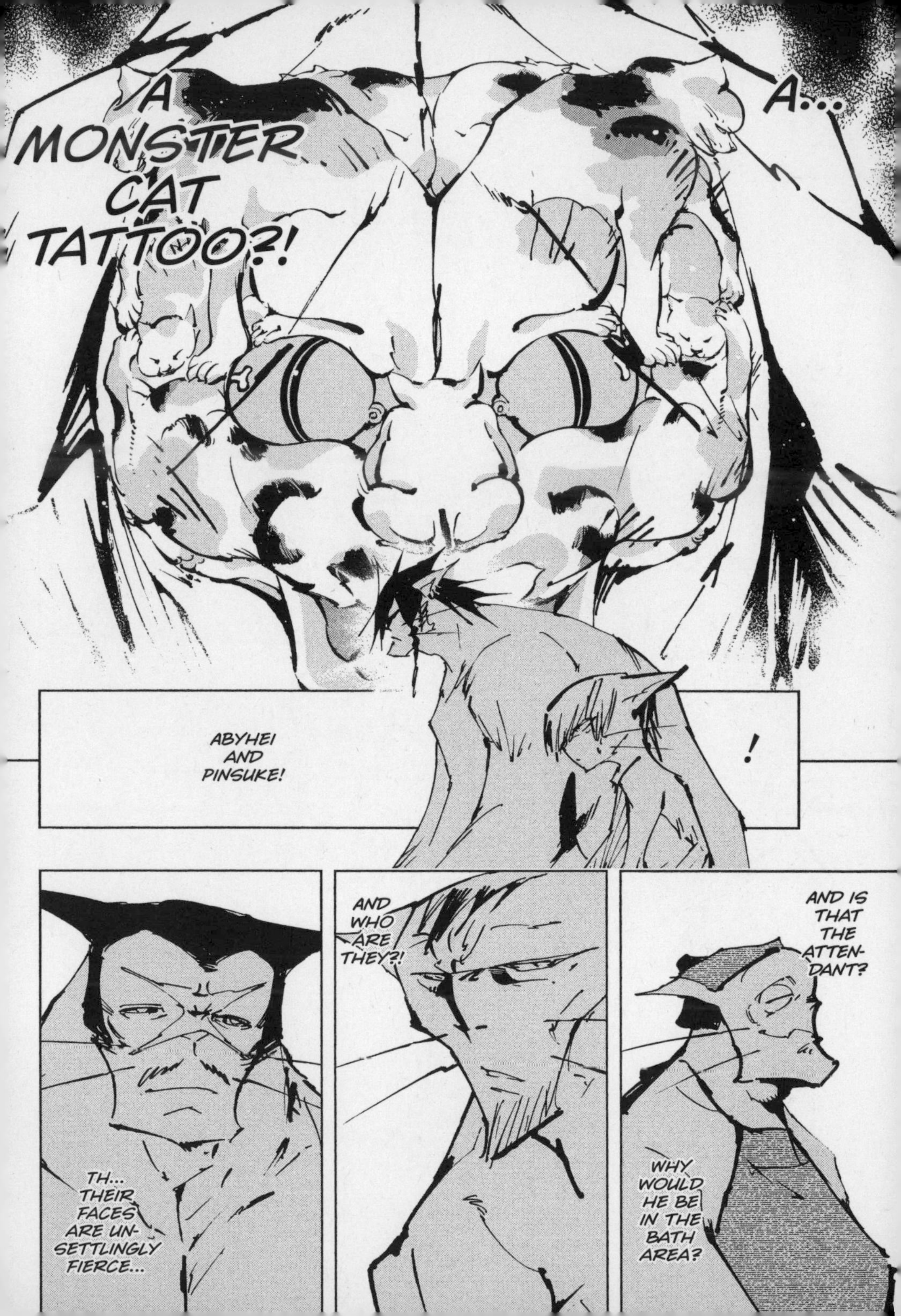
A...
A MONSTER CAT TATTOO?!
!
ABYHEI AND PINSUKE!
AND IS THAT THE ATTEN-DANT?
WHY WOULD HE BE IN THE BATH AREA?
AND WHO ARE THEY?!
TH... THEIR FACES ARE UN-SETTLINGLY FIERCE...

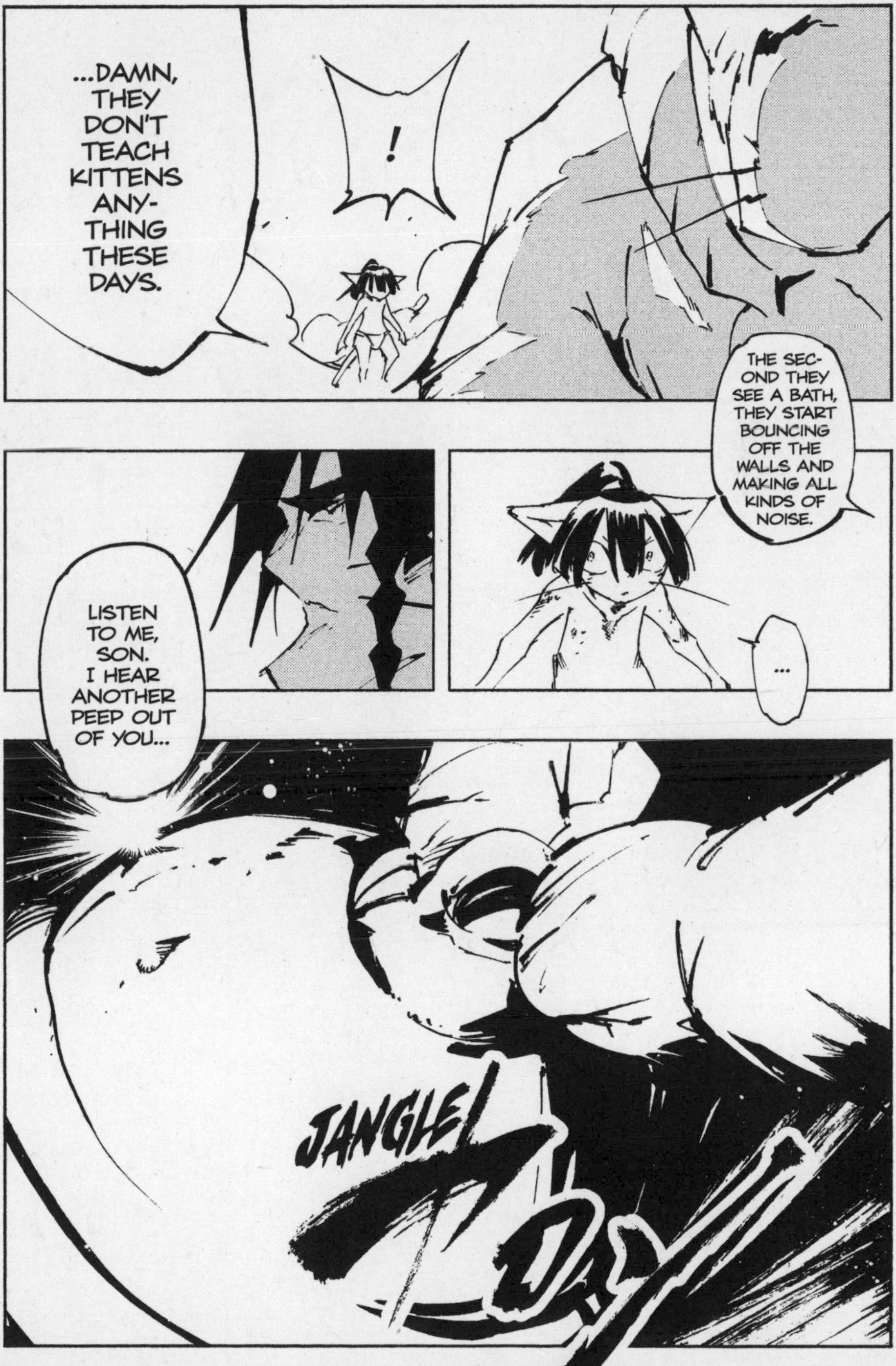
!
...DAMN, THEY DON'T TEACH KITTENS ANY-THING THESE DAYS.
THE SEC-OND THEY SEE A BATH, THEY START BOUNCING OFF THE WALLS AND MAKING ALL KINDS OF NOISE.
...
LISTEN TO ME, SON. I HEAR ANOTHER PEEP OUT OF YOU...
JANGLE

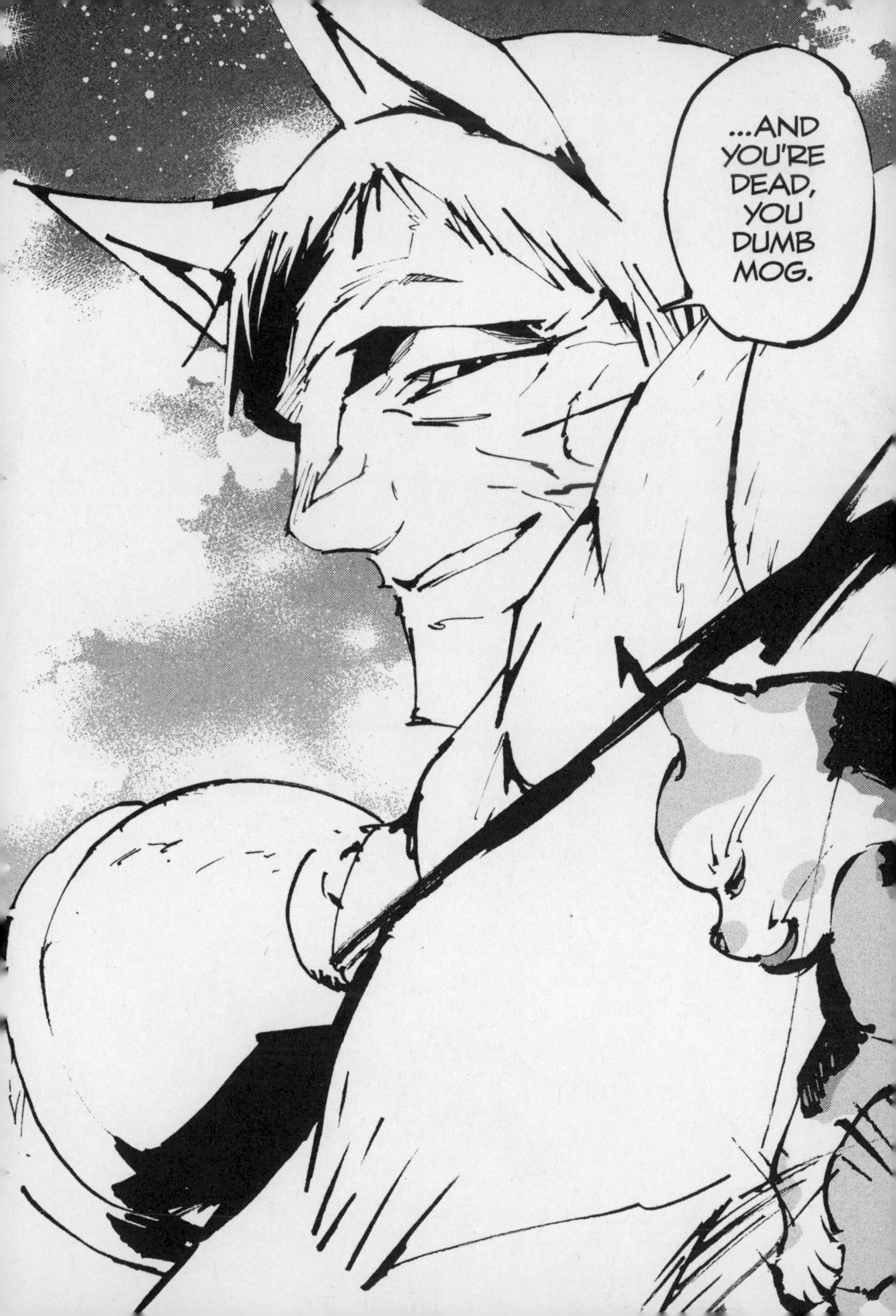
...AND YOU'RE DEAD, YOU DUMB MOG.

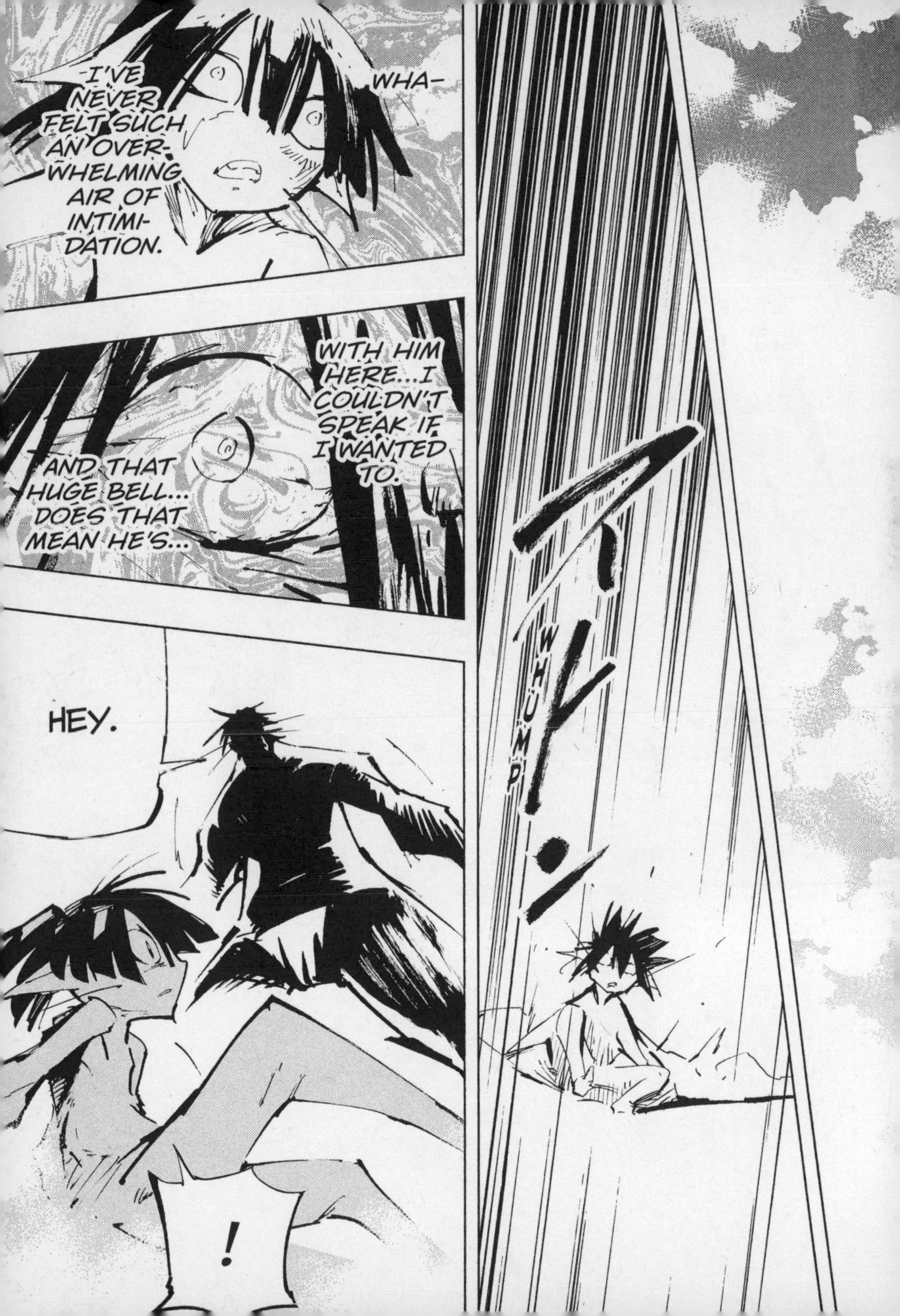
WHUMP
WHA-
I'VE NEVER FELT SUCH AN OVER-WHELMING AIR OF INTIMI-DATION.
WITH HIM HERE...I COULDN'T SPEAK IF I WANTED TO.
AND THAT HUGE BELL... DOES THAT MEAN HE'S...
HEY.
!

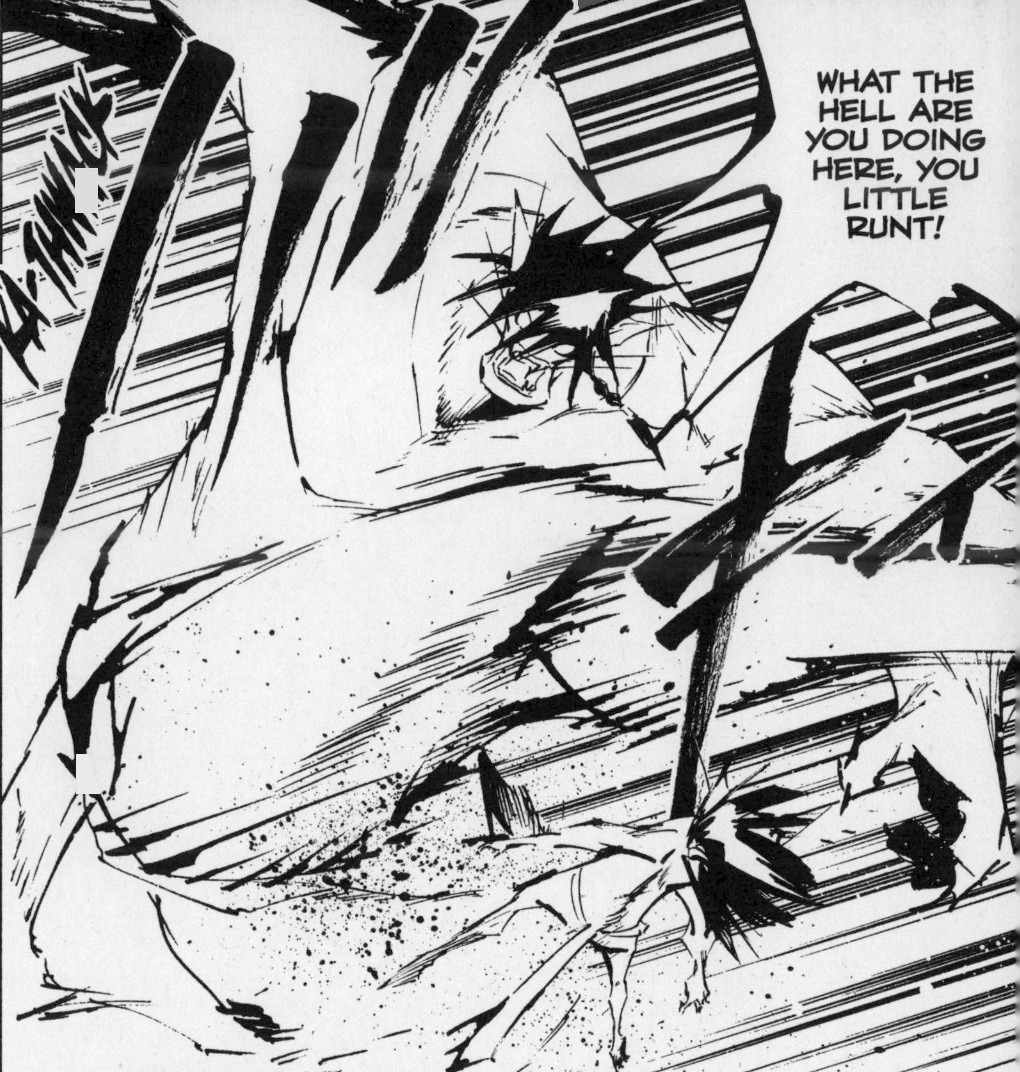
WHAT THE HELL ARE YOU DOING HERE, YOU LITTLE RUNT!
KA-THWACK

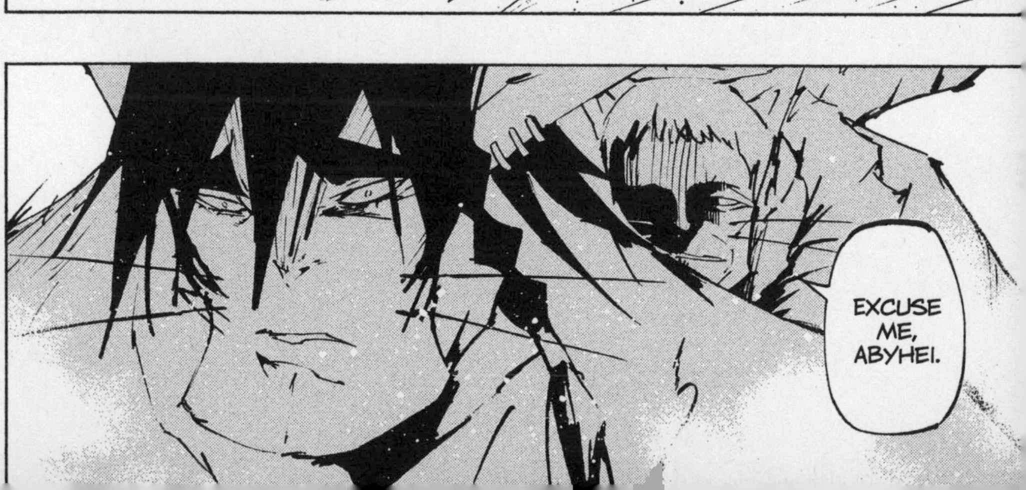
EXCUSE ME, ABYHEI.

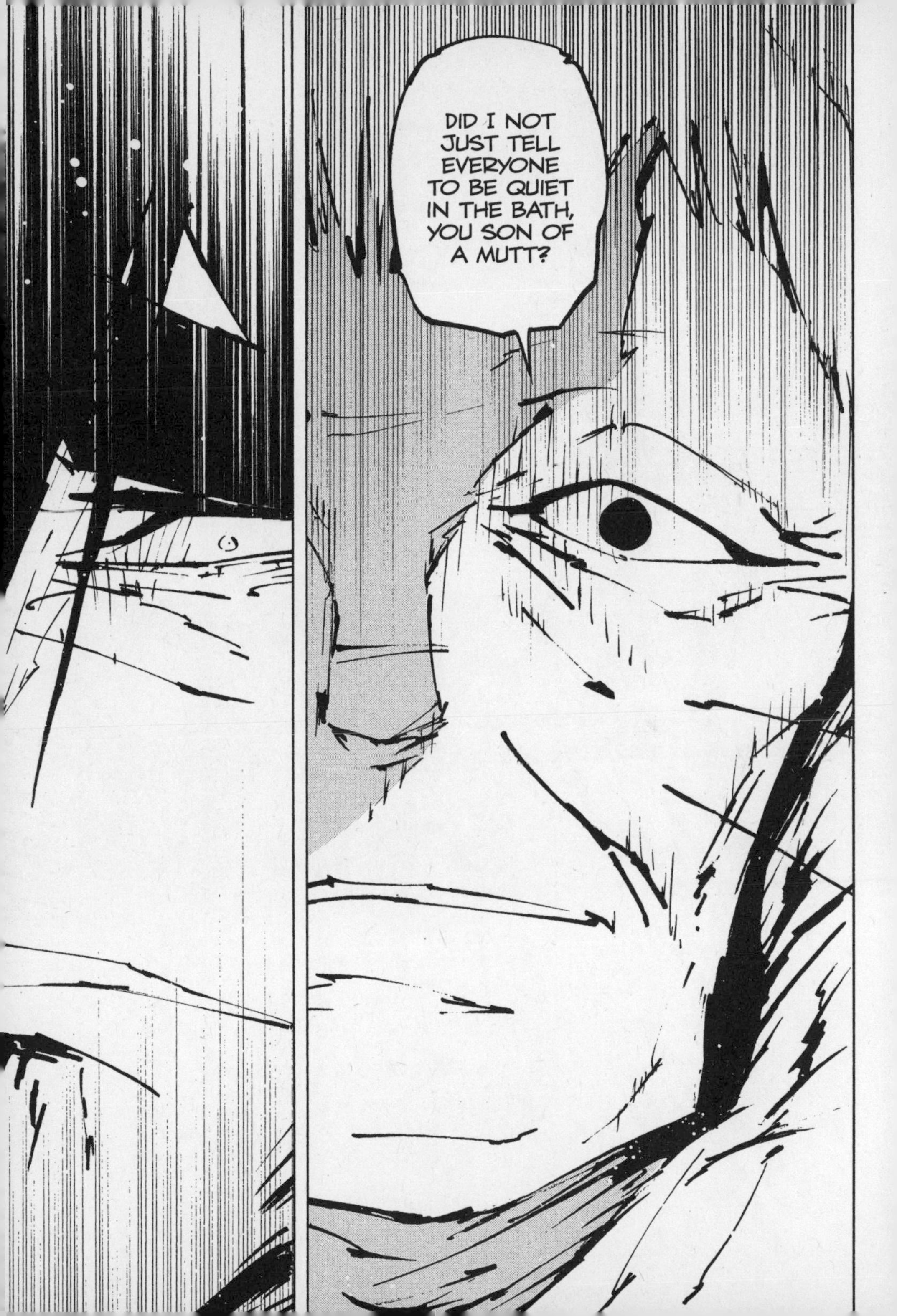
DID I NOT JUST TELL EVERYONE TO BE QUIET IN THE BATH, YOU SON OF A MUTT?

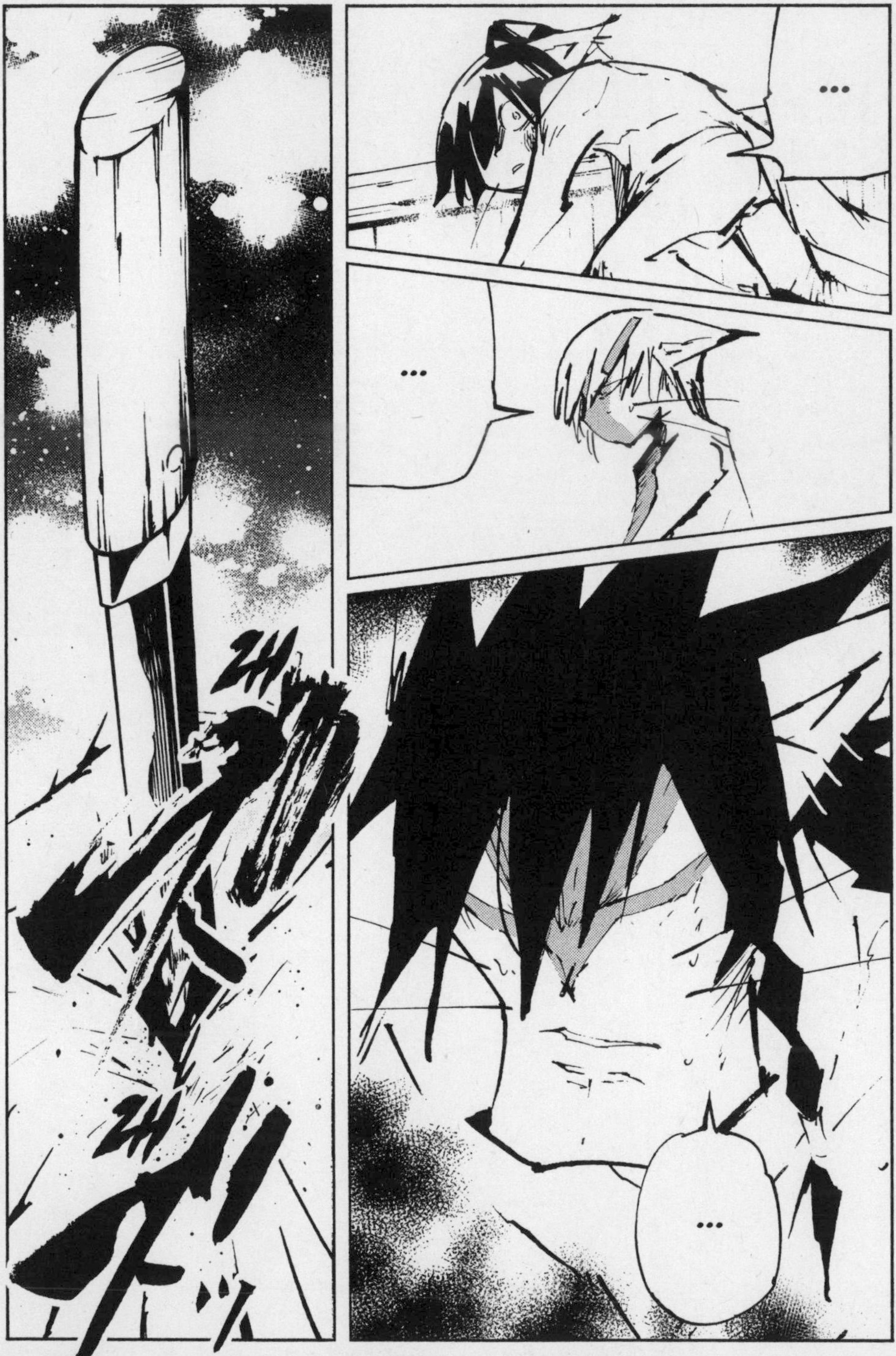
...
...
...
ZH
ZH

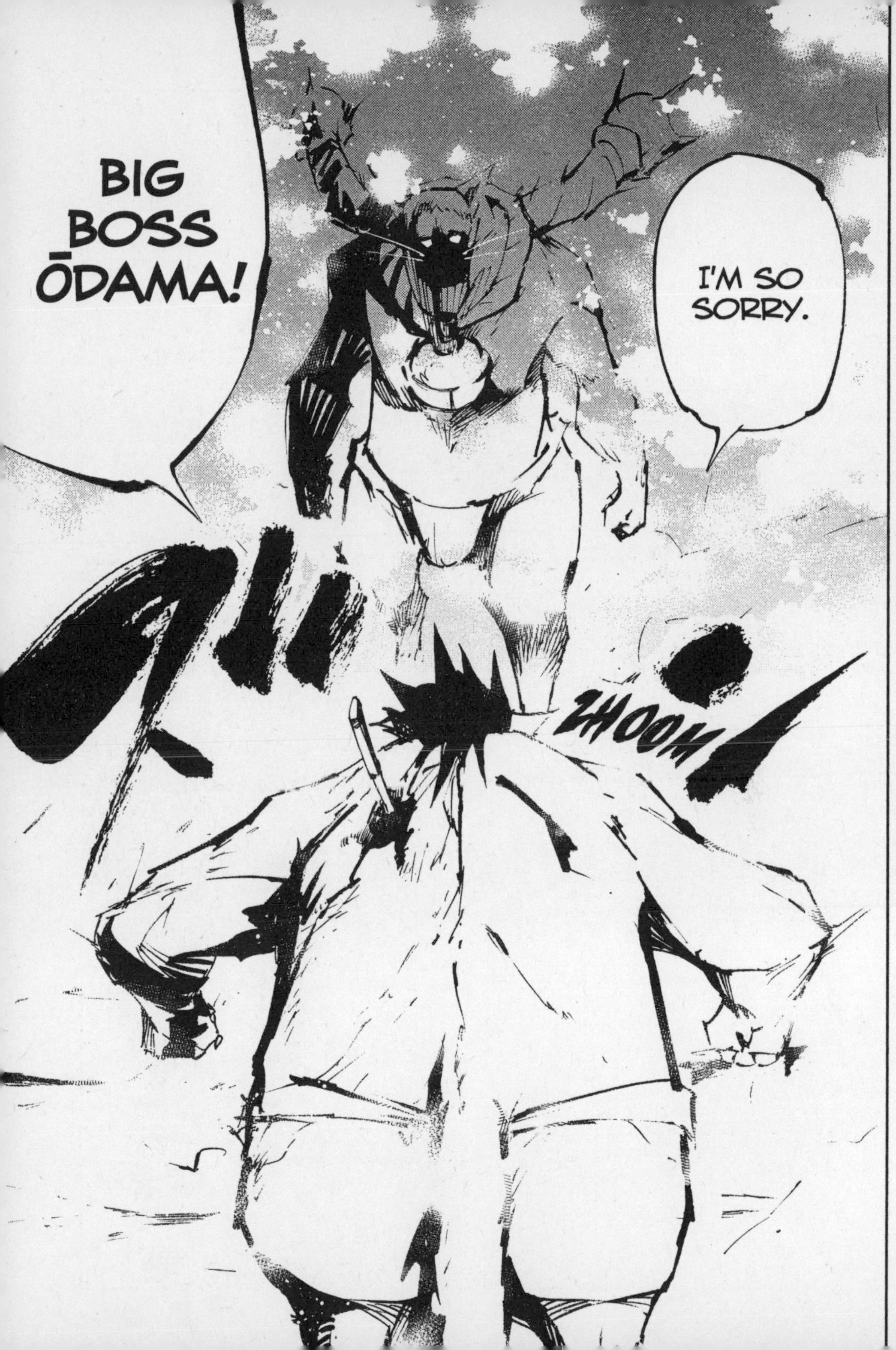
I'M SO SORRY.
BIG BOSS ŌDAMA!

猫ヶ原

NeKoGaHaRa

ネコガハラ

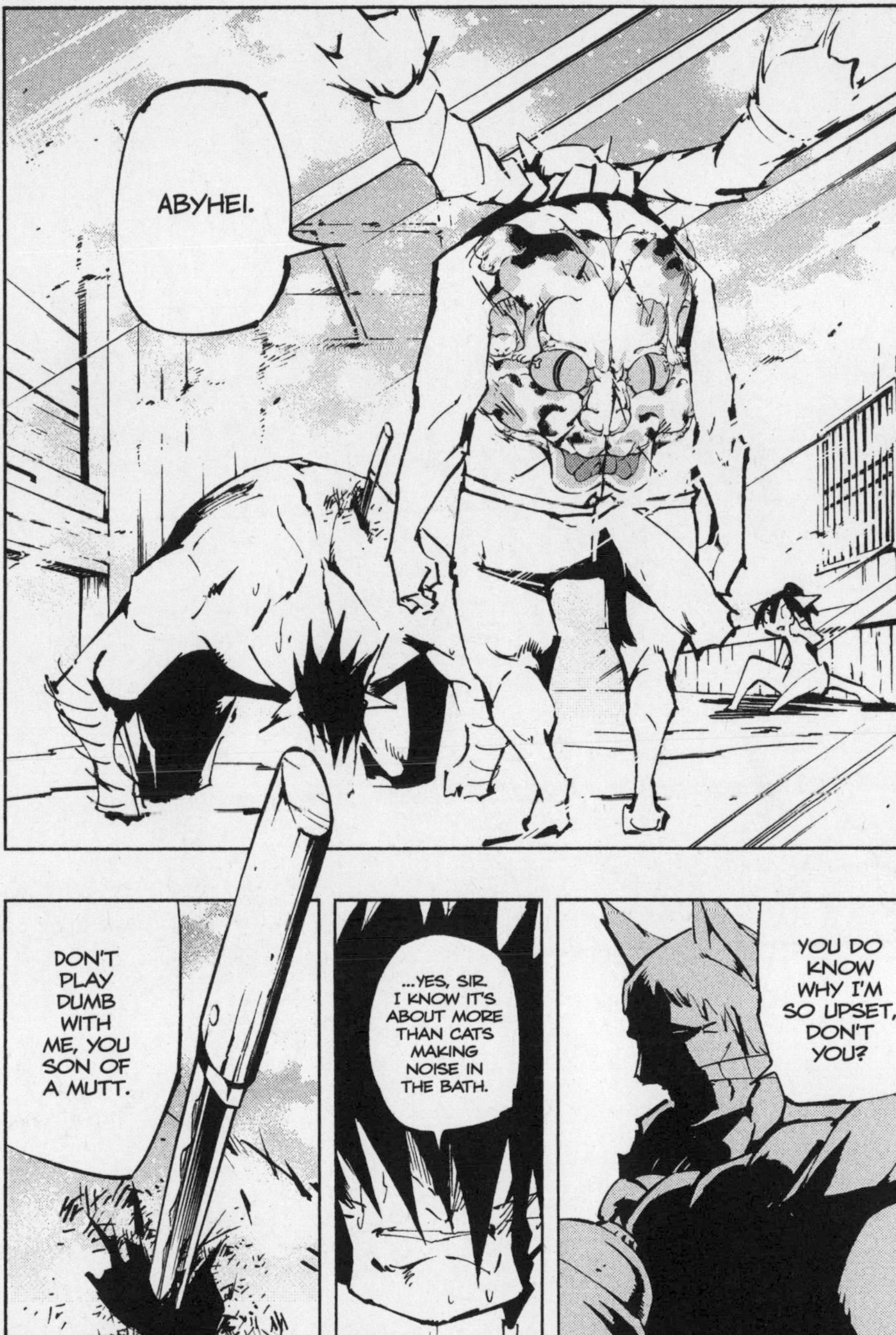
ABYHEI.
YOU DO KNOW WHY I'M SO UPSET, DON'T YOU?
...YES, SIR I KNOW IT'S ABOUT MORE THAN CATS MAKING NOISE IN THE BATH.
DON'T PLAY DUMB WITH ME, YOU SON OF A MUTT.

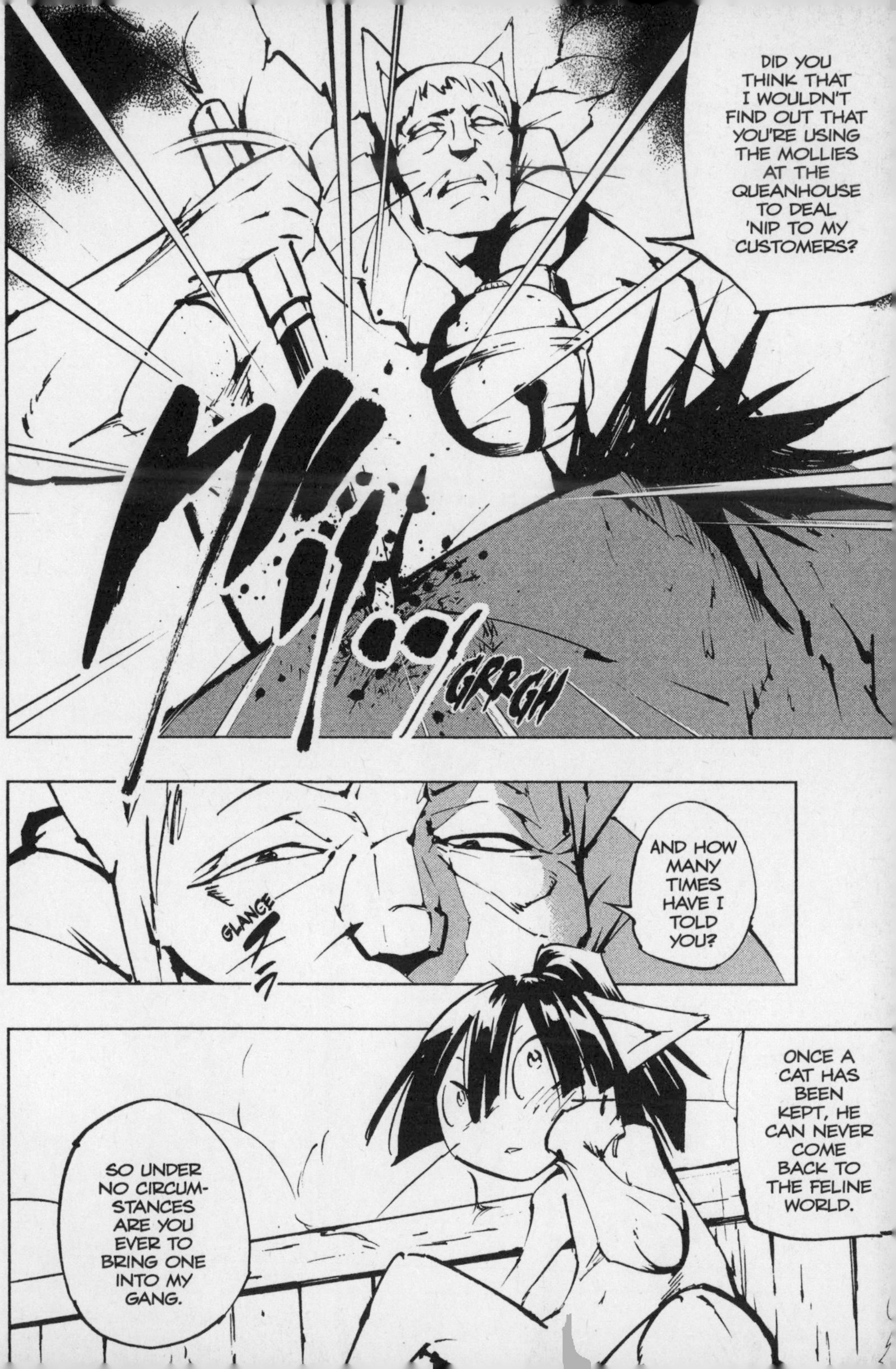
DID YOU THINK THAT I WOULDN'T FIND OUT THAT YOU'RE USING THE MOLLIES AT THE QUEANHOUSE TO DEAL 'NIP TO MY CUSTOMERS?
GRRGH
AND HOW MANY TIMES HAVE I TOLD YOU?
GLANCE
ONCE A CAT HAS BEEN KEPT, HE CAN NEVER COME BACK TO THE FELINE WORLD.
SO UNDER NO CIRCUM-STANCES ARE YOU EVER TO BRING ONE INTO MY GANG.

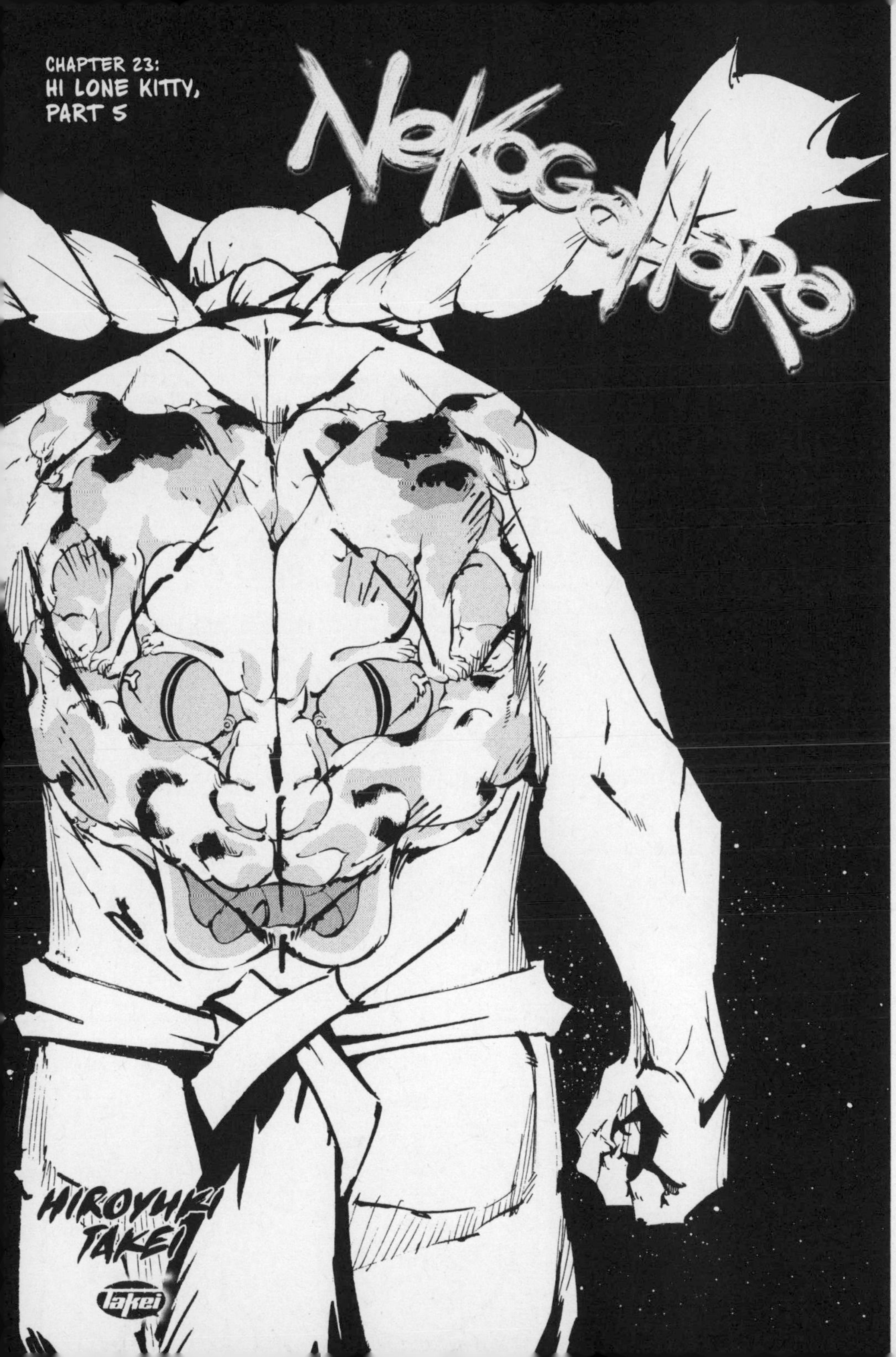
CHAPTER 23:
HI LONE KITTY,
PART 5
Nekogahara
HIROYUKI TAKEI
Takei

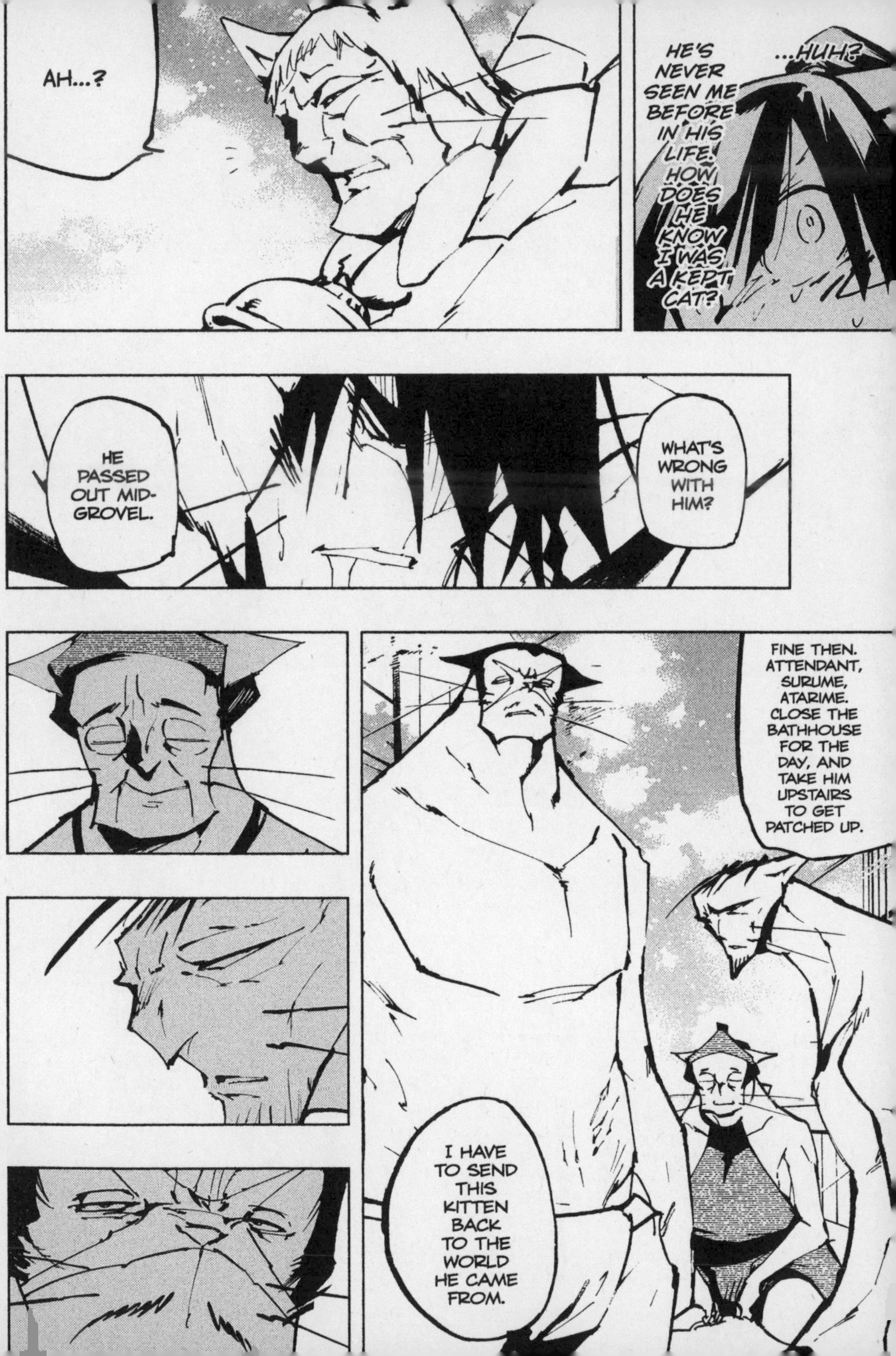
...HUH?
HE'S NEVER SEEN ME BEFORE IN HIS LIFE. HOW DOES HE KNOW I WAS A KEPT CAT?
AH...?
WHAT'S WRONG WITH HIM?
HE PASSED OUT MID-GROVEL.
FINE THEN. ATTENDANT, SURUME, ATARIME. CLOSE THE BATHHOUSE FOR THE DAY, AND TAKE HIM UPSTAIRS TO GET PATCHED UP.
I HAVE TO SEND THIS KITTEN BACK TO THE WORLD HE CAME FROM.

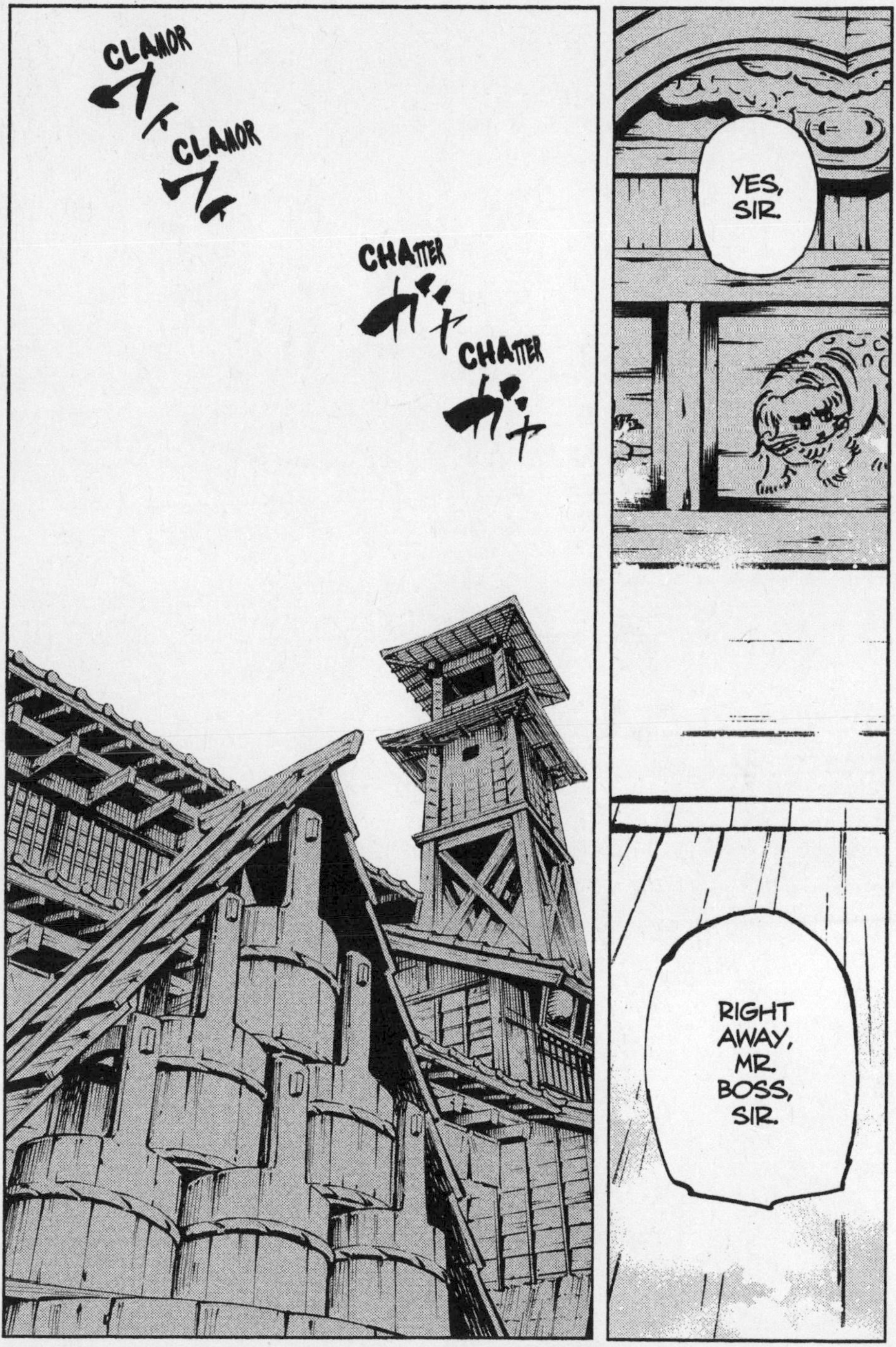
YES, SIR.
RIGHT AWAY, MR. BOSS, SIR.
CHATTER
ガヤ
CHATTER
ガヤ
CLAMOR
ワイ
CLAMOR
ワイ

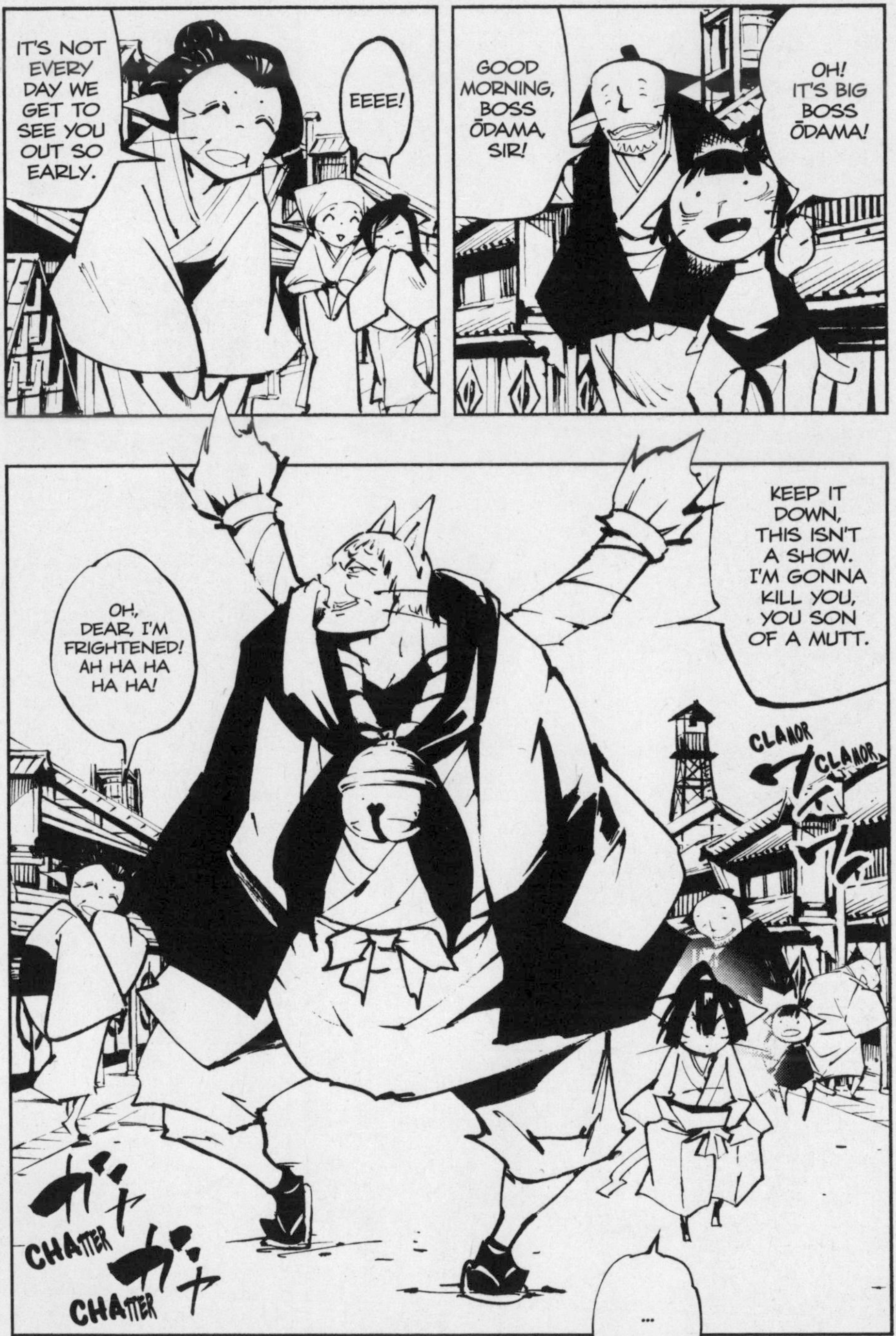
OH! IT'S BIG BOSS ŌDAMA!
GOOD MORNING, BOSS ŌDAMA, SIR!
EEEE!
IT'S NOT EVERY DAY WE GET TO SEE YOU OUT SO EARLY.
KEEP IT DOWN, THIS ISN'T A SHOW. I'M GONNA KILL YOU, YOU SON OF A MUTT.
OH, DEAR, I'M FRIGHTENED! AH HA HA HA HA!
CLAMOR
CLAMOR
CHATTER
CHATTER
...

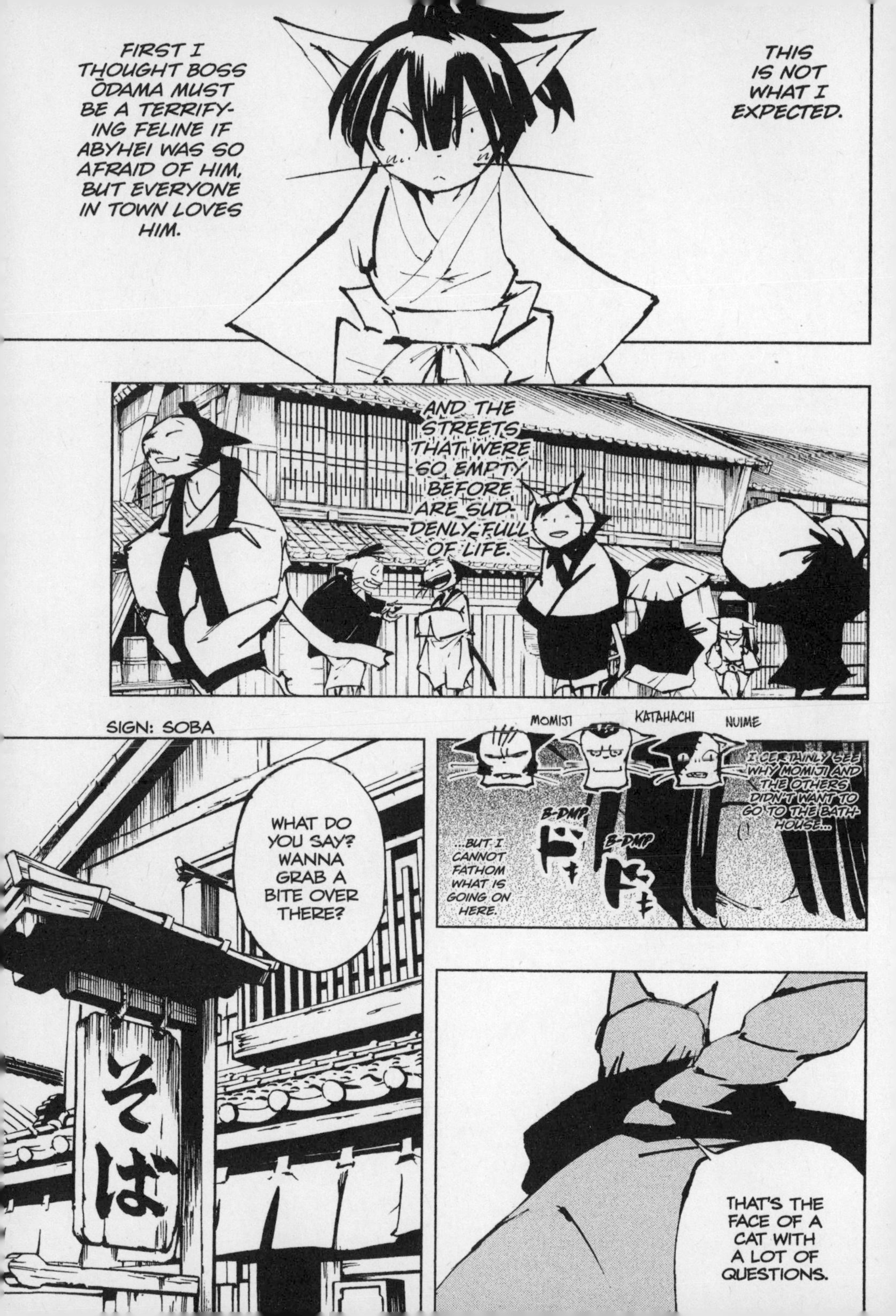

THIS IS NOT WHAT I EXPECTED.
FIRST I THOUGHT BOSS ŌDAMA MUST BE A TERRIFYING FELINE IF ABYHEI WAS SO AFRAID OF HIM, BUT EVERYONE IN TOWN LOVES HIM.
AND THE STREETS THAT WERE SO EMPTY BEFORE ARE SUDDENLY FULL OF LIFE.
NUIME
KATAHACHI
MOMIJI
I CERTAINLY SEE WHY MOMIJI AND THE OTHERS DIDN'T WANT TO GO TO THE BATHHOUSE...
B-DMP
B-DMP
...BUT I CANNOT FATHOM WHAT IS GOING ON HERE.
THAT'S THE FACE OF A CAT WITH A LOT OF QUESTIONS.
SIGN: SOBA
WHAT DO YOU SAY? WANNA GRAB A BITE OVER THERE?
そば

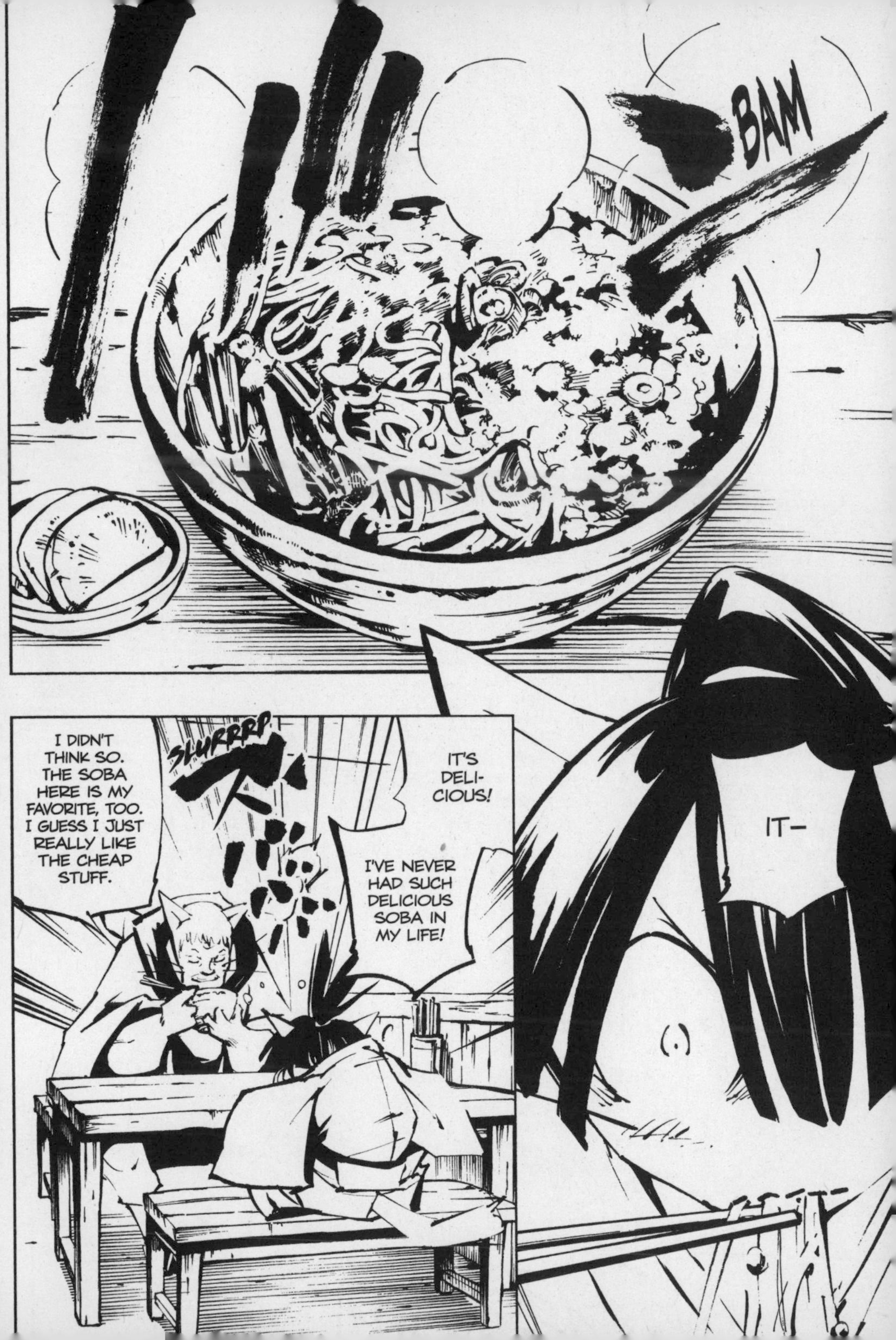
BAM
IT–
IT'S DELI-CIOUS!
I'VE NEVER HAD SUCH DELICIOUS SOBA IN MY LIFE!
SLURRRP
I DIDN'T THINK SO. THE SOBA HERE IS MY FAVORITE, TOO. I GUESS I JUST REALLY LIKE THE CHEAP STUFF.

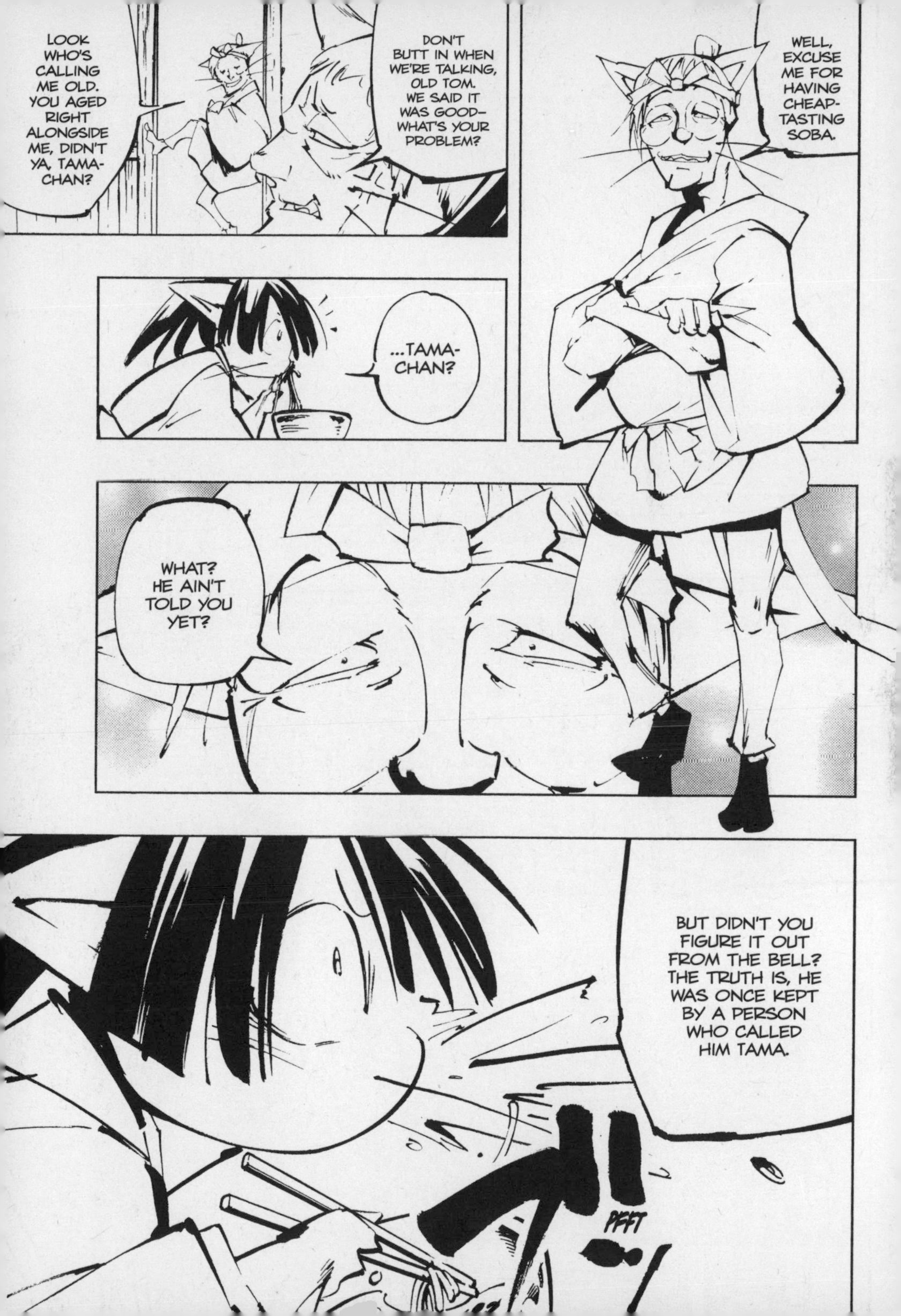
WELL, EXCUSE ME FOR HAVING CHEAP-TASTING SOBA.
DON'T BUTT IN WHEN WE'RE TALKING, OLD TOM. WE SAID IT WAS GOOD—WHAT'S YOUR PROBLEM?
LOOK WHO'S CALLING ME OLD. YOU AGED RIGHT ALONGSIDE ME, DIDN'T YA, TAMA-CHAN?
...TAMA-CHAN?
WHAT? HE AIN'T TOLD YOU YET?
BUT DIDN'T YOU FIGURE IT OUT FROM THE BELL? THE TRUTH IS, HE WAS ONCE KEPT BY A PERSON WHO CALLED HIM TAMA.
PFFT

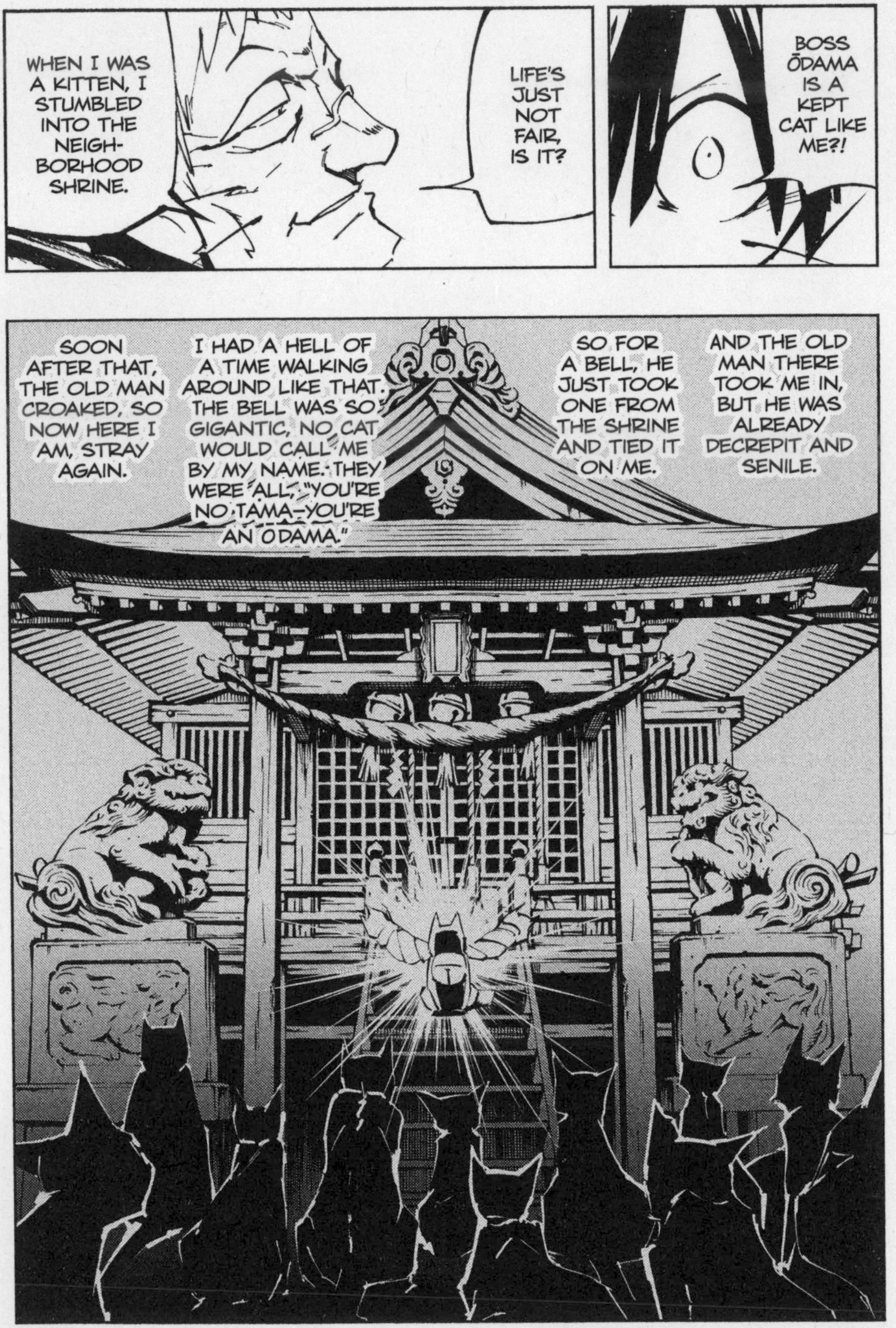
BOSS ŌDAMA IS A KEPT CAT LIKE ME?!
LIFE'S JUST NOT FAIR, IS IT?
WHEN I WAS A KITTEN, I STUMBLED INTO THE NEIGH-BORHOOD SHRINE.
AND THE OLD MAN THERE TOOK ME IN, BUT HE WAS ALREADY DECREPIT AND SENILE.
SO FOR A BELL, HE JUST TOOK ONE FROM THE SHRINE AND TIED IT ON ME.
I HAD A HELL OF A TIME WALKING AROUND LIKE THAT. THE BELL WAS SO GIGANTIC, NO CAT WOULD CALL ME BY MY NAME. THEY WERE ALL, "YOU'RE NO TAMA—YOU'RE AN ŌDAMA."
SOON AFTER THAT, THE OLD MAN CROAKED, SO NOW HERE I AM, STRAY AGAIN.

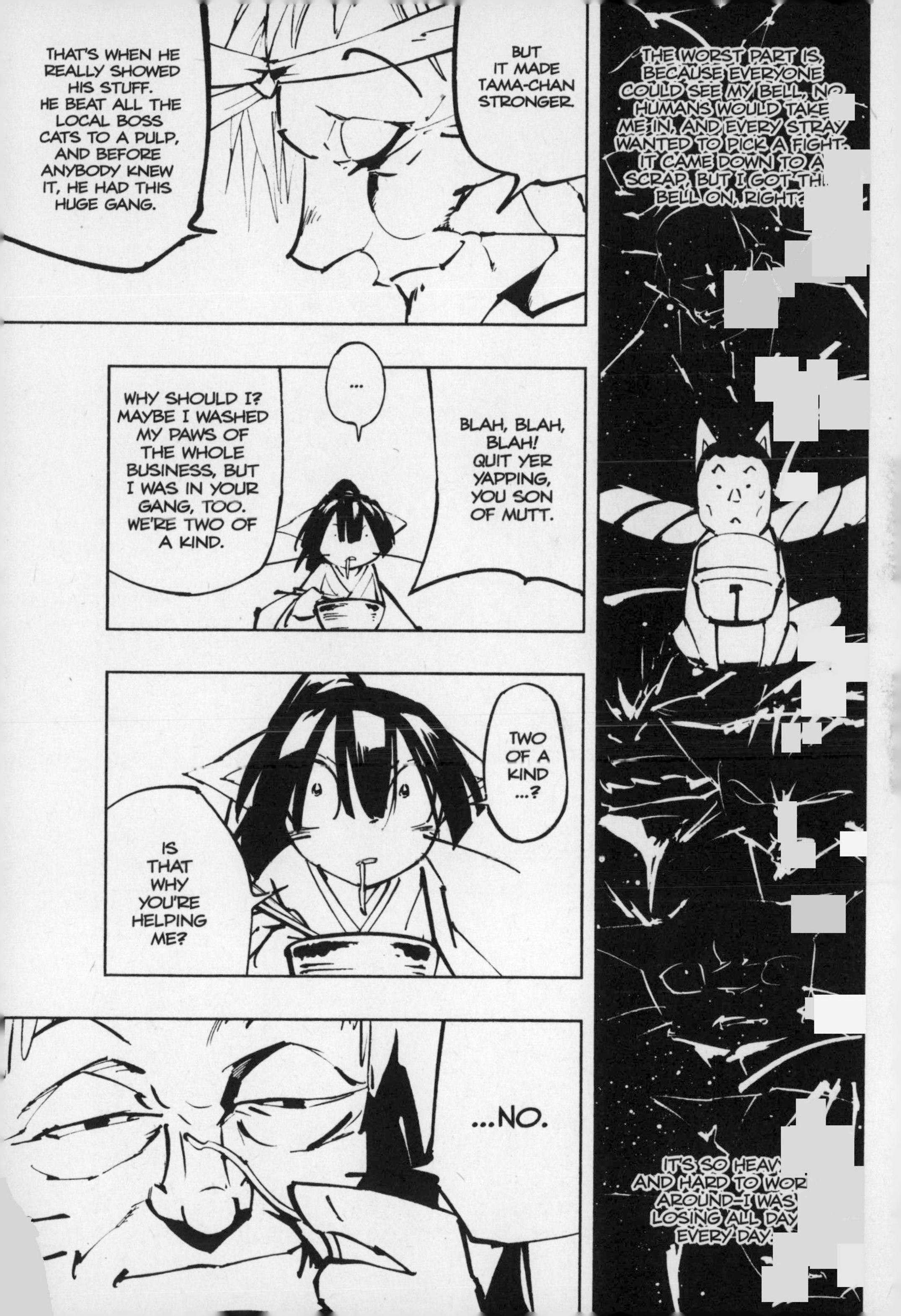

THE WORST PART IS, BECAUSE EVERYONE COULD SEE MY BELL, NO HUMANS WOULD TAKE ME IN, AND EVERY STRAY WANTED TO PICK A FIGHT. IT CAME DOWN TO A SCRAP, BUT I GOT TH BELL ON, RIGHT?
IT'S SO HEAV AND HARD TO WOR AROUND—I WAS LOSING ALL DAY EVERY DAY.
BUT IT MADE TAMA-CHAN STRONGER.
THAT'S WHEN HE REALLY SHOWED HIS STUFF. HE BEAT ALL THE LOCAL BOSS CATS TO A PULP, AND BEFORE ANYBODY KNEW IT, HE HAD THIS HUGE GANG.
...
BLAH, BLAH, BLAH! QUIT YER YAPPING, YOU SON OF MUTT.
WHY SHOULD I? MAYBE I WASHED MY PAWS OF THE WHOLE BUSINESS, BUT I WAS IN YOUR GANG, TOO. WE'RE TWO OF A KIND.
TWO OF A KIND ...?
IS THAT WHY YOU'RE HELPING ME?
...NO.

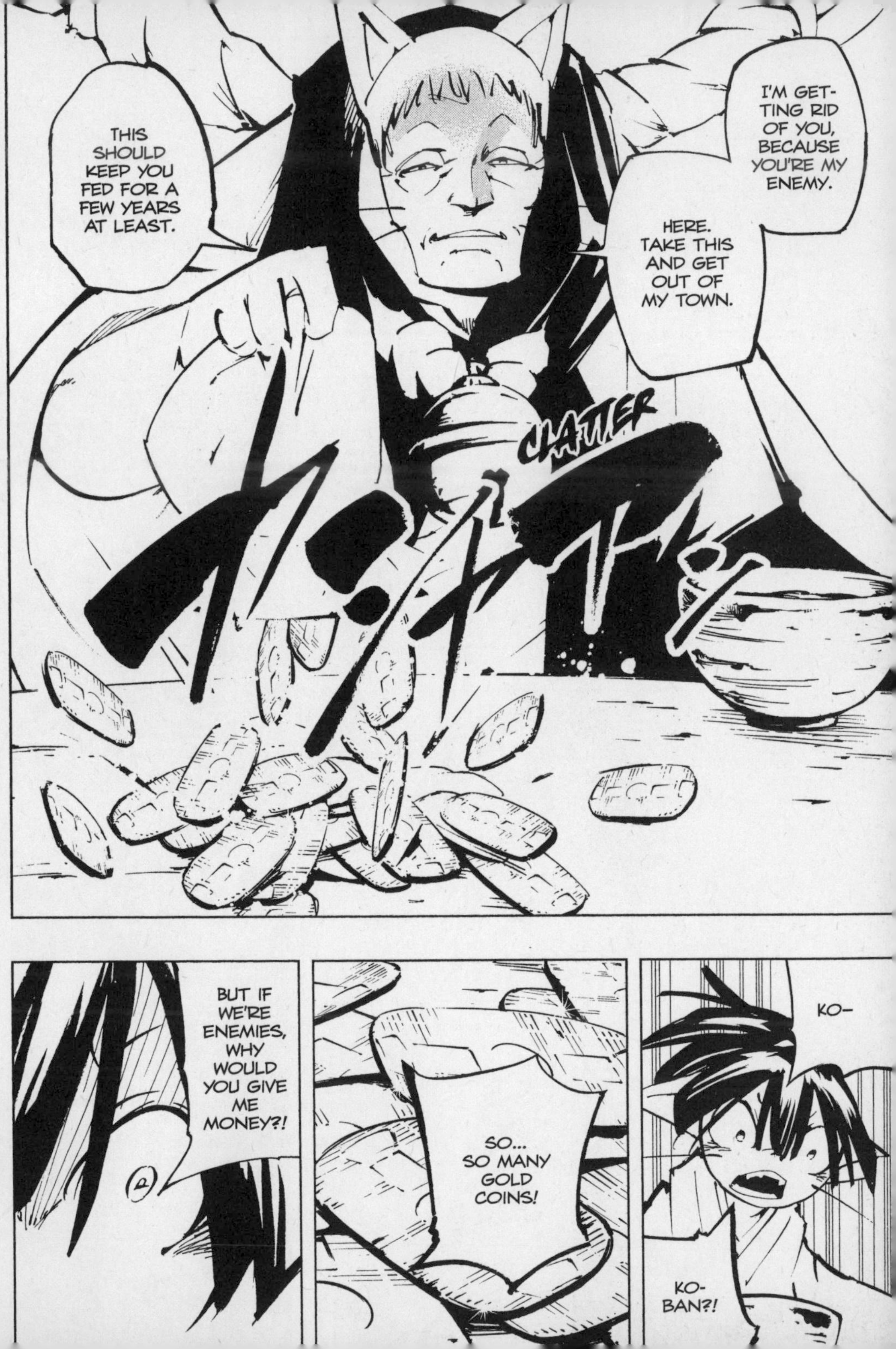
I'M GETTING RID OF YOU, BECAUSE YOU'RE MY ENEMY.
HERE. TAKE THIS AND GET OUT OF MY TOWN.
THIS SHOULD KEEP YOU FED FOR A FEW YEARS AT LEAST.
CLATTER
KO-
KO-BAN?!
SO... SO MANY GOLD COINS!
BUT IF WE'RE ENEMIES, WHY WOULD YOU GIVE ME MONEY?!

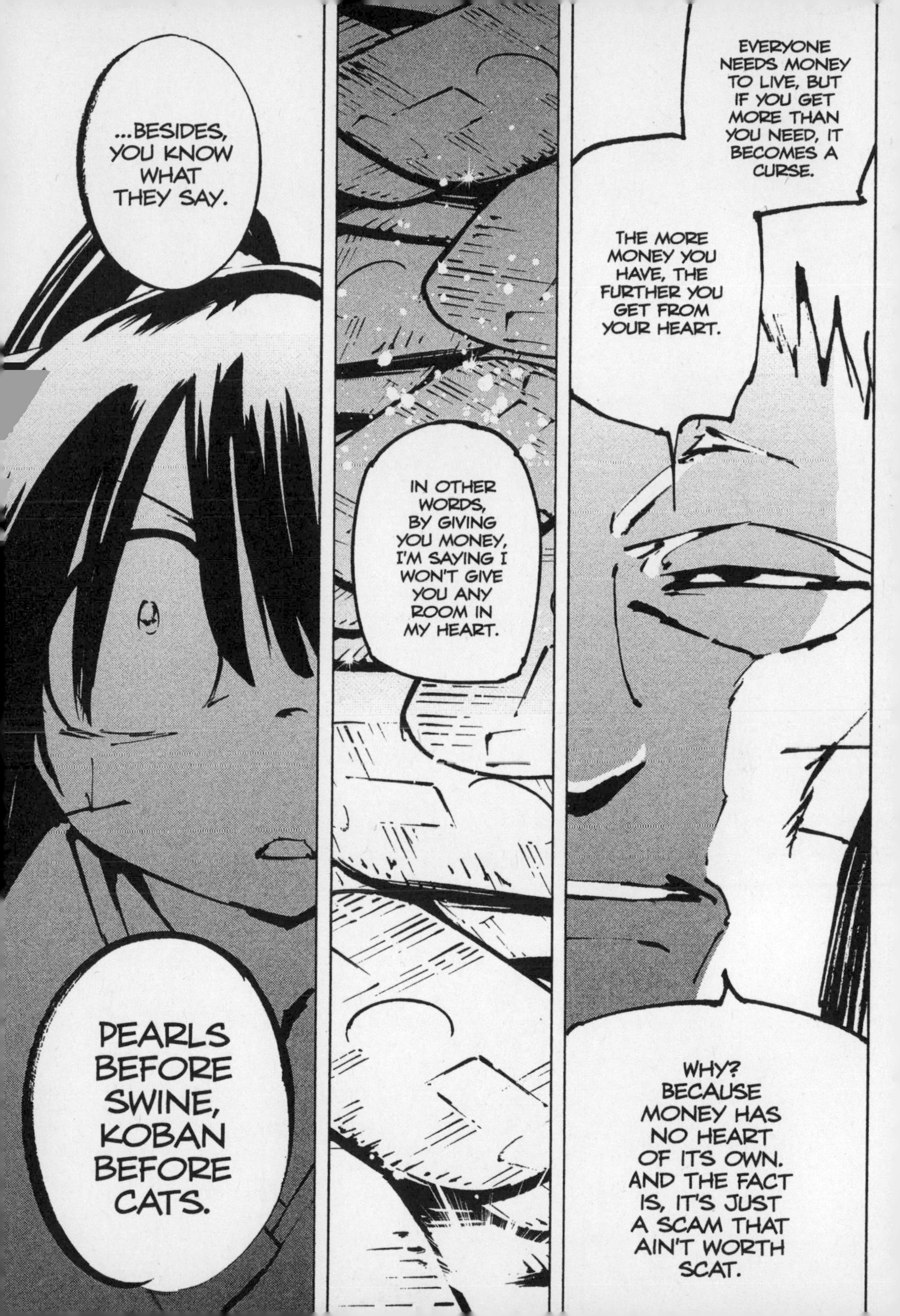
EVERYONE NEEDS MONEY TO LIVE, BUT IF YOU GET MORE THAN YOU NEED, IT BECOMES A CURSE.
THE MORE MONEY YOU HAVE, THE FURTHER YOU GET FROM YOUR HEART.
WHY? BECAUSE MONEY HAS NO HEART OF ITS OWN. AND THE FACT IS, IT'S JUST A SCAM THAT AIN'T WORTH SCAT.
IN OTHER WORDS, BY GIVING YOU MONEY, I'M SAYING I WON'T GIVE YOU ANY ROOM IN MY HEART.
...BESIDES, YOU KNOW WHAT THEY SAY.
PEARLS BEFORE SWINE, KOBAN BEFORE CATS.

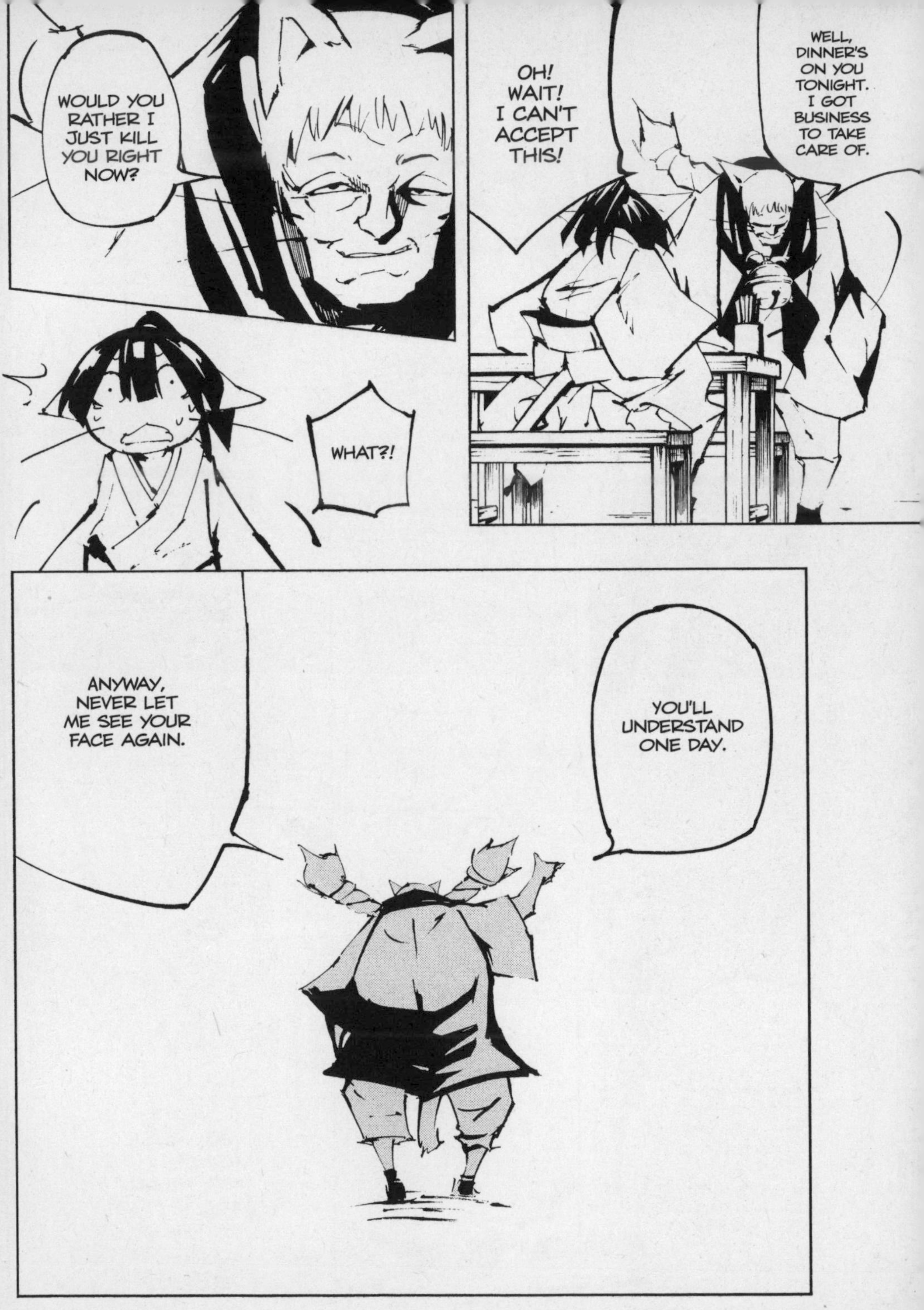
WELL, DINNER'S ON YOU TONIGHT. I GOT BUSINESS TO TAKE CARE OF.
OH! WAIT! I CAN'T ACCEPT THIS!
WOULD YOU RATHER I JUST KILL YOU RIGHT NOW?
WHAT?!
YOU'LL UNDERSTAND ONE DAY.
ANYWAY, NEVER LET ME SEE YOUR FACE AGAIN.

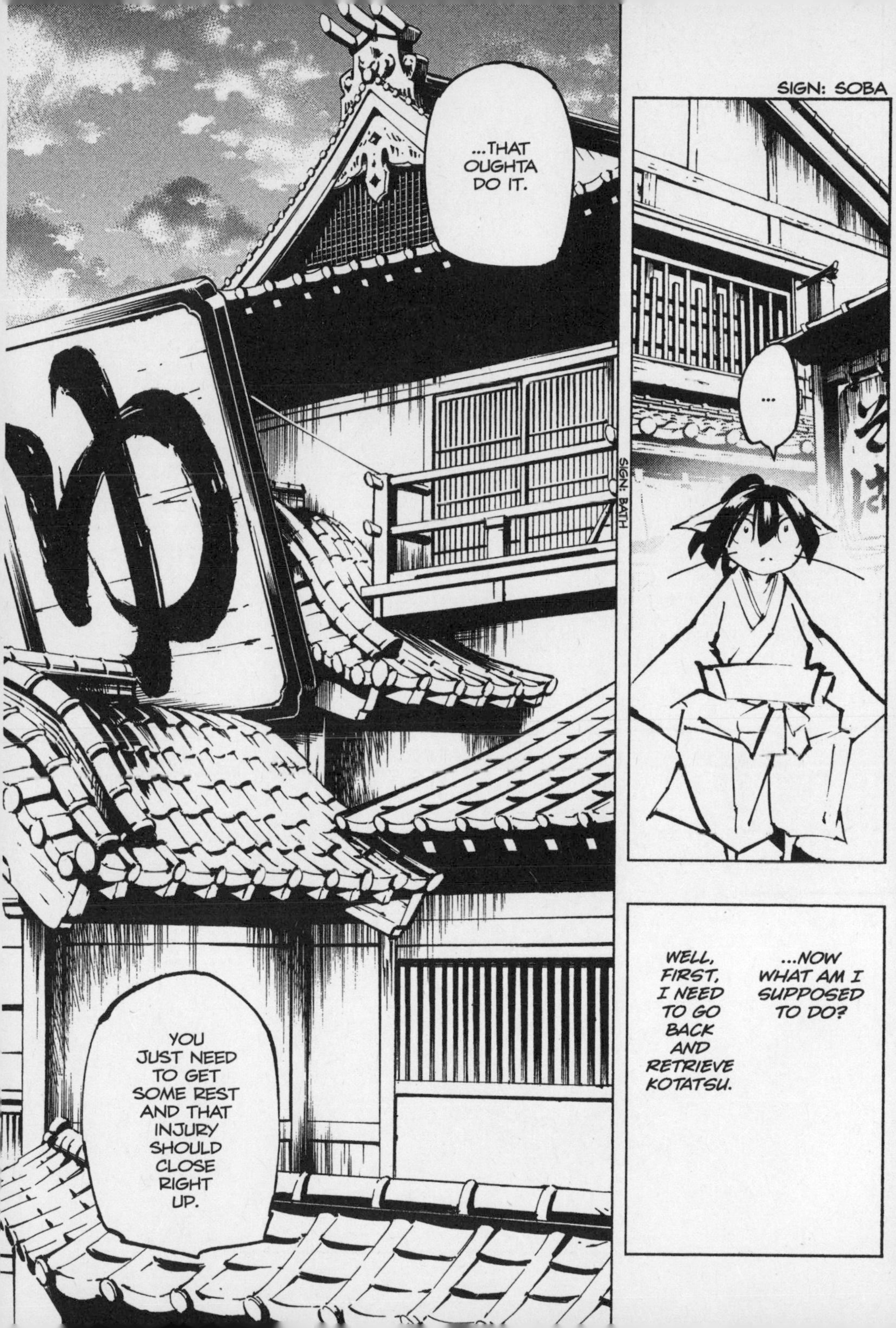
SIGN: SOBA
...
...NOW WHAT AM I SUPPOSED TO DO?
WELL, FIRST, I NEED TO GO BACK AND RETRIEVE KOTATSU.
...THAT OUGHTA DO IT.
SIGN: BATH
YOU JUST NEED TO GET SOME REST AND THAT INJURY SHOULD CLOSE RIGHT UP.

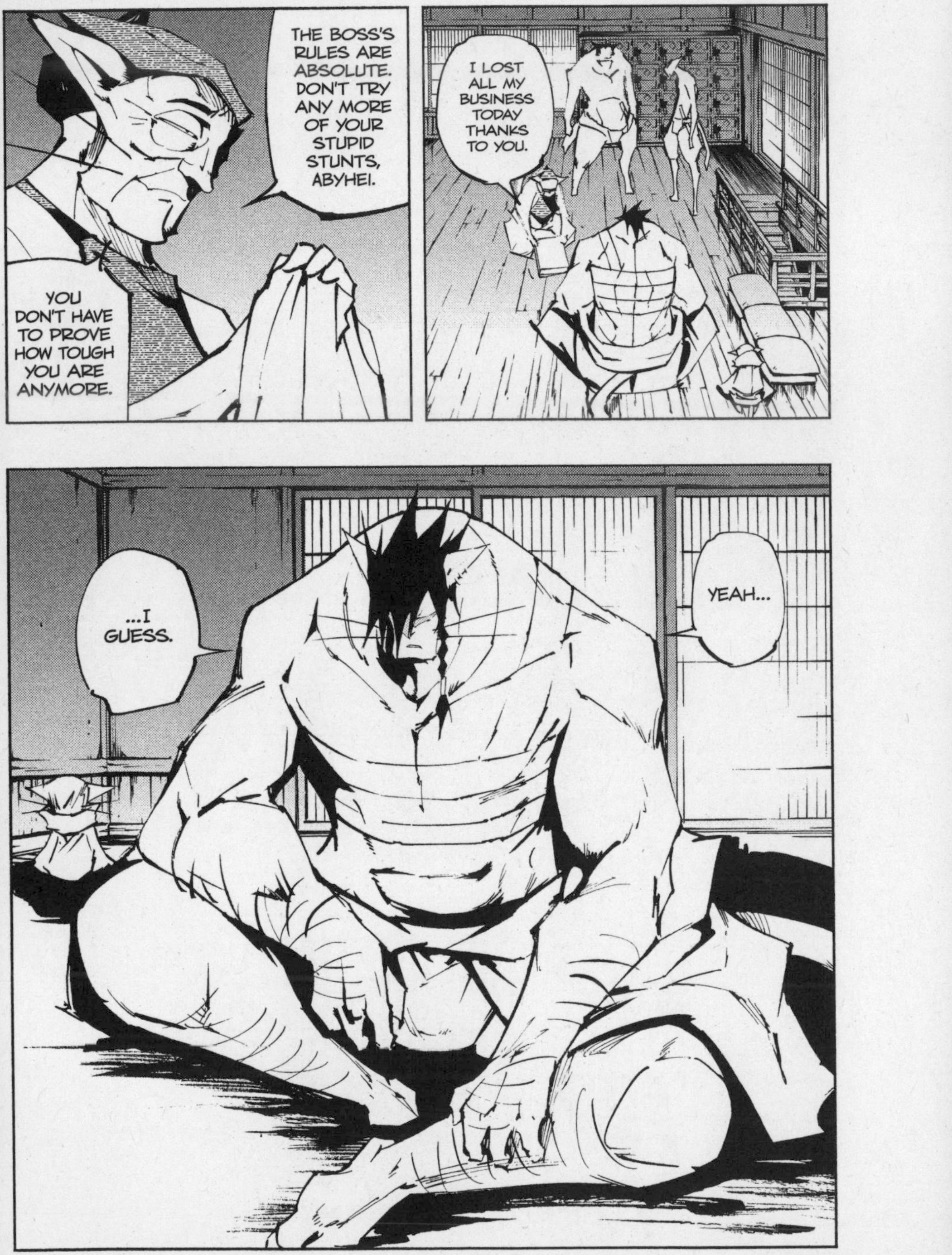
I LOST ALL MY BUSINESS TODAY THANKS TO YOU.
THE BOSS'S RULES ARE ABSOLUTE. DON'T TRY ANY MORE OF YOUR STUPID STUNTS, ABYHEI.
YOU DON'T HAVE TO PROVE HOW TOUGH YOU ARE ANYMORE.
YEAH...
...I GUESS.

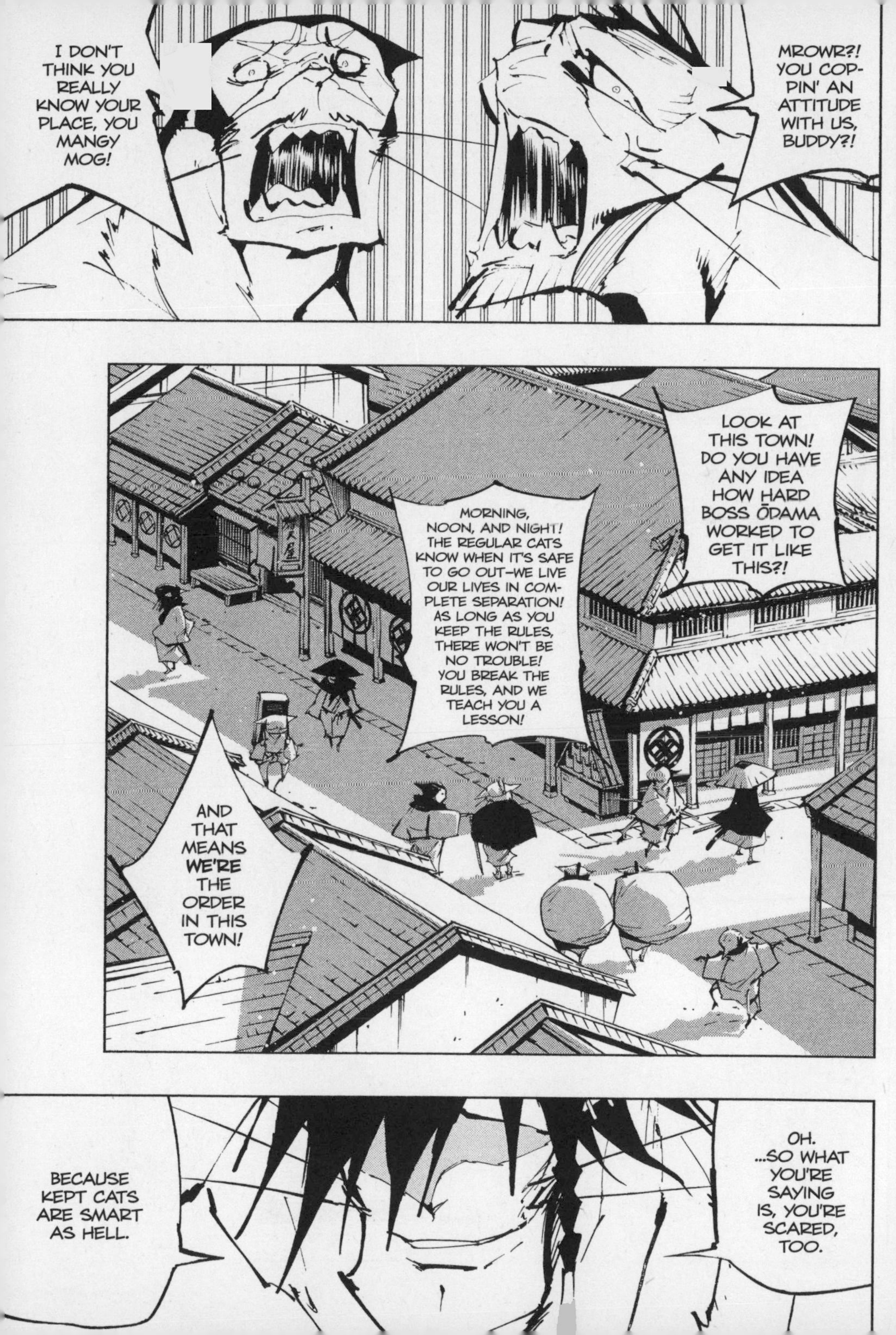
MROWR?! YOU COPPIN' AN ATTITUDE WITH US, BUDDY?!
I DON'T THINK YOU REALLY KNOW YOUR PLACE, YOU MANGY MOG!
LOOK AT THIS TOWN! DO YOU HAVE ANY IDEA HOW HARD BOSS ŌDAMA WORKED TO GET IT LIKE THIS?!
MORNING, NOON, AND NIGHT! THE REGULAR CATS KNOW WHEN IT'S SAFE TO GO OUT—WE LIVE OUR LIVES IN COMPLETE SEPARATION! AS LONG AS YOU KEEP THE RULES, THERE WON'T BE NO TROUBLE! YOU BREAK THE RULES, AND WE TEACH YOU A LESSON!
AND THAT MEANS **WE'RE** THE ORDER IN THIS TOWN!
OH. ...SO WHAT YOU'RE SAYING IS, YOU'RE SCARED, TOO.
BECAUSE KEPT CATS ARE SMART AS HELL.

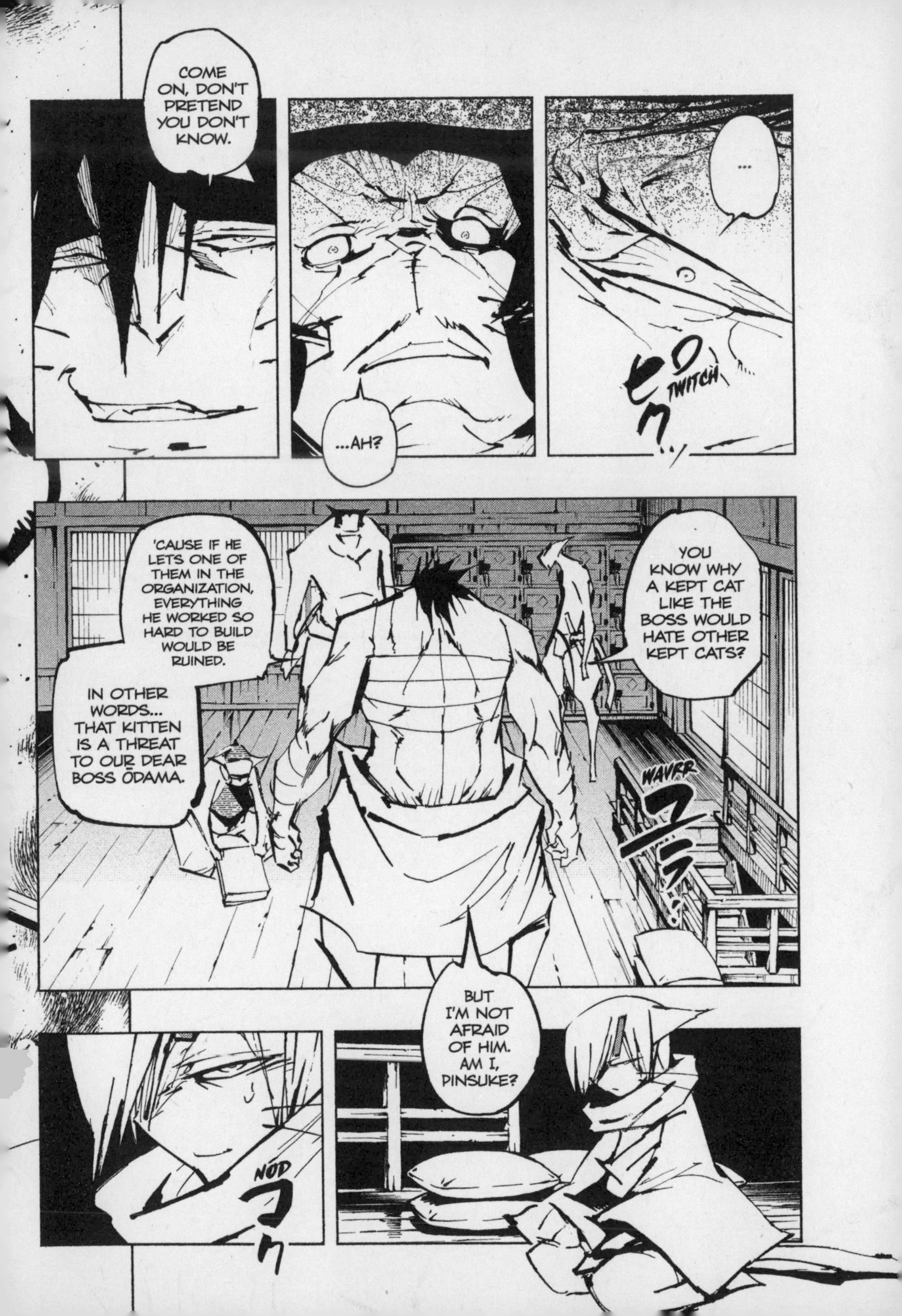
...
TWITCH
...AH?
COME ON, DON'T PRETEND YOU DON'T KNOW.
YOU KNOW WHY A KEPT CAT LIKE THE BOSS WOULD HATE OTHER KEPT CATS?
'CAUSE IF HE LETS ONE OF THEM IN THE ORGANIZATION, EVERYTHING HE WORKED SO HARD TO BUILD WOULD BE RUINED.
WAVRR
IN OTHER WORDS... THAT KITTEN IS A THREAT TO OUR DEAR BOSS ŌDAMA.
BUT I'M NOT AFRAID OF HIM. AM I, PINSUKE?
NOD

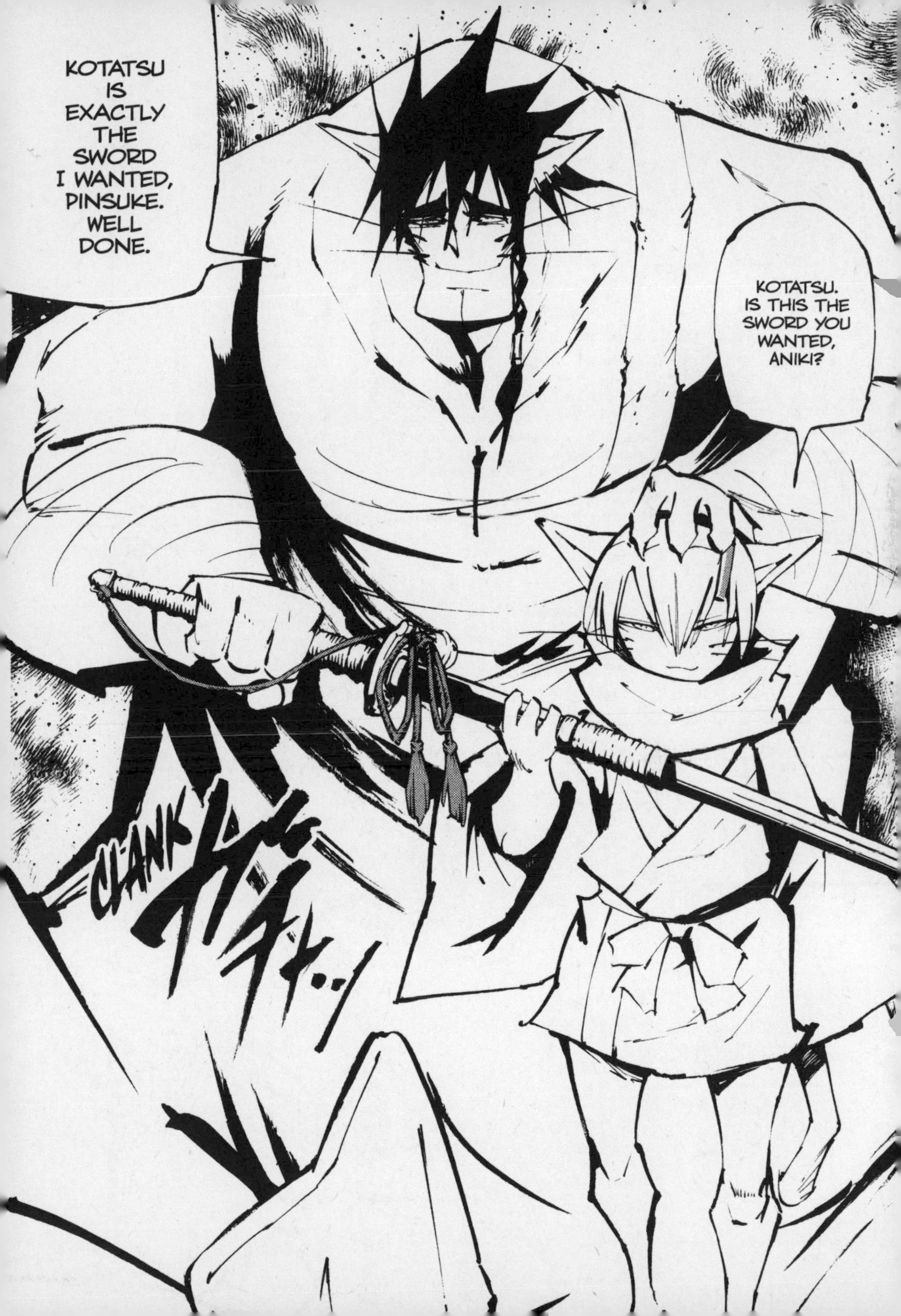
KOTATSU. IS THIS THE SWORD YOU WANTED, ANIKI?
KOTATSU IS EXACTLY THE SWORD I WANTED, PINSUKE. WELL DONE.
CLANK

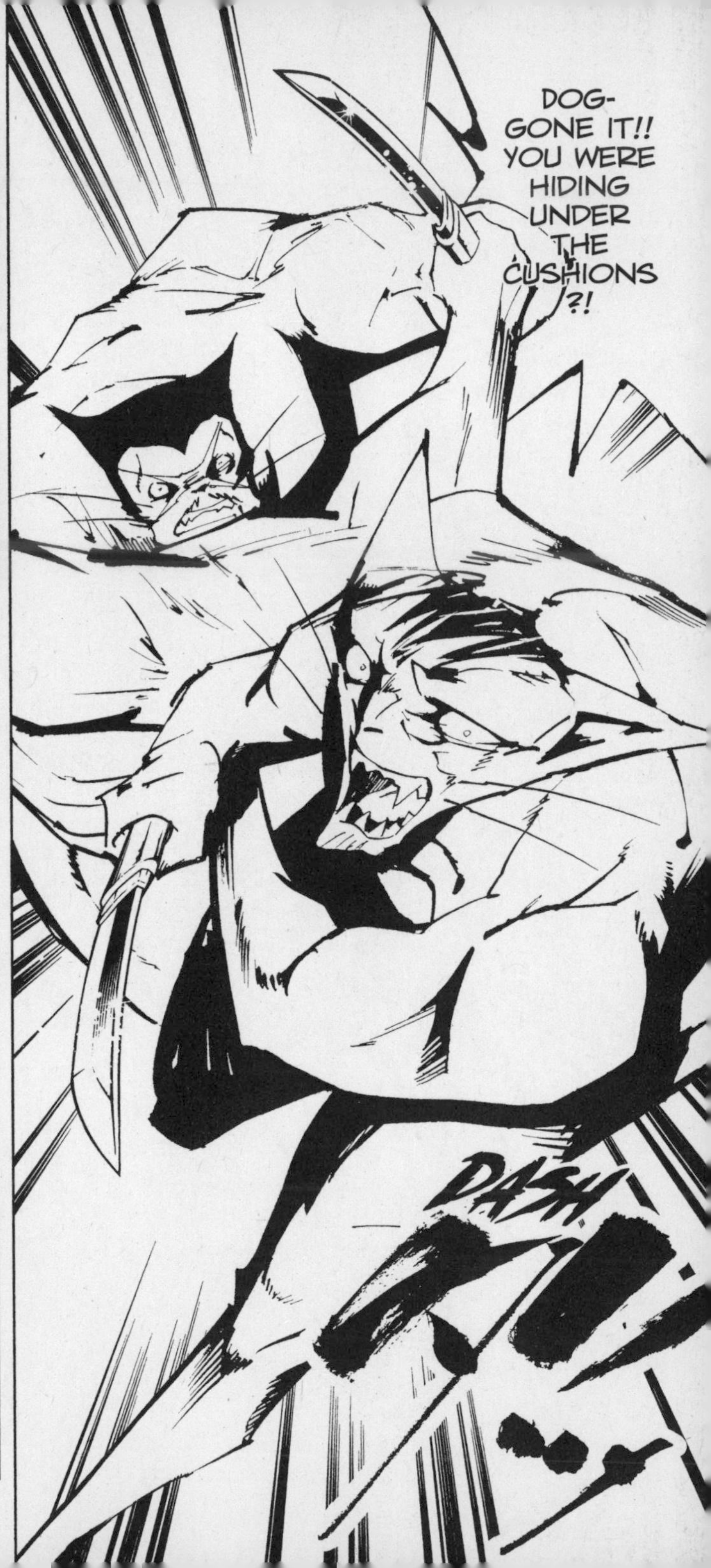
DOG-GONE IT!! YOU WERE HIDING UNDER THE CUSHIONS?!
DASH

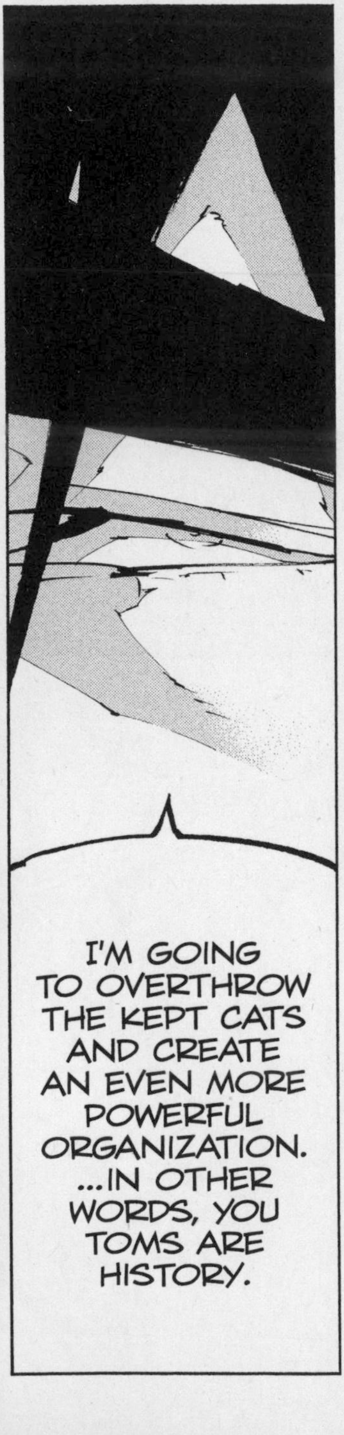
I'M GOING TO OVERTHROW THE KEPT CATS AND CREATE AN EVEN MORE POWERFUL ORGANIZATION. ...IN OTHER WORDS, YOU TOMS ARE HISTORY.

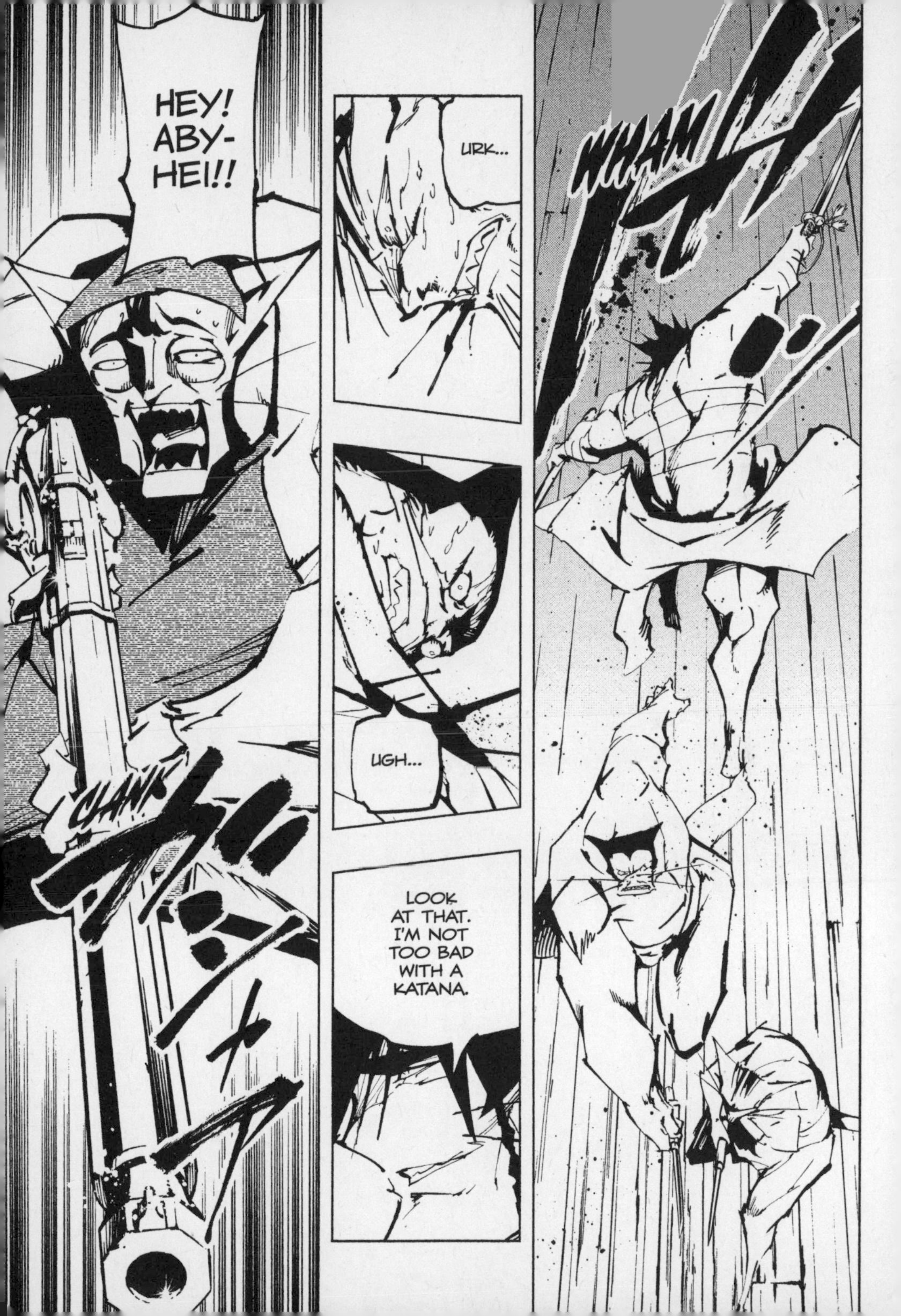
WHAM
URK...
UGH...
LOOK AT THAT. I'M NOT TOO BAD WITH A KATANA.
HEY! ABY-HEI!!
CLANK

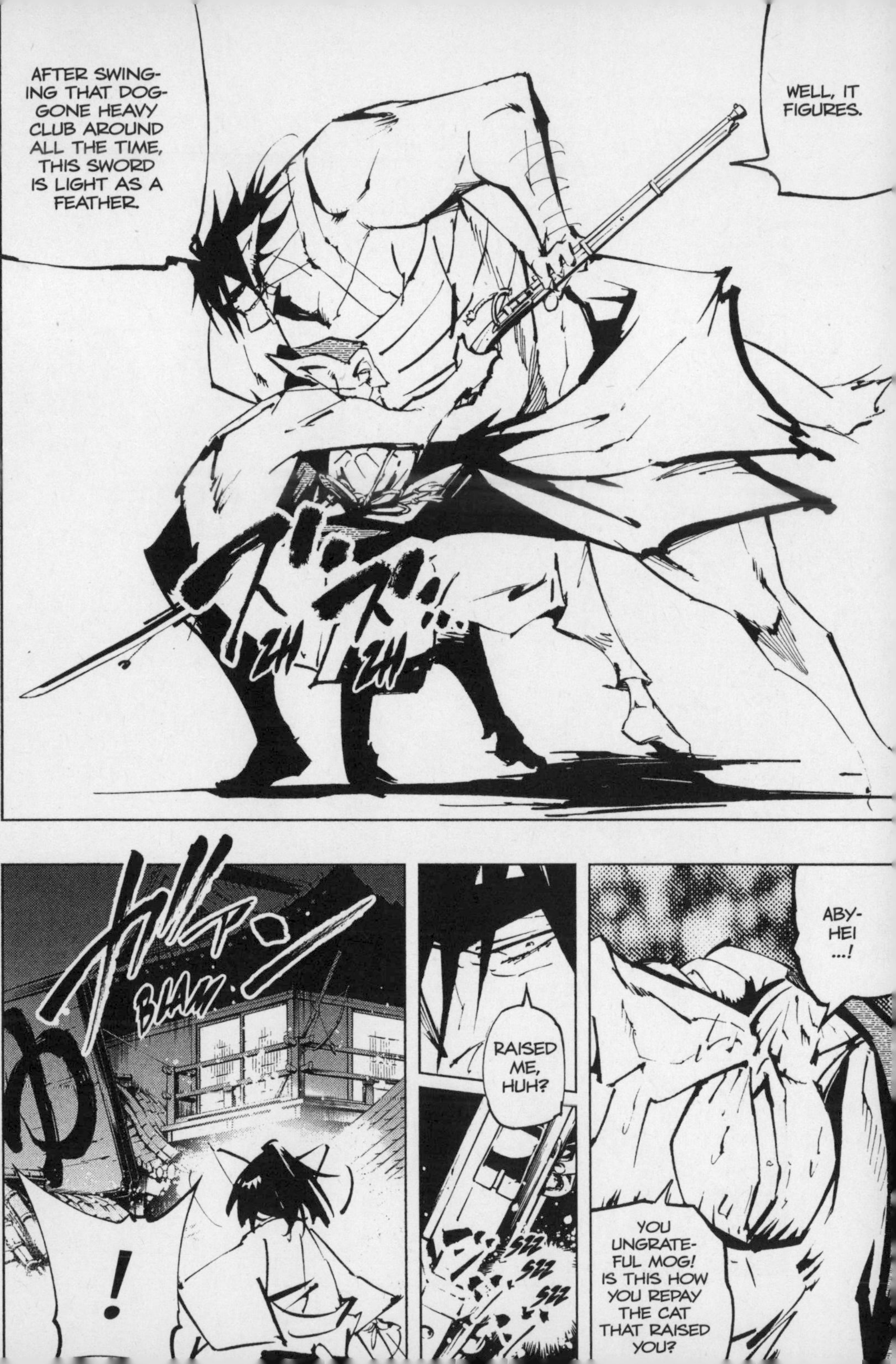
WELL, IT FIGURES.
AFTER SWINGING THAT DOGGONE HEAVY CLUB AROUND ALL THE TIME, THIS SWORD IS LIGHT AS A FEATHER.
ZH
ZH
ABY-HEI ...!
YOU UNGRATEFUL MOG! IS THIS HOW YOU REPAY THE CAT THAT RAISED YOU?
RAISED ME, HUH?
SSS
SSS
SSS
BLAM
!
SIGN: BATH

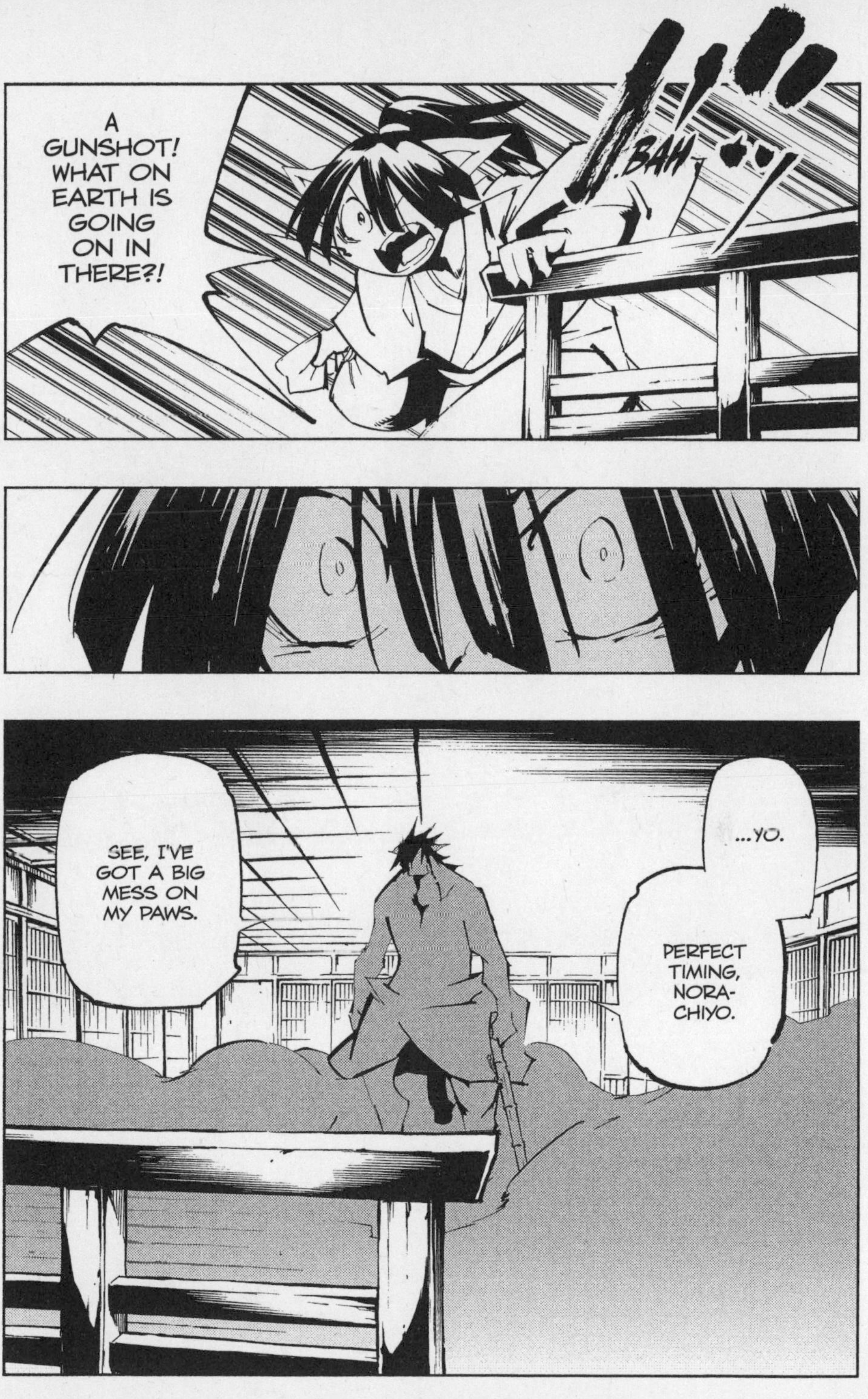
BAH-
A GUNSHOT! WHAT ON EARTH IS GOING ON IN THERE?!
...YO.
PERFECT TIMING, NORA-CHIYO.
SEE, I'VE GOT A BIG MESS ON MY PAWS.

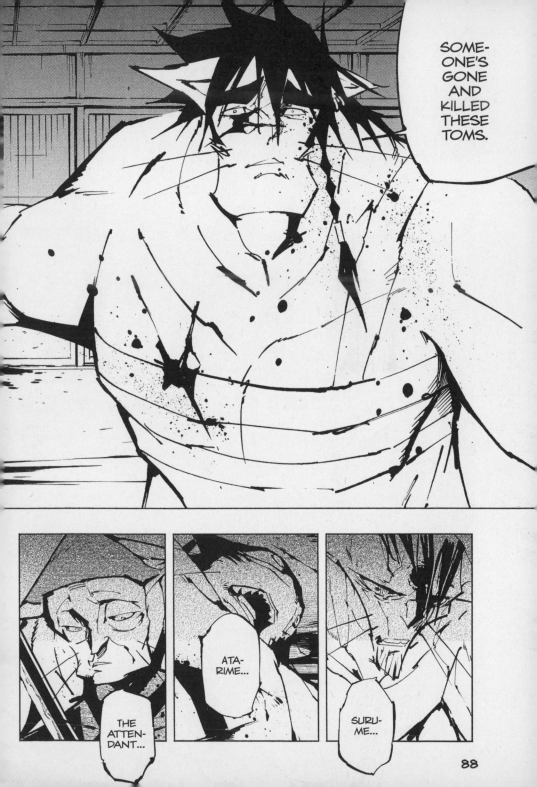

SOME-ONE'S GONE AND KILLED THESE TOMS.

THE ATTEN-DANT...

ATA-RIME...

SURU-ME...

88

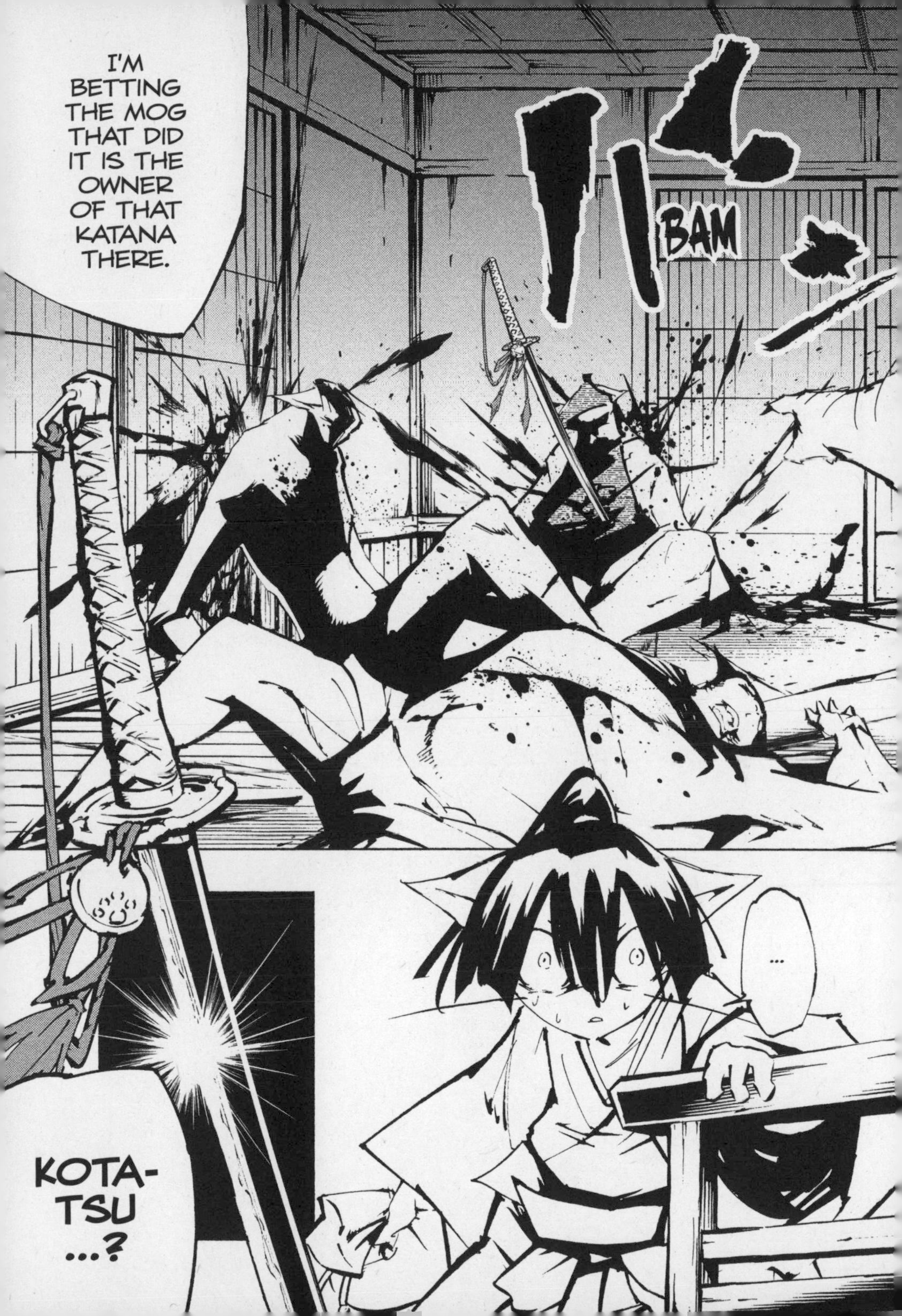
BAM
I'M BETTING THE MOG THAT DID IT IS THE OWNER OF THAT KATANA THERE.
...
KOTA-TSU ...?

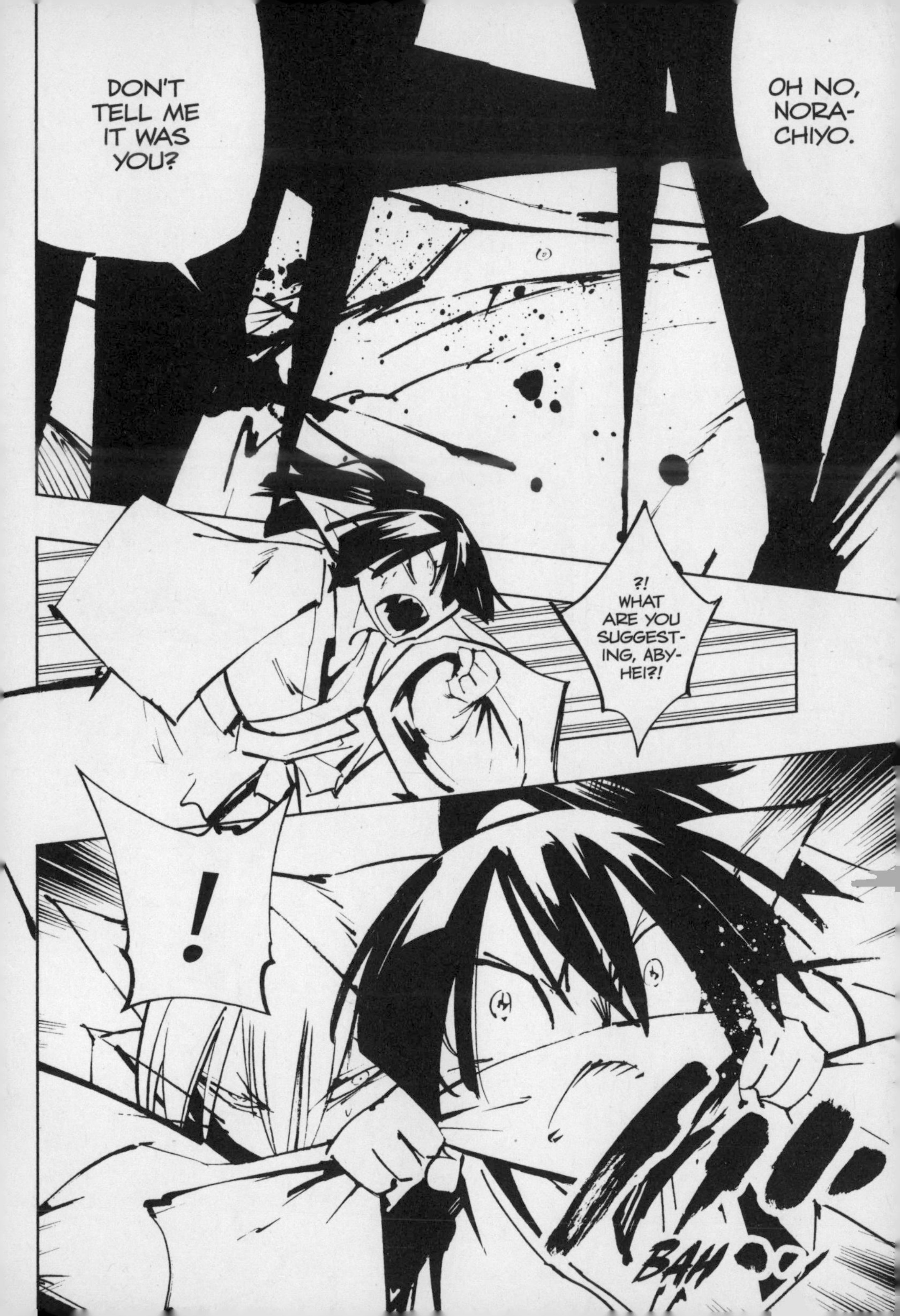
OH NO, NORA-CHIYO.
DON'T TELL ME IT WAS YOU?
?! WHAT ARE YOU SUGGEST-ING, ABY-HEI?!
!
BAH

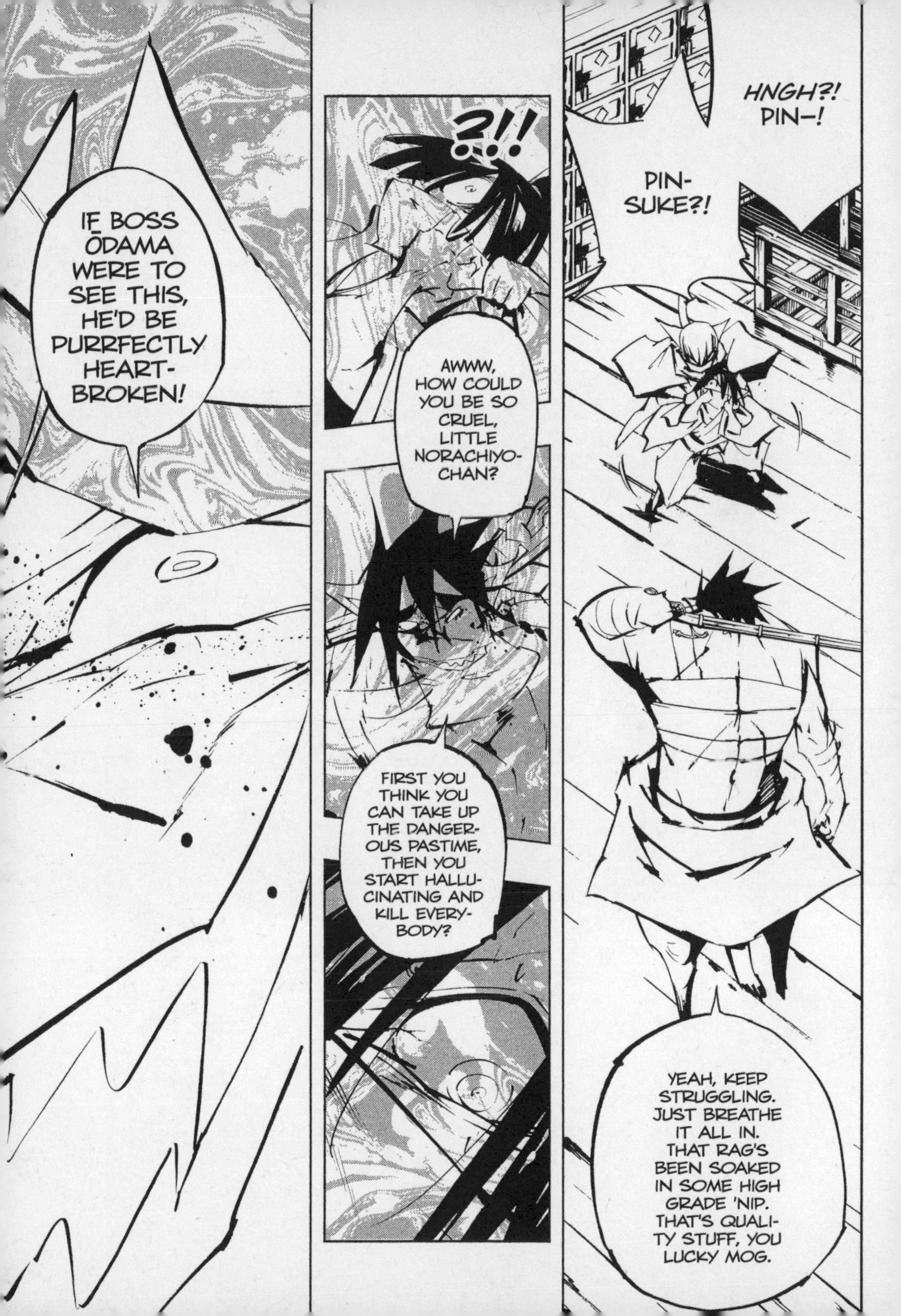
HNGH?! PIN-!
PIN-SUKE?!
YEAH, KEEP STRUGGLING. JUST BREATHE IT ALL IN. THAT RAG'S BEEN SOAKED IN SOME HIGH GRADE 'NIP. THAT'S QUALITY STUFF, YOU LUCKY MOG.
?!!
AWWW, HOW COULD YOU BE SO CRUEL, LITTLE NORACHIYO-CHAN?
FIRST YOU THINK YOU CAN TAKE UP THE DANGEROUS PASTIME, THEN YOU START HALLUCINATING AND KILL EVERYBODY?
IF BOSS ŌDAMA WERE TO SEE THIS, HE'D BE PURRFECTLY HEARTBROKEN!

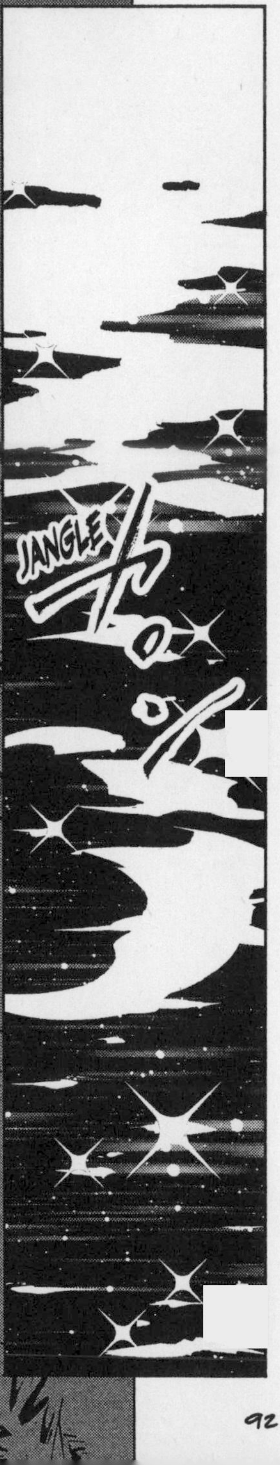
JANGLE
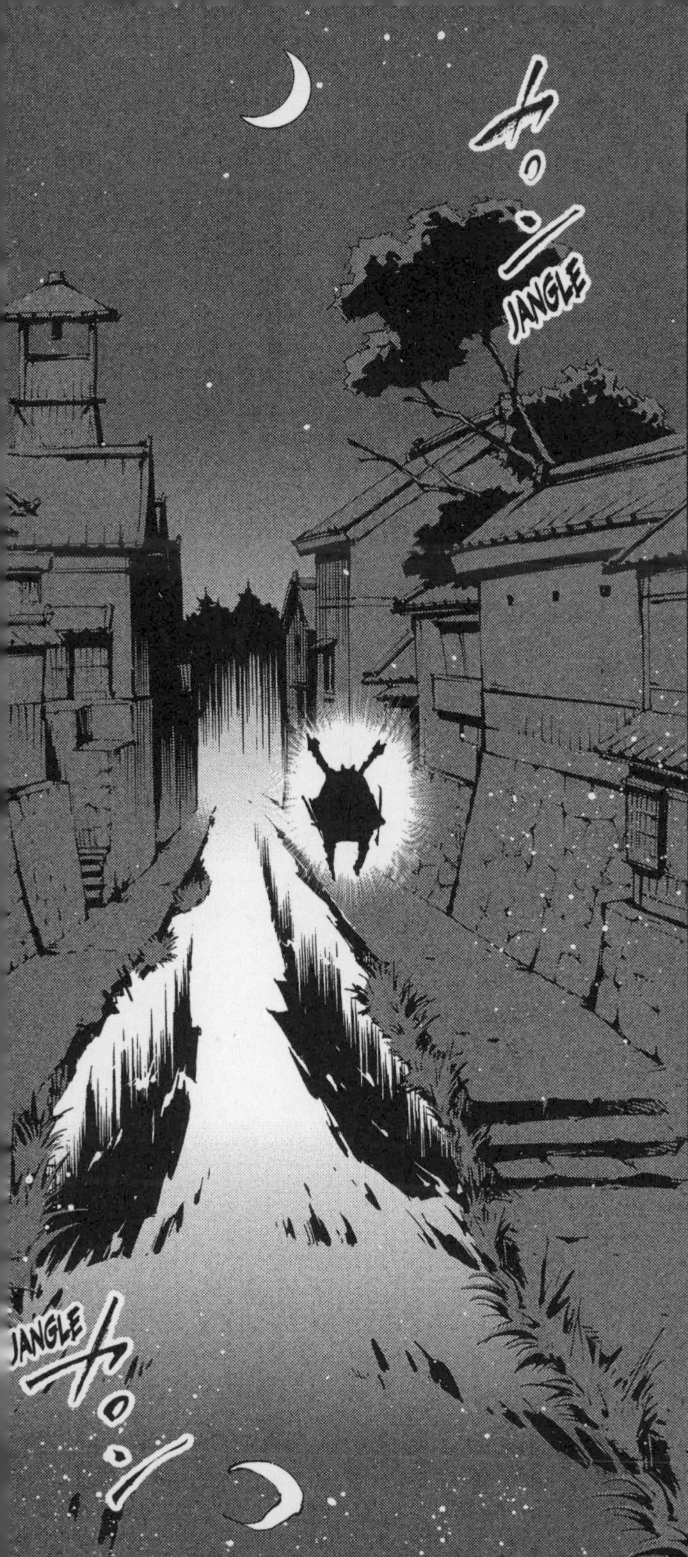
JANGLE
JANGLE

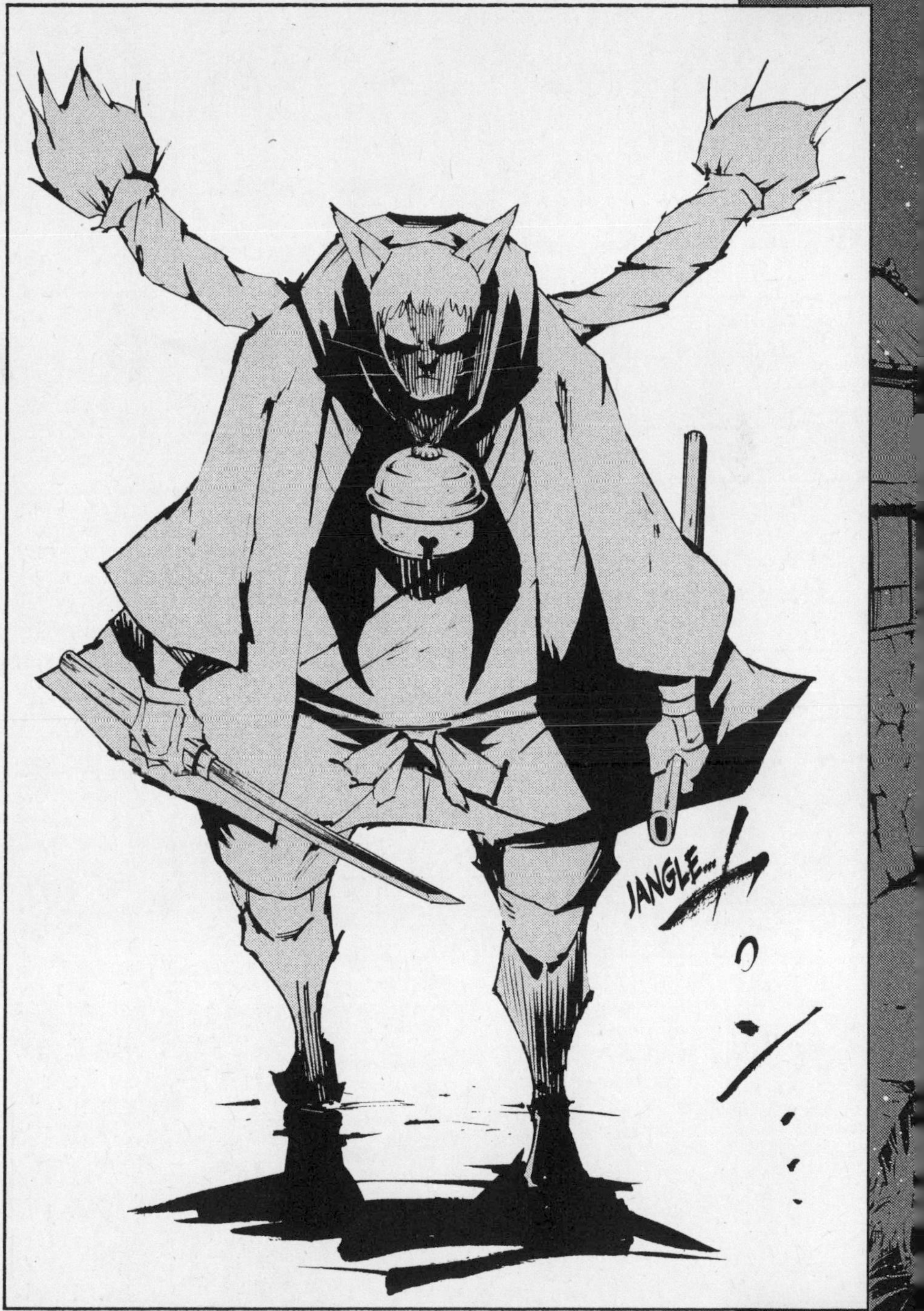
JANGLE...

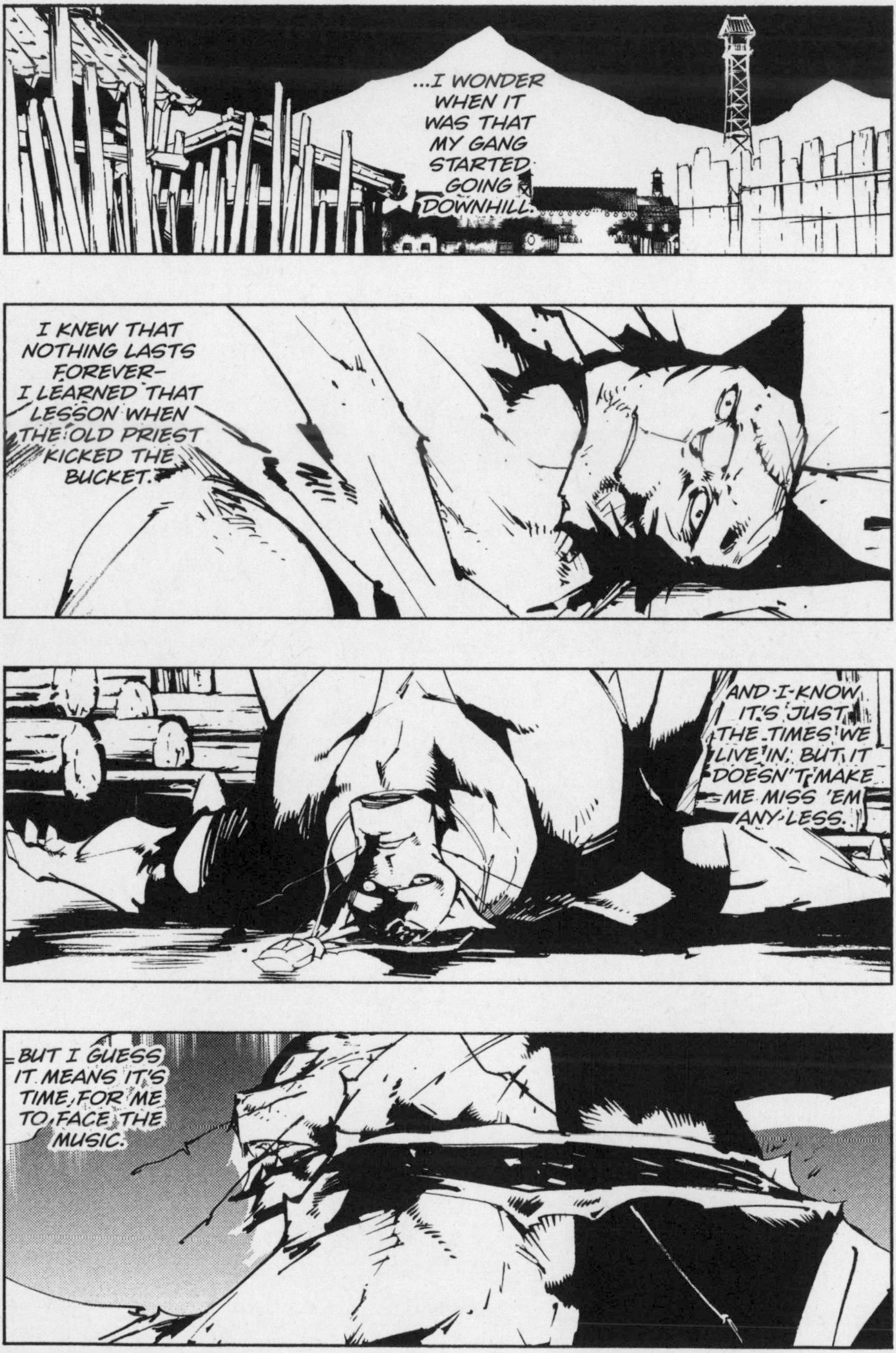
...I WONDER WHEN IT WAS THAT MY GANG STARTED GOING DOWNHILL.
I KNEW THAT NOTHING LASTS FOREVER– I LEARNED THAT LESSON WHEN THE OLD PRIEST KICKED THE BUCKET.
AND I KNOW IT'S JUST THE TIMES WE LIVE IN, BUT IT DOESN'T MAKE ME MISS 'EM ANY LESS.
BUT I GUESS IT MEANS IT'S TIME FOR ME TO FACE THE MUSIC.

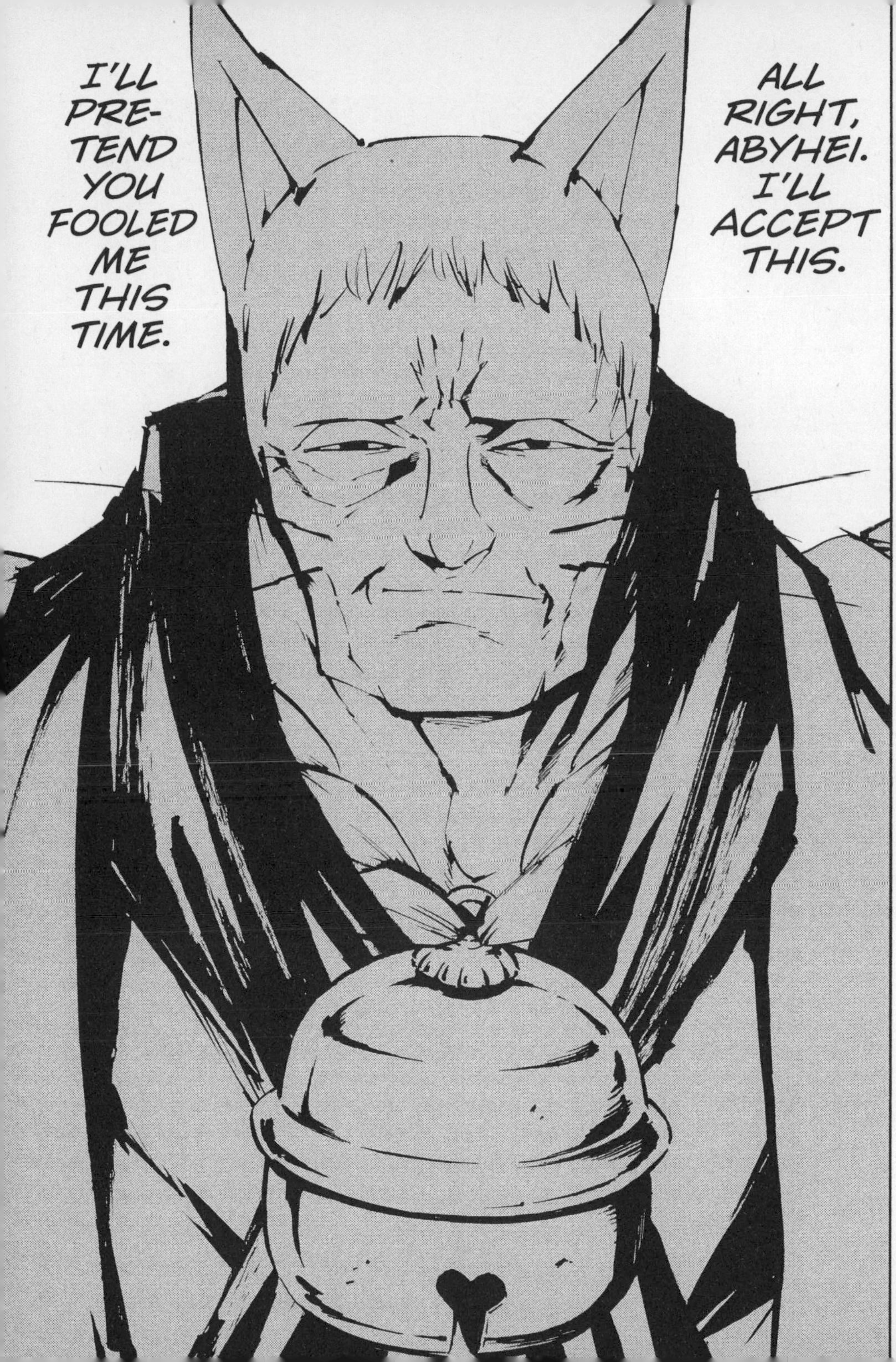
ALL RIGHT, ABYHEI. I'LL ACCEPT THIS.
I'LL PRE-TEND YOU FOOLED ME THIS TIME.

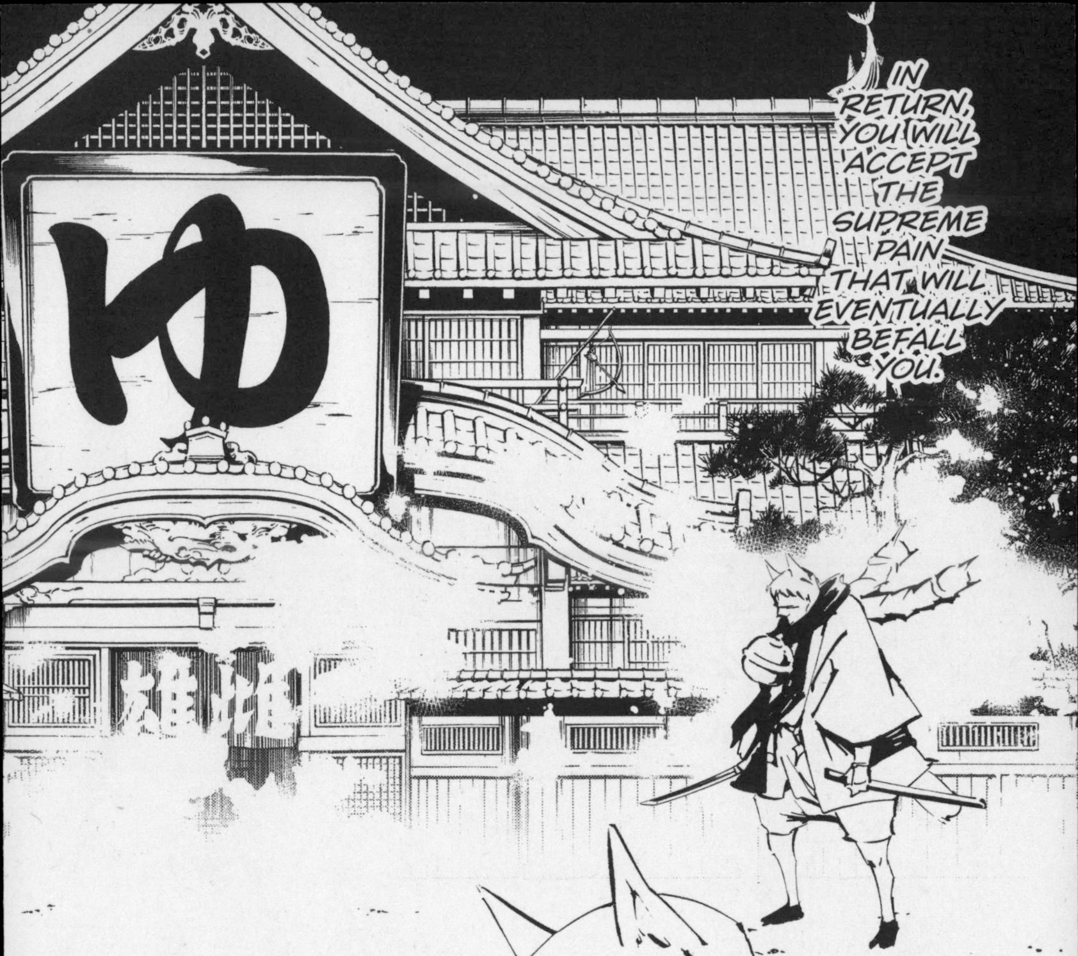
IN RETURN, YOU WILL ACCEPT THE SUPREME PAIN THAT WILL EVENTUALLY BEFALL YOU.

SIGN: BATH, LEFT: TOMS, RIGHT: MOLLIES

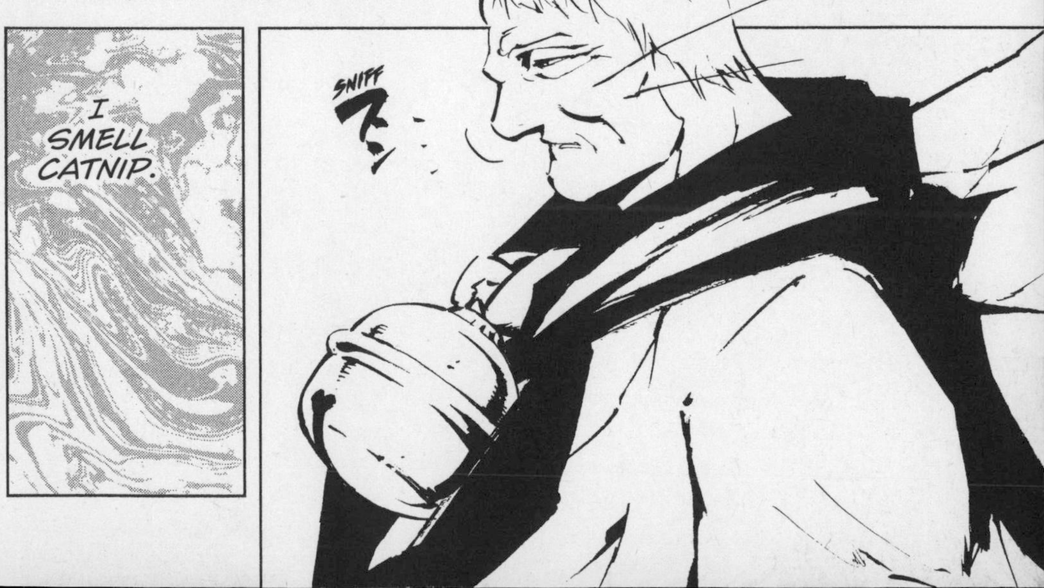
SNIFF
I SMELL CATNIP.

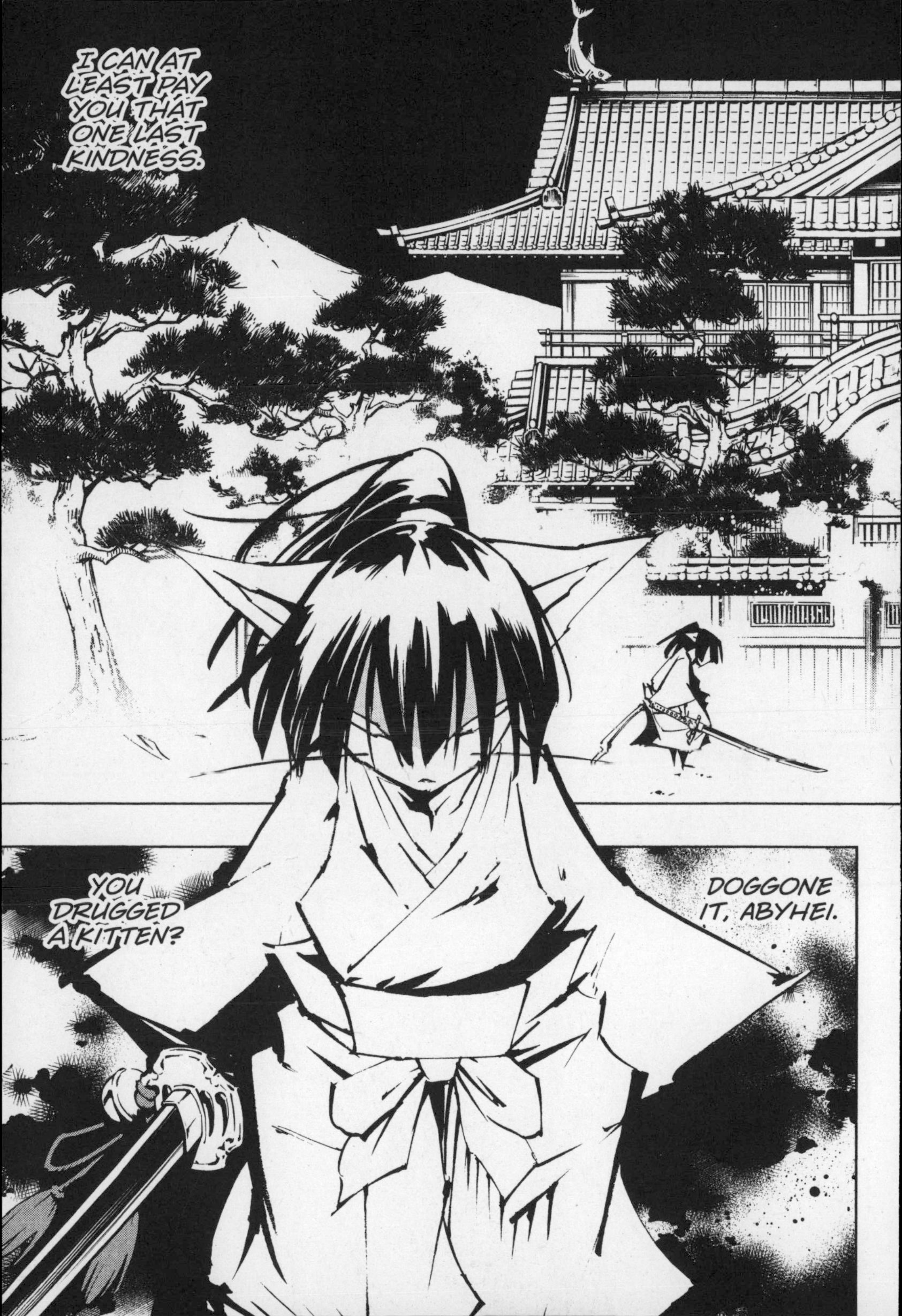
I CAN AT LEAST PAY YOU THAT ONE LAST KINDNESS.
DOGGONE IT, ABYHEI.
YOU DRUGGED A KITTEN?

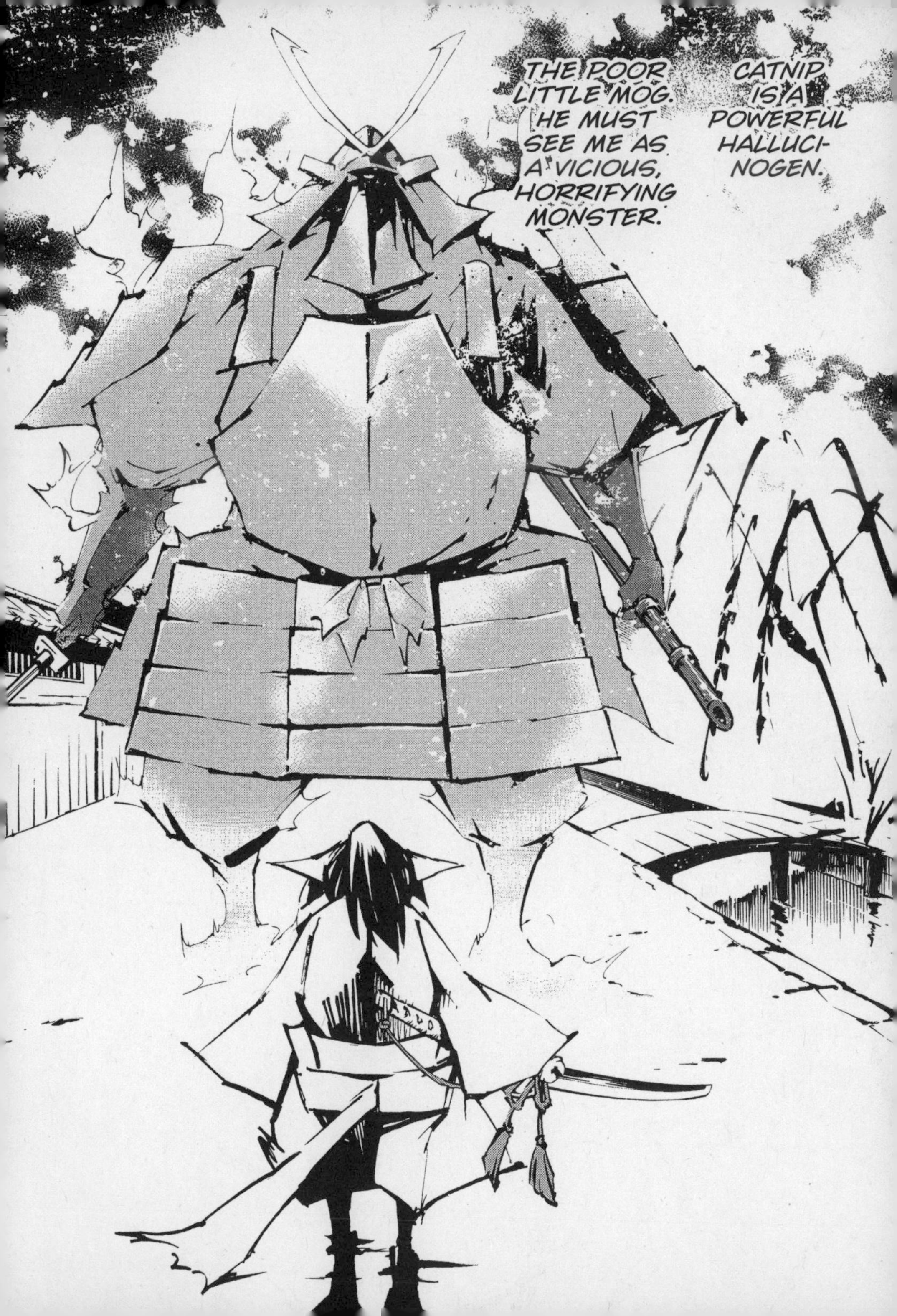
THE POOR LITTLE MOG. HE MUST SEE ME AS A VICIOUS, HORRIFYING MONSTER.
CATNIP IS A POWERFUL HALLUCI-NOGEN.

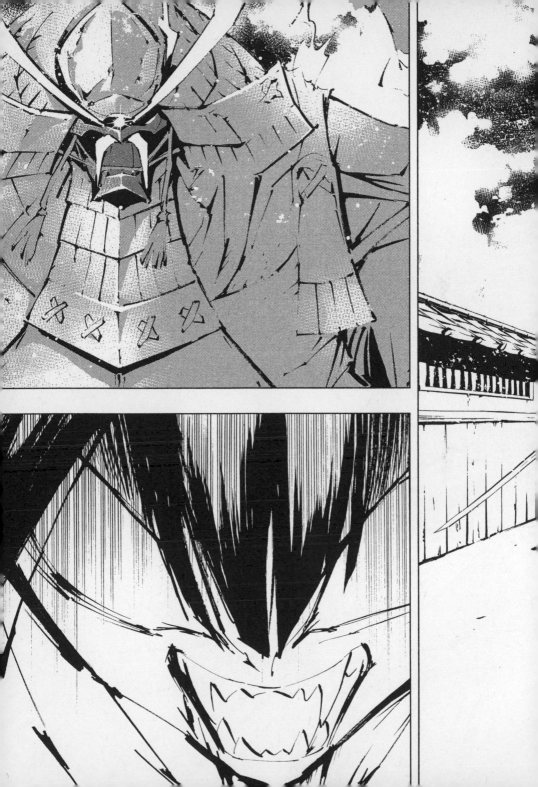

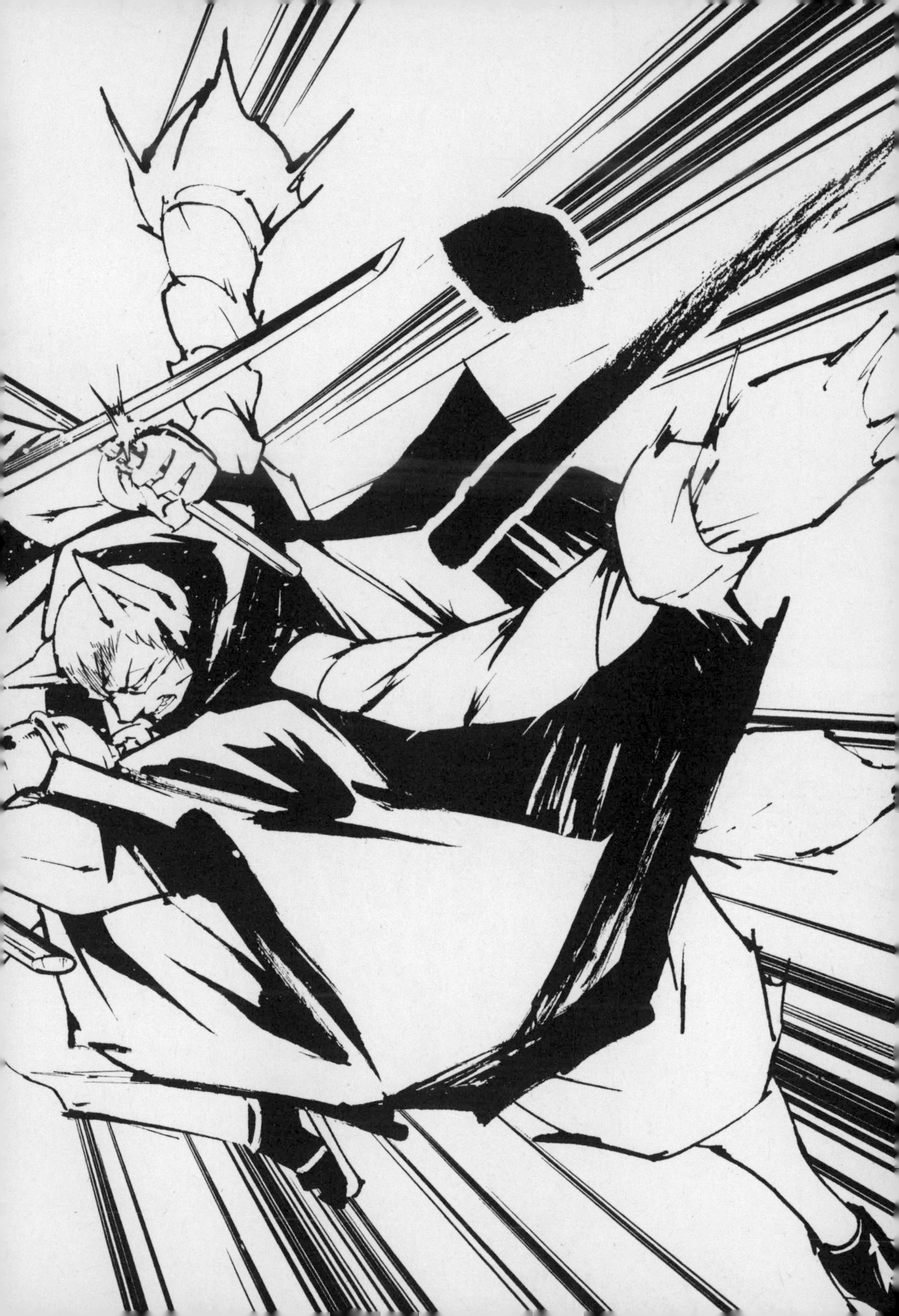

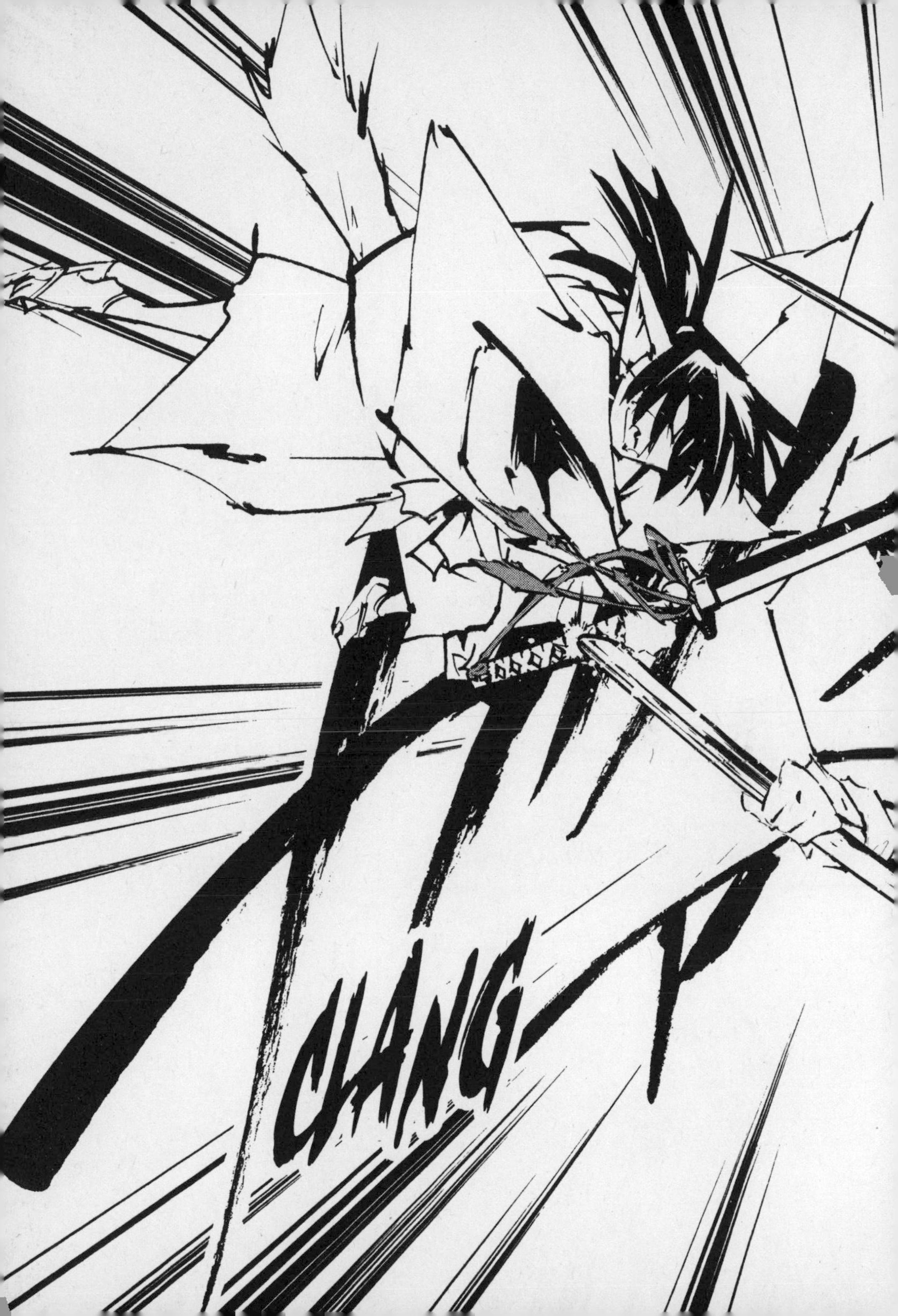
CLANG

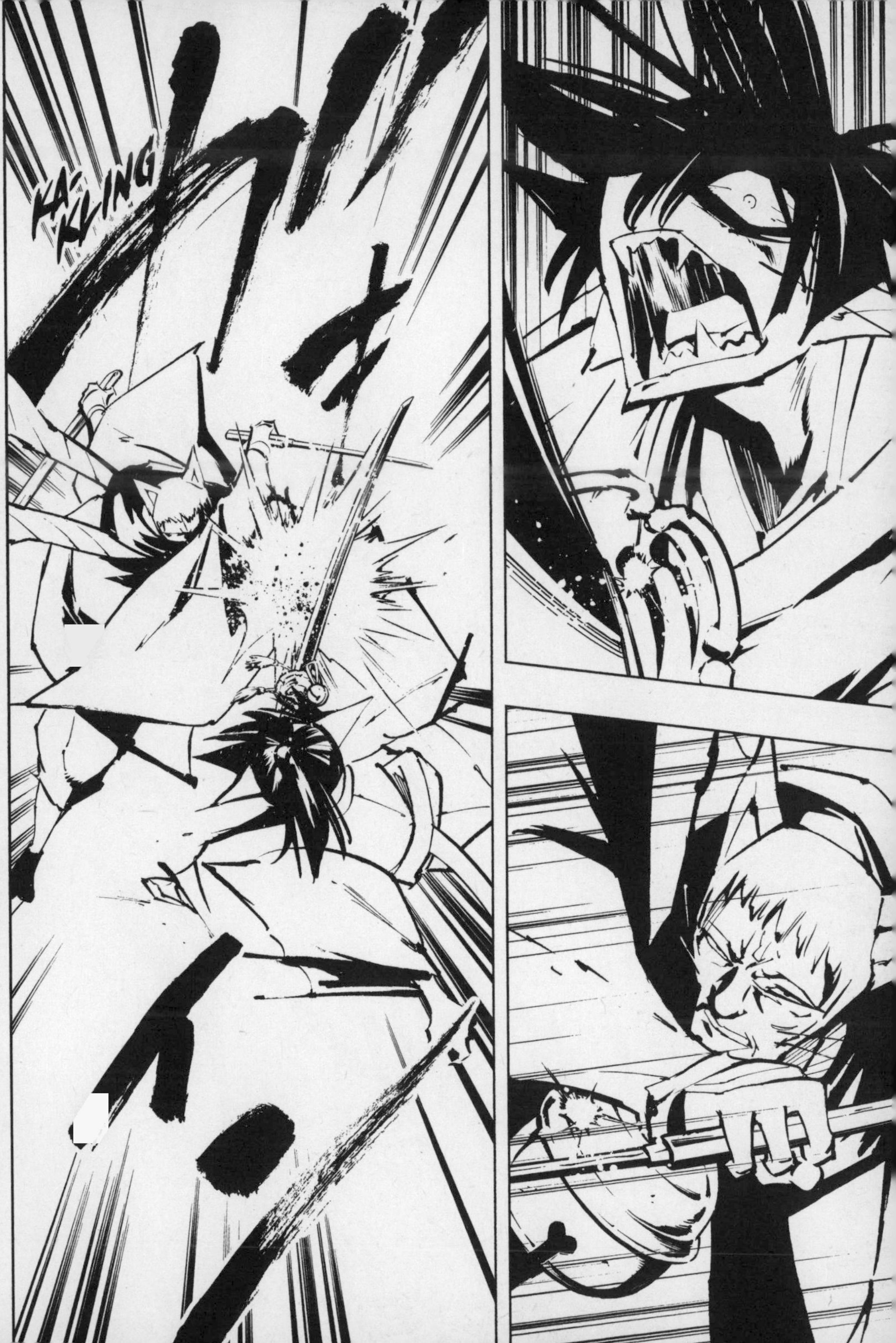
KA-KLING

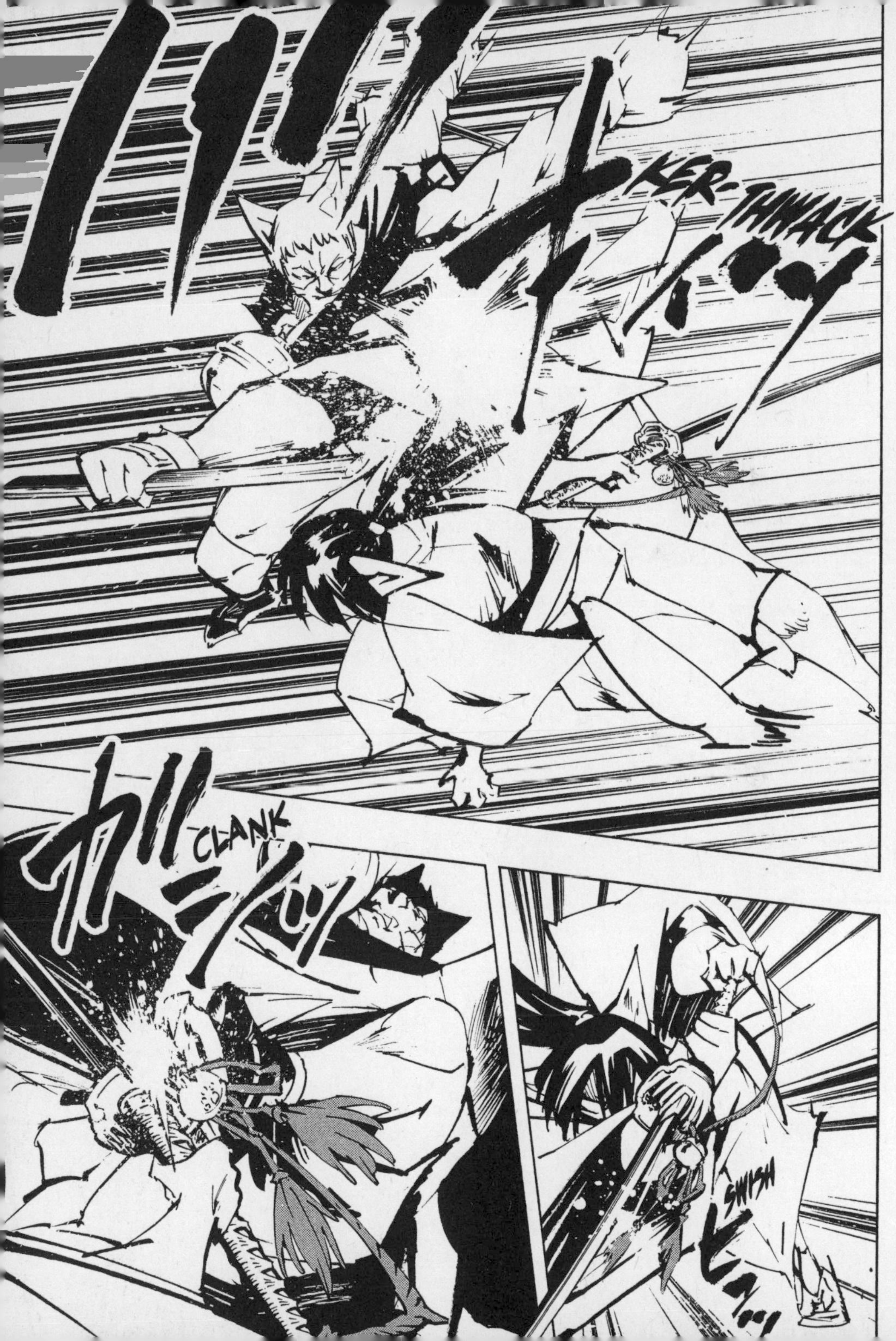
KER-THWACK
SWISH
CLANK

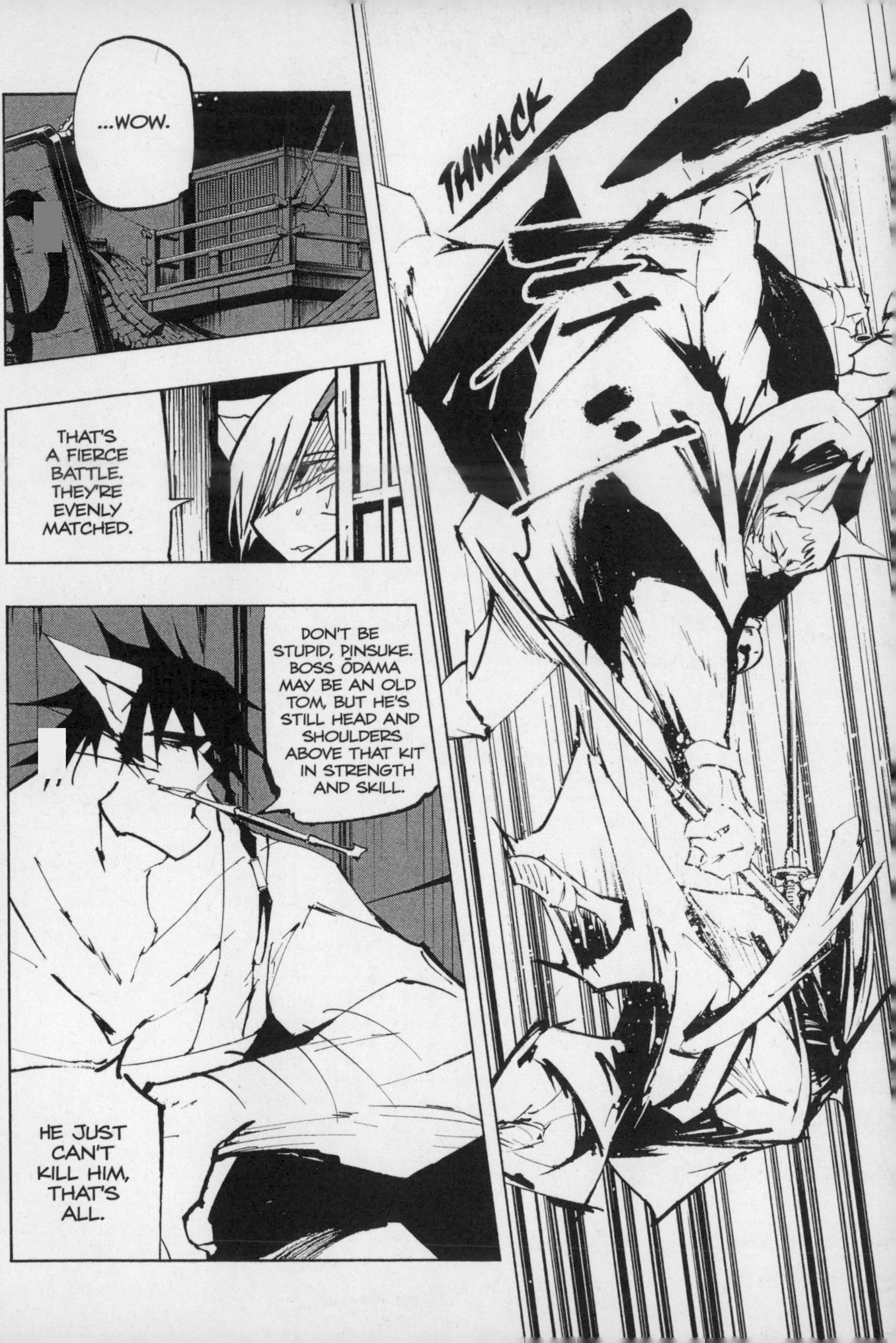
THWACK
...WOW.
THAT'S A FIERCE BATTLE. THEY'RE EVENLY MATCHED.
DON'T BE STUPID, PINSUKE. BOSS ŌDAMA MAY BE AN OLD TOM, BUT HE'S STILL HEAD AND SHOULDERS ABOVE THAT KIT IN STRENGTH AND SKILL.
HE JUST CAN'T KILL HIM, THAT'S ALL.

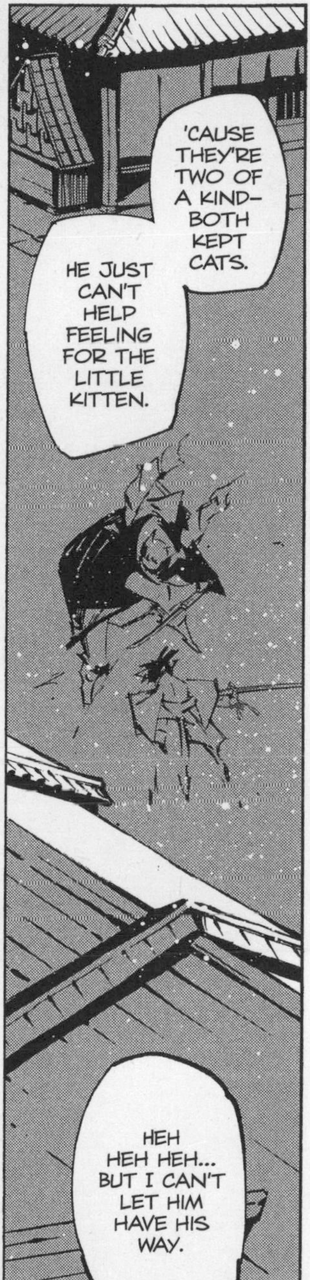
'CAUSE THEY'RE TWO OF A KIND–BOTH KEPT CATS.
HE JUST CAN'T HELP FEELING FOR THE LITTLE KITTEN.
HEH HEH HEH... BUT I CAN'T LET HIM HAVE HIS WAY.
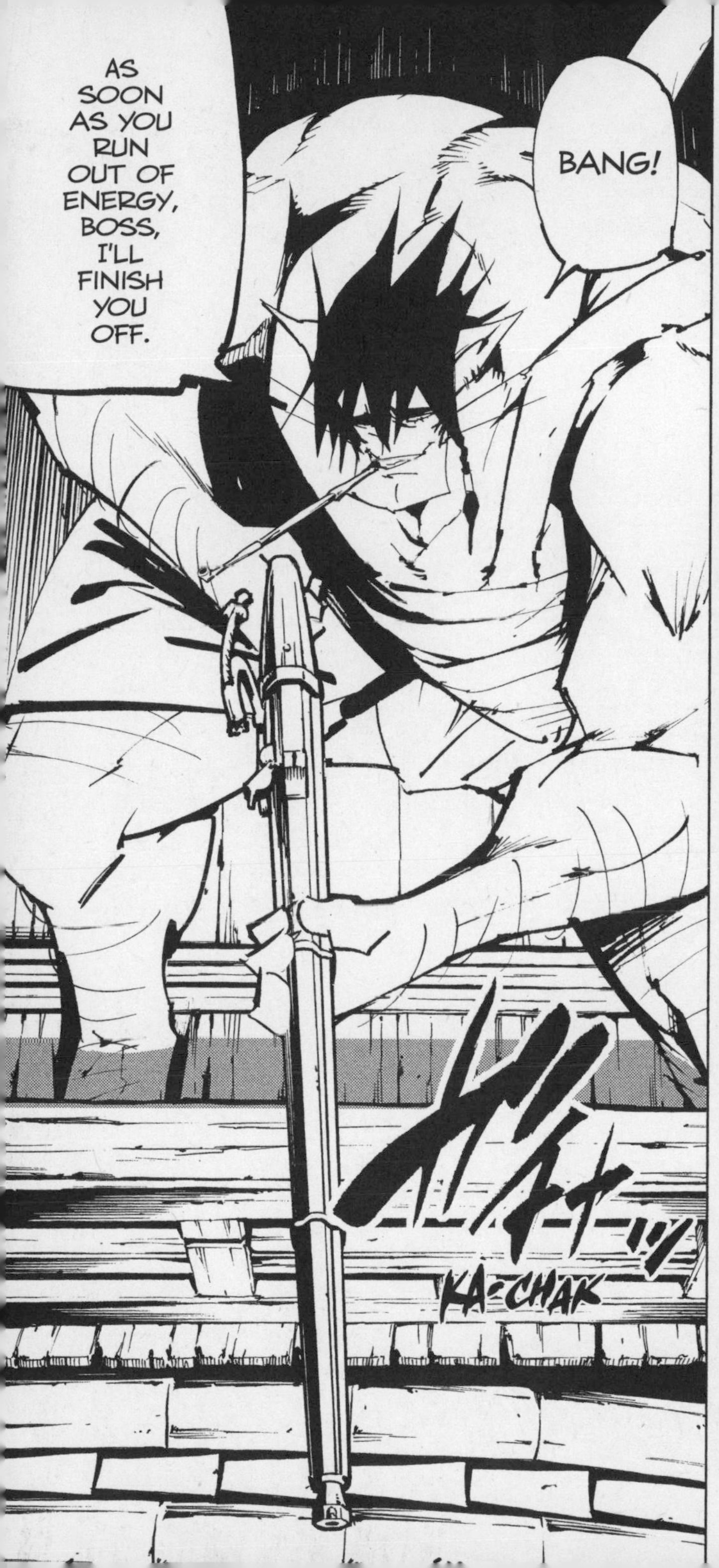
BANG!
AS SOON AS YOU RUN OUT OF ENERGY, BOSS, I'LL FINISH YOU OFF.
KA-CHAK

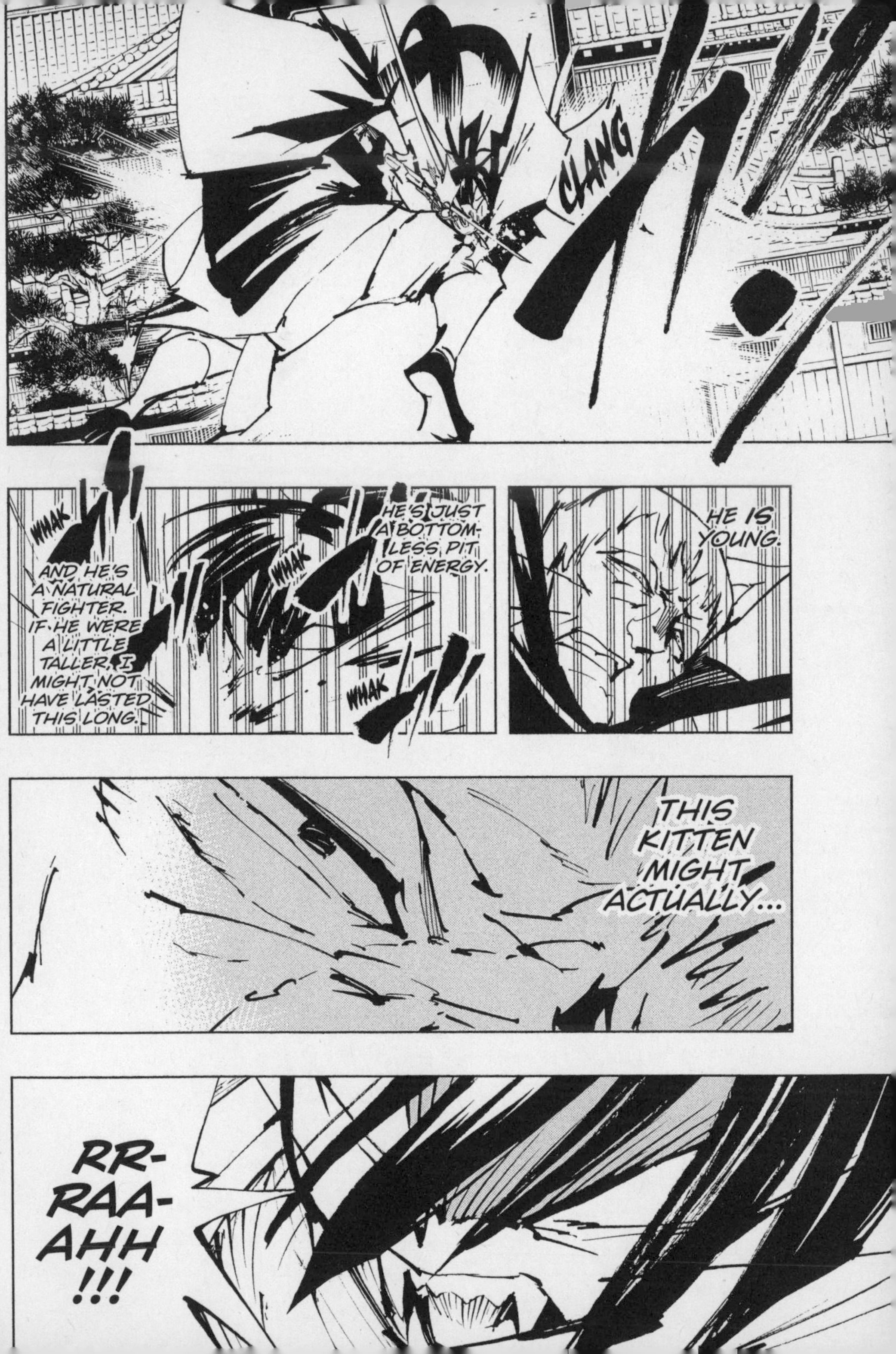
CLANG
HE IS YOUNG.
HE'S JUST A BOTTOMLESS PIT OF ENERGY.
WHAK
WHAK
AND HE'S A NATURAL FIGHTER. IF HE WERE A LITTLE TALLER, I MIGHT NOT HAVE LASTED THIS LONG.
WHAK
THIS KITTEN MIGHT ACTUALLY...
RR-RAA-AHH!!!

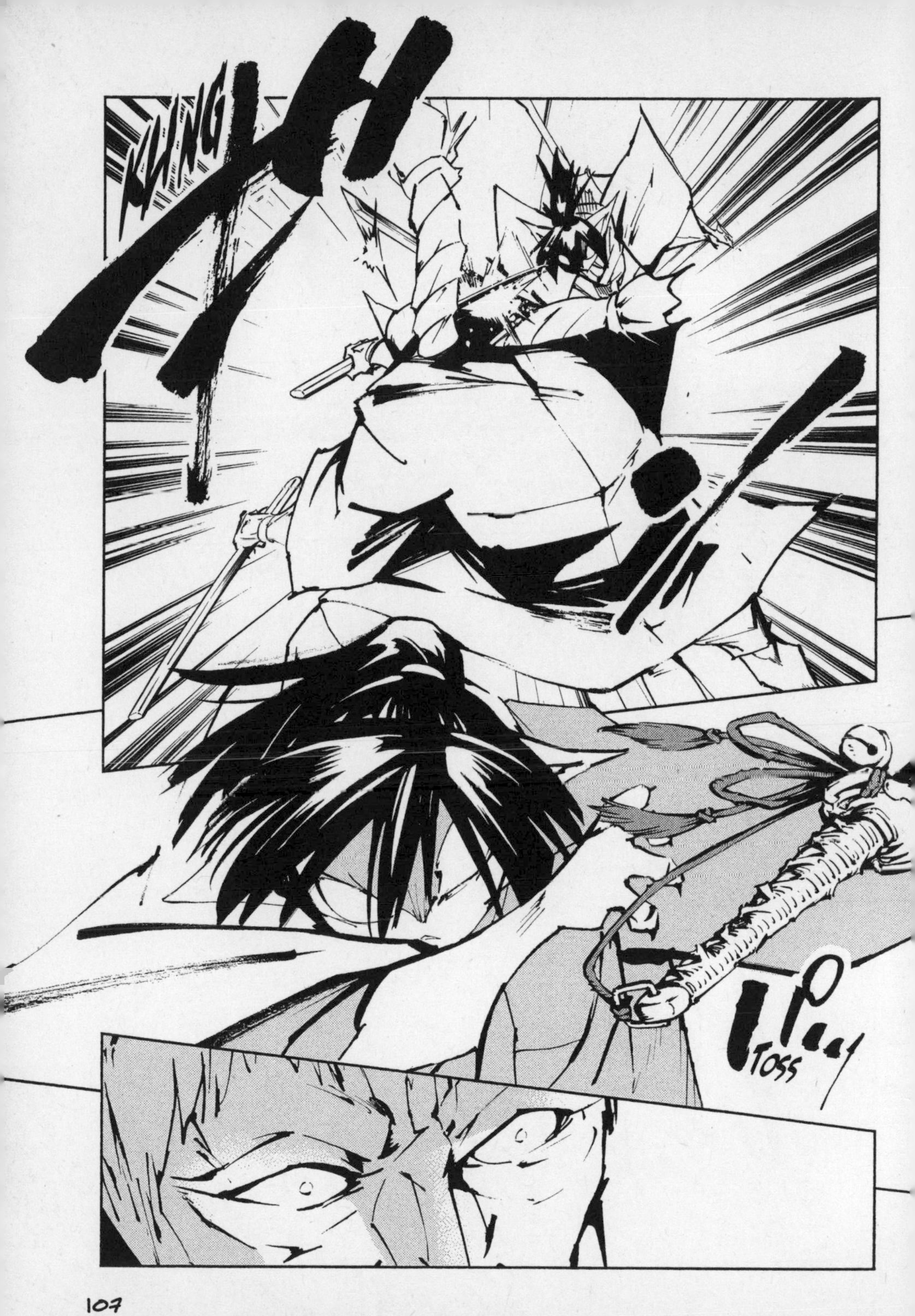
KLING
TOSS

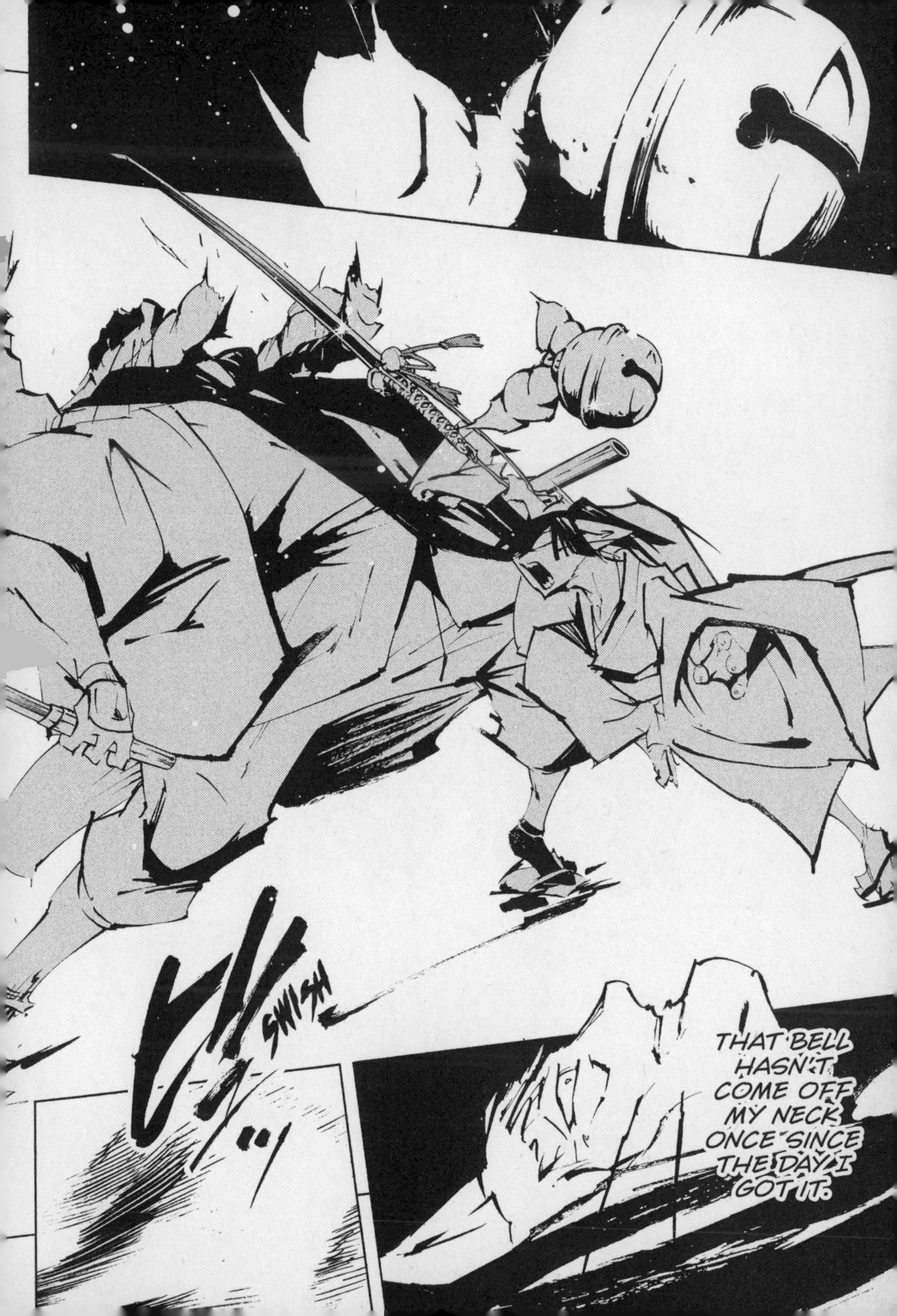
SWISH
THAT BELL HASN'T COME OFF MY NECK ONCE SINCE THE DAY I GOT IT.

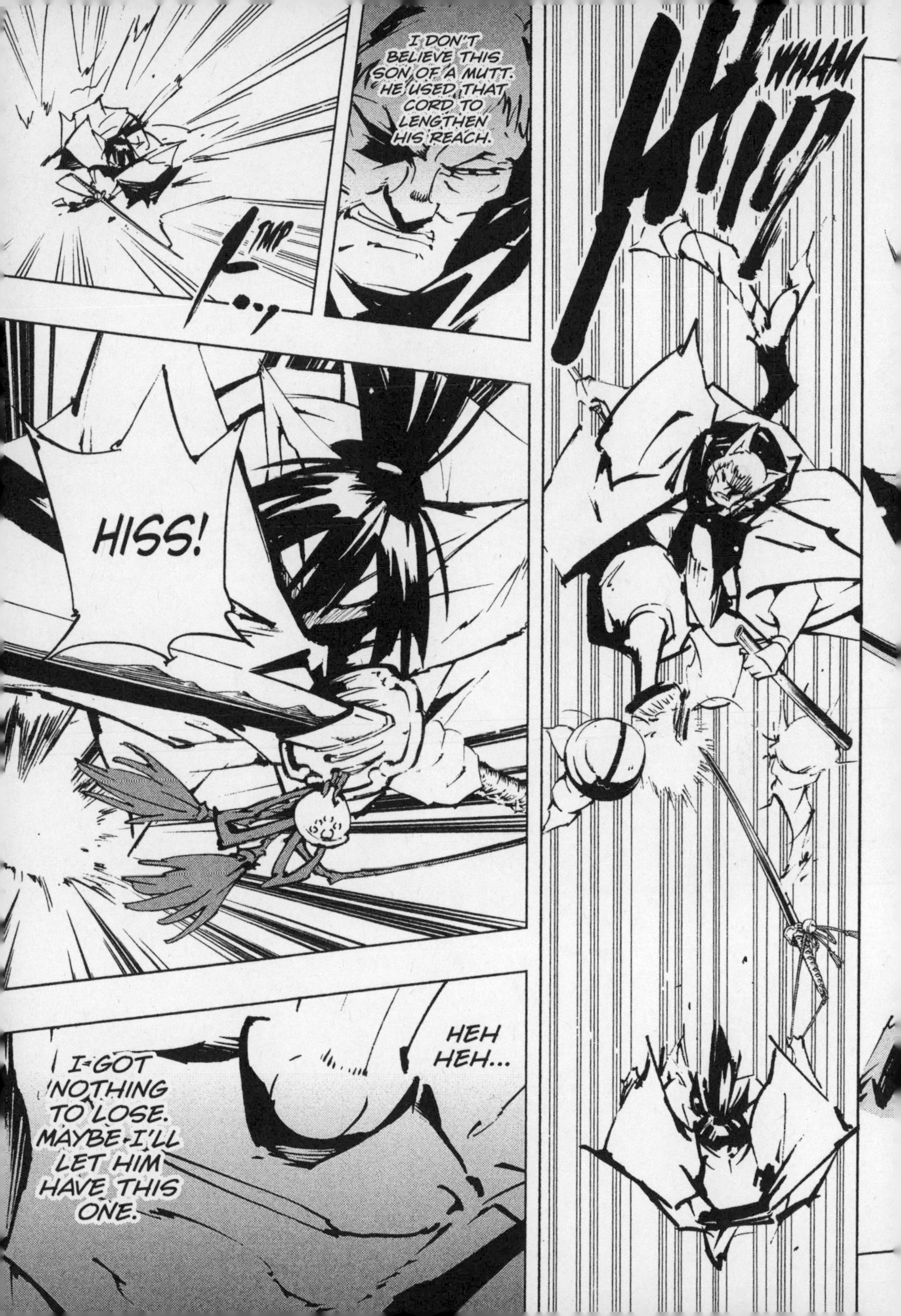
WHAM
I DON'T BELIEVE THIS SON OF A MUTT. HE USED THAT CORD TO LENGTHEN HIS REACH.
TMP
...
HISS!
HEH HEH...
I GOT NOTHING TO LOSE. MAYBE I'LL LET HIM HAVE THIS ONE.

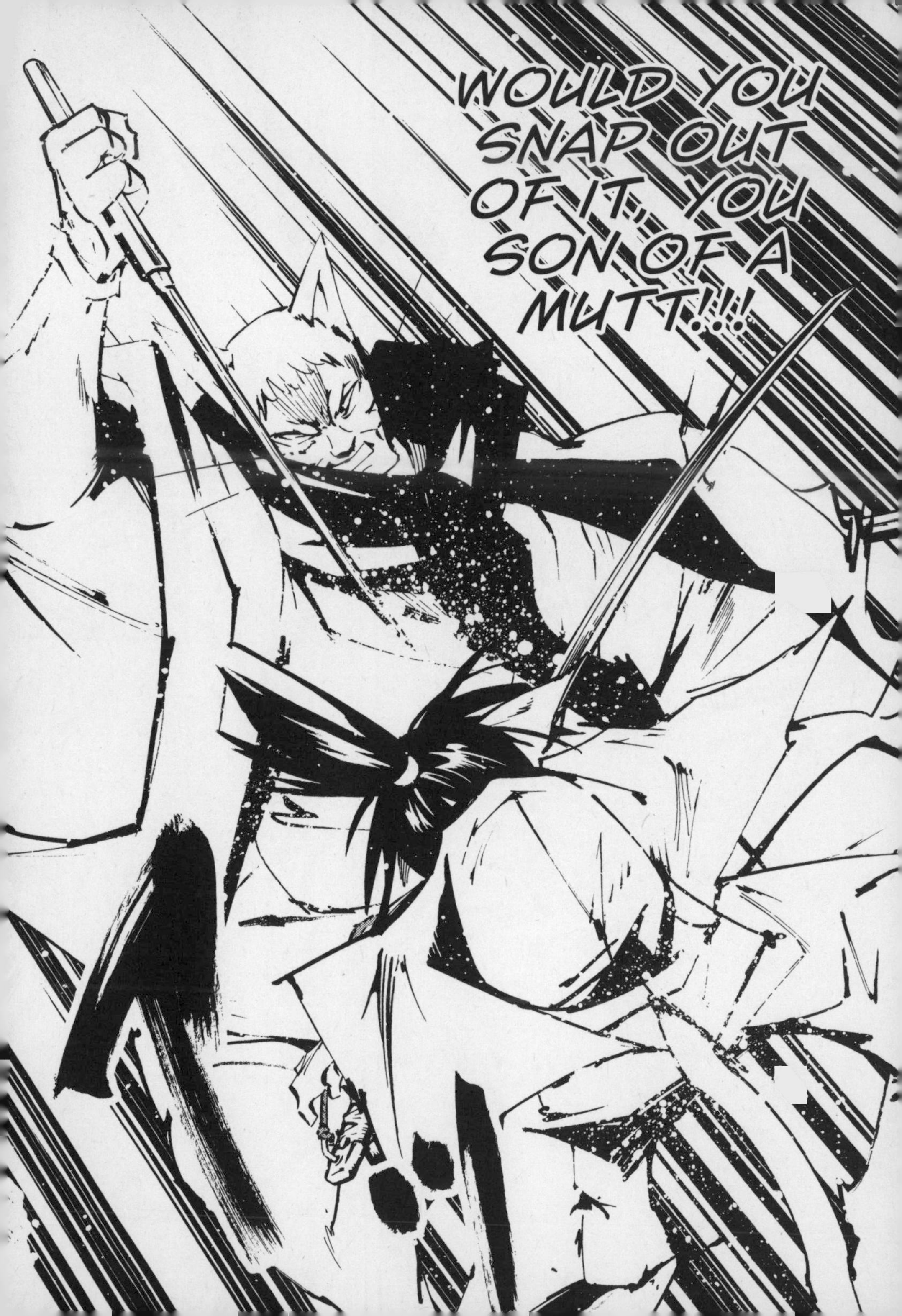
WOULD YOU SNAP OUT OF IT, YOU SON OF A MUTT!!!

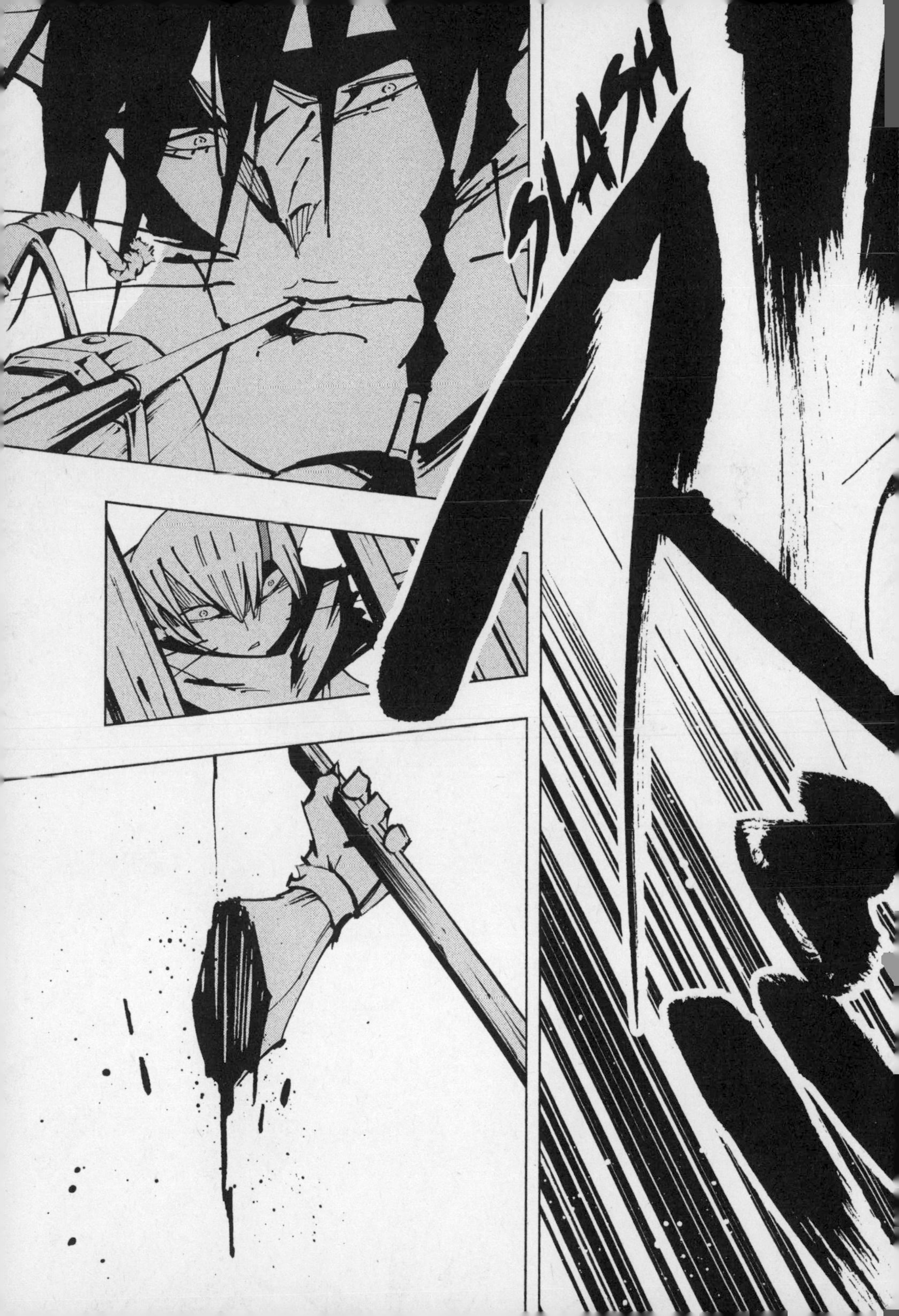
SLASH

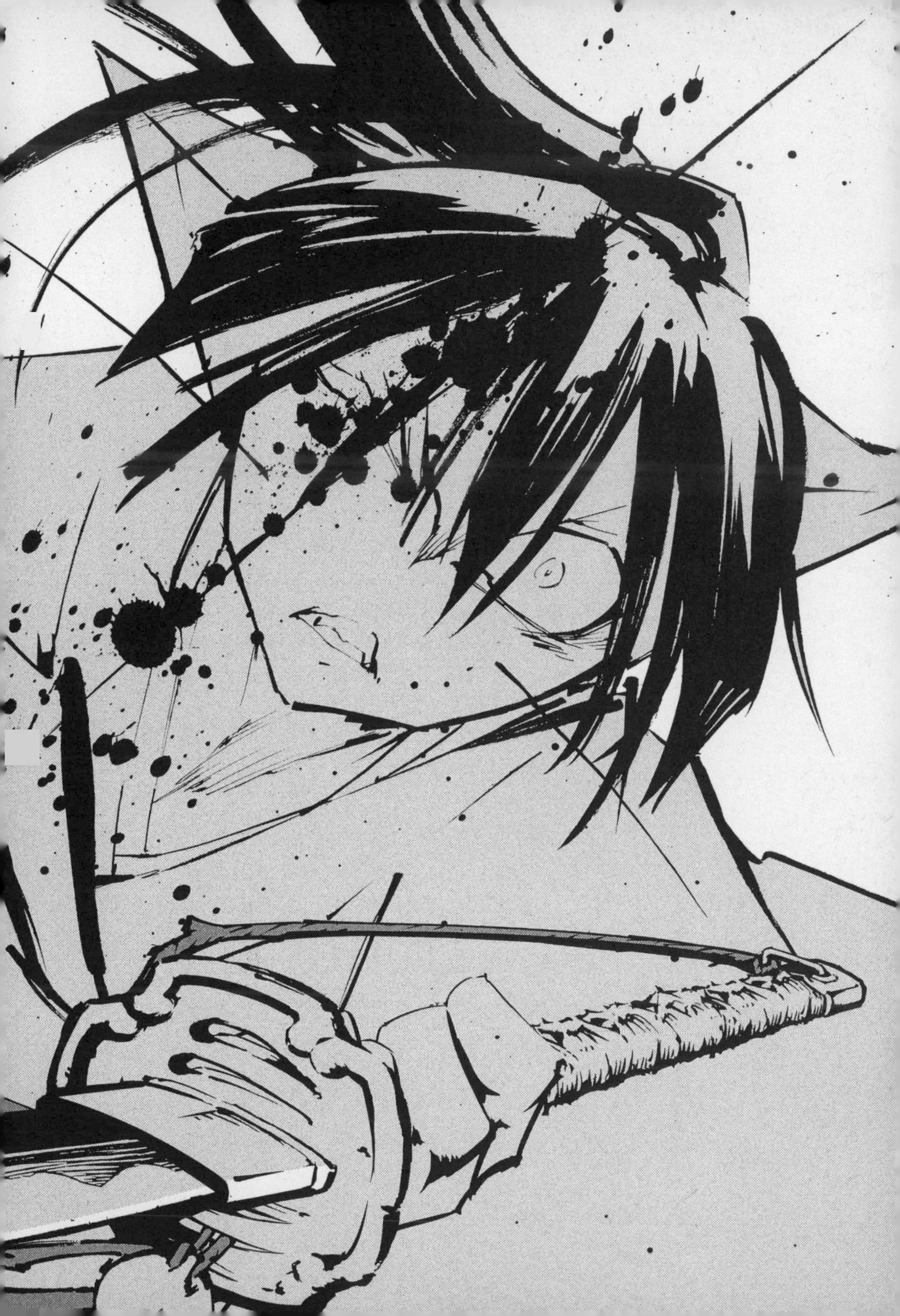

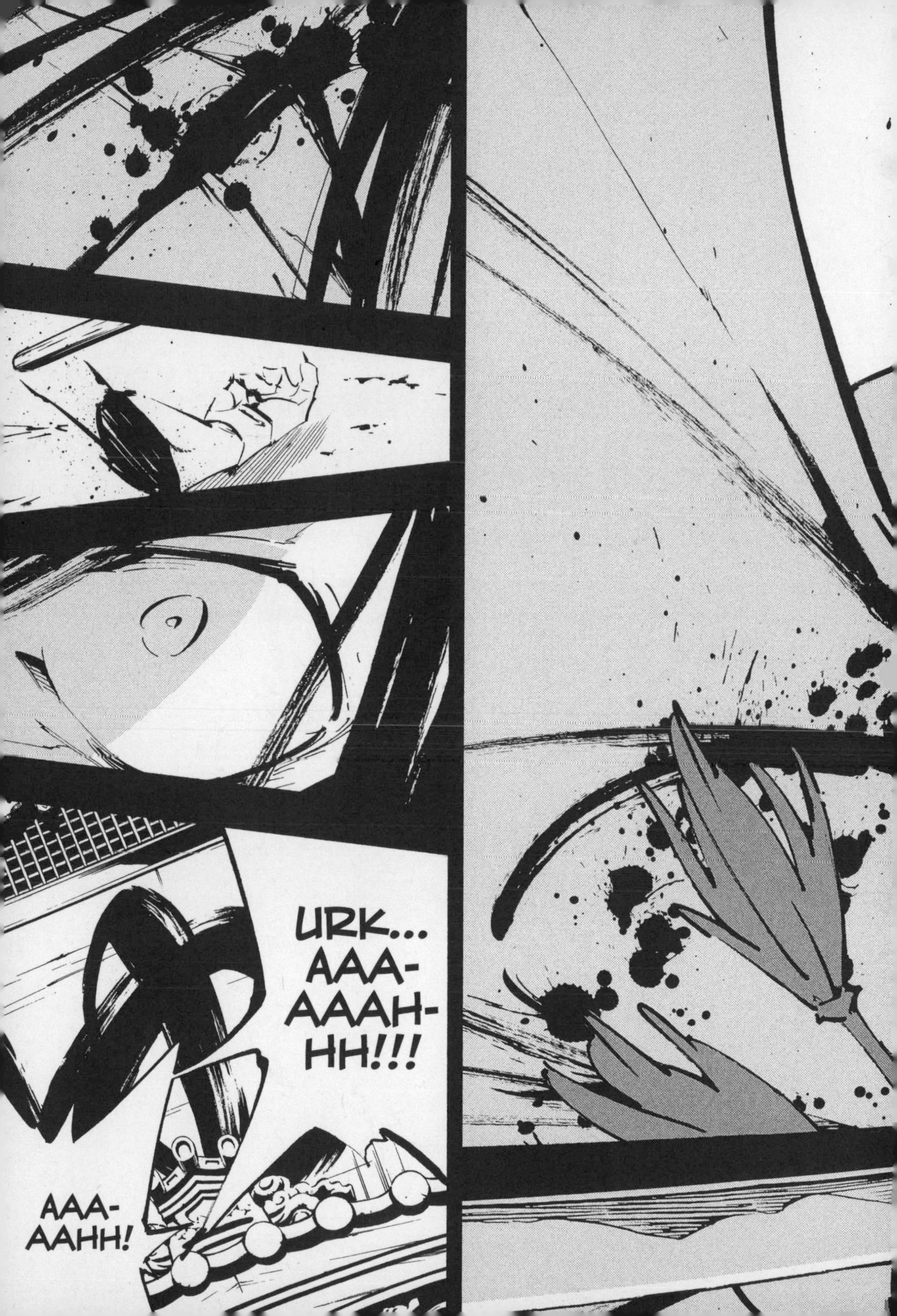
URK... AAA-AAAH-HH!!!
AAA-AAHH!

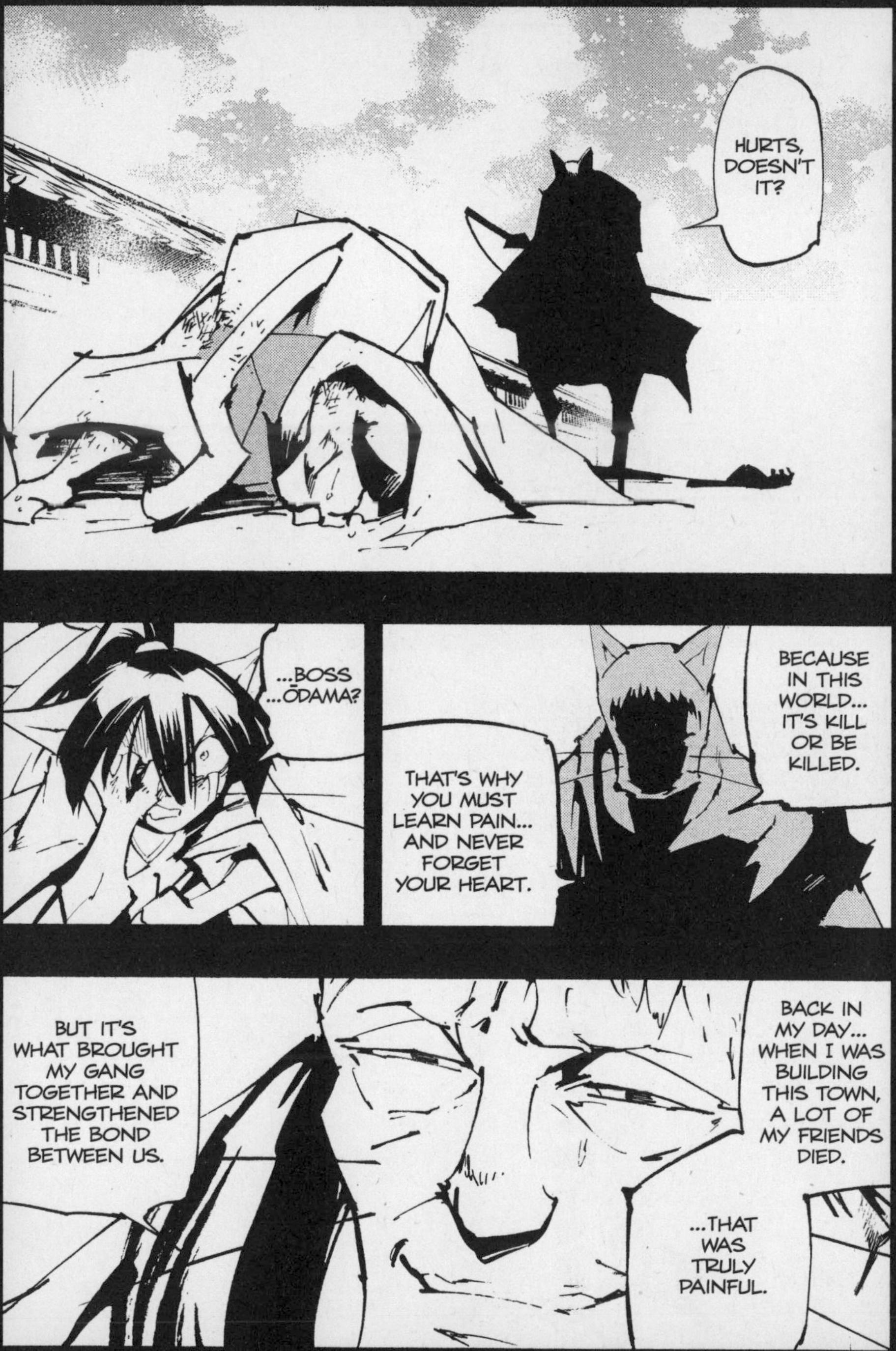
HURTS, DOESN'T IT?
BECAUSE IN THIS WORLD... IT'S KILL OR BE KILLED.
THAT'S WHY YOU MUST LEARN PAIN... AND NEVER FORGET YOUR HEART.
...BOSS ...ŌDAMA?
BACK IN MY DAY... WHEN I WAS BUILDING THIS TOWN, A LOT OF MY FRIENDS DIED.
BUT IT'S WHAT BROUGHT MY GANG TOGETHER AND STRENGTHENED THE BOND BETWEEN US.
...THAT WAS TRULY PAINFUL.

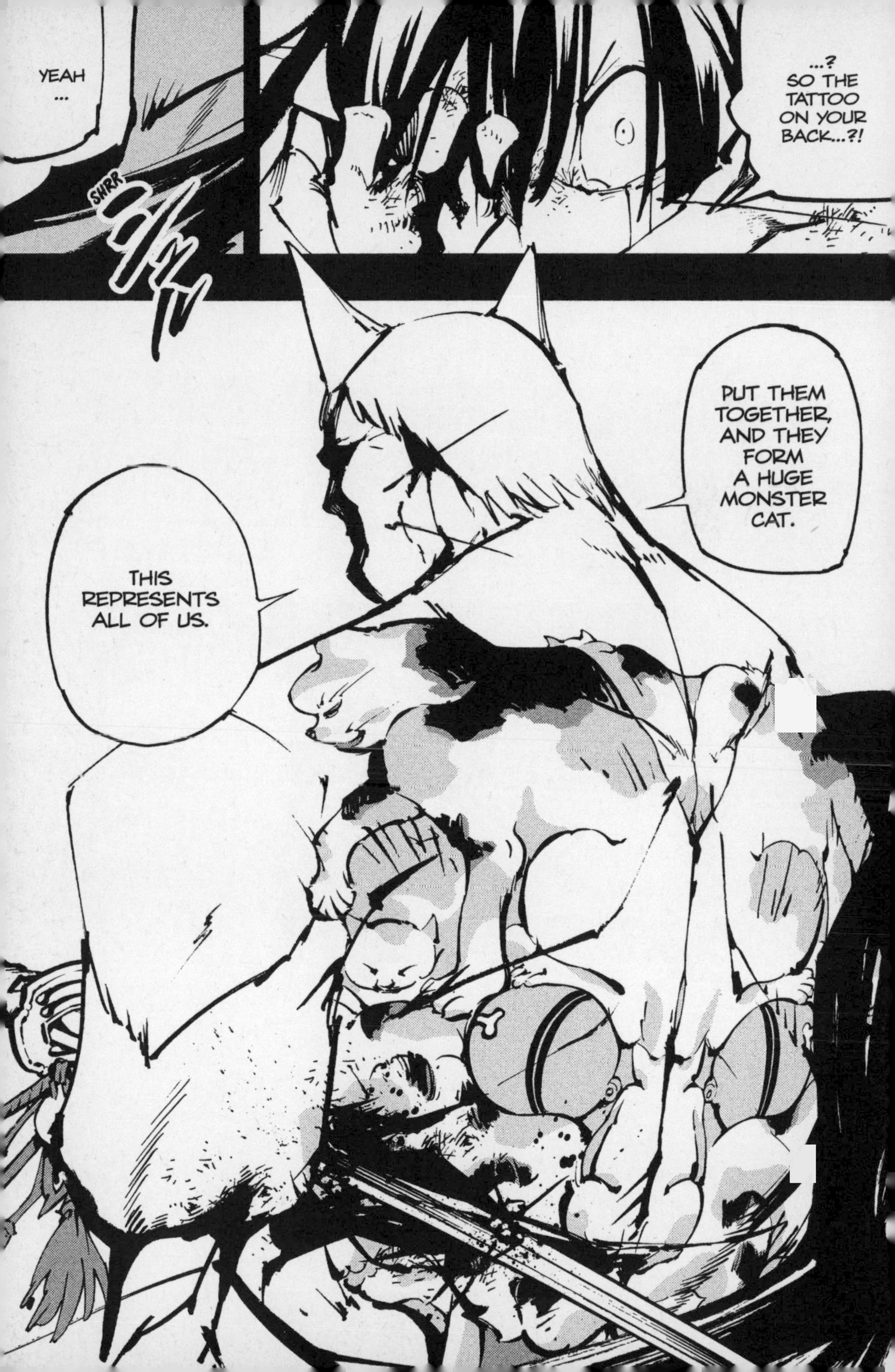
...?
SO THE TATTOO ON YOUR BACK...?!
YEAH ...
SHRR
PUT THEM TOGETHER, AND THEY FORM A HUGE MONSTER CAT.
THIS REPRESENTS ALL OF US.

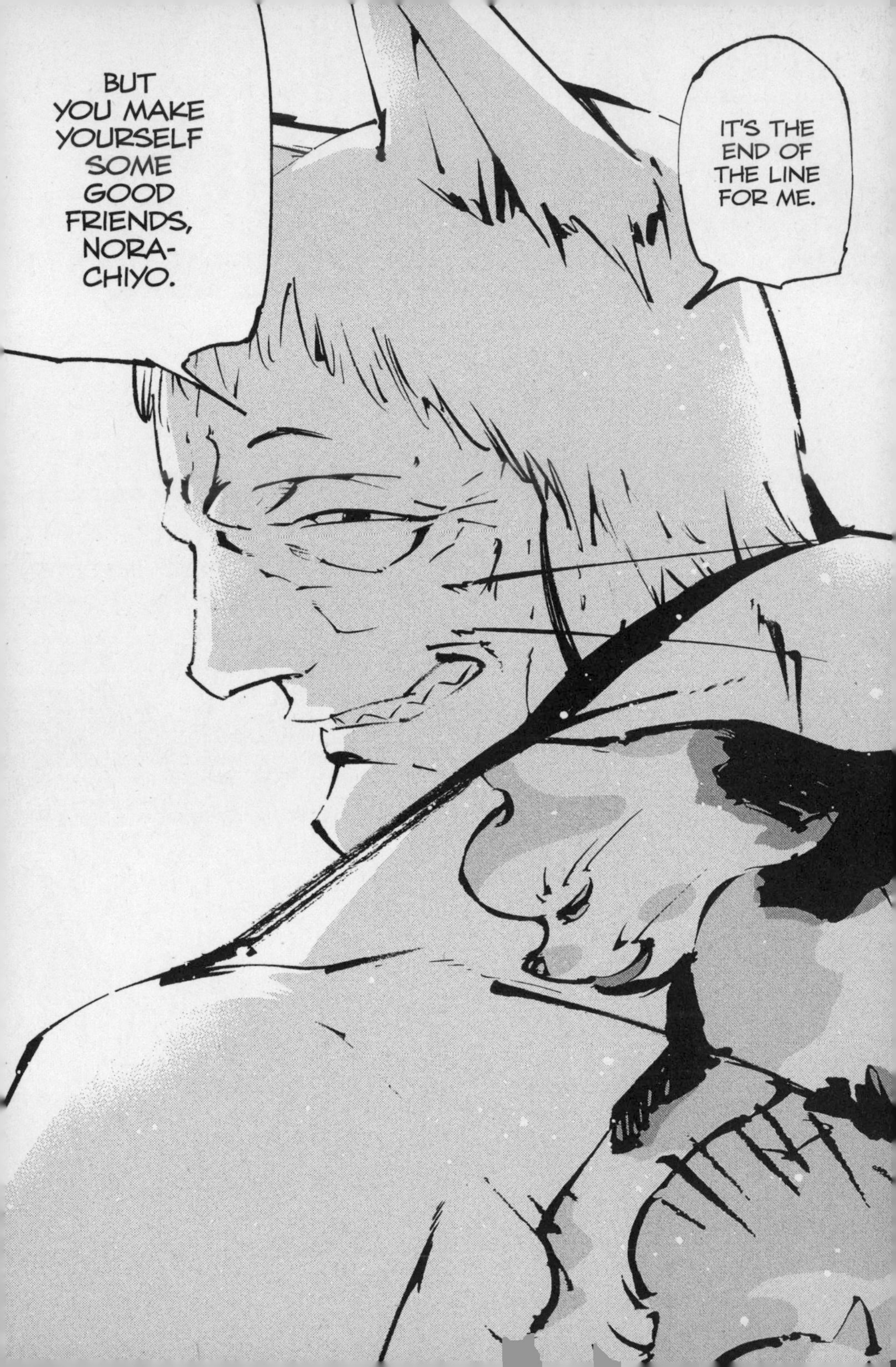
IT'S THE END OF THE LINE FOR ME.
BUT YOU MAKE YOURSELF SOME GOOD FRIENDS, NORA-CHIYO.

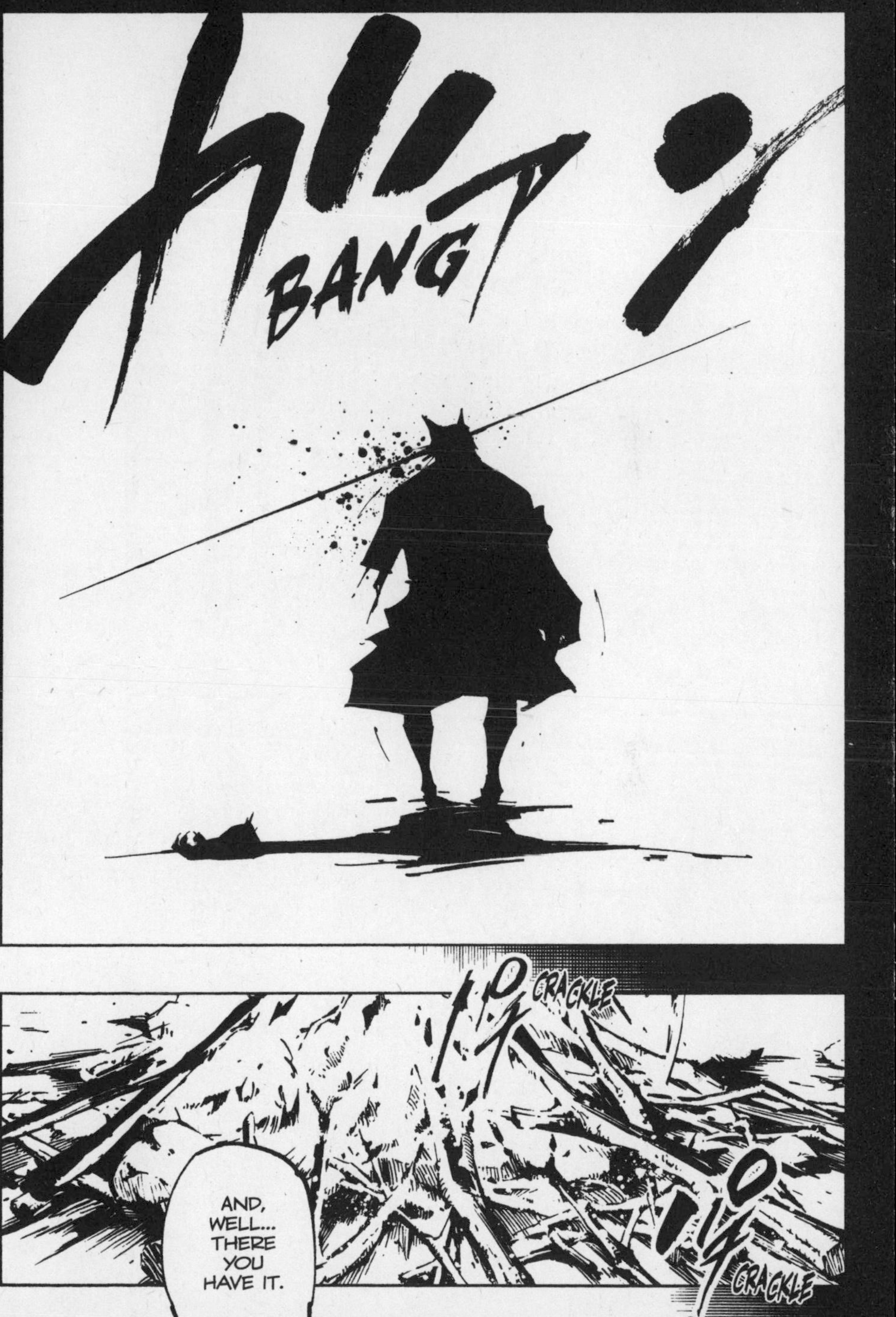
BANG
CRACKLE
CRACKLE
AND, WELL... THERE YOU HAVE IT.

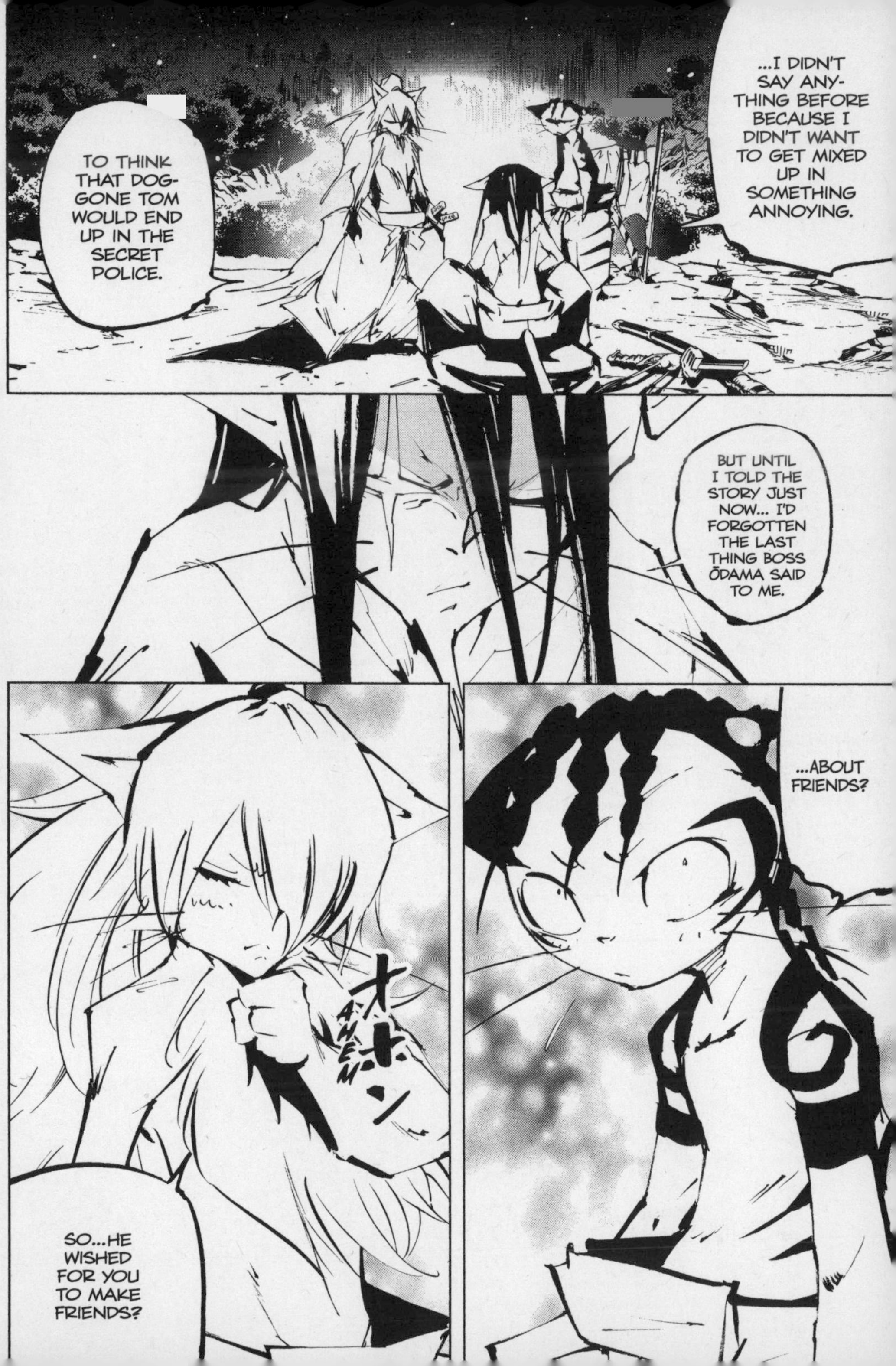
...I DIDN'T SAY ANY-THING BEFORE BECAUSE I DIDN'T WANT TO GET MIXED UP IN SOMETHING ANNOYING.
TO THINK THAT DOG-GONE TOM WOULD END UP IN THE SECRET POLICE.
BUT UNTIL I TOLD THE STORY JUST NOW... I'D FORGOTTEN THE LAST THING BOSS ŌDAMA SAID TO ME.
...ABOUT FRIENDS?
AHEM
SO...HE WISHED FOR YOU TO MAKE FRIENDS?

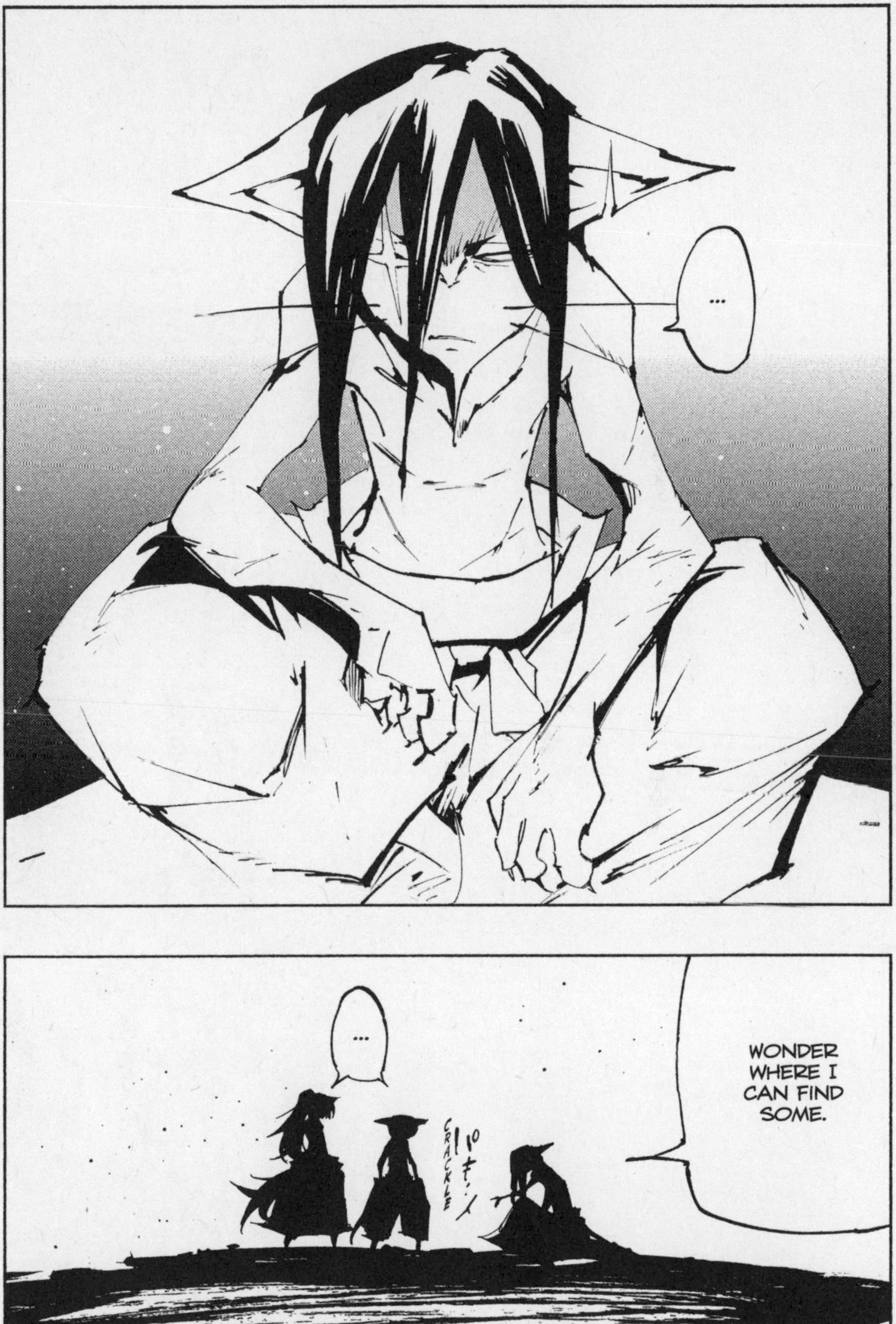
...
WONDER WHERE I CAN FIND SOME.
CRACKLE
...

猫ヶ原

ネコガハラ

NeKoGaHaRa

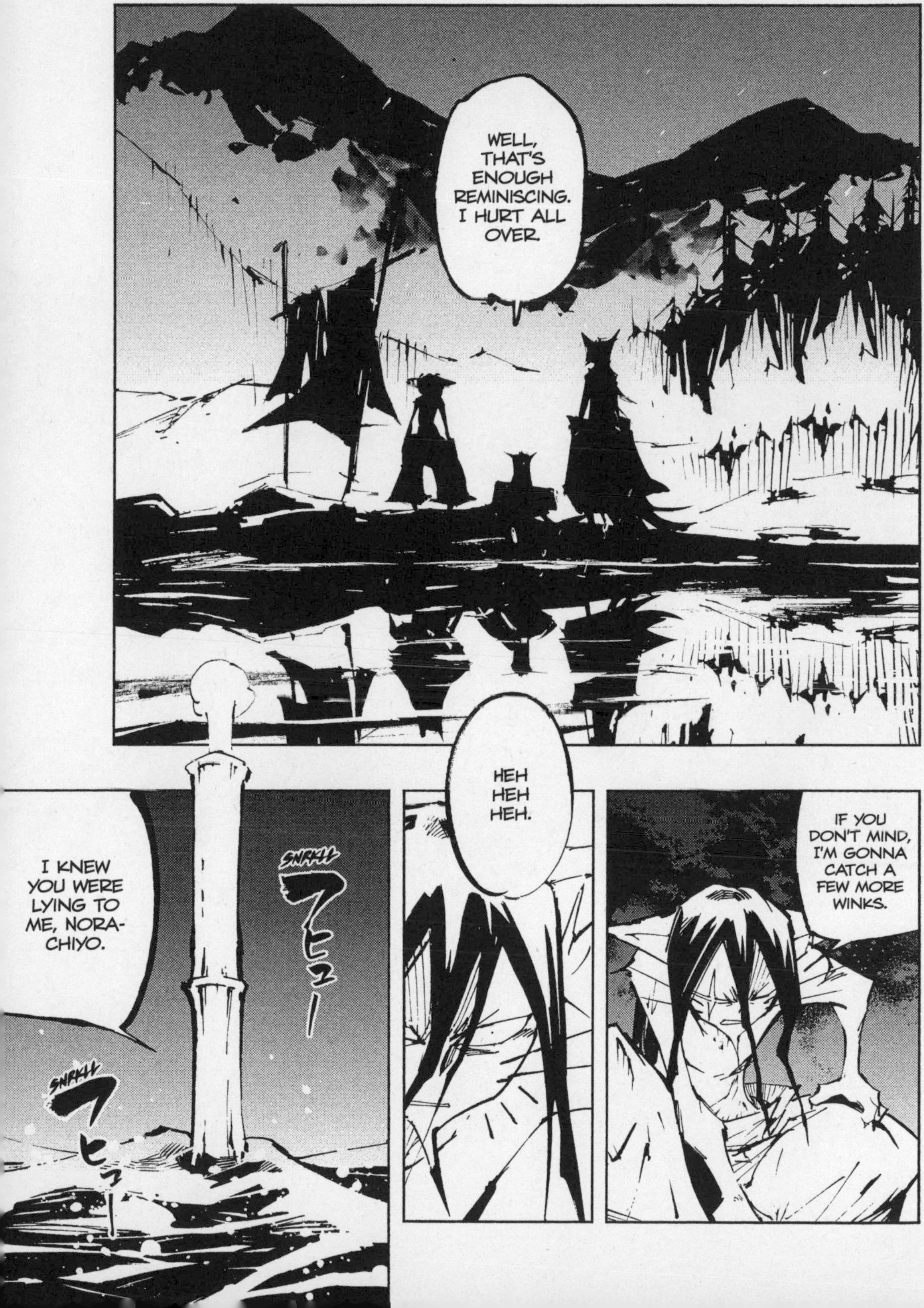
WELL, THAT'S ENOUGH REMINISCING. I HURT ALL OVER.
IF YOU DON'T MIND, I'M GONNA CATCH A FEW MORE WINKS.
HEH HEH HEH.
SNRKLL
フヒュー
I KNEW YOU WERE LYING TO ME, NORA-CHIYO.
SNRKLL
フヒュー

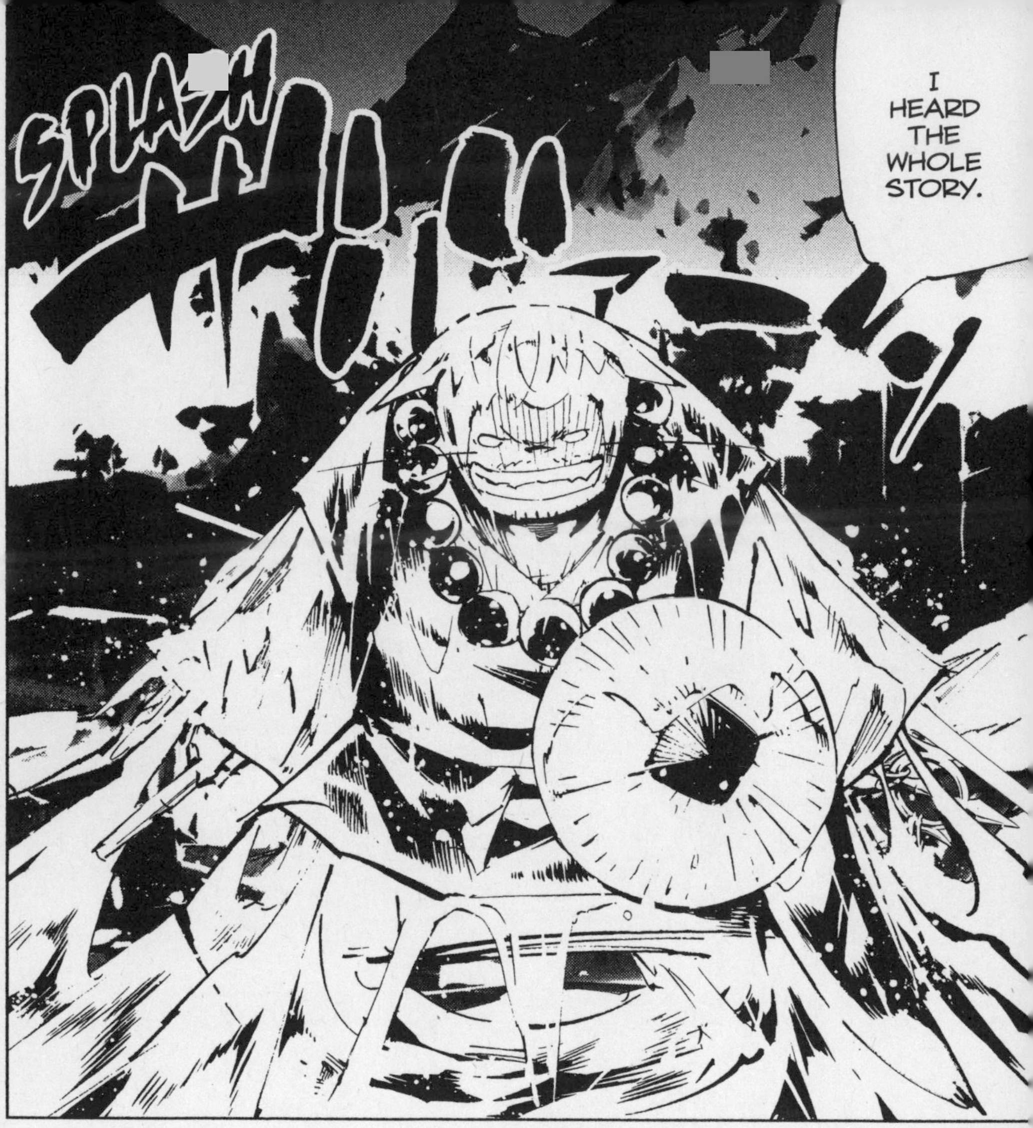
SPLASH
I HEARD THE WHOLE STORY.
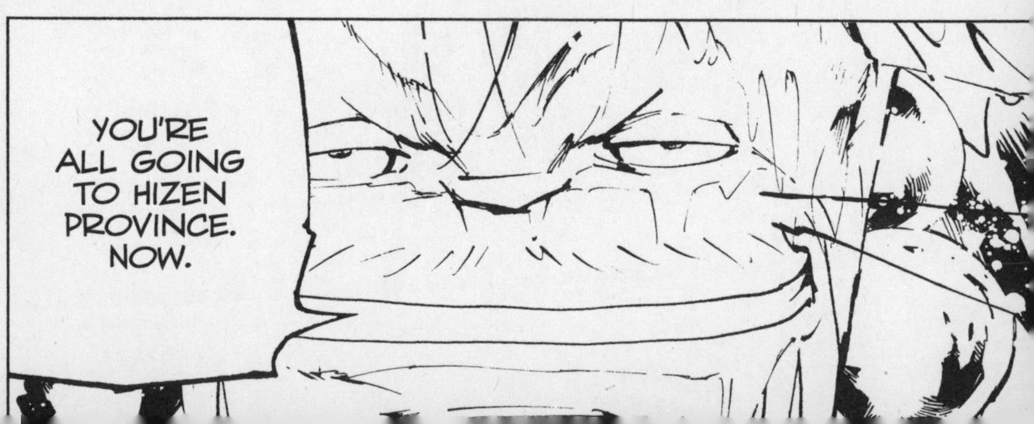
YOU'RE ALL GOING TO HIZEN PROVINCE. NOW.

NEKOGAHARA

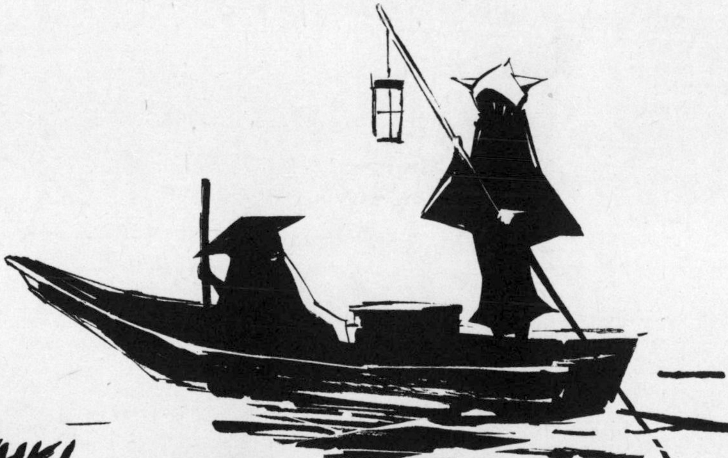

HIROYUKI
TAKEI

Takei

CHAPTER 24:
MEW UPON
THE SEA

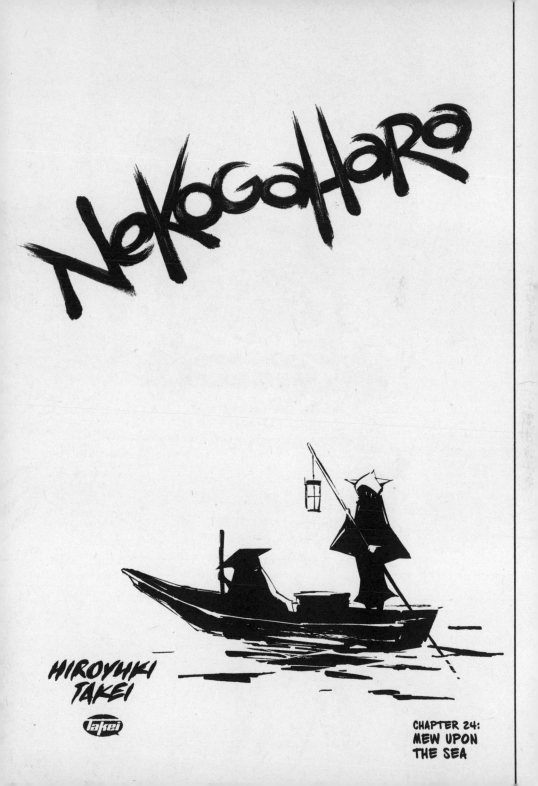

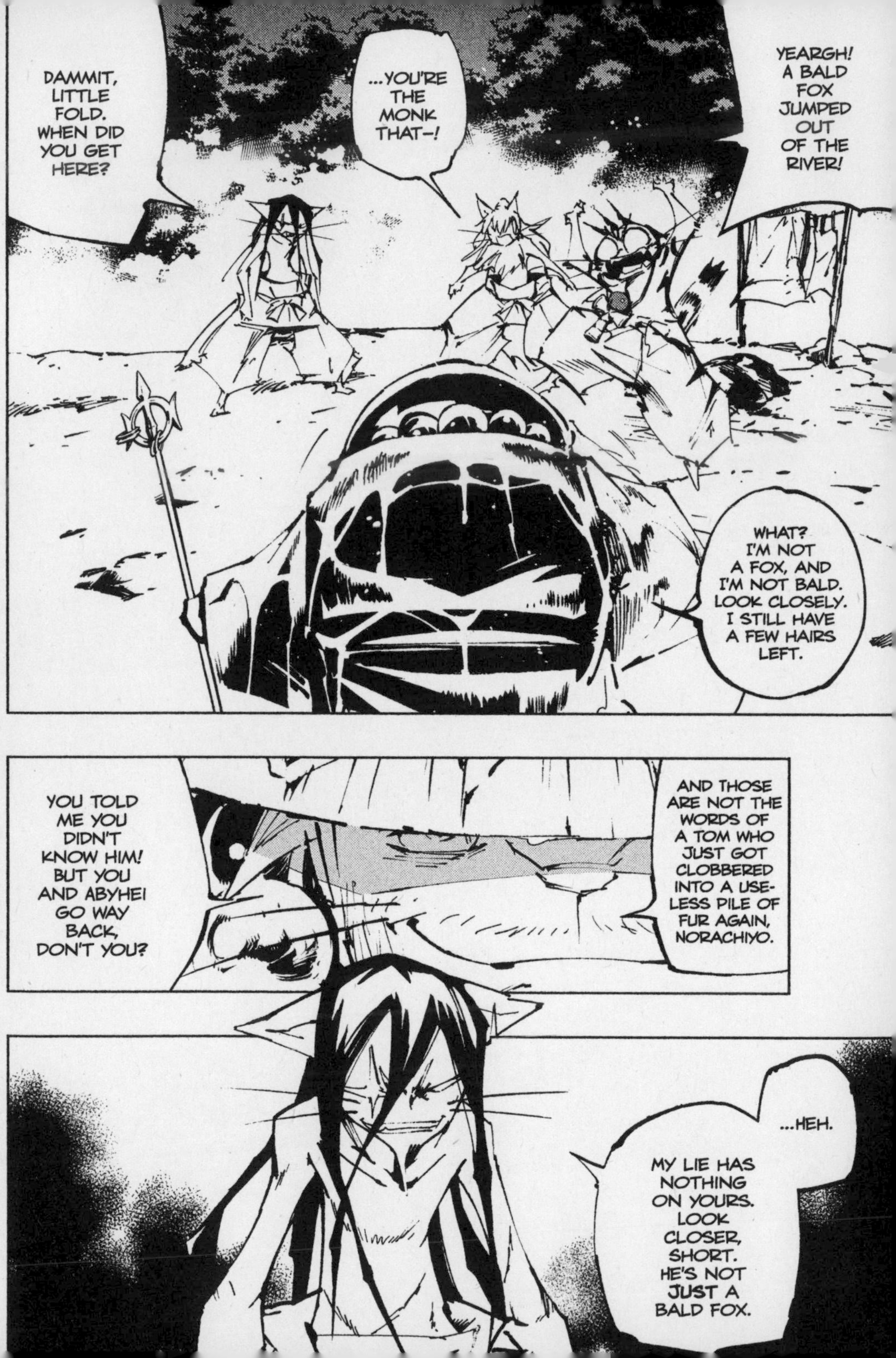
YEARGH! A BALD FOX JUMPED OUT OF THE RIVER!
...YOU'RE THE MONK THAT—!
DAMMIT, LITTLE FOLD. WHEN DID YOU GET HERE?
WHAT? I'M NOT A FOX, AND I'M NOT BALD. LOOK CLOSELY. I STILL HAVE A FEW HAIRS LEFT.
AND THOSE ARE NOT THE WORDS OF A TOM WHO JUST GOT CLOBBERED INTO A USELESS PILE OF FUR AGAIN, NORACHIYO.
YOU TOLD ME YOU DIDN'T KNOW HIM! BUT YOU AND ABYHEI GO WAY BACK, DON'T YOU?
...HEH.
MY LIE HAS NOTHING ON YOURS. LOOK CLOSER, SHORT. HE'S NOT JUST A BALD FOX.

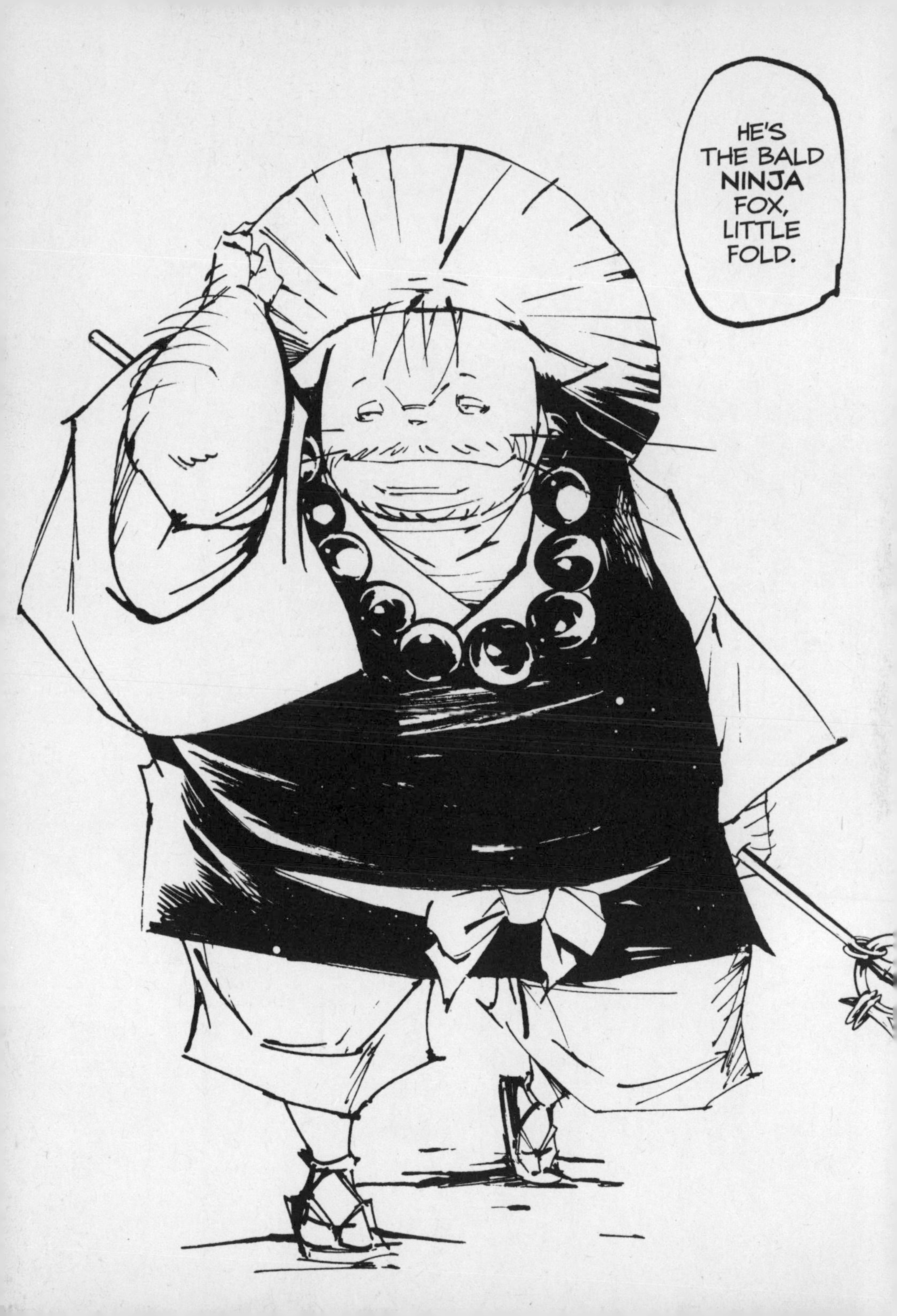
HE'S THE BALD NINJA FOX, LITTLE FOLD.

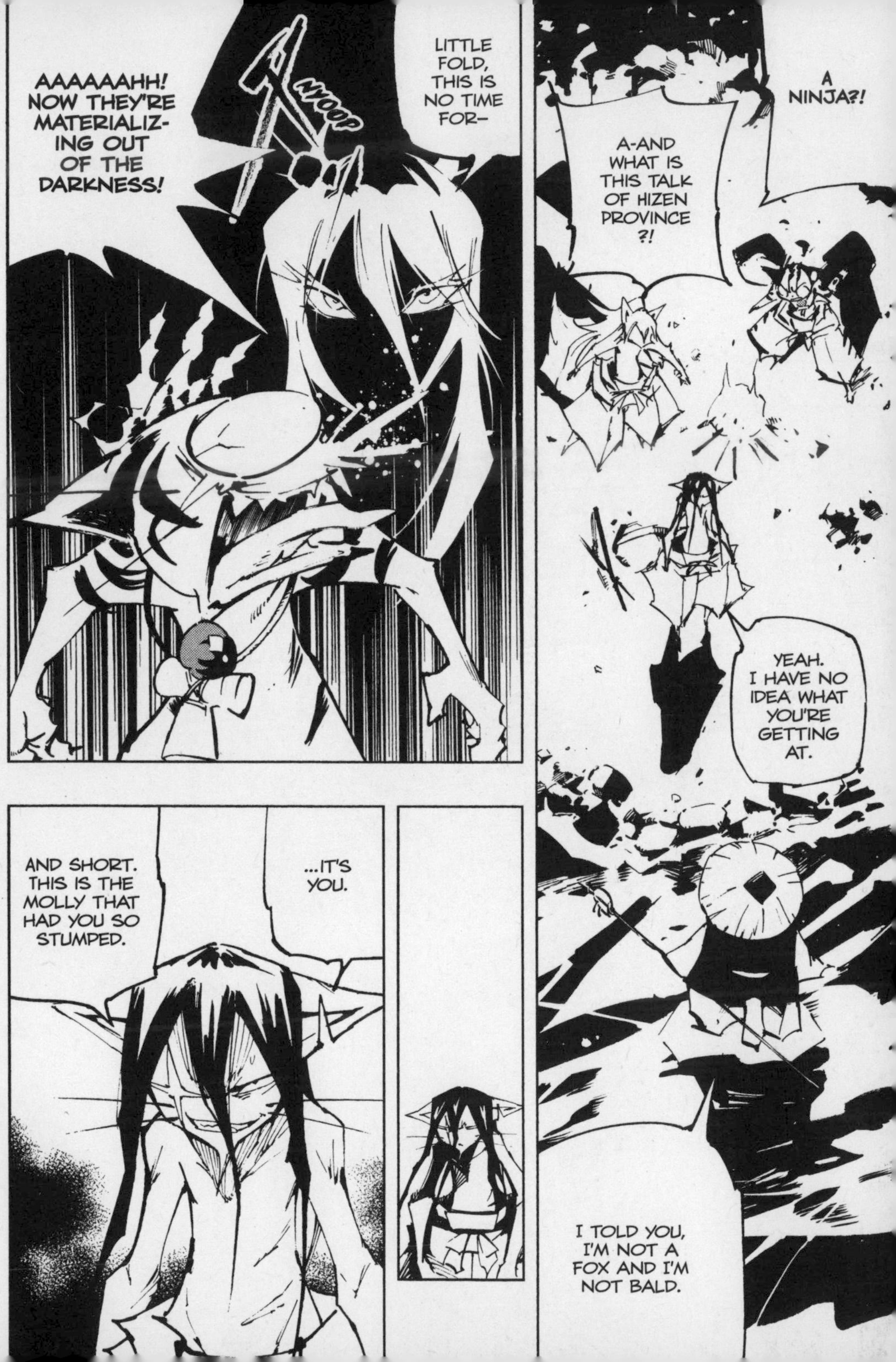
A NINJA?!
A-AND WHAT IS THIS TALK OF HIZEN PROVINCE ?!
YEAH. I HAVE NO IDEA WHAT YOU'RE GETTING AT.
I TOLD YOU, I'M NOT A FOX AND I'M NOT BALD.
LITTLE FOLD, THIS IS NO TIME FOR–
NYOOP
AAAAAAHH! NOW THEY'RE MATERIALIZ-ING OUT OF THE DARKNESS!
...IT'S YOU.
AND SHORT. THIS IS THE MOLLY THAT HAD YOU SO STUMPED.

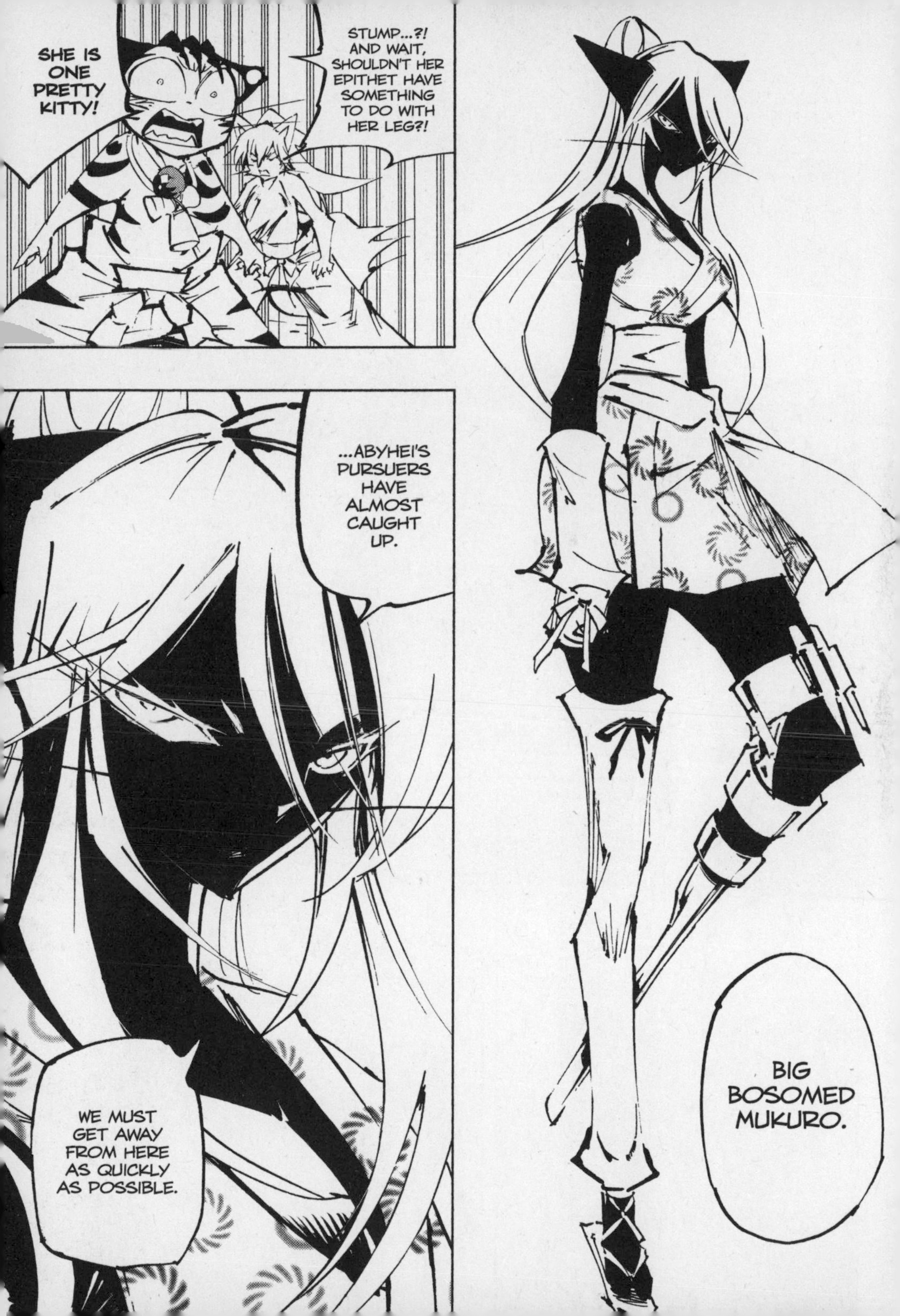
BIG BOSOMED MUKURO.
STUMP...?! AND WAIT, SHOULDN'T HER EPITHET HAVE SOMETHING TO DO WITH HER LEG?!
SHE IS ONE PRETTY KITTY!
...ABYHEI'S PURSUERS HAVE ALMOST CAUGHT UP.
WE MUST GET AWAY FROM HERE AS QUICKLY AS POSSIBLE.

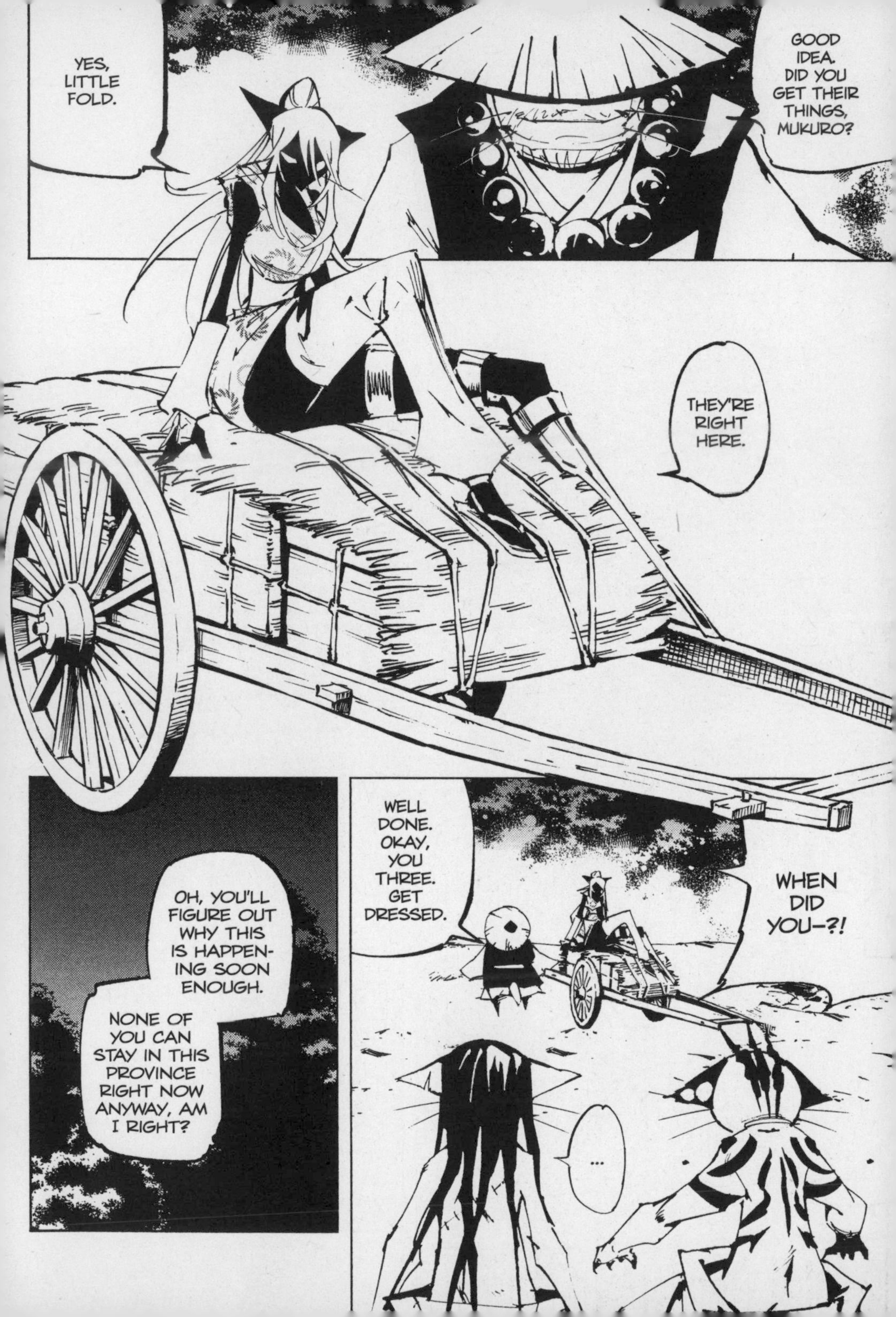
GOOD IDEA. DID YOU GET THEIR THINGS, MUKURO?
YES, LITTLE FOLD.
THEY'RE RIGHT HERE.
WELL DONE. OKAY, YOU THREE. GET DRESSED.
WHEN DID YOU–?!
...
OH, YOU'LL FIGURE OUT WHY THIS IS HAPPEN-ING SOON ENOUGH.
NONE OF YOU CAN STAY IN THIS PROVINCE RIGHT NOW ANYWAY, AM I RIGHT?

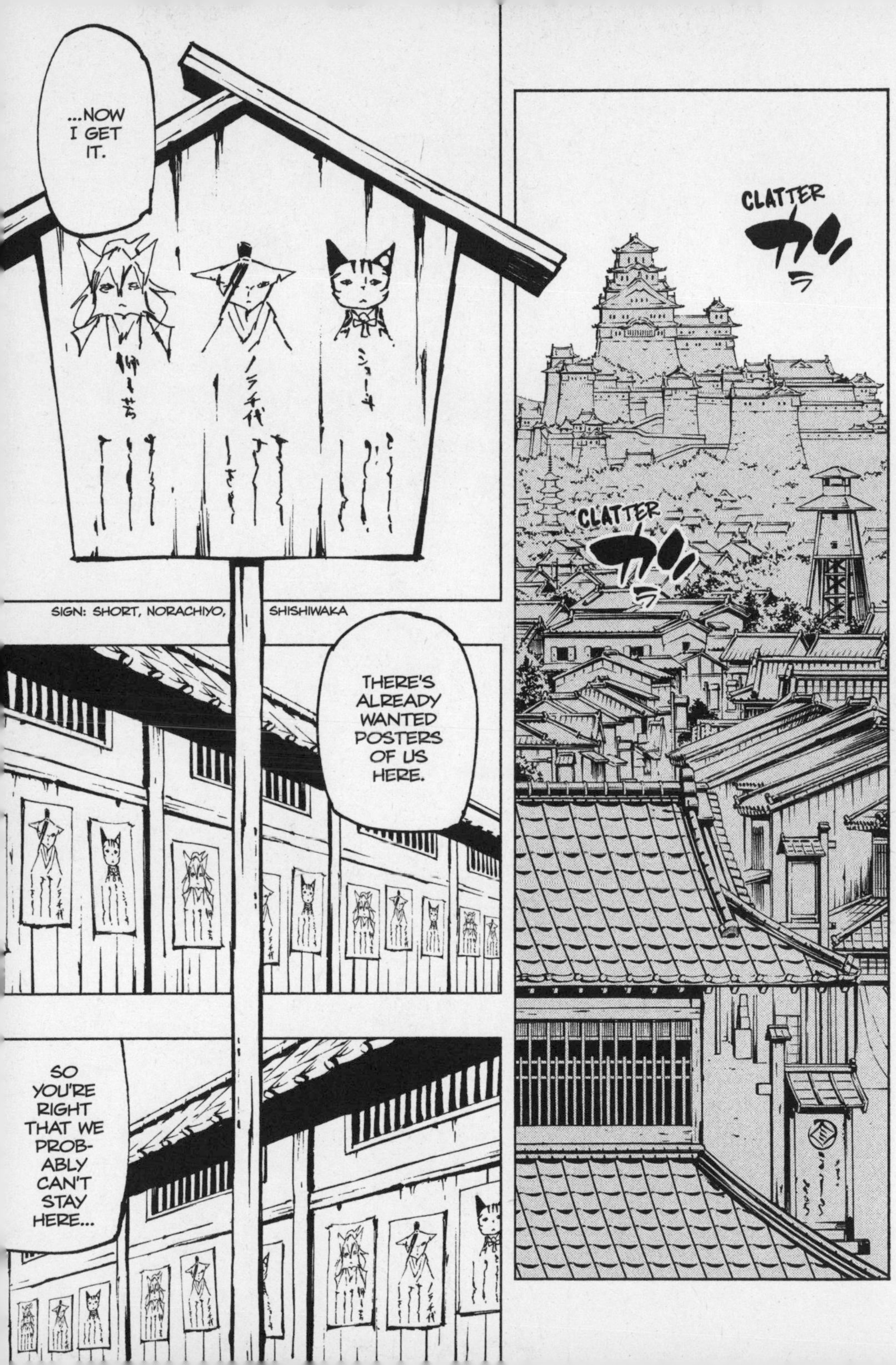
CLATTER
CLATTER
...NOW I GET IT.
SIGN: SHORT, NORACHIYO, SHISHIWAKA
THERE'S ALREADY WANTED POSTERS OF US HERE.
SO YOU'RE RIGHT THAT WE PROB-ABLY CAN'T STAY HERE...

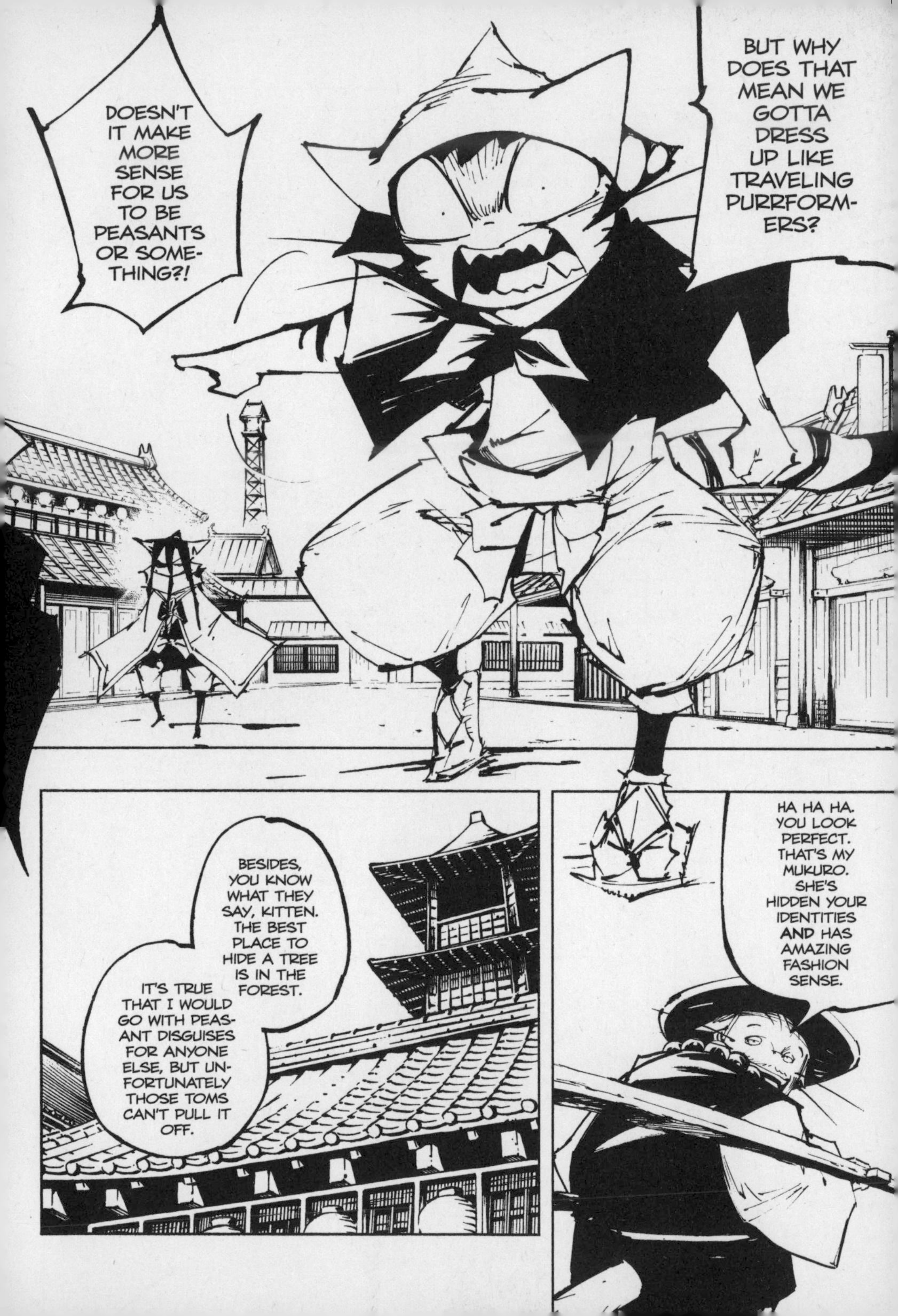
BUT WHY DOES THAT MEAN WE GOTTA DRESS UP LIKE TRAVELING PURRFORM-ERS?
DOESN'T IT MAKE MORE SENSE FOR US TO BE PEASANTS OR SOME-THING?!
HA HA HA. YOU LOOK PERFECT. THAT'S MY MUKURO. SHE'S HIDDEN YOUR IDENTITIES AND HAS AMAZING FASHION SENSE.
BESIDES, YOU KNOW WHAT THEY SAY, KITTEN. THE BEST PLACE TO HIDE A TREE IS IN THE FOREST.
IT'S TRUE THAT I WOULD GO WITH PEAS-ANT DISGUISES FOR ANYONE ELSE, BUT UN-FORTUNATELY THOSE TOMS CAN'T PULL IT OFF.

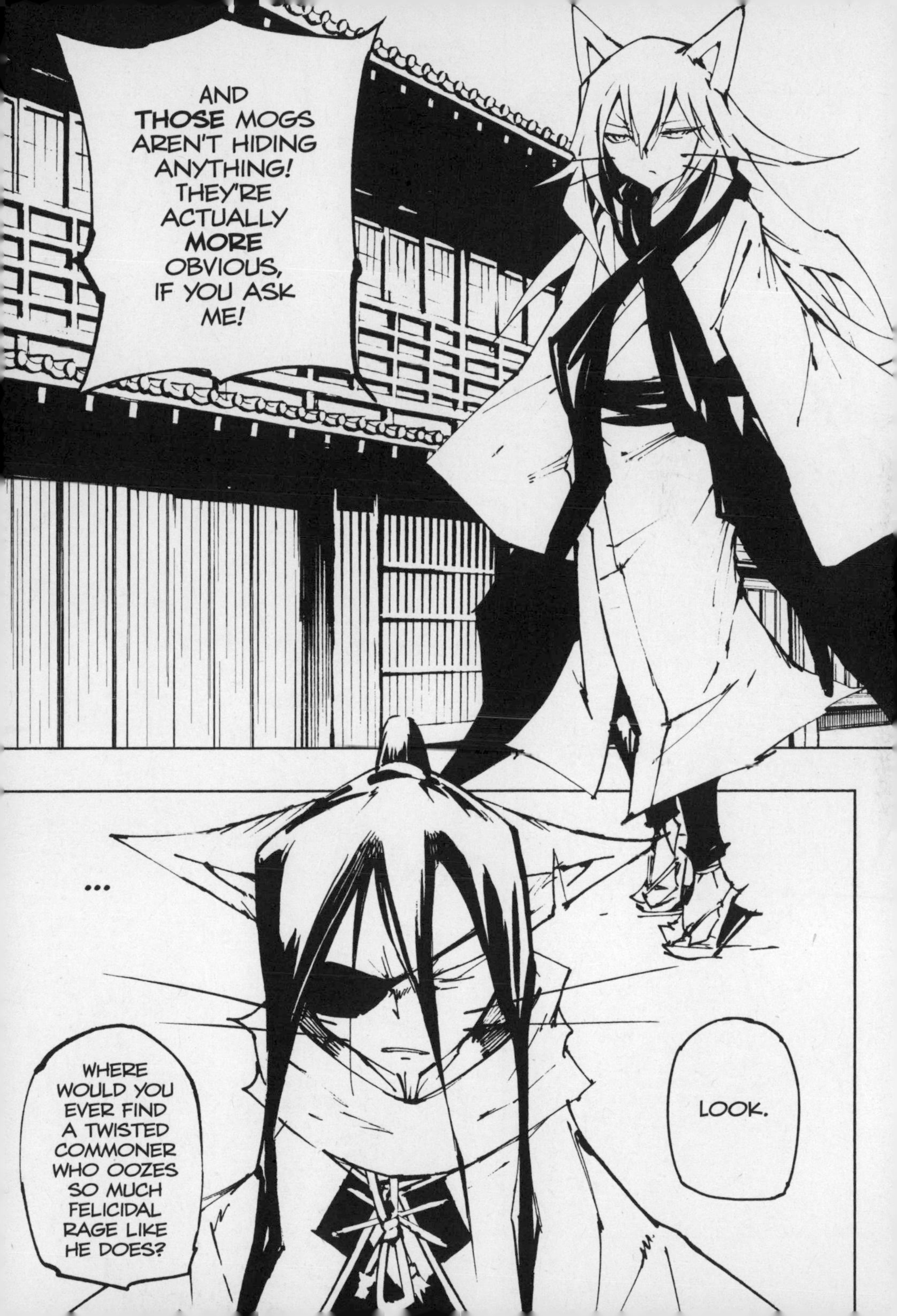
AND THOSE MOGS AREN'T HIDING ANYTHING! THEY'RE ACTUALLY MORE OBVIOUS, IF YOU ASK ME!
...
LOOK.
WHERE WOULD YOU EVER FIND A TWISTED COMMONER WHO OOZES SO MUCH FELICIDAL RAGE LIKE HE DOES?

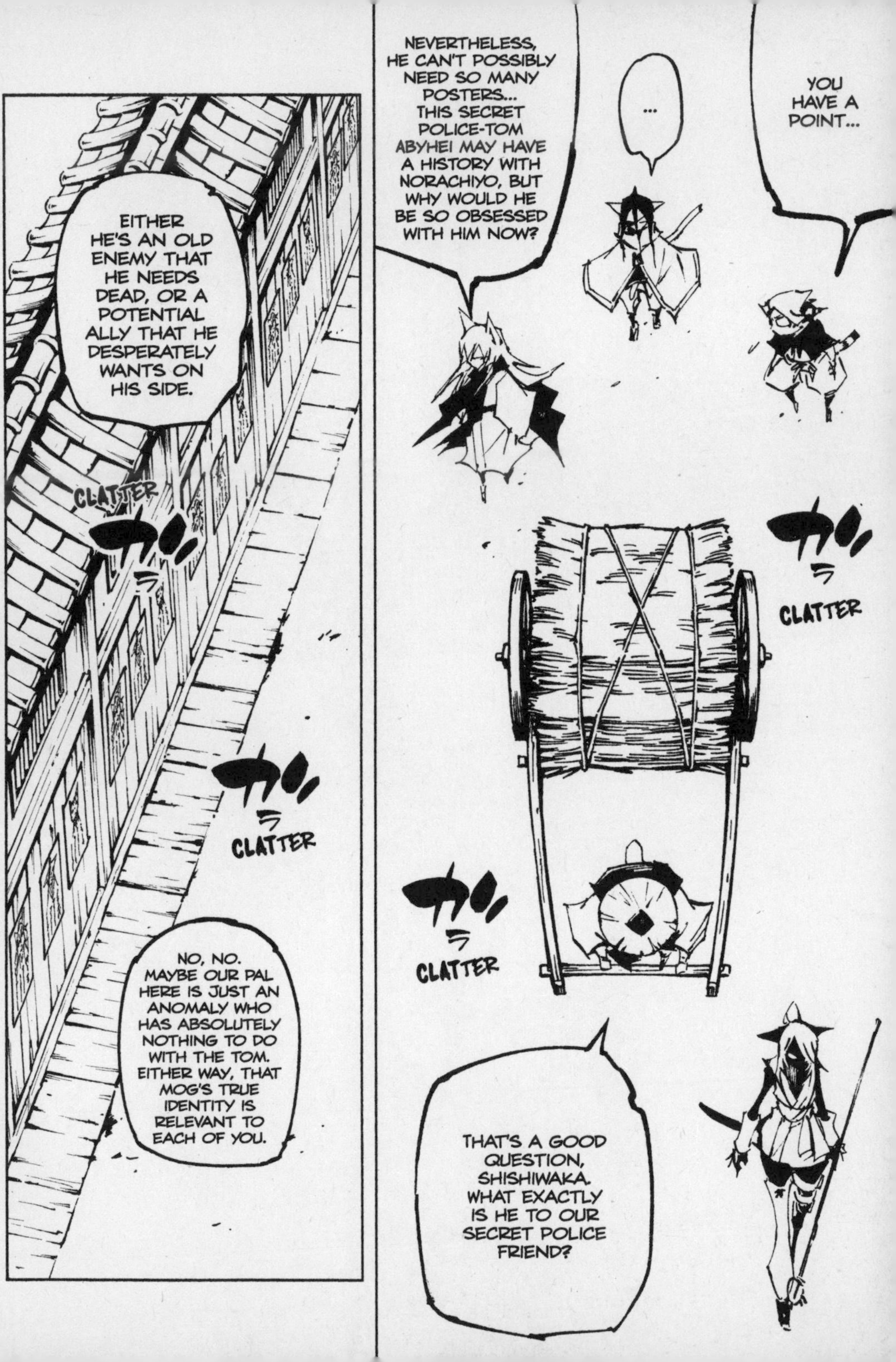
NEVERTHELESS, HE CAN'T POSSIBLY NEED SO MANY POSTERS... THIS SECRET POLICE-TOM ABYHEI MAY HAVE A HISTORY WITH NORACHIYO, BUT WHY WOULD HE BE SO OBSESSED WITH HIM NOW?
...
YOU HAVE A POINT...
CLATTER
CLATTER
THAT'S A GOOD QUESTION, SHISHIWAKA. WHAT EXACTLY IS HE TO OUR SECRET POLICE FRIEND?
EITHER HE'S AN OLD ENEMY THAT HE NEEDS DEAD, OR A POTENTIAL ALLY THAT HE DESPERATELY WANTS ON HIS SIDE.
CLATTER
CLATTER
NO, NO. MAYBE OUR PAL HERE IS JUST AN ANOMALY WHO HAS ABSOLUTELY NOTHING TO DO WITH THE TOM. EITHER WAY, THAT MOG'S TRUE IDENTITY IS RELEVANT TO EACH OF YOU.

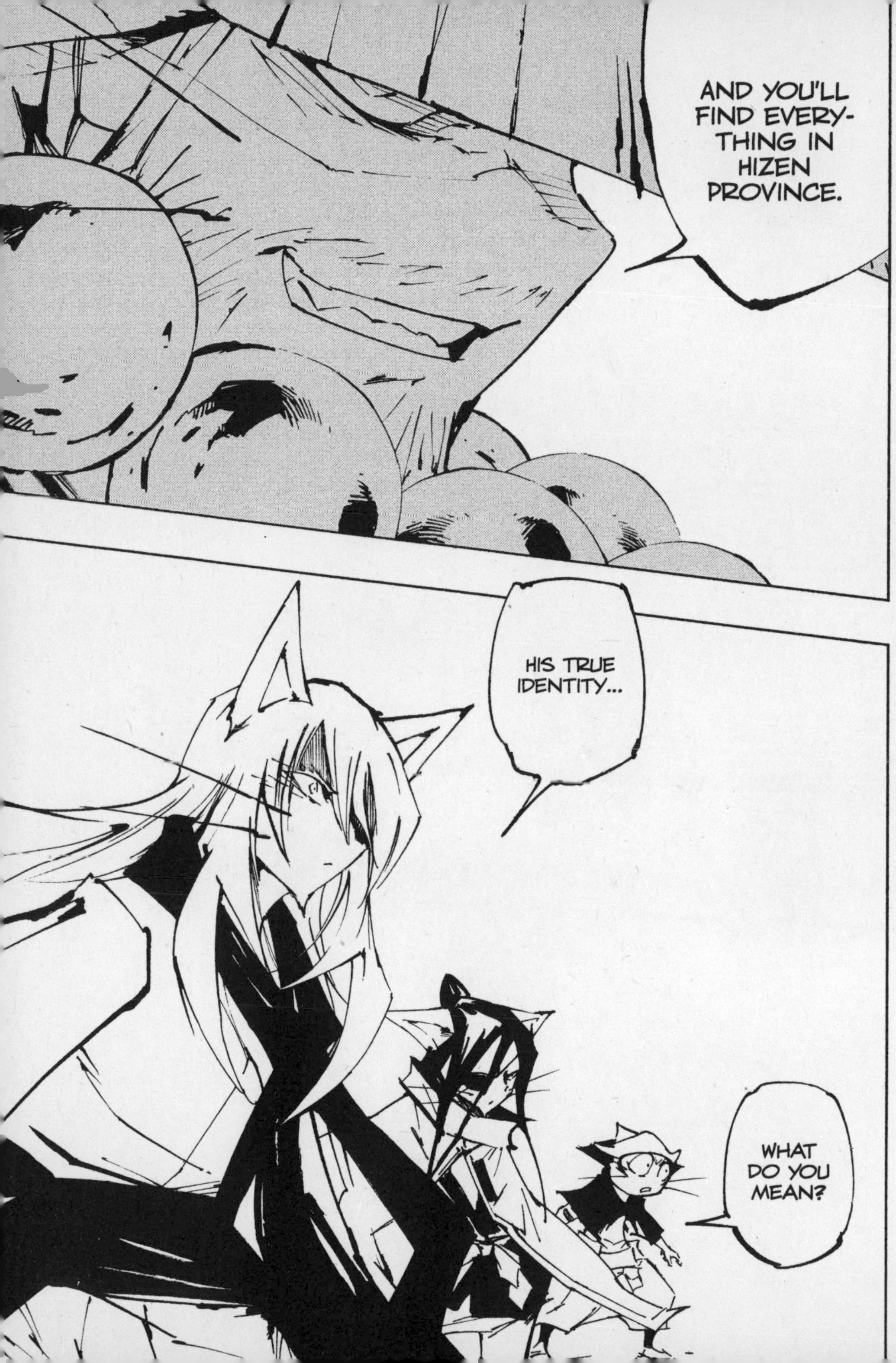
AND YOU'LL FIND EVERY-THING IN HIZEN PROVINCE.
HIS TRUE IDENTITY...
WHAT DO YOU MEAN?

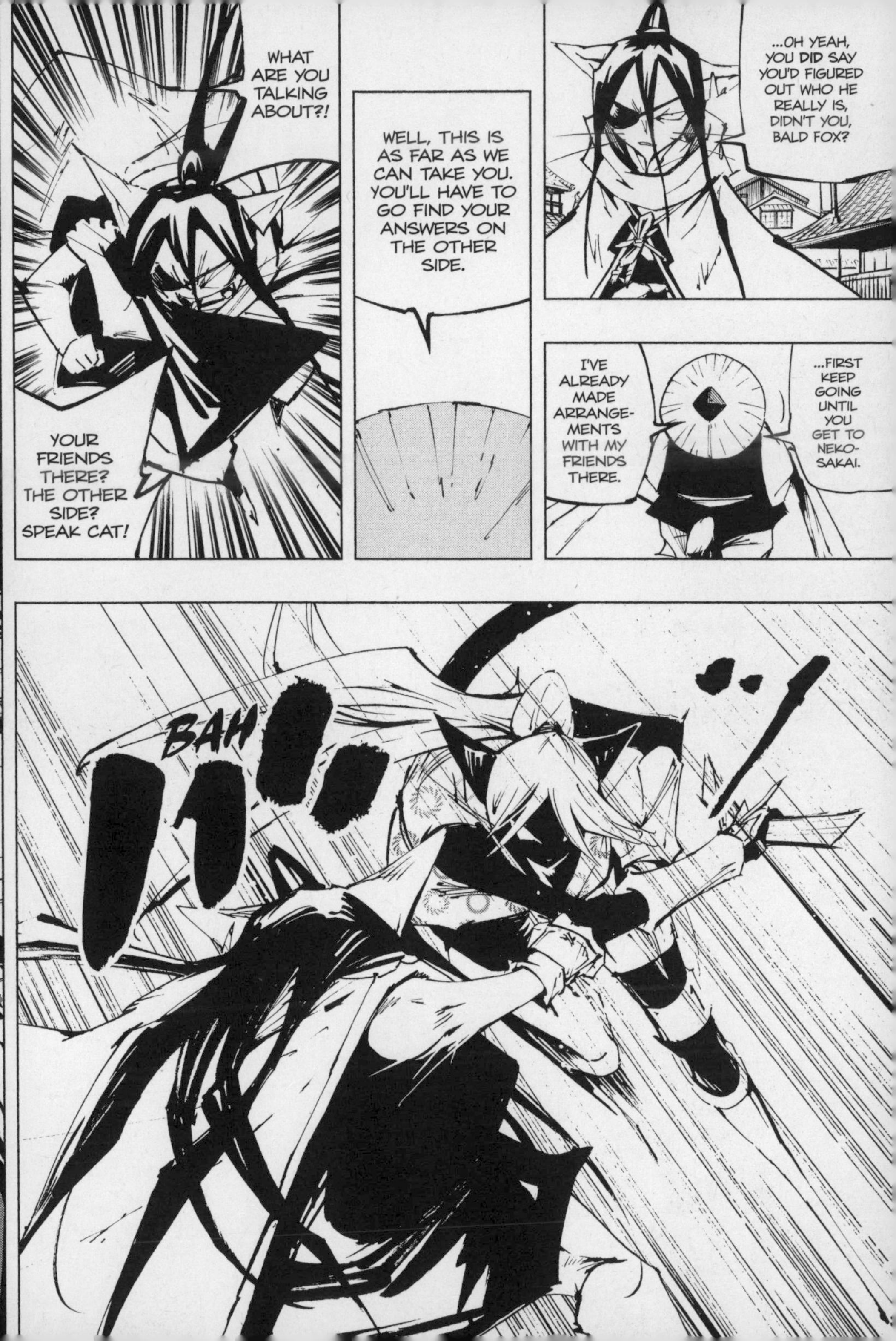
...OH YEAH, YOU DID SAY YOU'D FIGURED OUT WHO HE REALLY IS, DIDN'T YOU, BALD FOX?
...FIRST KEEP GOING UNTIL YOU GET TO NEKO-SAKAI.
I'VE ALREADY MADE ARRANGEMENTS WITH MY FRIENDS THERE.
WELL, THIS IS AS FAR AS WE CAN TAKE YOU. YOU'LL HAVE TO GO FIND YOUR ANSWERS ON THE OTHER SIDE.
WHAT ARE YOU TALKING ABOUT?!
YOUR FRIENDS THERE? THE OTHER SIDE? SPEAK CAT!
BAH

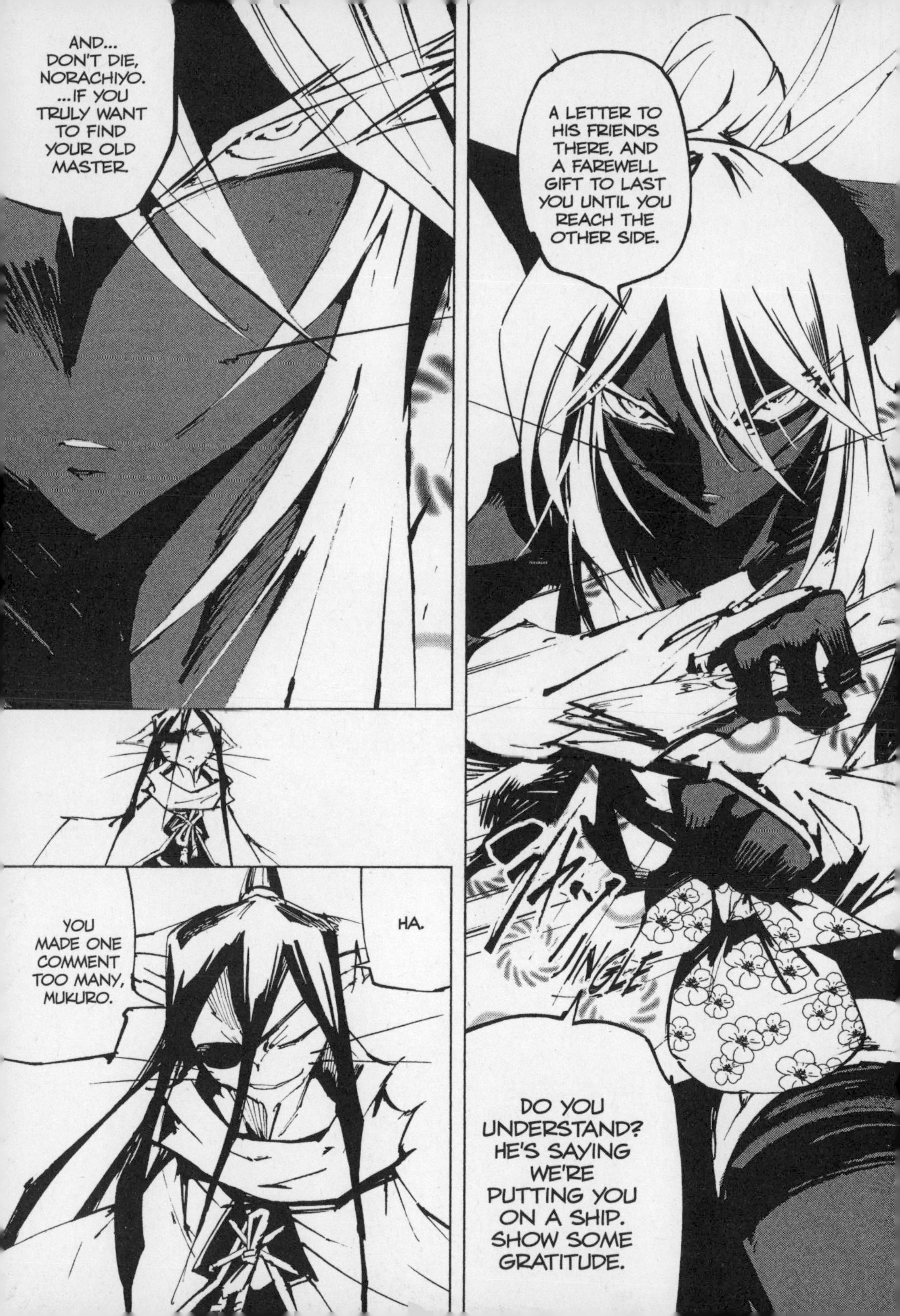
A LETTER TO HIS FRIENDS THERE, AND A FAREWELL GIFT TO LAST YOU UNTIL YOU REACH THE OTHER SIDE.
JINGLE
DO YOU UNDERSTAND? HE'S SAYING WE'RE PUTTING YOU ON A SHIP. SHOW SOME GRATITUDE.
AND... DON'T DIE, NORACHIYO. ...IF YOU TRULY WANT TO FIND YOUR OLD MASTER.
HA.
YOU MADE ONE COMMENT TOO MANY, MUKURO.

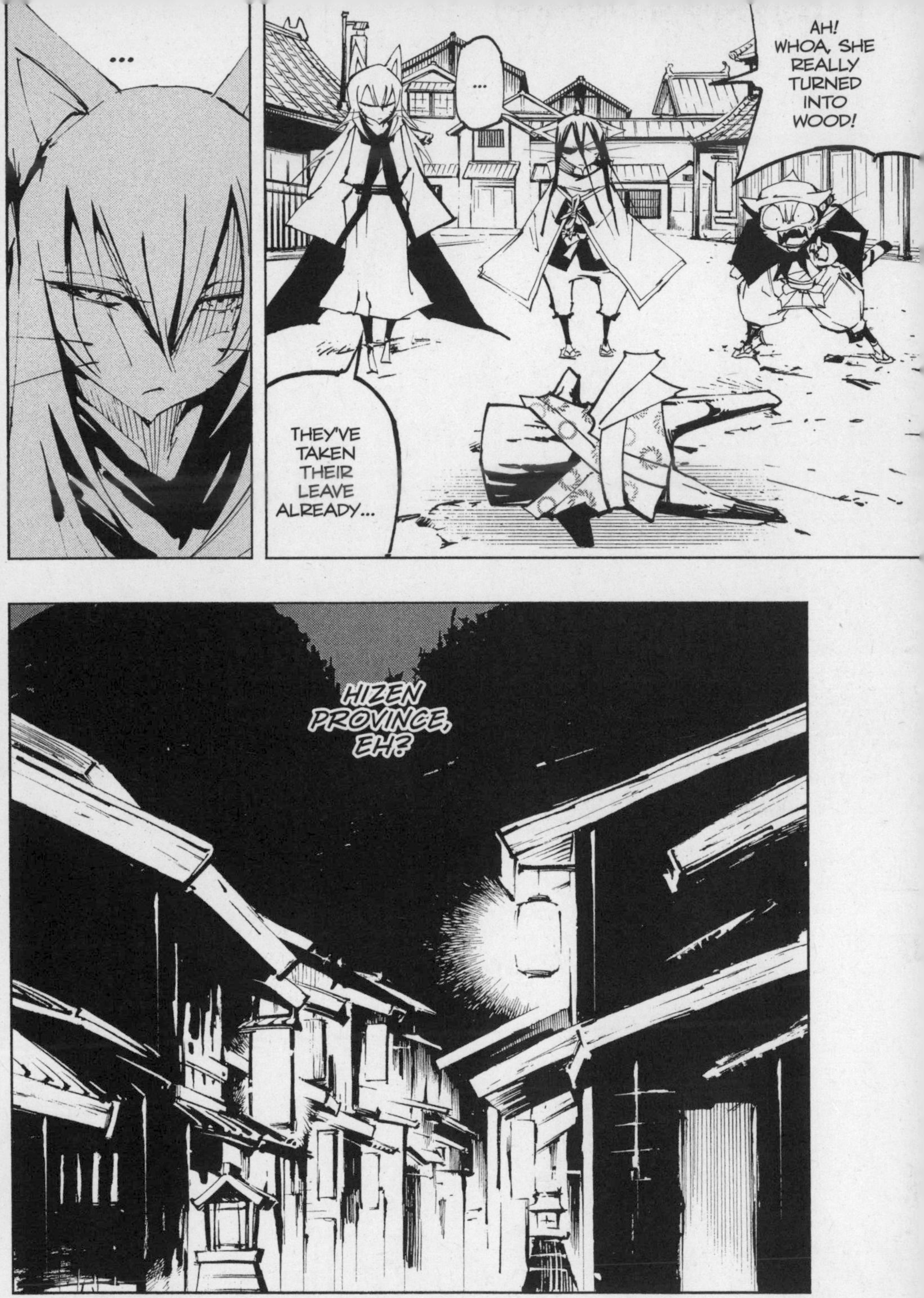
AH! WHOA, SHE REALLY TURNED INTO WOOD!
...
THEY'VE TAKEN THEIR LEAVE ALREADY...
...
HIZEN PROVINCE, EH?

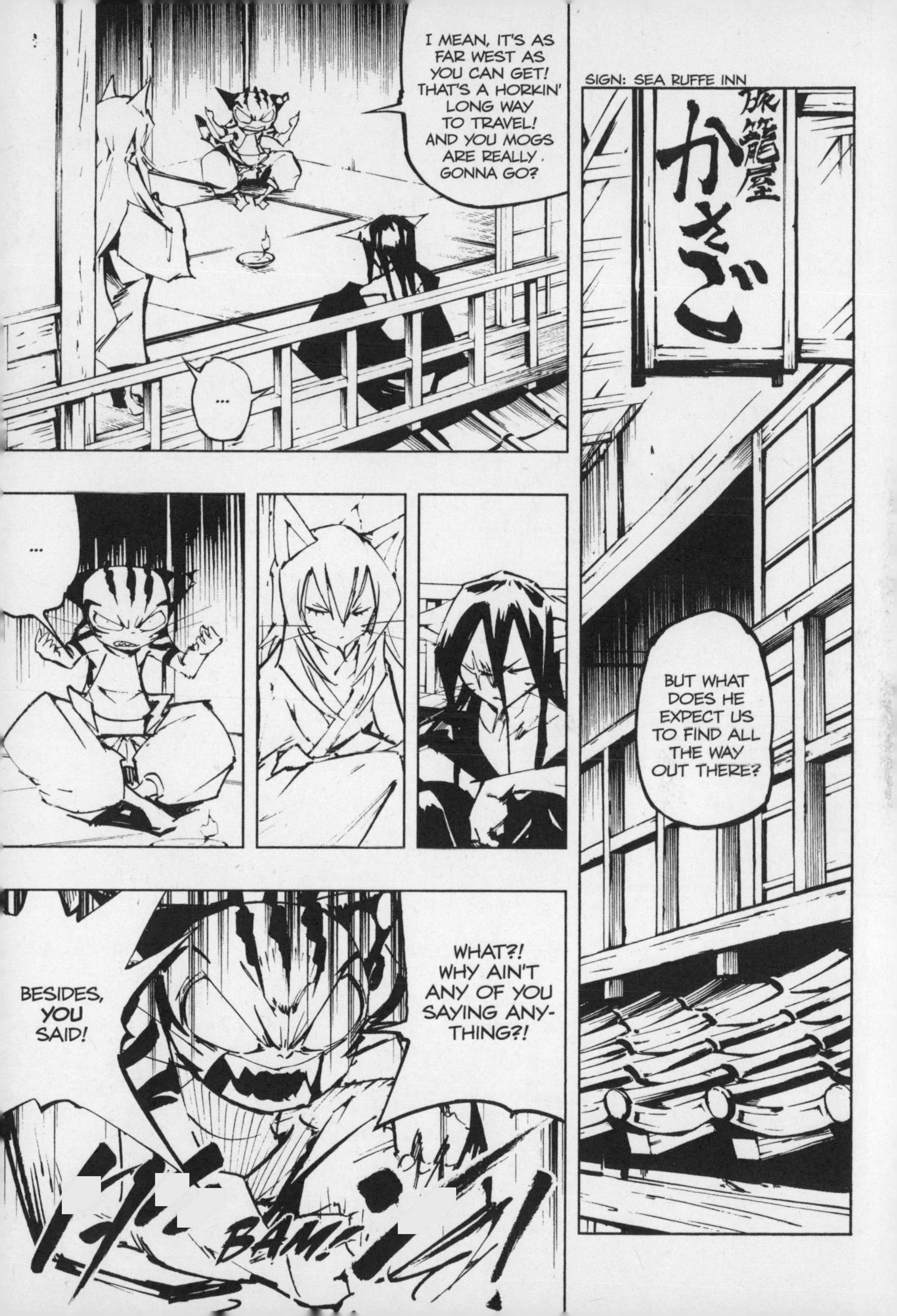
SIGN: SEA RUFFE INN
旅籠屋
かさご
BUT WHAT DOES HE EXPECT US TO FIND ALL THE WAY OUT THERE?
I MEAN, IT'S AS FAR WEST AS YOU CAN GET! THAT'S A HORKIN' LONG WAY TO TRAVEL! AND YOU MOGS ARE REALLY GONNA GO?
...
...
WHAT?! WHY AIN'T ANY OF YOU SAYING ANY-THING?!
BESIDES, YOU SAID!
BAM!

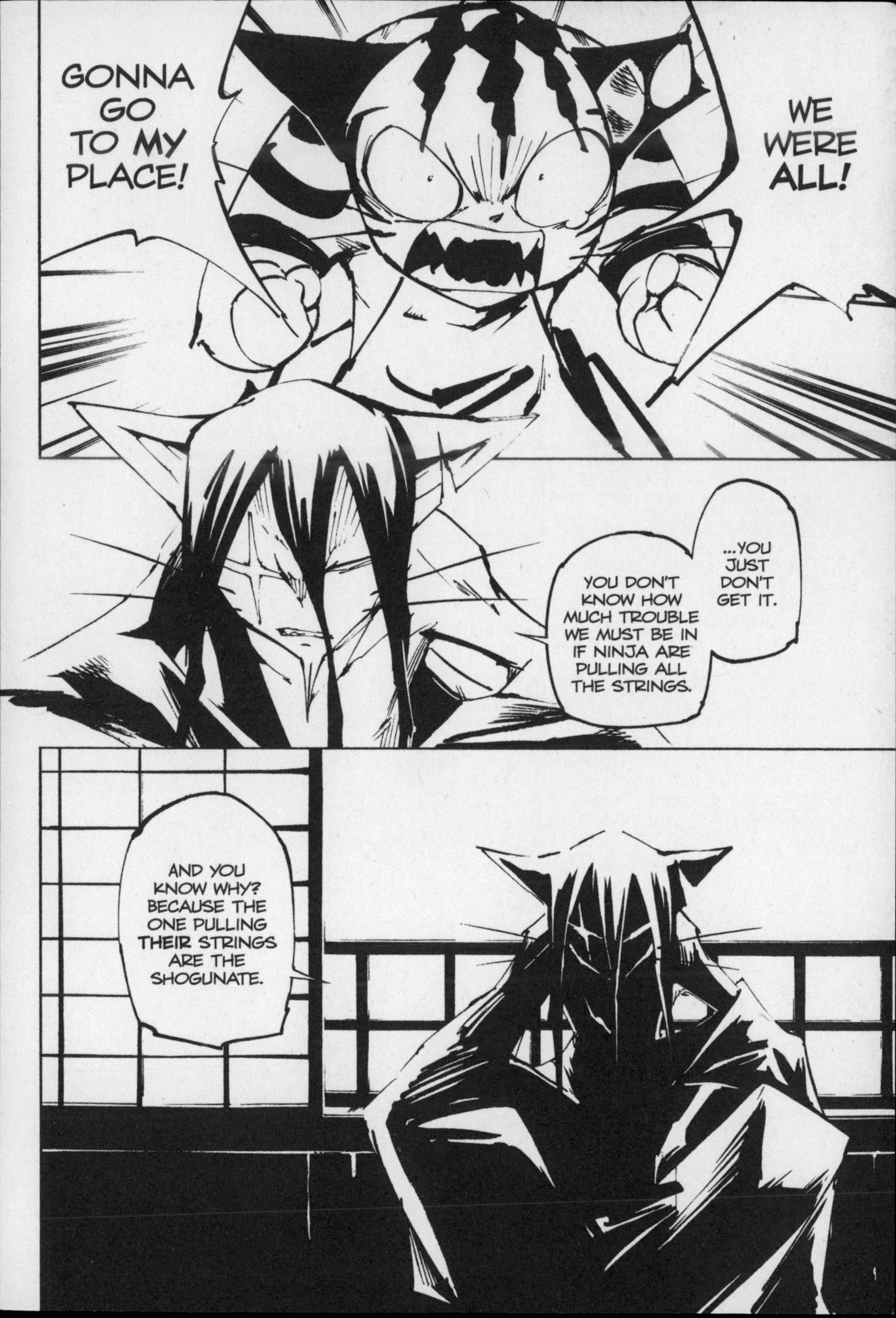
WE WERE ALL!
GONNA GO TO MY PLACE!
...YOU JUST DON'T GET IT.
YOU DON'T KNOW HOW MUCH TROUBLE WE MUST BE IN IF NINJA ARE PULLING ALL THE STRINGS.
AND YOU KNOW WHY? BECAUSE THE ONE PULLING THEIR STRINGS ARE THE SHOGUNATE.

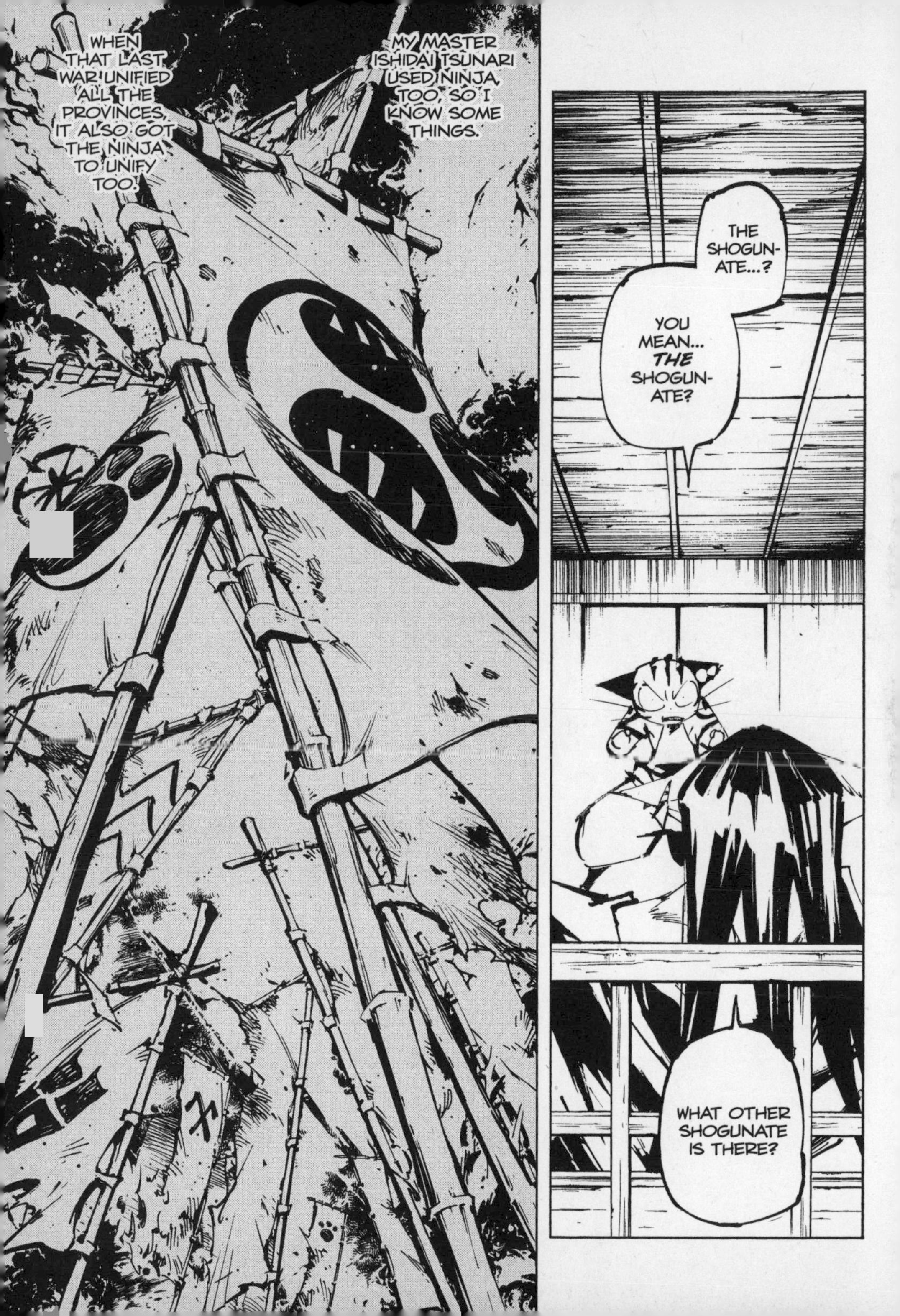
THE SHOGUN-ATE...?
YOU MEAN... *THE* SHOGUN-ATE?
WHAT OTHER SHOGUNATE IS THERE?
MY MASTER ISHIDAI TSUNARI USED NINJA, TOO, SO I KNOW SOME THINGS.
WHEN THAT LAST WAR UNIFIED ALL THE PROVINCES, IT ALSO GOT THE NINJA TO UNIFY TOO!

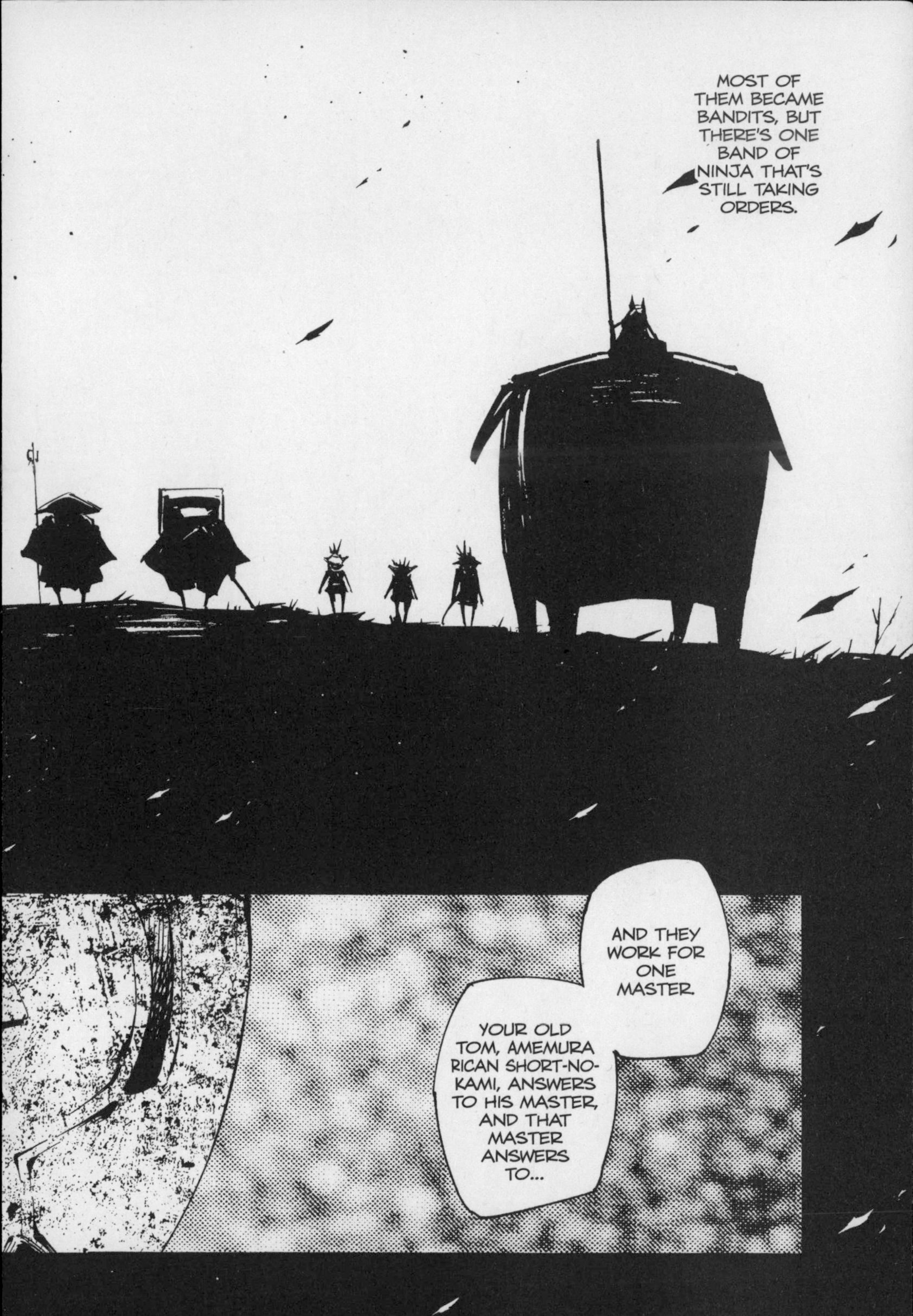
MOST OF THEM BECAME BANDITS, BUT THERE'S ONE BAND OF NINJA THAT'S STILL TAKING ORDERS.
AND THEY WORK FOR ONE MASTER.
YOUR OLD TOM, AMEMURA RICAN SHORT-NO-KAMI, ANSWERS TO HIS MASTER, AND THAT MASTER ANSWERS TO...

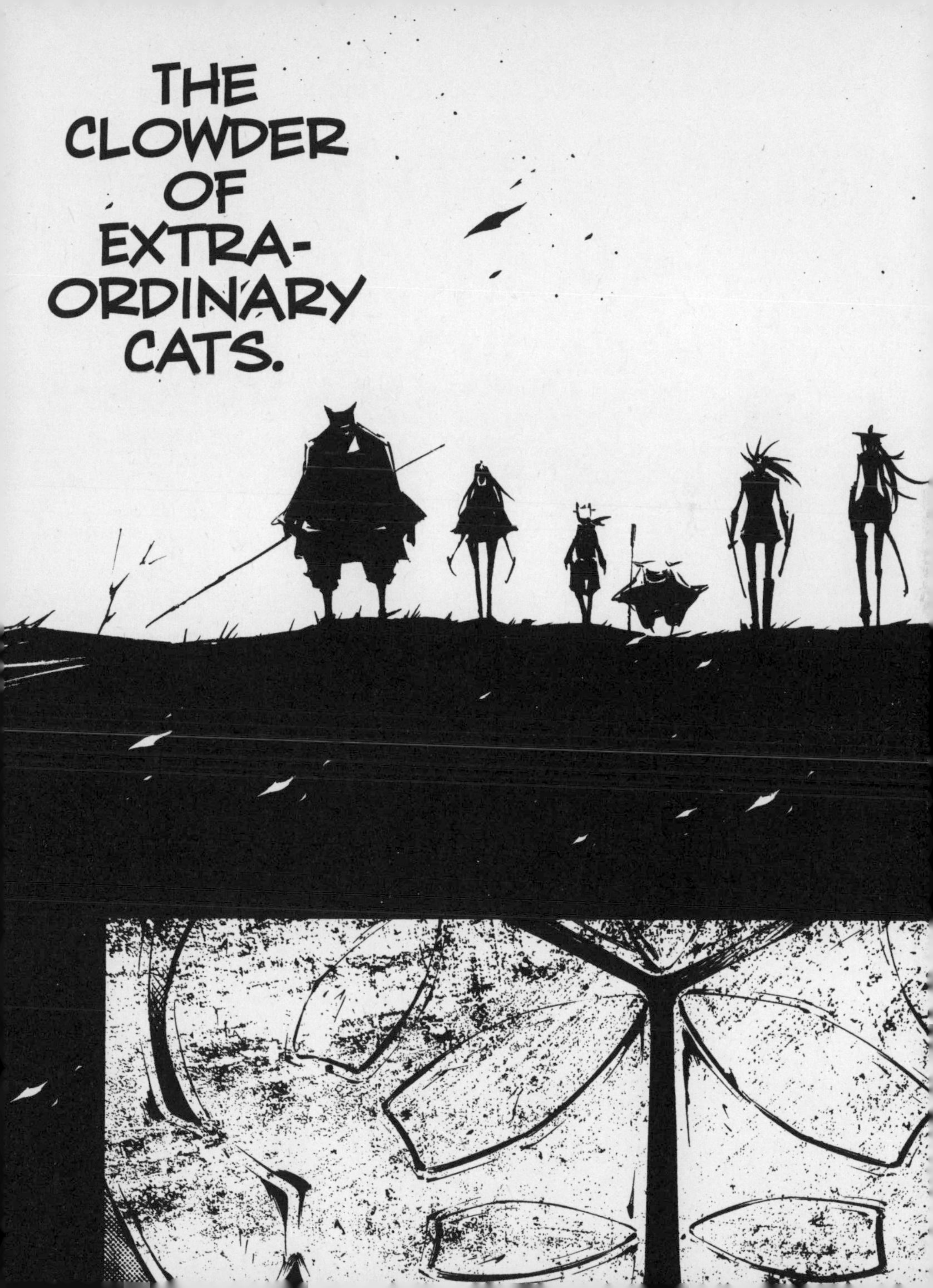
THE CLOWDER OF EXTRA-ORDINARY CATS.

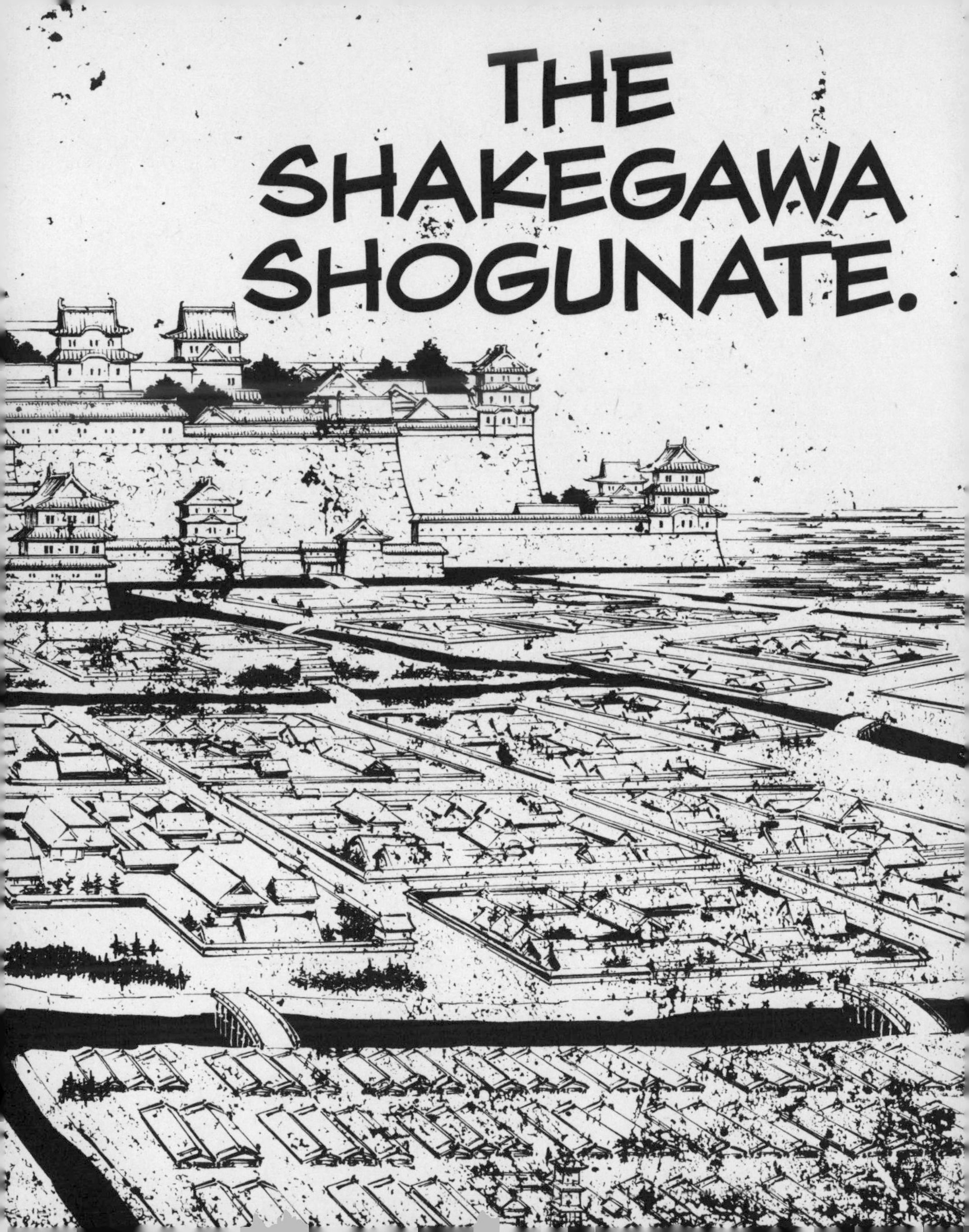
THE SHAKEGAWA SHOGUNATE.

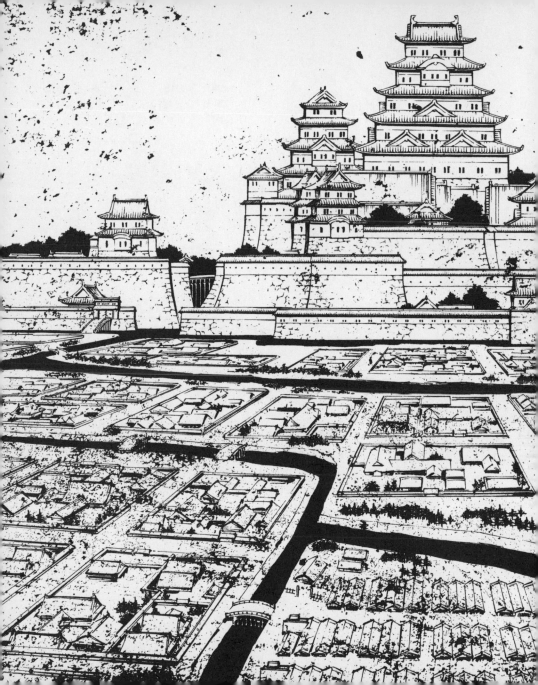

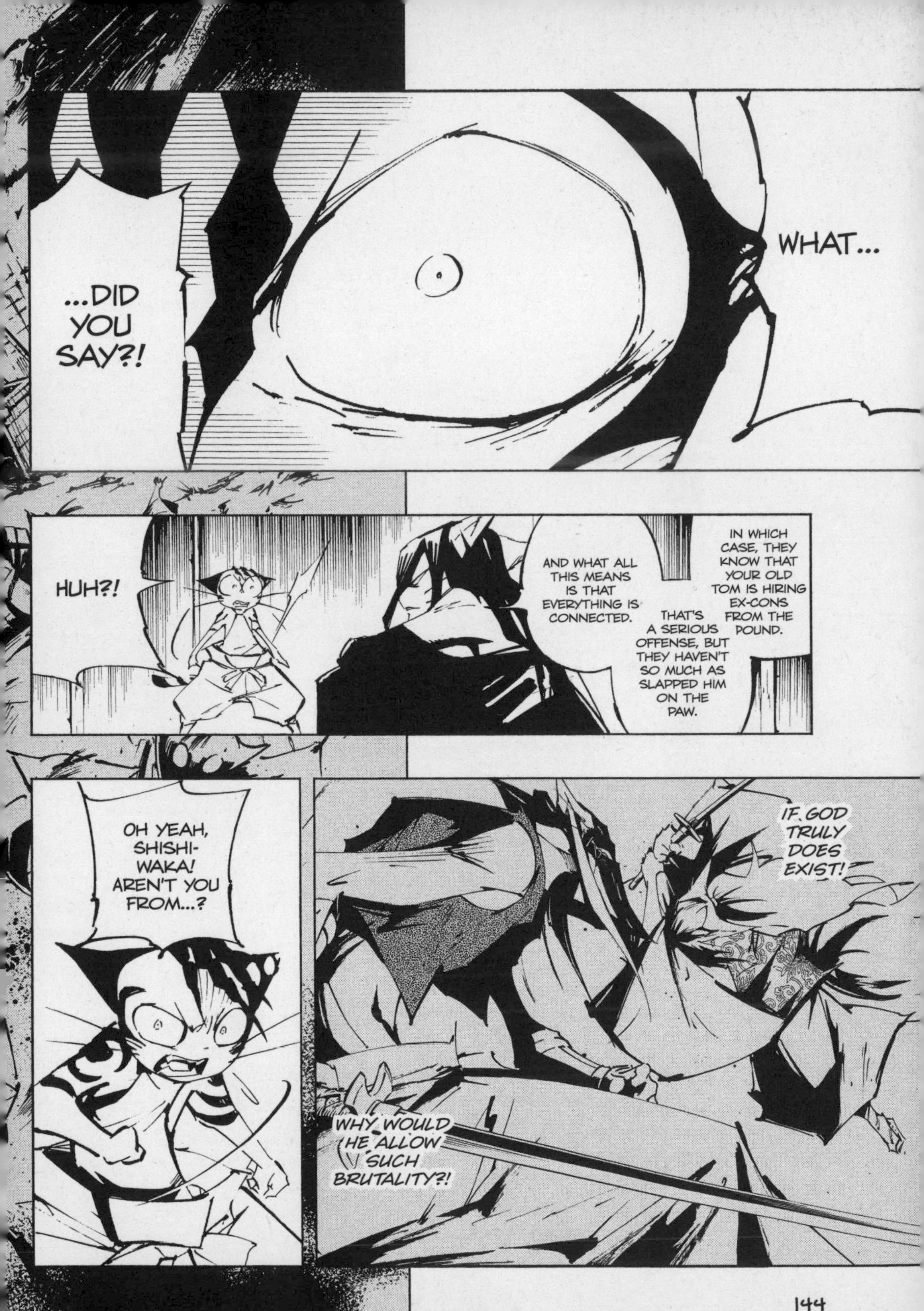
WHAT...
...DID YOU SAY?!
IN WHICH CASE, THEY KNOW THAT YOUR OLD TOM IS HIRING EX-CONS FROM THE POUND.
AND WHAT ALL THIS MEANS IS THAT EVERYTHING IS CONNECTED.
THAT'S A SERIOUS OFFENSE, BUT THEY HAVEN'T SO MUCH AS SLAPPED HIM ON THE PAW.
HUH?!
IF GOD TRULY DOES EXIST!
WHY WOULD HE ALLOW SUCH BRUTALITY?!
OH YEAH, SHISHI-WAKA! AREN'T YOU FROM...?

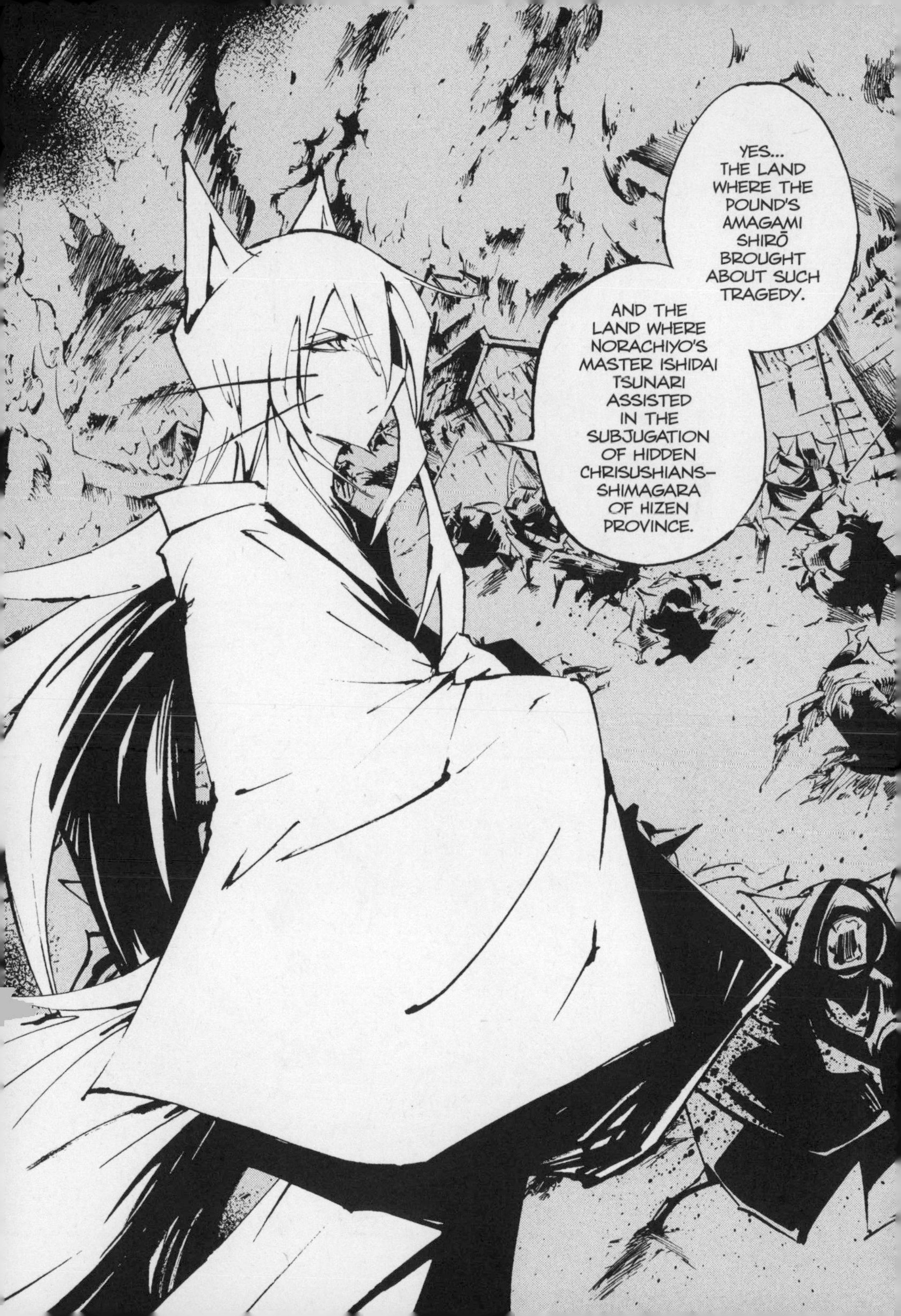
YES... THE LAND WHERE THE POUND'S AMAGAMI SHIRŌ BROUGHT ABOUT SUCH TRAGEDY.
AND THE LAND WHERE NORACHIYO'S MASTER ISHIDAI TSUNARI ASSISTED IN THE SUBJUGATION OF HIDDEN CHRISUSHIANS– SHIMAGARA OF HIZEN PROVINCE.

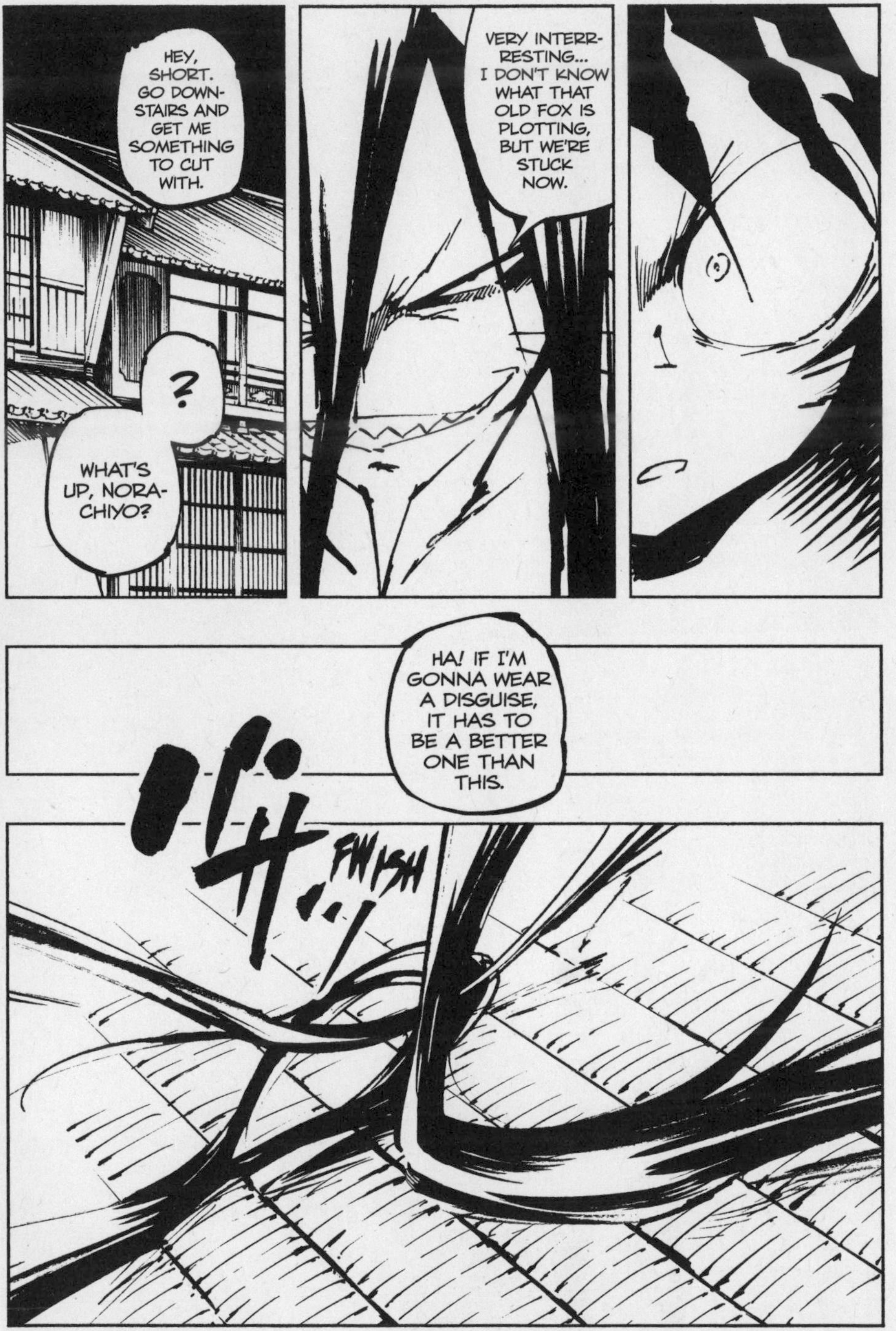
VERY INTERR-RESTING... I DON'T KNOW WHAT THAT OLD FOX IS PLOTTING, BUT WE'RE STUCK NOW.
HEY, SHORT. GO DOWN-STAIRS AND GET ME SOMETHING TO CUT WITH.
?
WHAT'S UP, NORA-CHIYO?
HA! IF I'M GONNA WEAR A DISGUISE, IT HAS TO BE A BETTER ONE THAN THIS.
FWISH

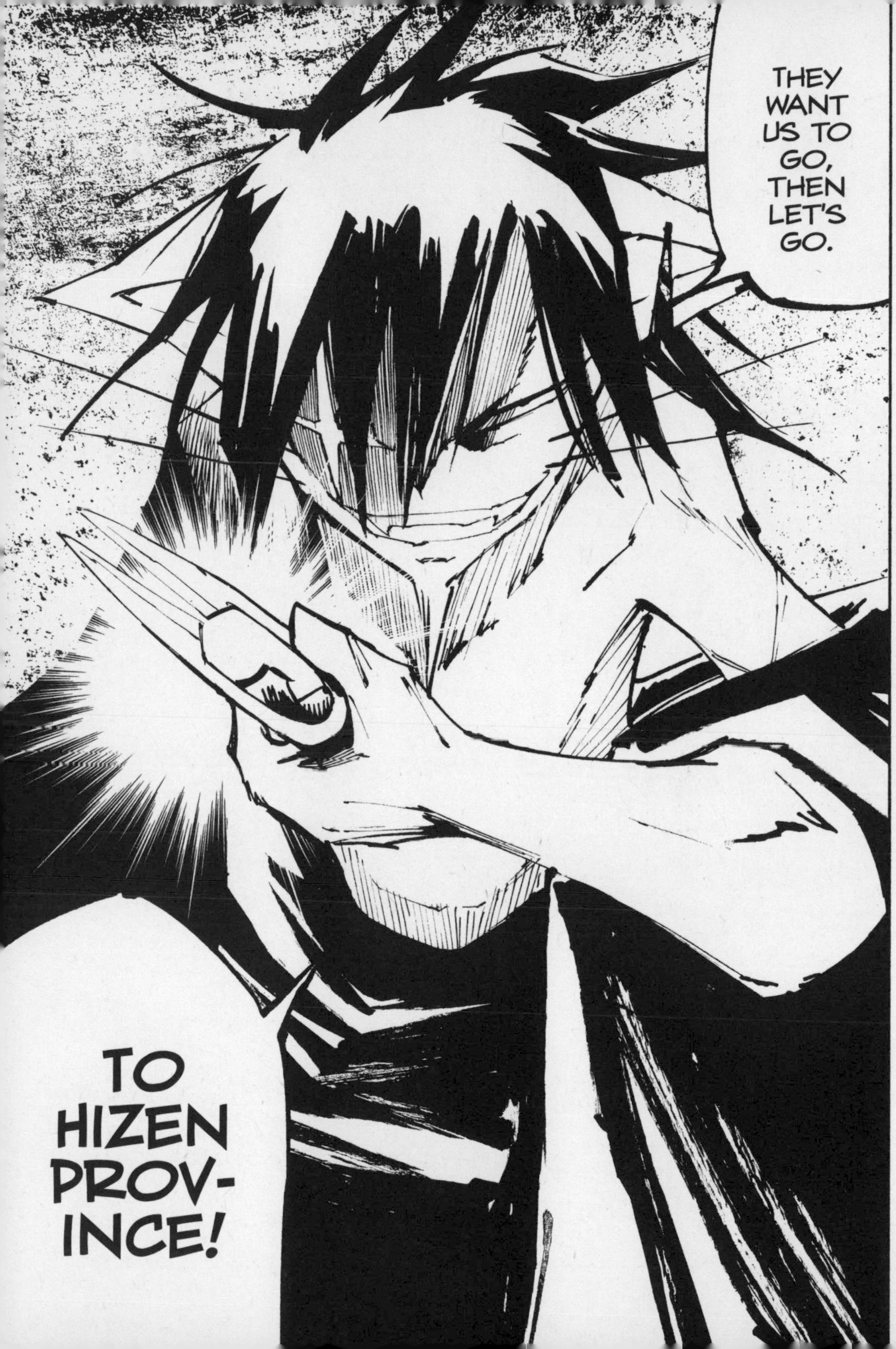
THEY WANT US TO GO, THEN LET'S GO.
TO HIZEN PROV-INCE!

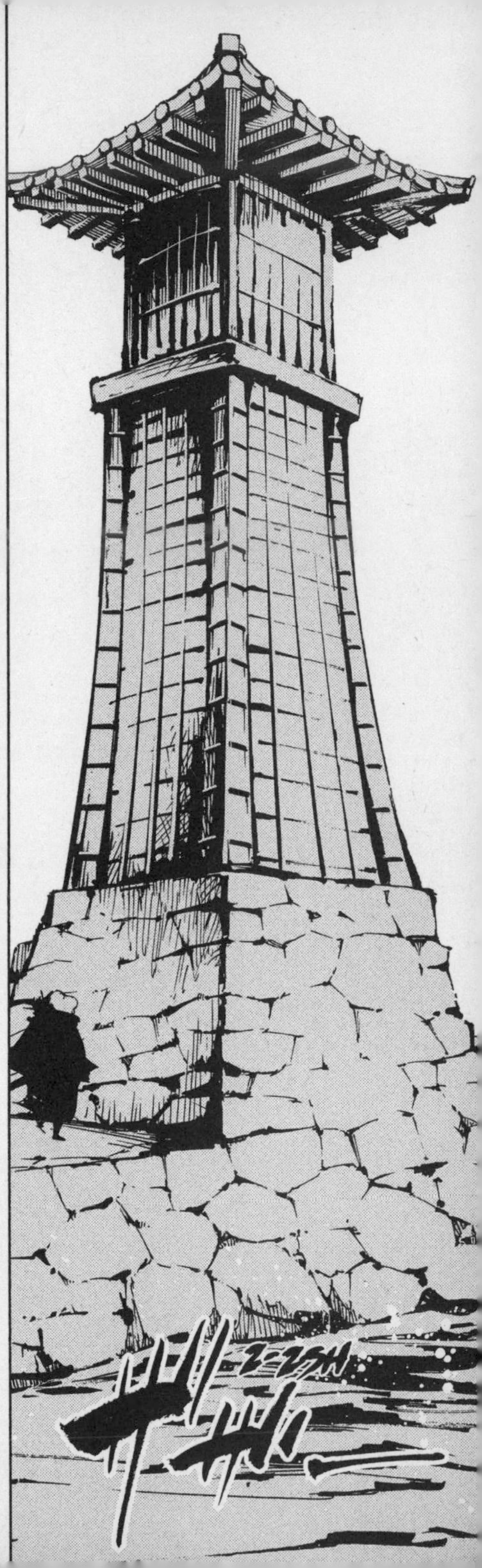
Z-ZSH
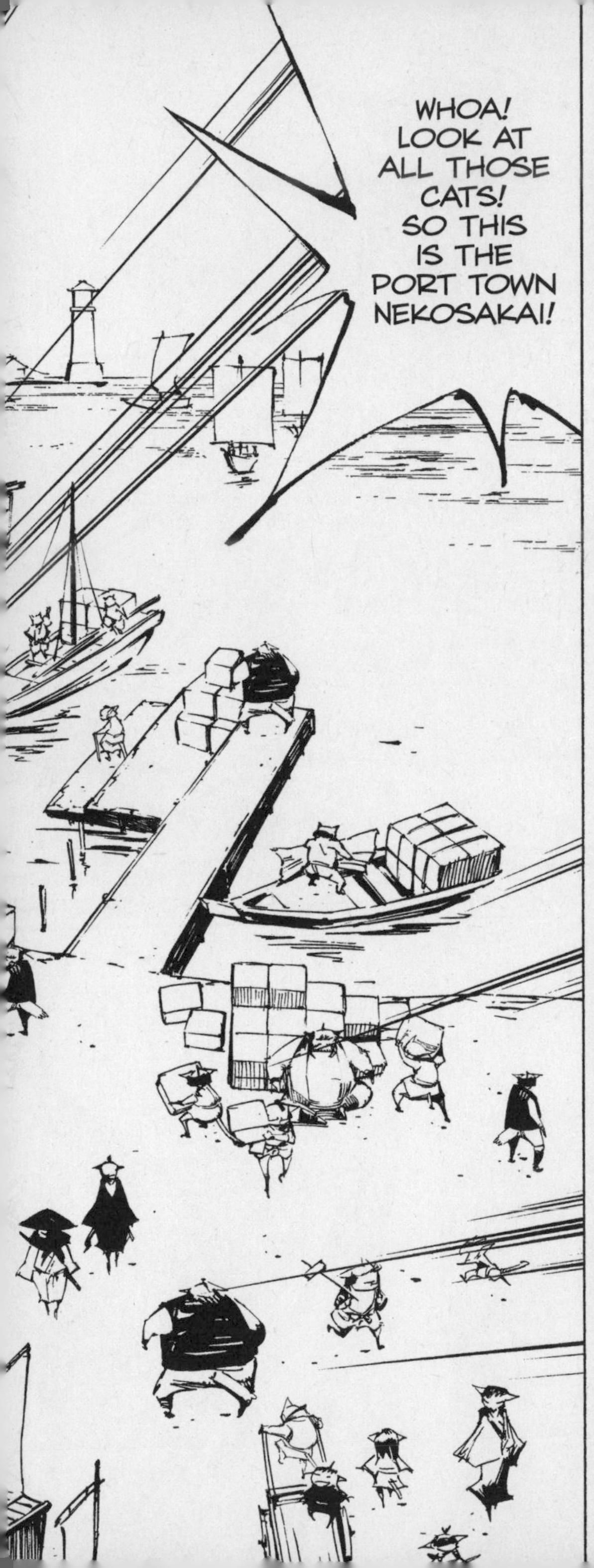
WHOA! LOOK AT ALL THOSE CATS! SO THIS IS THE PORT TOWN NEKOSAKAI!

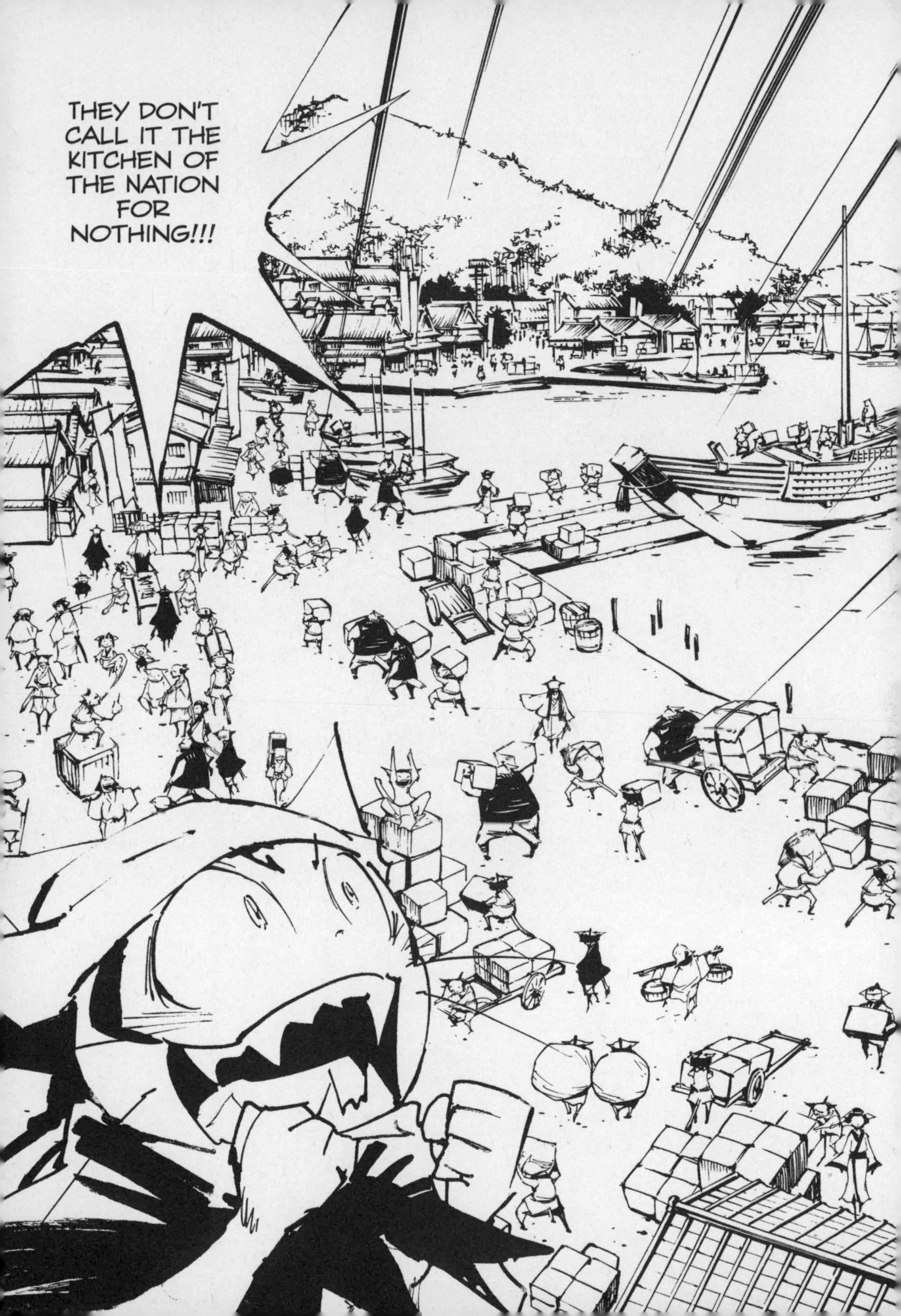
THEY DON'T CALL IT THE KITCHEN OF THE NATION FOR NOTHING!!!

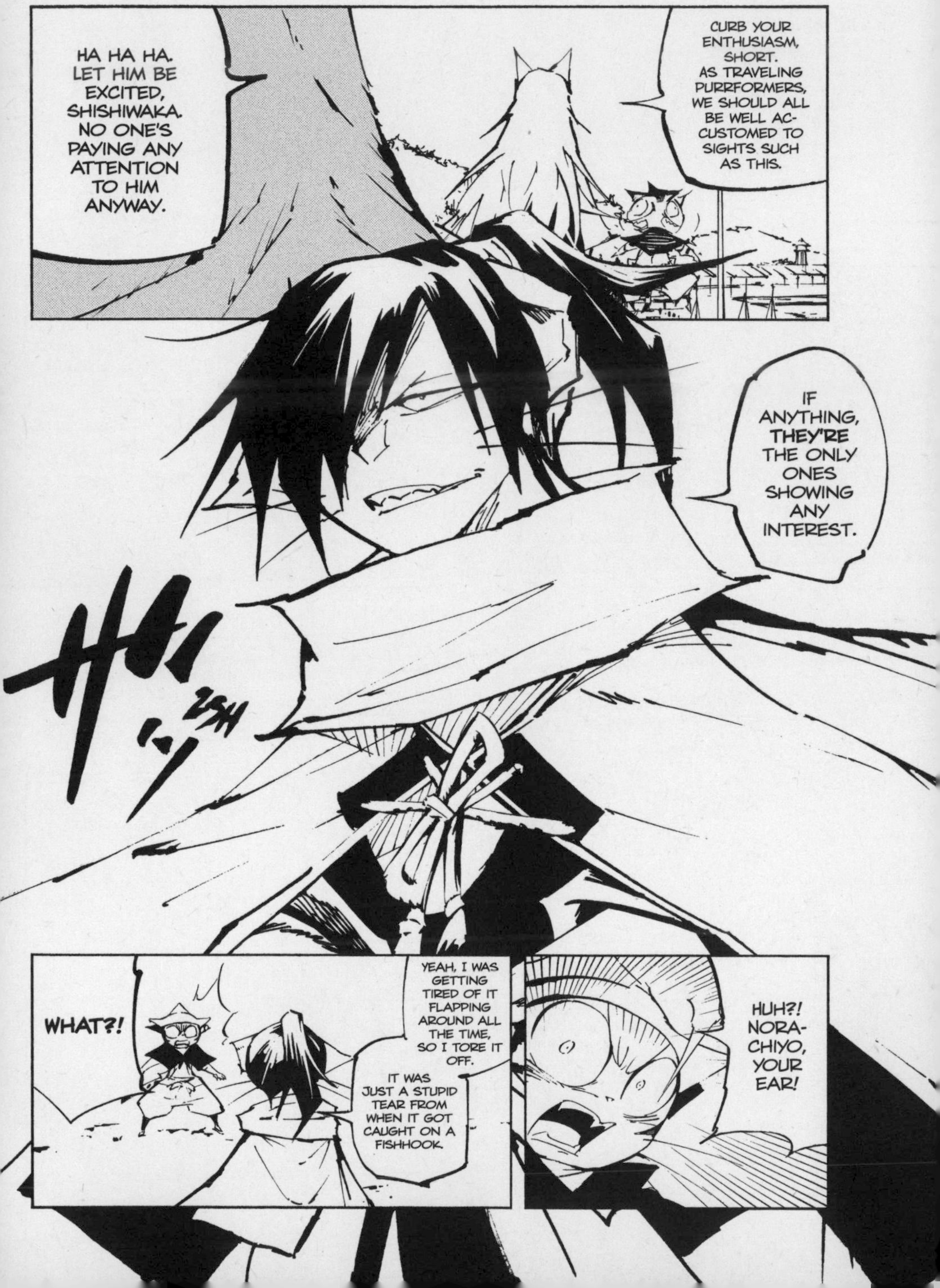
CURB YOUR ENTHUSIASM, SHORT. AS TRAVELING PURRFORMERS, WE SHOULD ALL BE WELL AC-CUSTOMED TO SIGHTS SUCH AS THIS.
HA HA HA. LET HIM BE EXCITED, SHISHIWAKA. NO ONE'S PAYING ANY ATTENTION TO HIM ANYWAY.
IF ANYTHING, THEY'RE THE ONLY ONES SHOWING ANY INTEREST.
ZSH
HUH?! NORA-CHIYO, YOUR EAR!
YEAH, I WAS GETTING TIRED OF IT FLAPPING AROUND ALL THE TIME, SO I TORE IT OFF.
IT WAS JUST A STUPID TEAR FROM WHEN IT GOT CAUGHT ON A FISHHOOK.
WHAT?!

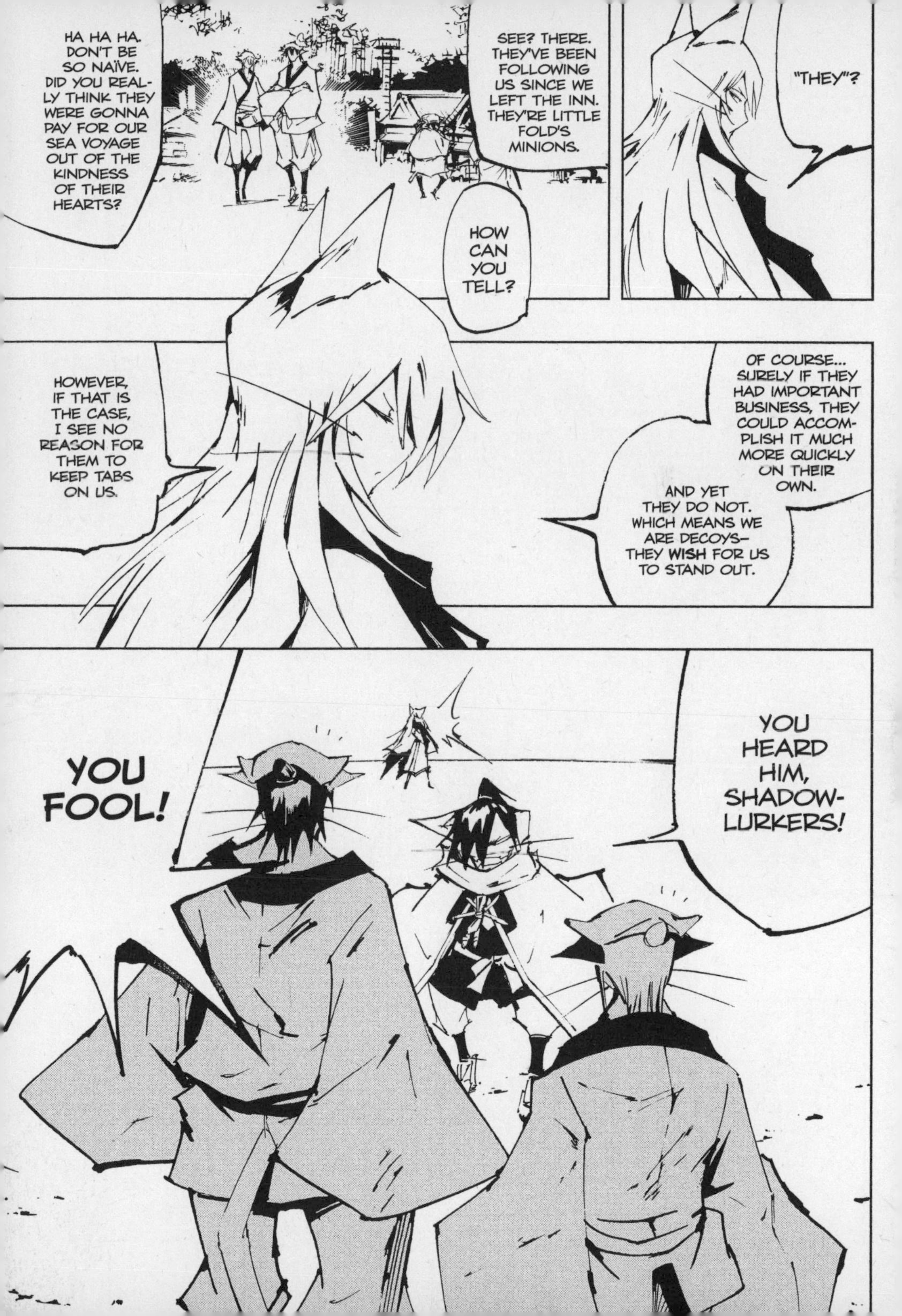
HA HA HA. DON'T BE SO NAÏVE. DID YOU REALLY THINK THEY WERE GONNA PAY FOR OUR SEA VOYAGE OUT OF THE KINDNESS OF THEIR HEARTS?
SEE? THERE. THEY'VE BEEN FOLLOWING US SINCE WE LEFT THE INN. THEY'RE LITTLE FOLD'S MINIONS.
"THEY"?
HOW CAN YOU TELL?
HOWEVER, IF THAT IS THE CASE, I SEE NO REASON FOR THEM TO KEEP TABS ON US.
OF COURSE... SURELY IF THEY HAD IMPORTANT BUSINESS, THEY COULD ACCOMPLISH IT MUCH MORE QUICKLY ON THEIR OWN.
AND YET THEY DO NOT. WHICH MEANS WE ARE DECOYS— THEY **WISH** FOR US TO STAND OUT.
YOU FOOL!
YOU HEARD HIM, SHADOW-LURKERS!

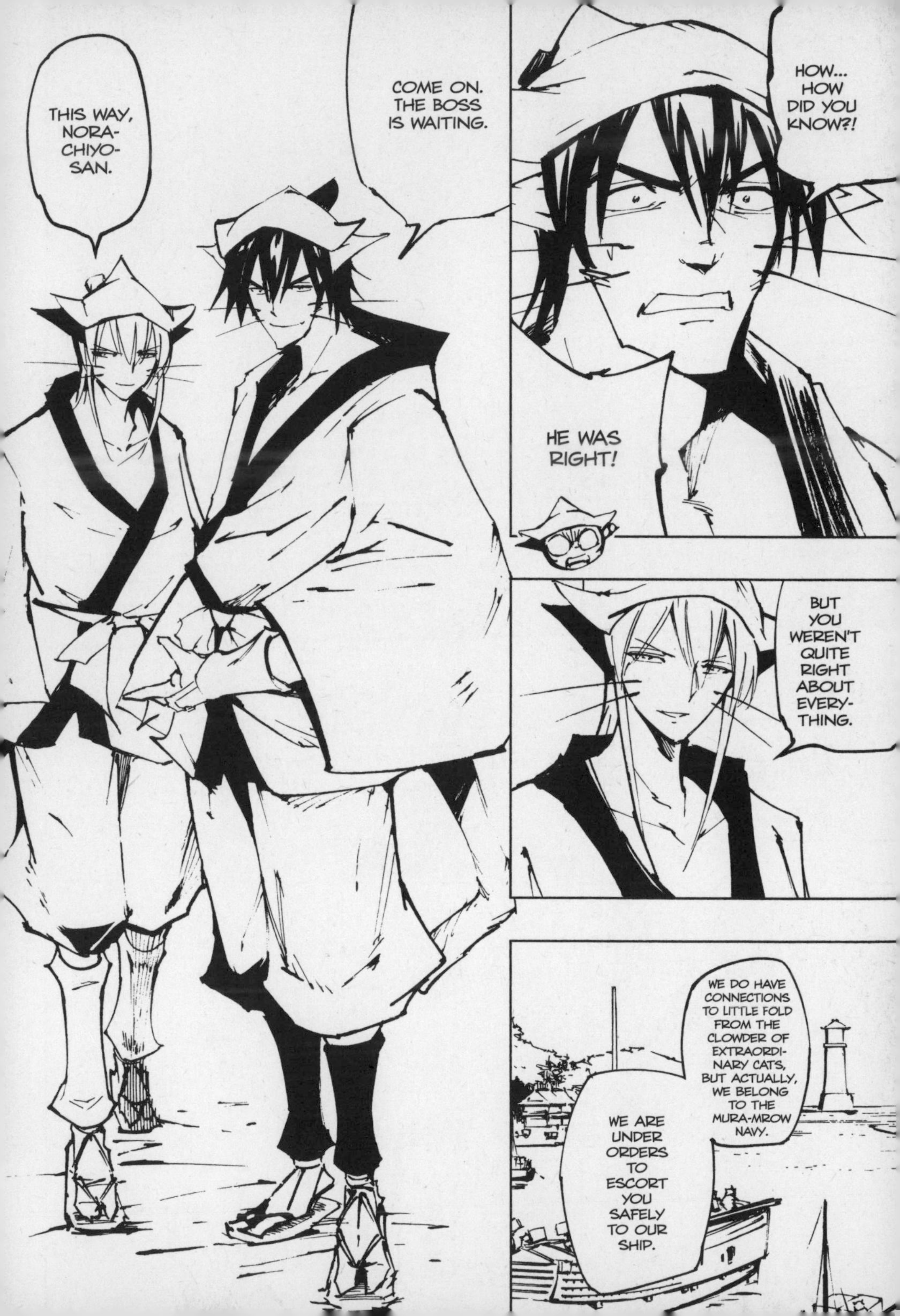
HOW... HOW DID YOU KNOW?!
HE WAS RIGHT!
BUT YOU WEREN'T QUITE RIGHT ABOUT EVERYTHING.
WE DO HAVE CONNECTIONS TO LITTLE FOLD FROM THE CLOWDER OF EXTRAORDINARY CATS, BUT ACTUALLY, WE BELONG TO THE MURA-MROW NAVY.
WE ARE UNDER ORDERS TO ESCORT YOU SAFELY TO OUR SHIP.
COME ON. THE BOSS IS WAITING.
THIS WAY, NORA-CHIYO-SAN.

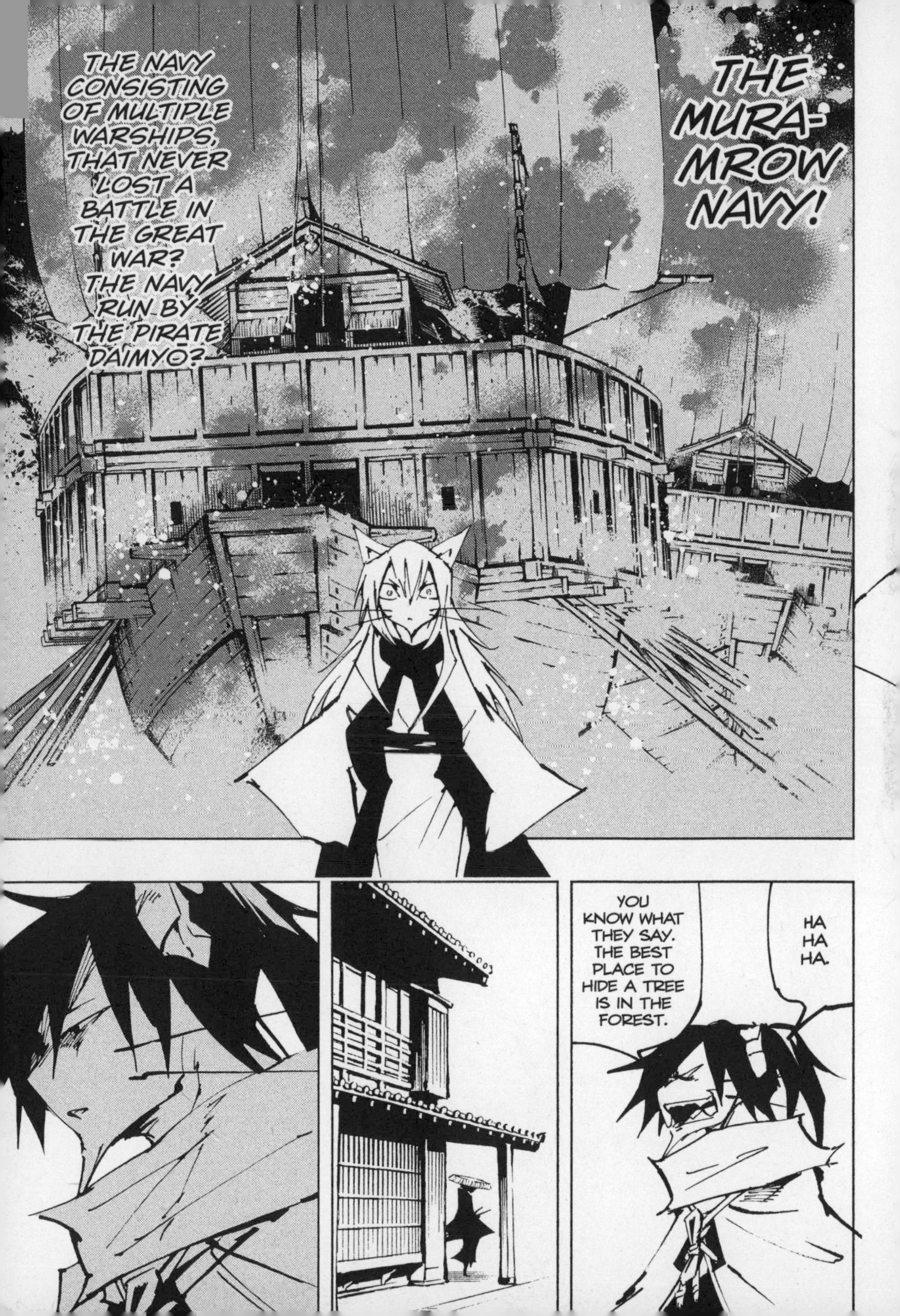
THE MURA-MROW NAVY!
THE NAVY CONSISTING OF MULTIPLE WARSHIPS, THAT NEVER LOST A BATTLE IN THE GREAT WAR? THE NAVY RUN BY THE PIRATE DAIMYŌ?
HA HA HA.
YOU KNOW WHAT THEY SAY. THE BEST PLACE TO HIDE A TREE IS IN THE FOREST.

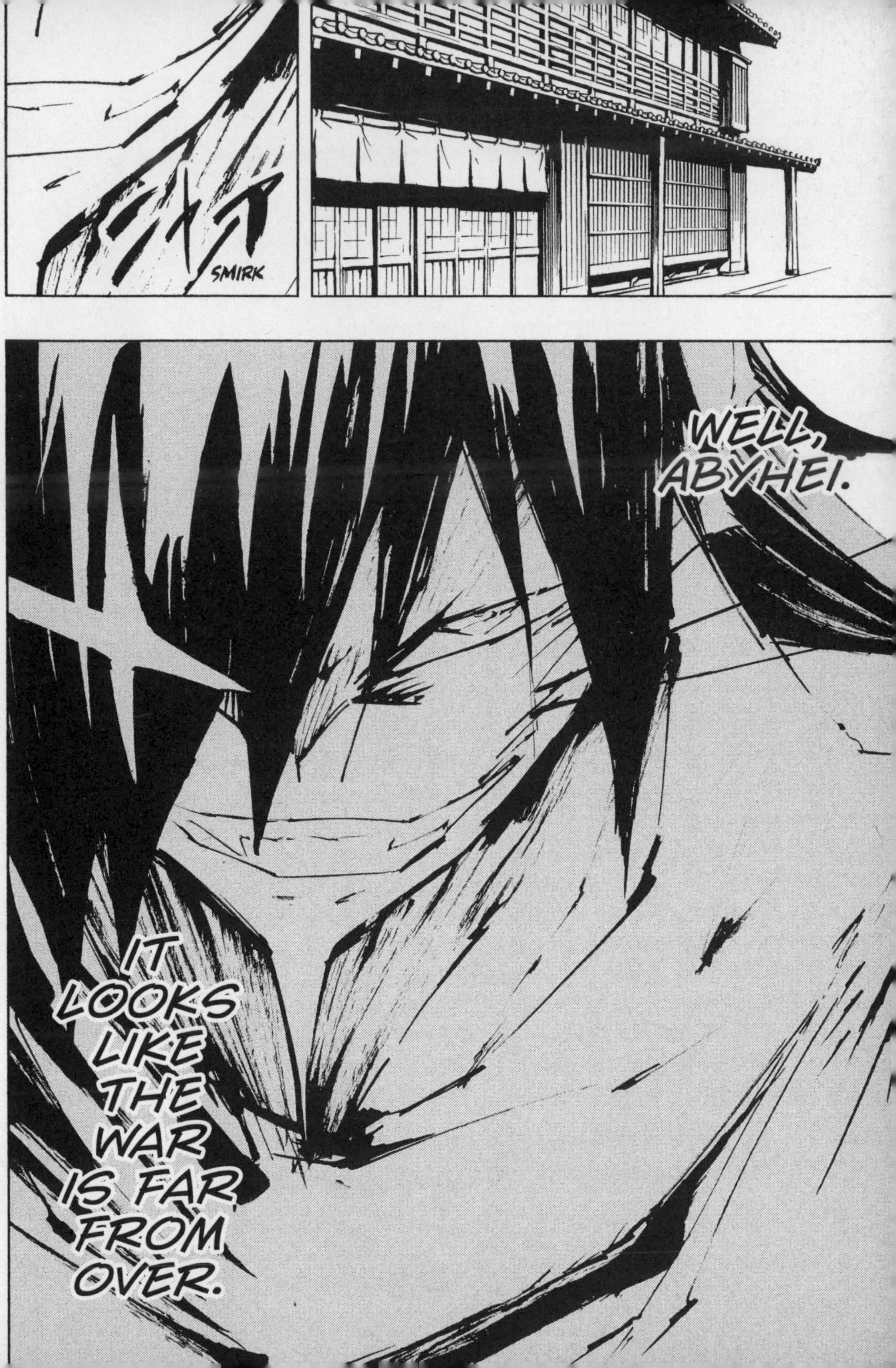
SMIRK
WELL, ABYHEI.
IT LOOKS LIKE THE WAR IS FAR FROM OVER.

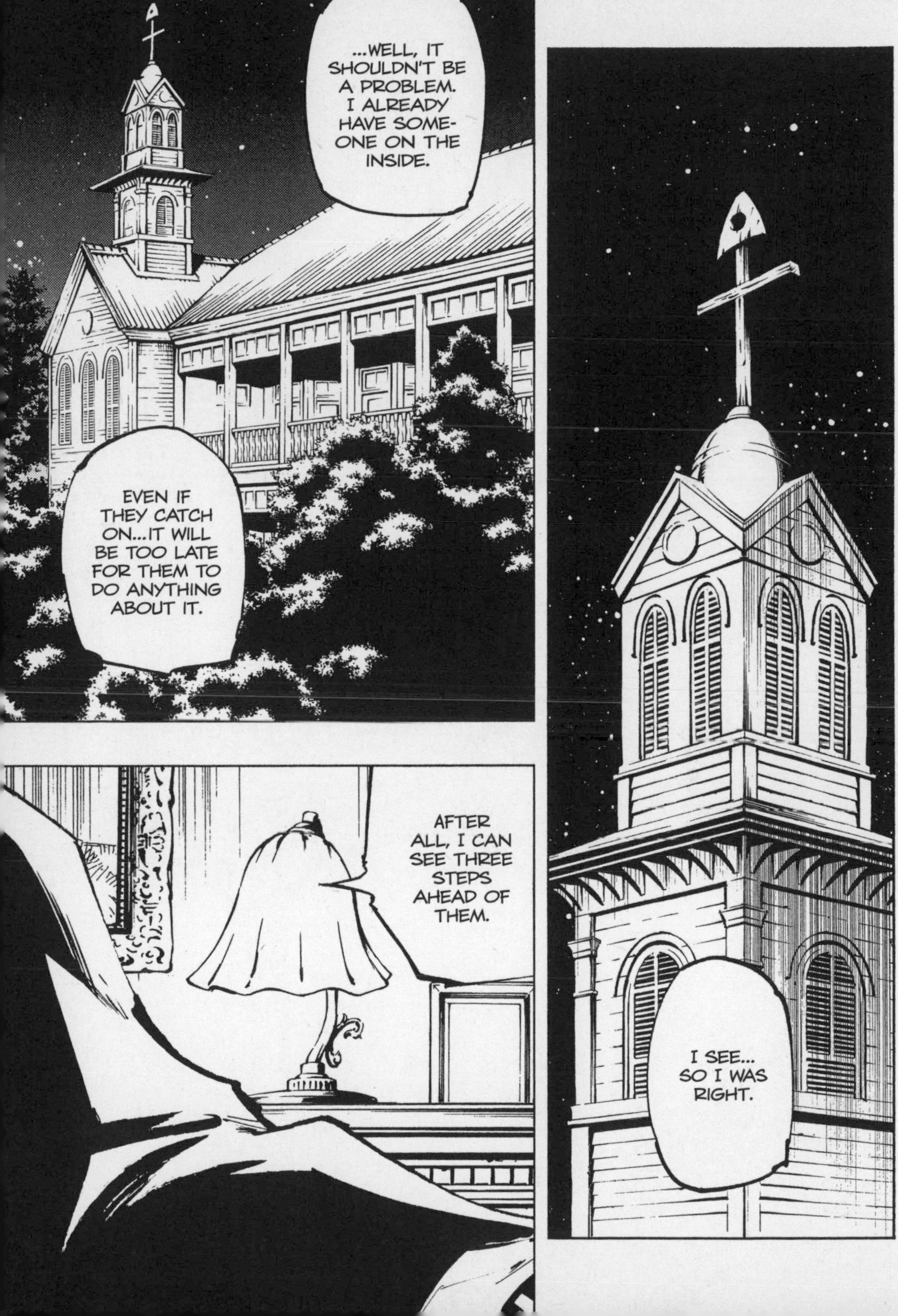
I SEE... SO I WAS RIGHT.
...WELL, IT SHOULDN'T BE A PROBLEM. I ALREADY HAVE SOME-ONE ON THE INSIDE.
EVEN IF THEY CATCH ON...IT WILL BE TOO LATE FOR THEM TO DO ANYTHING ABOUT IT.
AFTER ALL, I CAN SEE THREE STEPS AHEAD OF THEM.

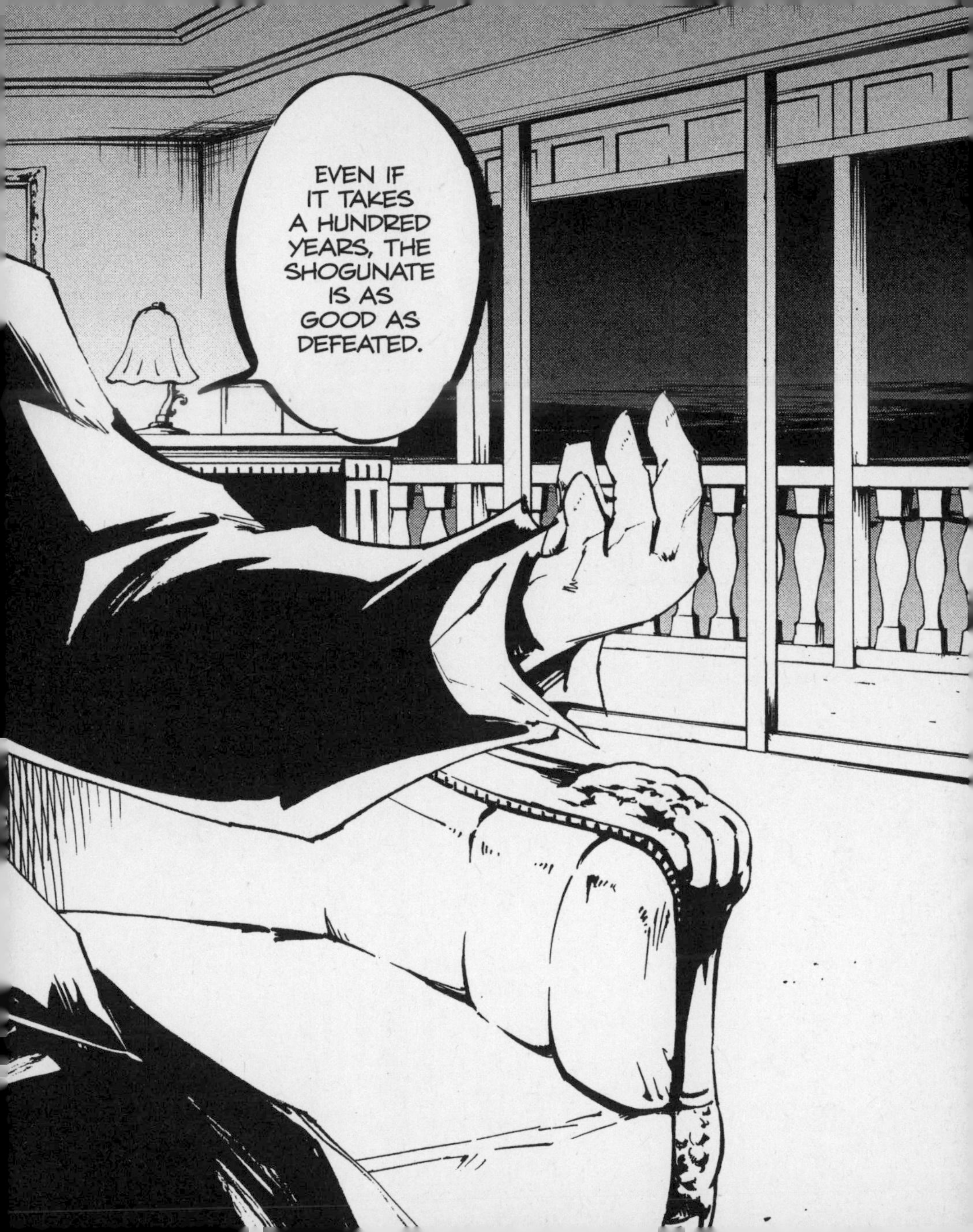
EVEN IF IT TAKES A HUNDRED YEARS, THE SHOGUNATE IS AS GOOD AS DEFEATED.

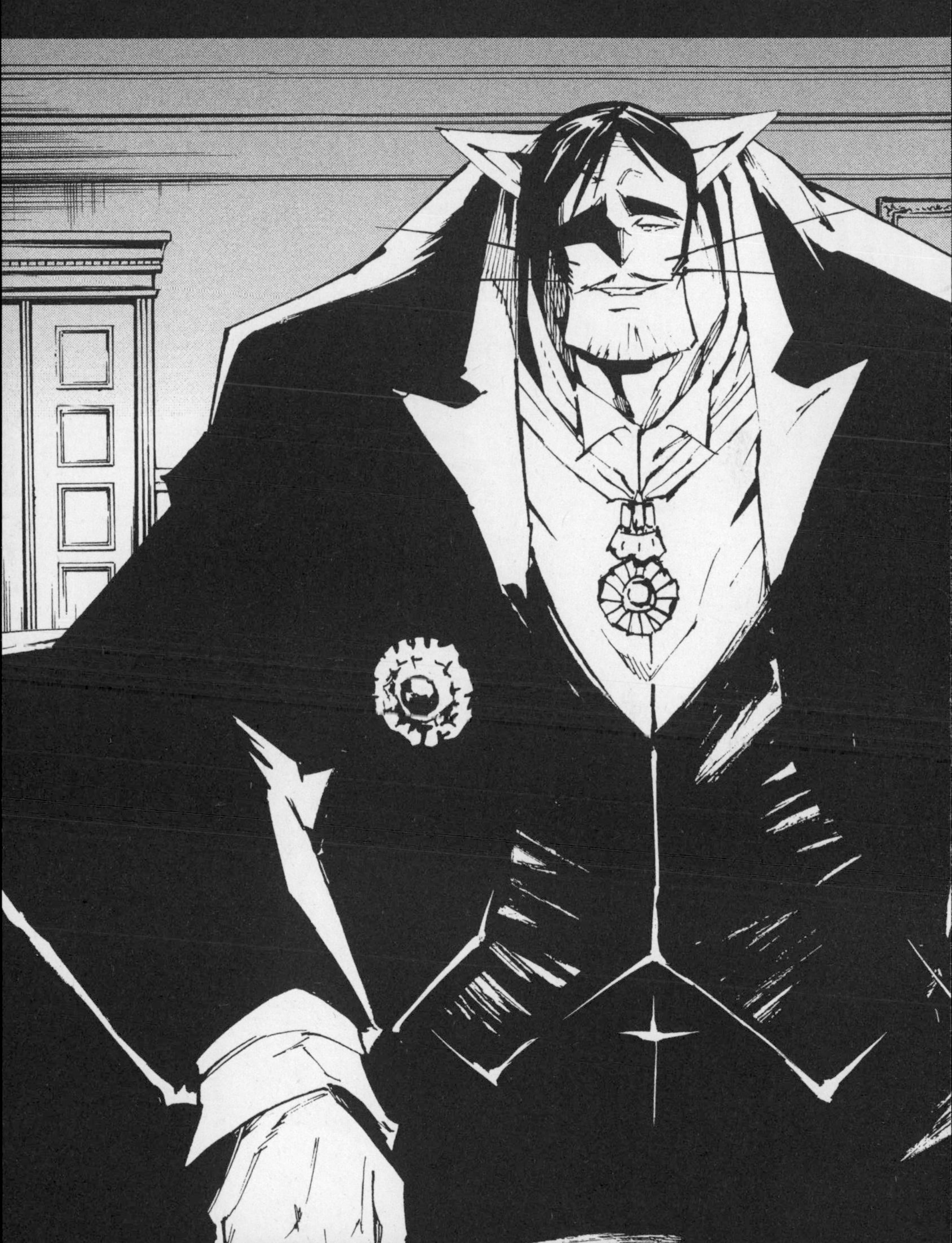

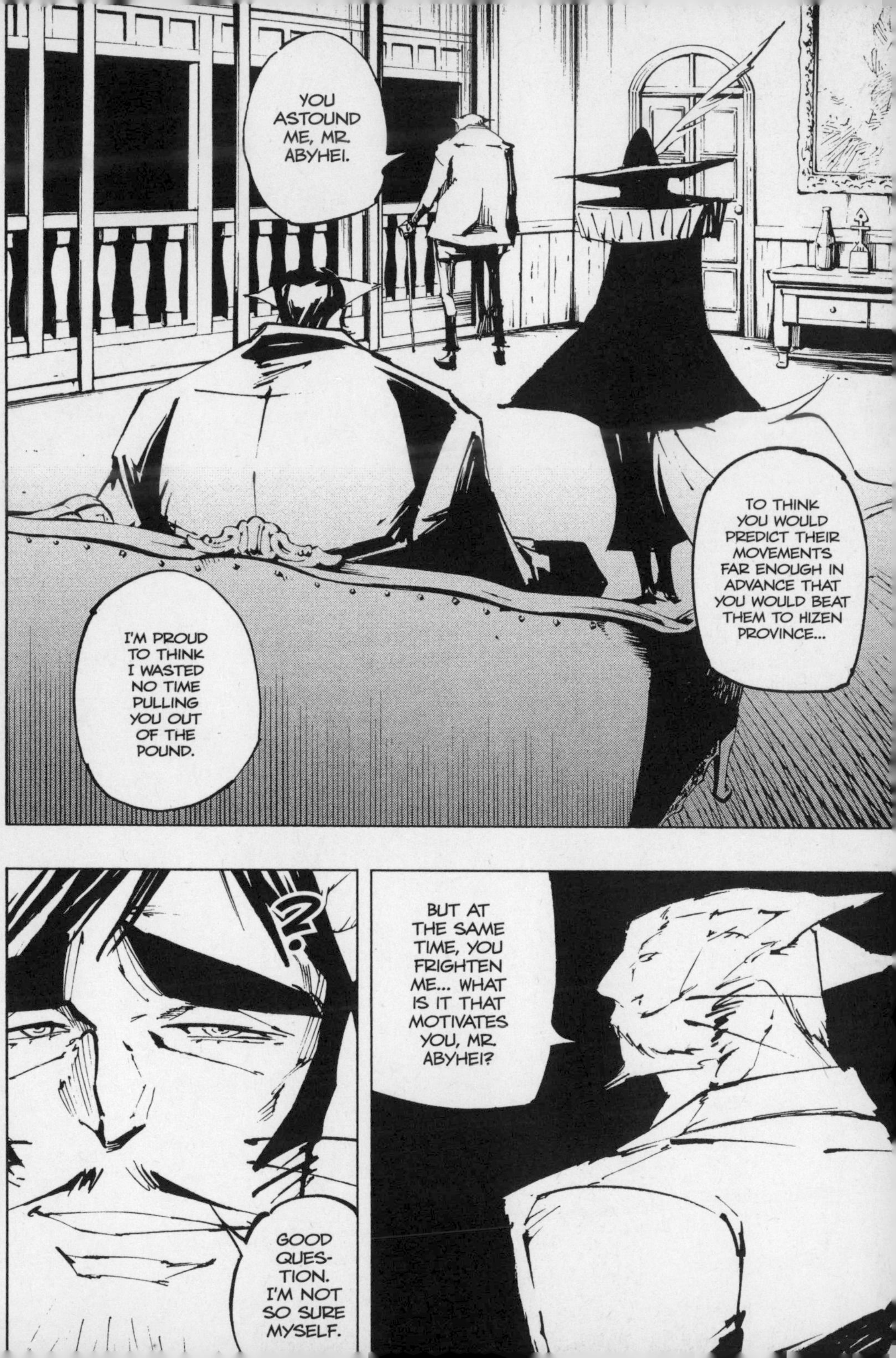
YOU ASTOUND ME, MR. ABYHEI.
TO THINK YOU WOULD PREDICT THEIR MOVEMENTS FAR ENOUGH IN ADVANCE THAT YOU WOULD BEAT THEM TO HIZEN PROVINCE...
I'M PROUD TO THINK I WASTED NO TIME PULLING YOU OUT OF THE POUND.
BUT AT THE SAME TIME, YOU FRIGHTEN ME... WHAT IS IT THAT MOTIVATES YOU, MR. ABYHEI?
?
GOOD QUES-TION. I'M NOT SO SURE MYSELF.

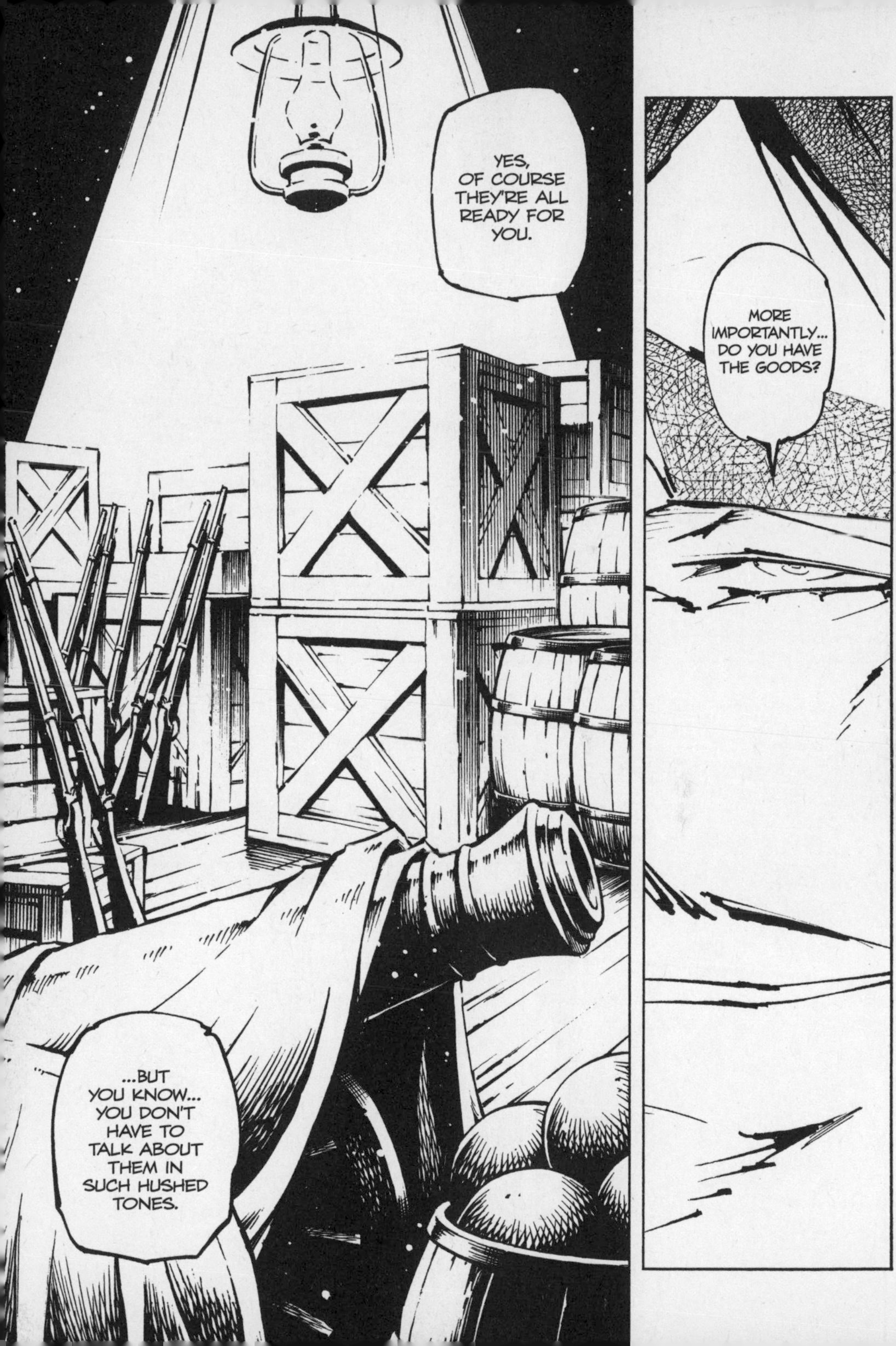
MORE IMPORTANTLY... DO YOU HAVE THE GOODS?
YES, OF COURSE THEY'RE ALL READY FOR YOU.
...BUT YOU KNOW... YOU DON'T HAVE TO TALK ABOUT THEM IN SUCH HUSHED TONES.

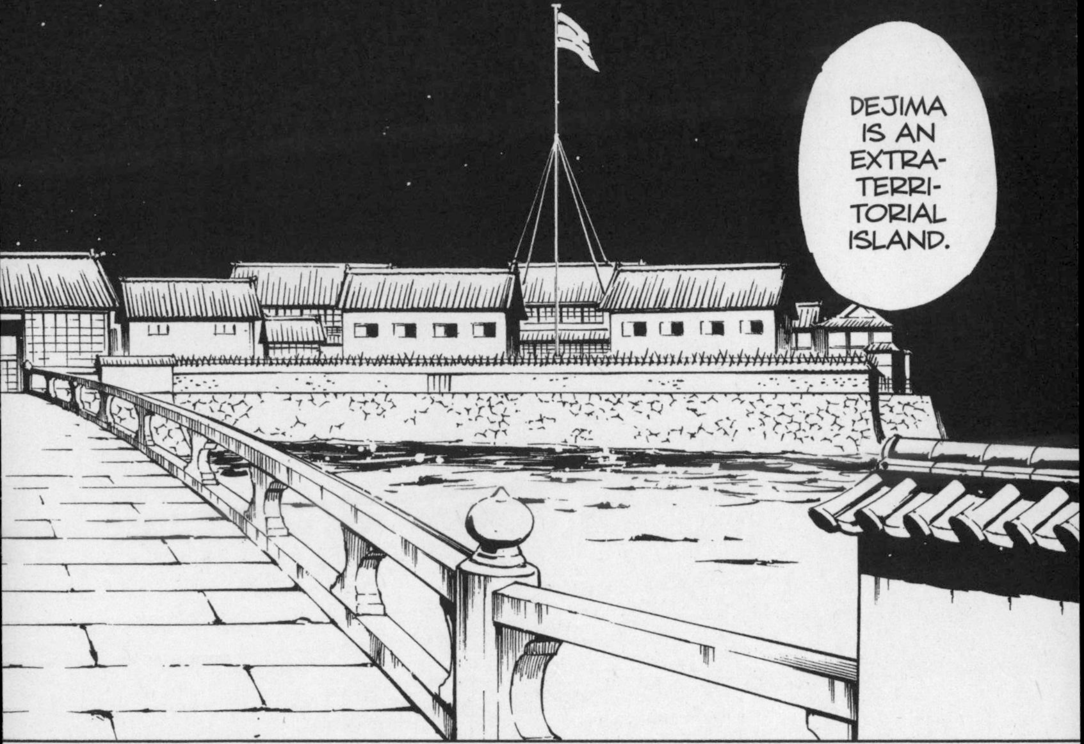
DEJIMA IS AN EXTRA-TERRITORIAL ISLAND.
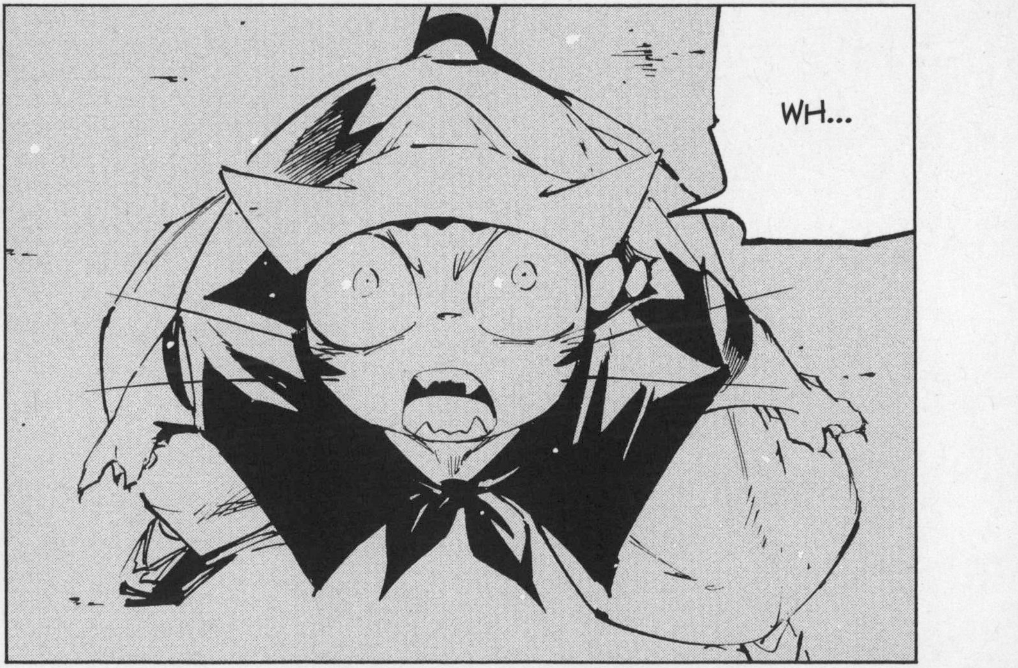
WH...

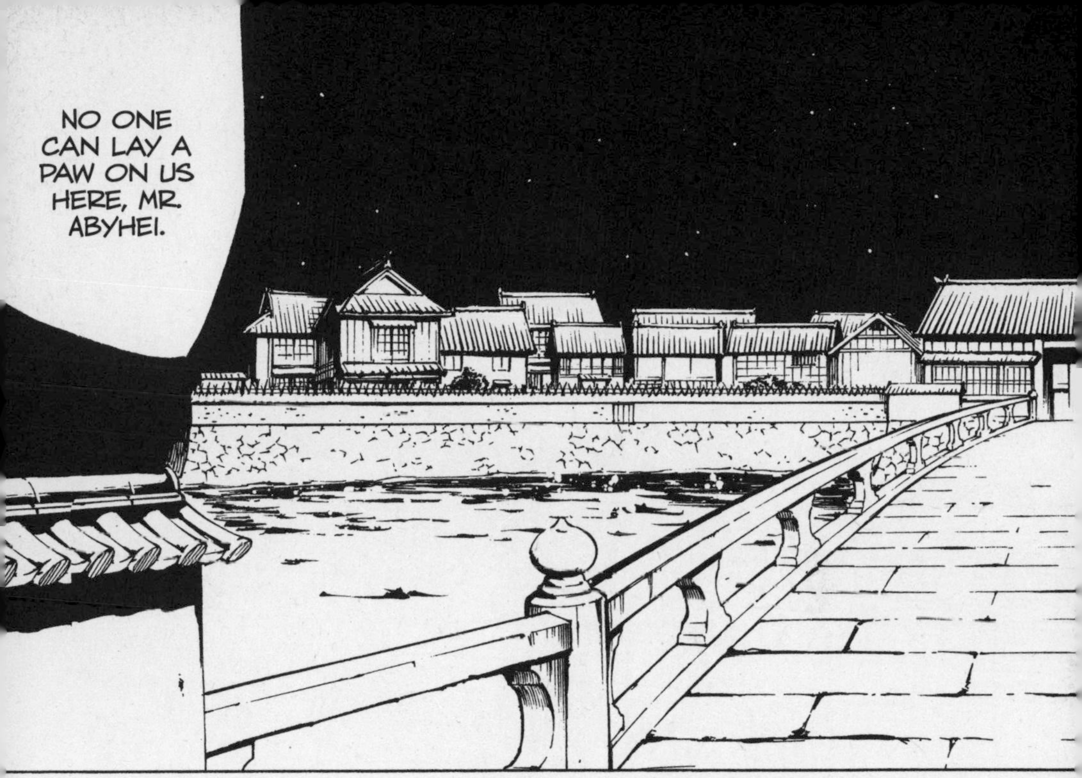
NO ONE CAN LAY A PAW ON US HERE, MR. ABYHEI.

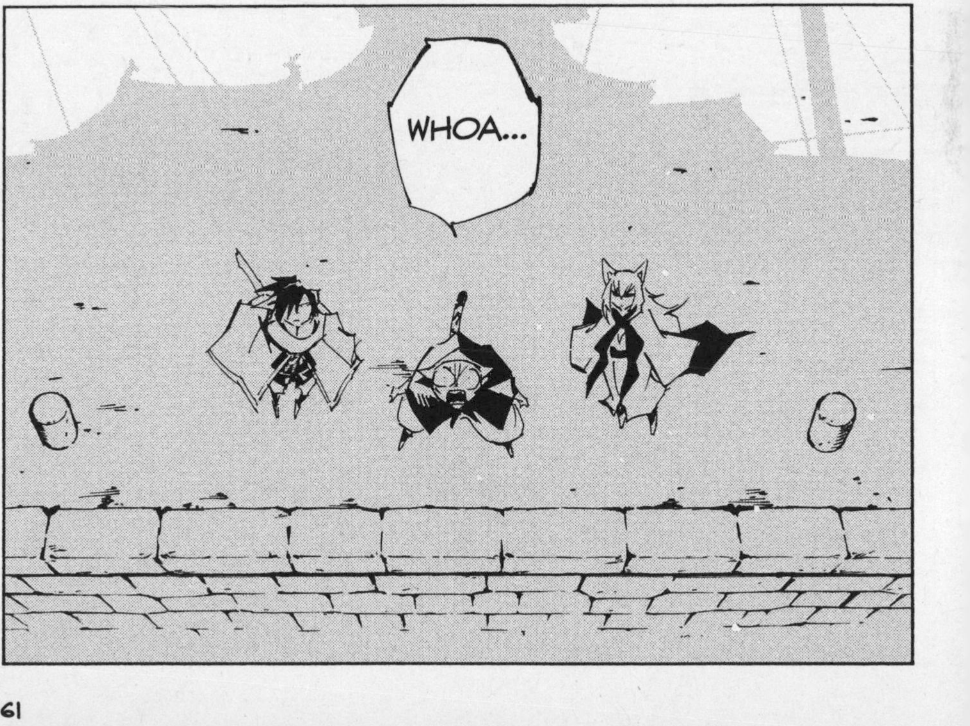
WHOA...

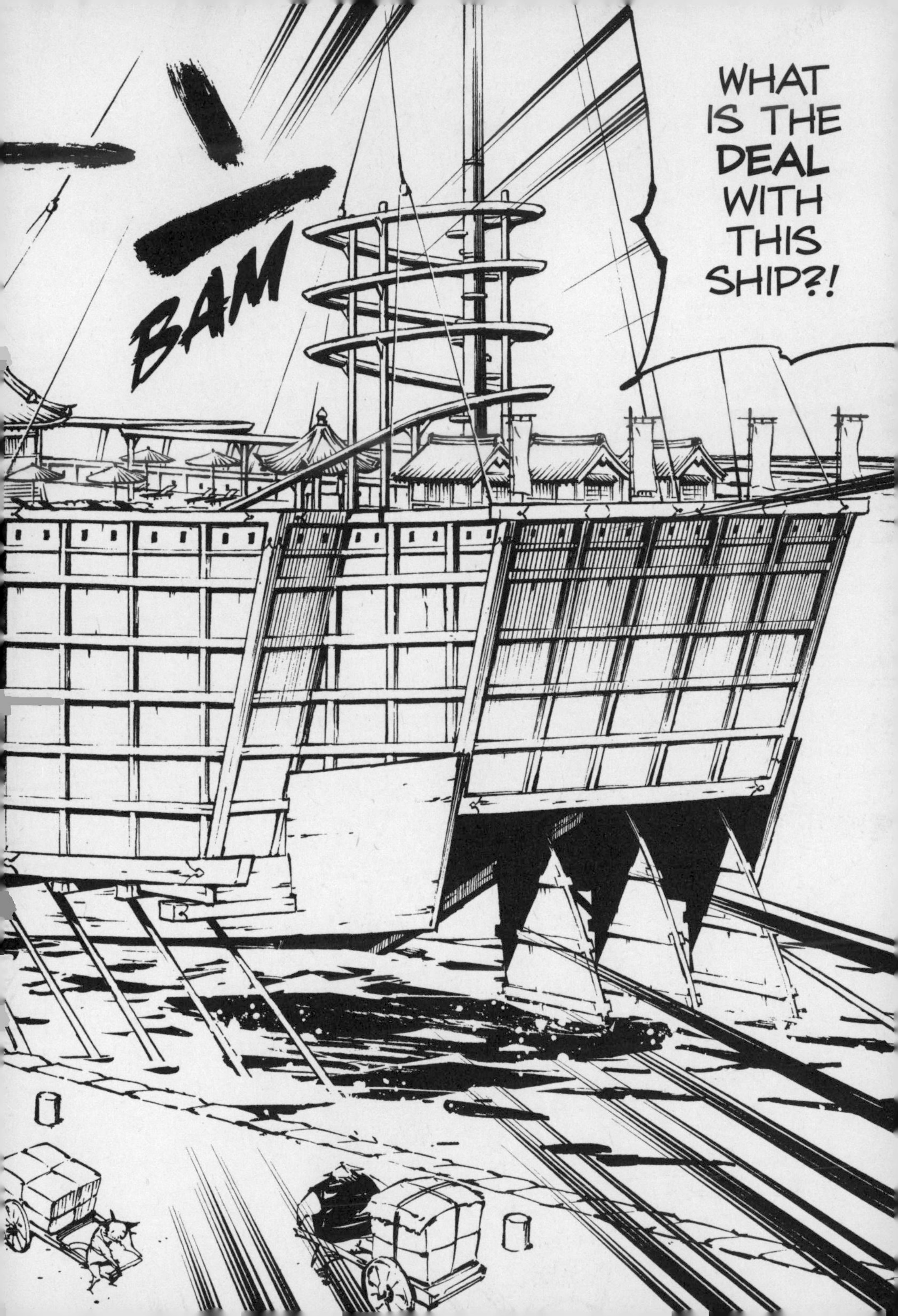
WHAT IS THE **DEAL** WITH THIS SHIP?!
BAM

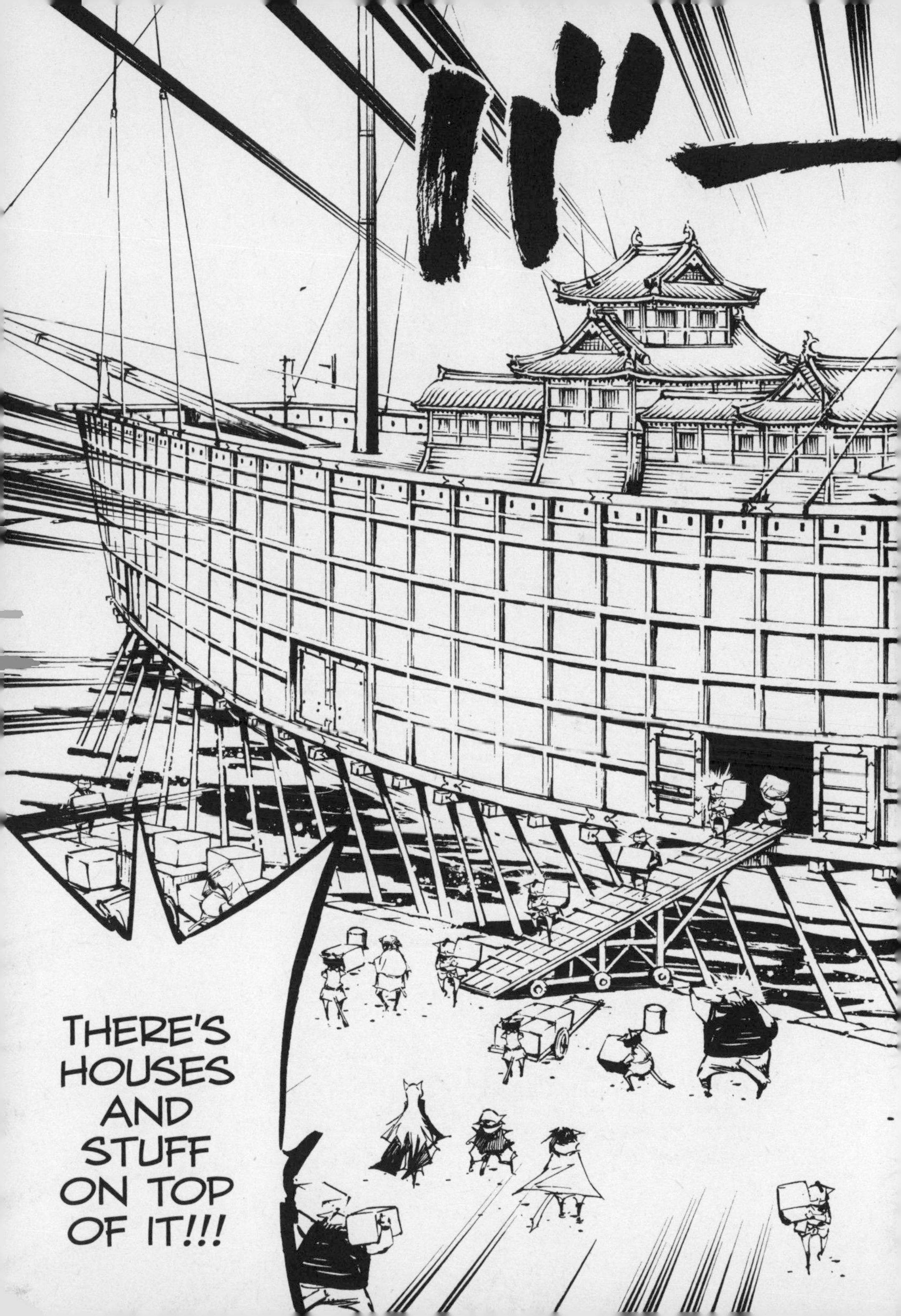
THERE'S HOUSES AND STUFF ON TOP OF IT!!!

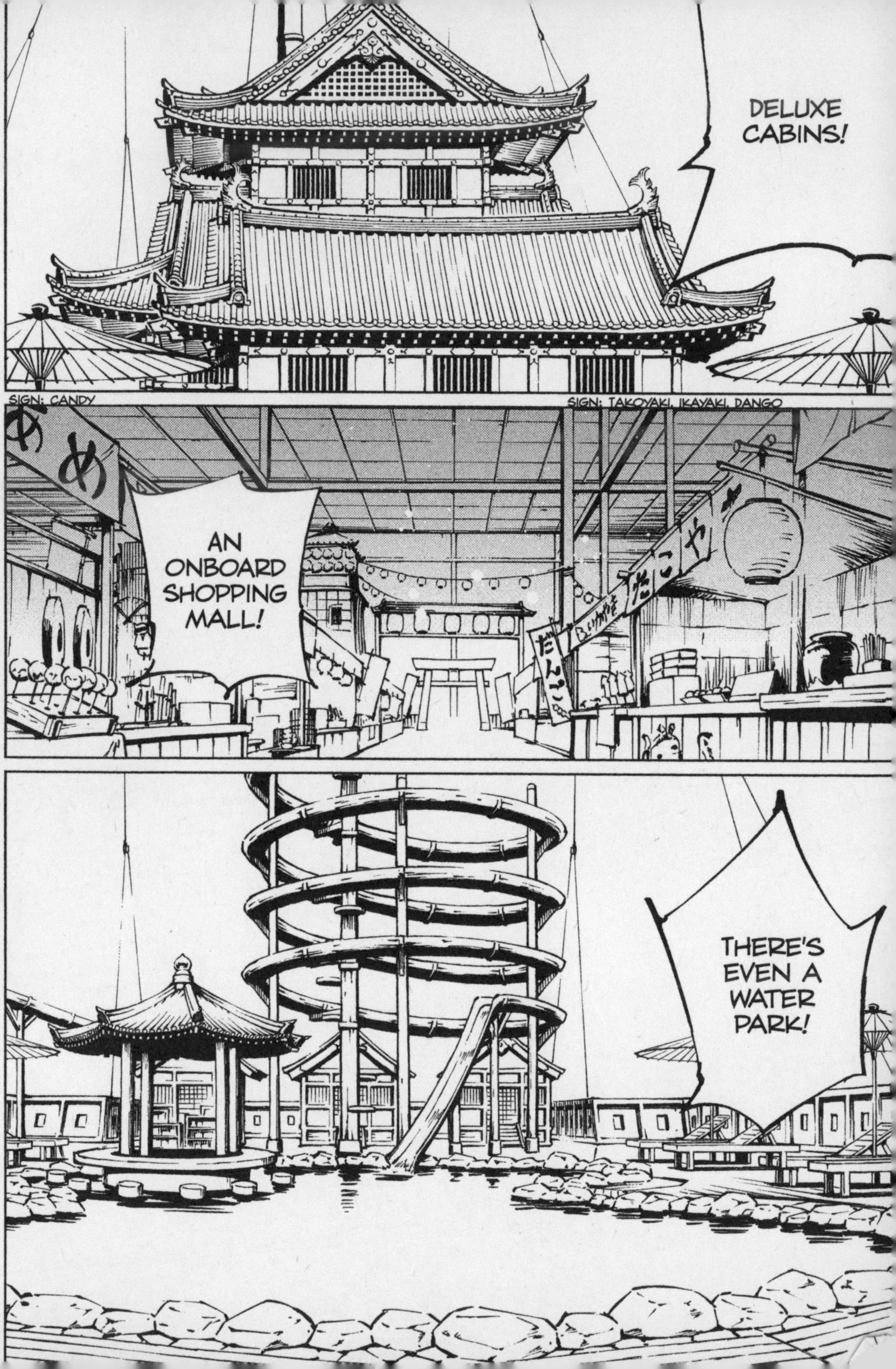
DELUXE CABINS!
SIGN: TAKOYAKI, IKAYAKI, DANGO
SIGN: CANDY
AN ONBOARD SHOPPING MALL!
THERE'S EVEN A WATER PARK!

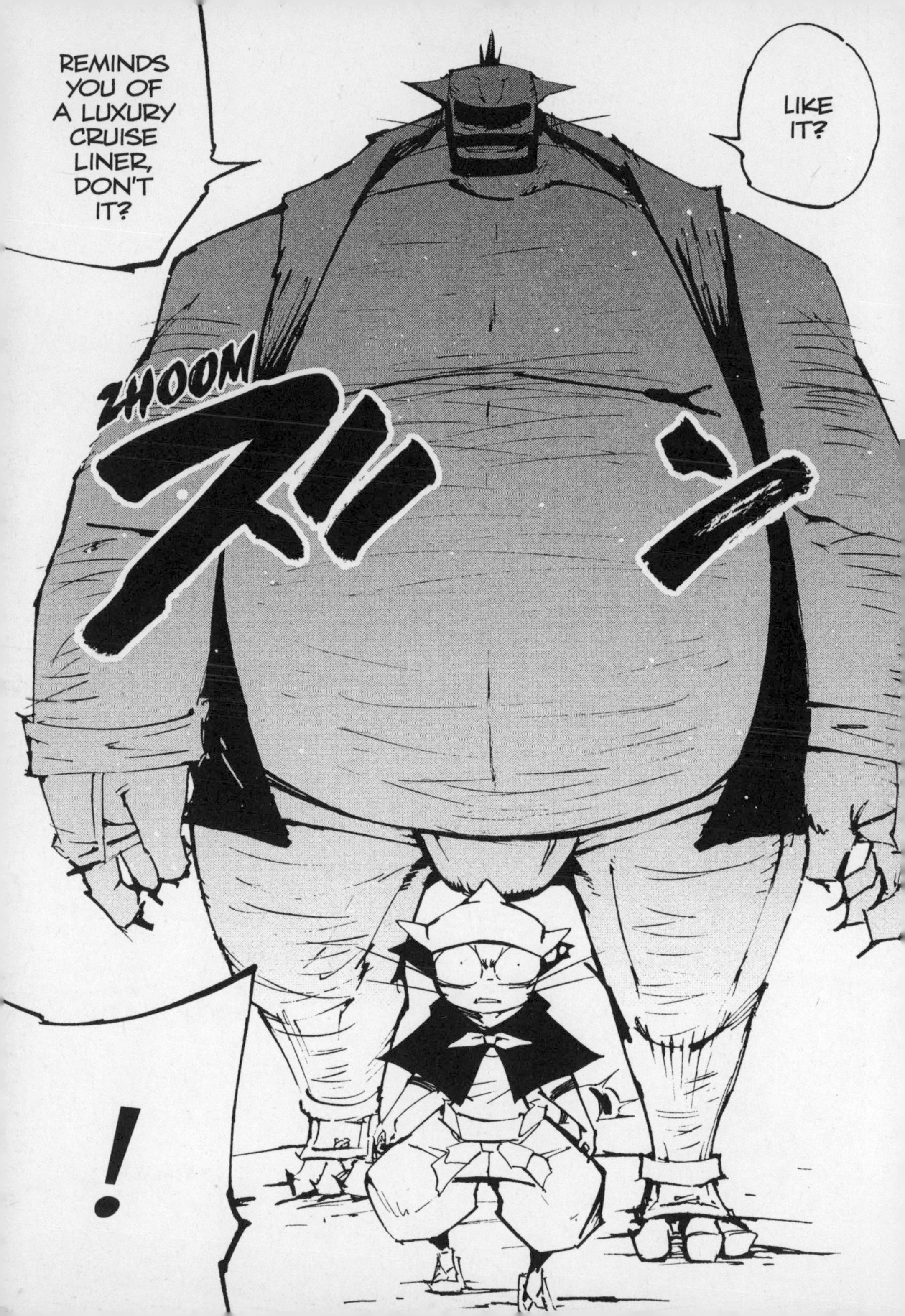
LIKE IT?
REMINDS YOU OF A LUXURY CRUISE LINER, DON'T IT?
ZHOOM
ズーン
!

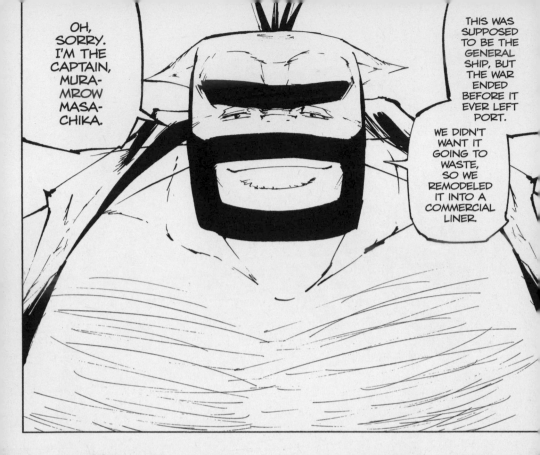

THIS WAS SUPPOSED TO BE THE GENERAL SHIP, BUT THE WAR ENDED BEFORE IT EVER LEFT PORT.
OH, SORRY. I'M THE CAPTAIN, MURA-MROW MASA-CHIKA.
WE DIDN'T WANT IT GOING TO WASTE, SO WE REMODELED IT INTO A COMMERCIAL LINER.
I AGREED TO LET YOU SAIL WITH ME FOR CHEAP AS A SPECIAL FAVOR TO ME BEST MATE LITTLE FOLD... BUT YOU'RE... YOU KNOW.
ANYWAY, LET'S ENJOY OUR TWO-WEEK CRUISE, EH, LITTLE ARISTO-CAT?
Y...
YEAH...

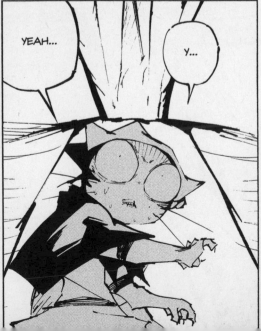

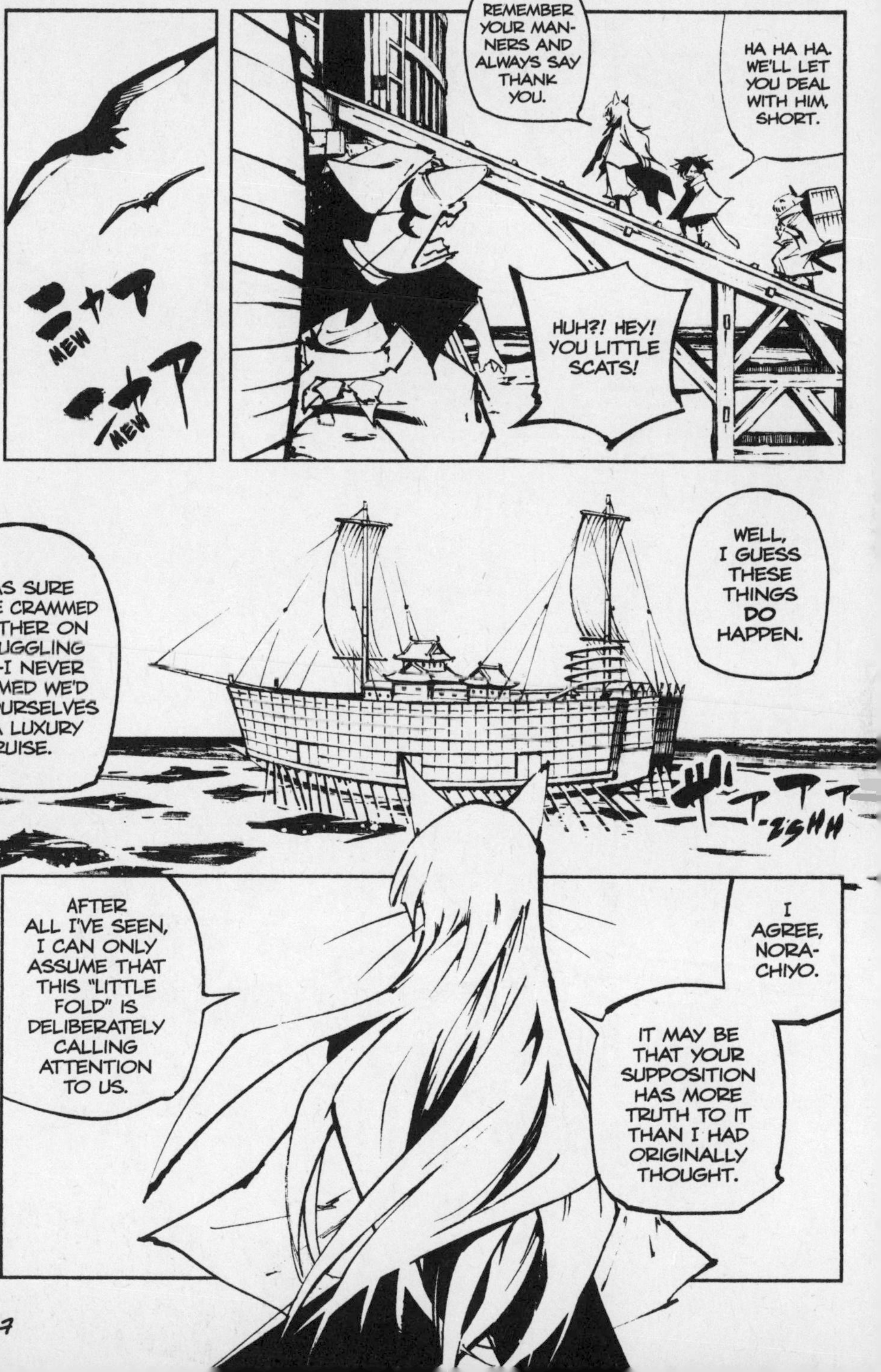
HA HA HA. WE'LL LET YOU DEAL WITH HIM, SHORT.
REMEMBER YOUR MANNERS AND ALWAYS SAY THANK YOU.
HUH?! HEY! YOU LITTLE SCATS!
ニャア
MEW
ニャア
MEW
WELL, I GUESS THESE THINGS DO HAPPEN.
I WAS SURE WE'D BE CRAMMED TOGETHER ON A SMUGGLING SHIP—I NEVER DREAMED WE'D FIND OURSELVES ON A LUXURY CRUISE.
ザァァァ
ZSHH
I AGREE, NORA-CHIYO.
IT MAY BE THAT YOUR SUPPOSITION HAS MORE TRUTH TO IT THAN I HAD ORIGINALLY THOUGHT.
AFTER ALL I'VE SEEN, I CAN ONLY ASSUME THAT THIS "LITTLE FOLD" IS DELIBERATELY CALLING ATTENTION TO US.

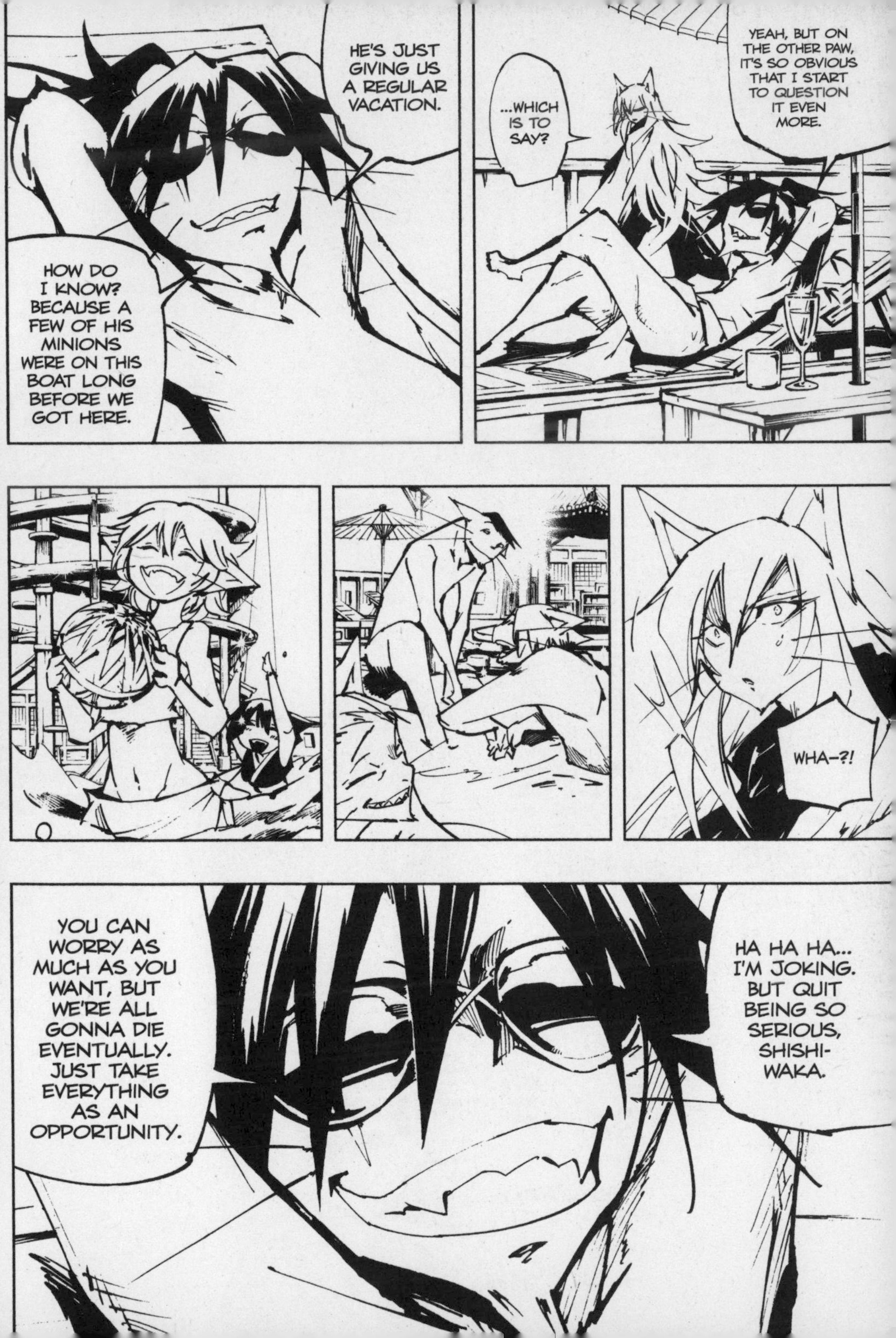
YEAH, BUT ON THE OTHER PAW, IT'S SO OBVIOUS THAT I START TO QUESTION IT EVEN MORE.
...WHICH IS TO SAY?
HE'S JUST GIVING US A REGULAR VACATION.
HOW DO I KNOW? BECAUSE A FEW OF HIS MINIONS WERE ON THIS BOAT LONG BEFORE WE GOT HERE.
WHA-?!
HA HA HA... I'M JOKING. BUT QUIT BEING SO SERIOUS, SHISHI-WAKA.
YOU CAN WORRY AS MUCH AS YOU WANT, BUT WE'RE ALL GONNA DIE EVENTUALLY. JUST TAKE EVERYTHING AS AN OPPORTUNITY.

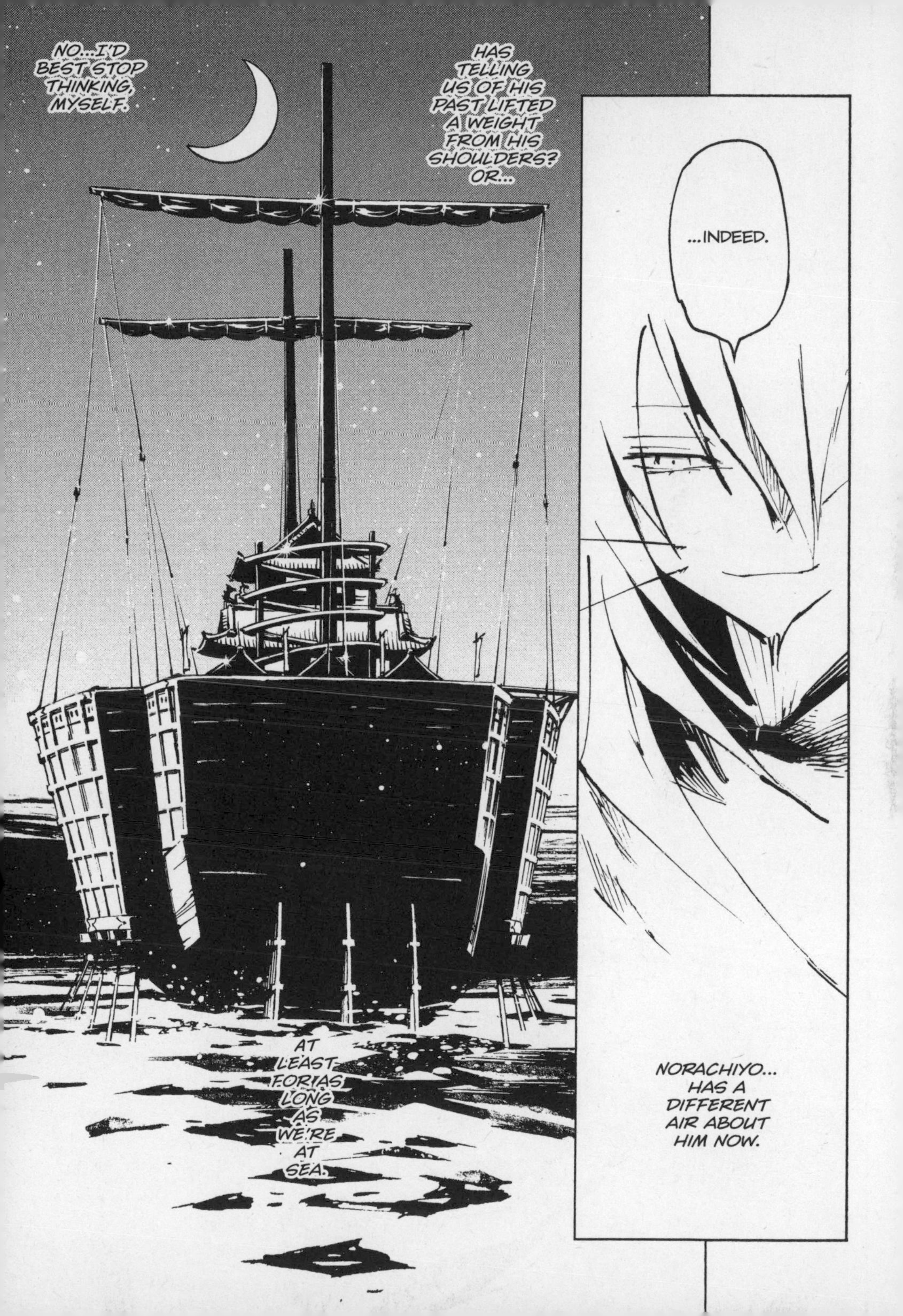
...INDEED.
NORACHIYO... HAS A DIFFERENT AIR ABOUT HIM NOW.
HAS TELLING US OF HIS PAST LIFTED A WEIGHT FROM HIS SHOULDERS? OR...
NO...I'D BEST STOP THINKING, MYSELF.
AT LEAST FOR AS LONG AS WE'RE AT SEA.

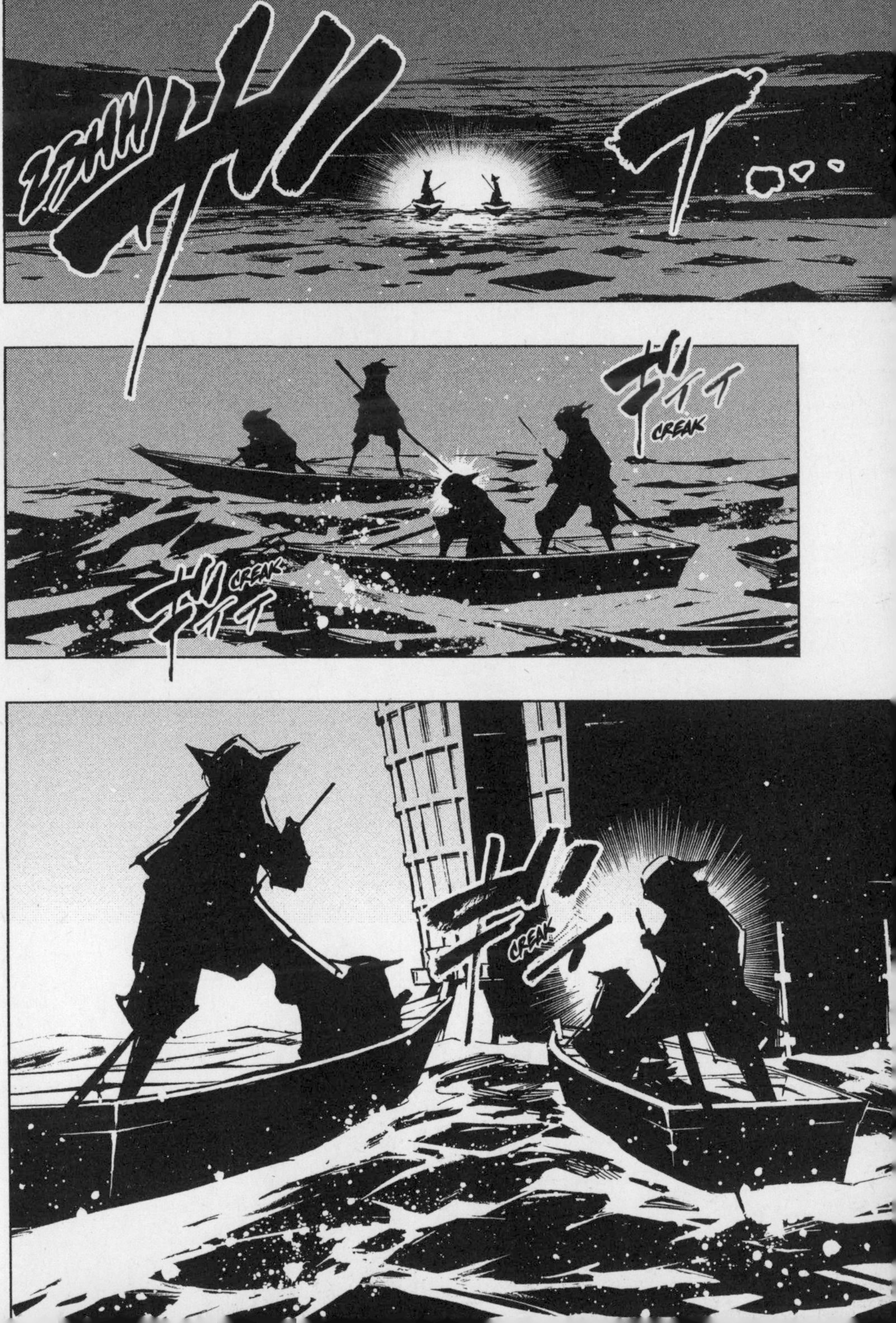

ギイイ
CREAK
CREAK
ギイイ
CREAK

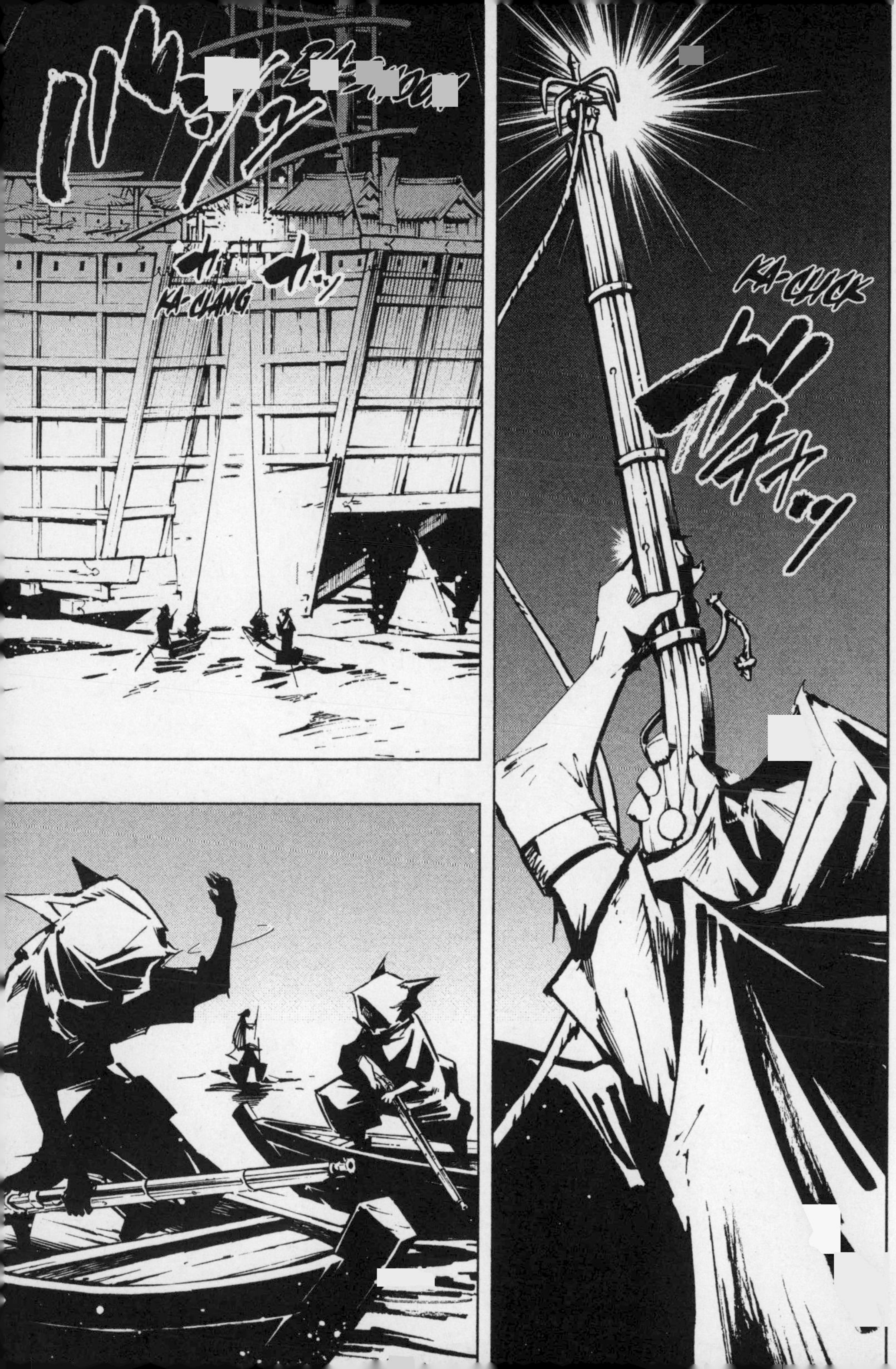
KA-CHICK
KA-CLANG

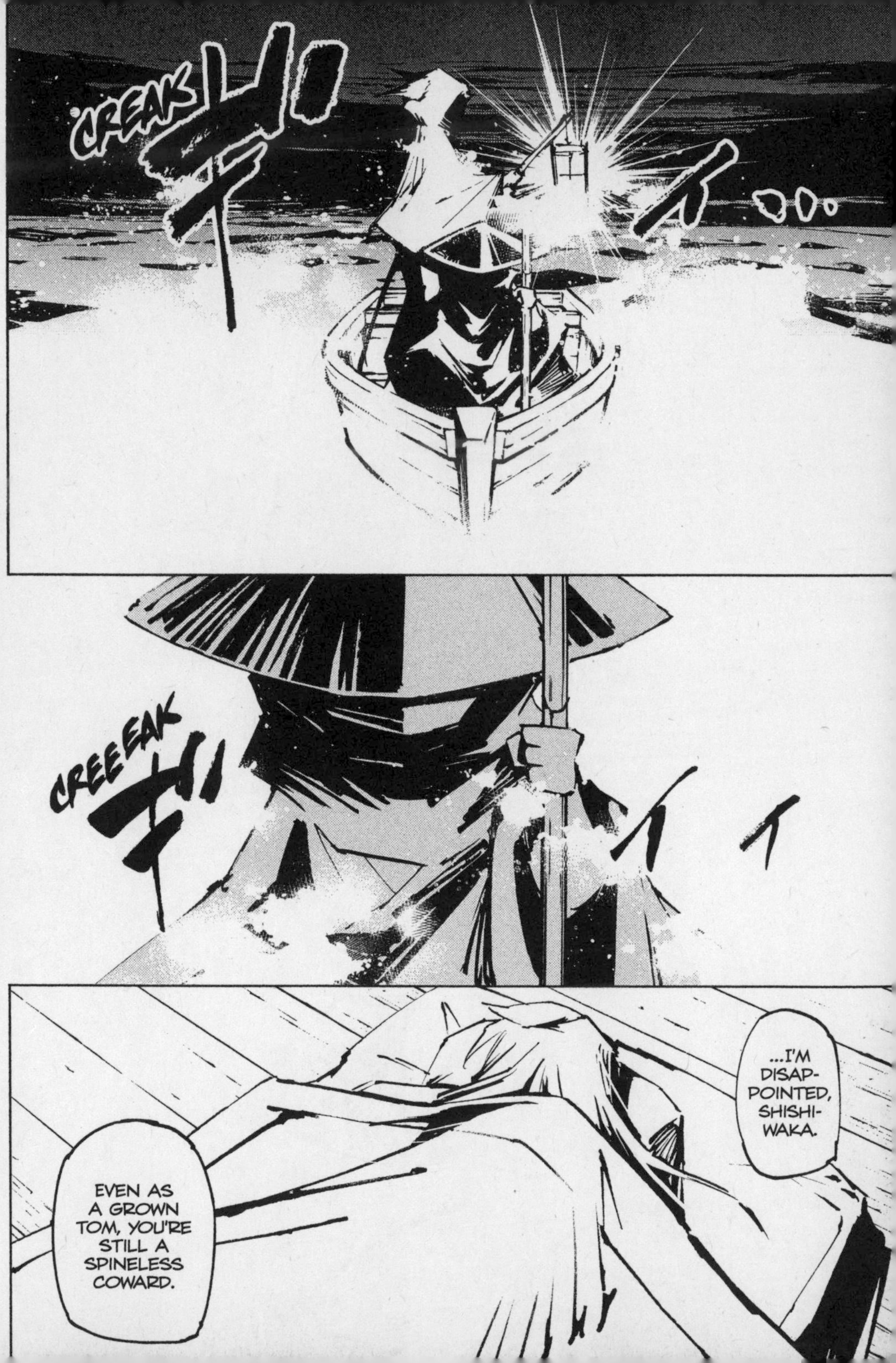
CREAK
CREEEAK
...I'M DISAPPOINTED, SHISHIWAKA.
EVEN AS A GROWN TOM, YOU'RE STILL A SPINELESS COWARD.

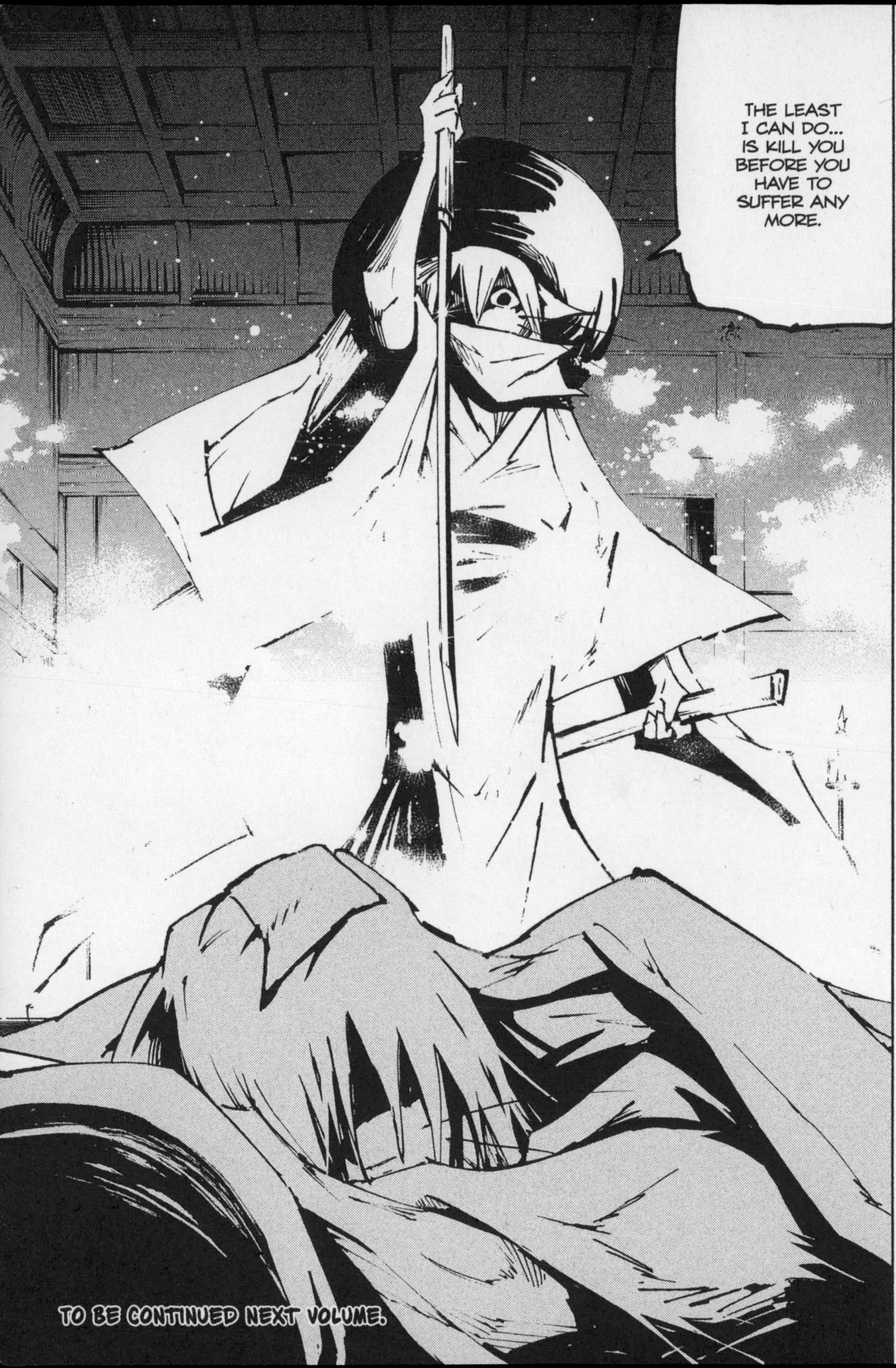
THE LEAST I CAN DO... IS KILL YOU BEFORE YOU HAVE TO SUFFER ANY MORE.
TO BE CONTINUED NEXT VOLUME.

猫ヶ原

NeKoGaHara

ネコガハラ

TRANSLATION NOTES

Quean house, page 10

THIS IS THE QUEAN-HOUSE ŌDAMAYA.

大玉屋

The Japanese word used here is yūkaku, which literally means "pleasure quarters," and refers to the district in town where the licensed brothels were situated until all prostitution was outlawed. While searching for a term for brothel that seemed most likely to be used by felines, the translators came across the US slang "cathouse." This seemed like the perfect word for it until the translators realized that any house inhabited by a character in this series could reasonably be called a cathouse, with or without prostitutes, and so they have substituted another obscure word for a lady of leisure, which is also homonymous with a word for an experienced female cat.

Tama, page 73

BUT DIDN'T YOU FIGURE IT OUT FROM THE BELL? THE TRUTH IS, HE WAS ONCE KEPT BY A PERSON WHO CALLED HIM TAMA.

Perhaps because of their tendency to curl up into near-spherical shapes, cats in Japan are commonly named Tama, meaning "ball." Maybe it was the absurd size of the round bell on Tama's neck, or maybe it was the size of a certain part of his anatomy, that inspired his friends and acquaintances to call him Ōdama, meaning "big ball(s)."

Koban, page 76

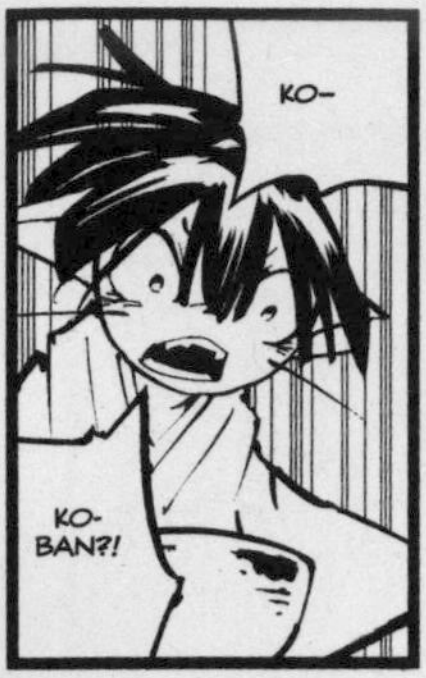
KO-
KO-BAN?!

In the Edo Era, oval-shaped koban gold coins were used as a form of currency. Originally, one koban would be enough to buy enough rice to eat for at least a year. The coins are frequently associated with cats, not only because they are carved into maneki neko (lucky cat) statues and figures, but also because of the saying "koban before cats." This phrase is the Japanese equivalent to "pearls before swine," and refers to giving something of value to someone who cannot understand its worth.

Tanegashima, page 85

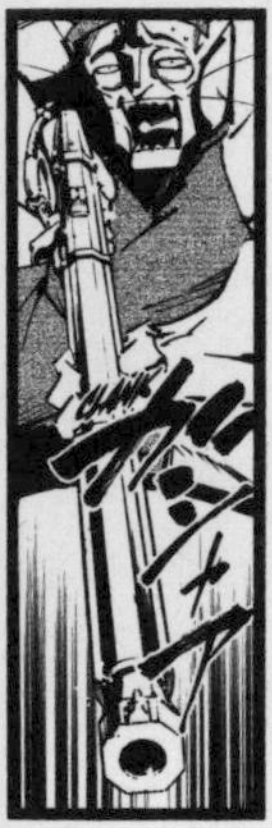

Here the foreman of the bathhouse is equipped with a Tanegashima, or Hinawajū, matchlock gun. This model of firearm was based on the matchlock guns that were brought to Japan by Portuguese sailors in 1543.

A bald fox, page 124

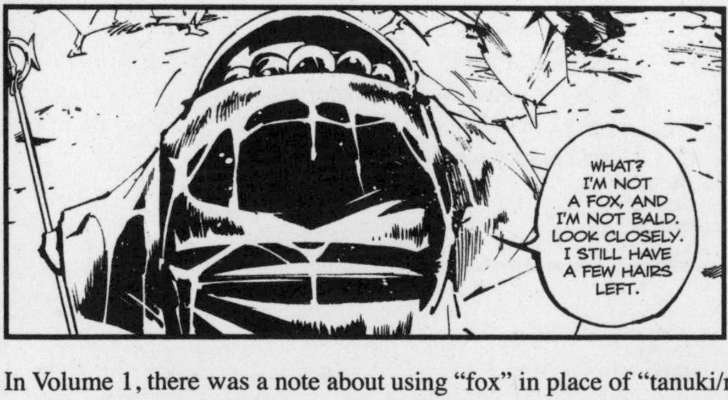
WHAT? I'M NOT A FOX, AND I'M NOT BALD. LOOK CLOSELY. I STILL HAVE A FEW HAIRS LEFT.

In Volume 1, there was a note about using "fox" in place of "tanuki/raccoon-dog" to express a sly and cunning animal that would be easily recognized by Western readers, and for consistency, this usage was retained in this volume. However, the use of "tanuki" in this scene may also play into the fact that Little Fold is a rather portly cat, as statues and other images of tanuki often portray them as having large bellies.

Shimagara, page 145

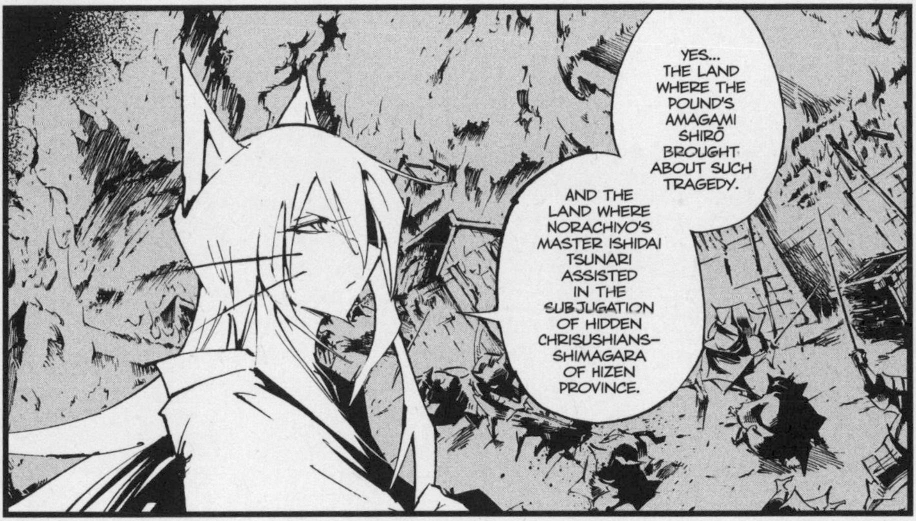
YES... THE LAND WHERE THE POUND'S AMAGAMI SHIRŌ BROUGHT ABOUT SUCH TRAGEDY.
AND THE LAND WHERE NORACHIYO'S MASTER ISHIDAI TSUNARI ASSISTED IN THE SUBJUGATION OF HIDDEN CHRISUSHIANS– SHIMAGARA OF HIZEN PROVINCE.

The name of Shishiwaka's home island is remarkably similar to the real-life island of Shimabara, where a young man named Amakusa Shirō led a band of Christians in a rebellion against the local government. This rebellion had little to do with the subjugation of Christians led by Norachiyo's master's real-life counterpart, Ishida Mitsunari, who was following orders from a shogun who feared that the Christians were plotting to take over Japan.
It may also be noted that the island name here, Shimagara, is a homophone for a word meaning "striped pattern," like the one you might find on a tabby cat.

Kitchen of the Nation, page 149

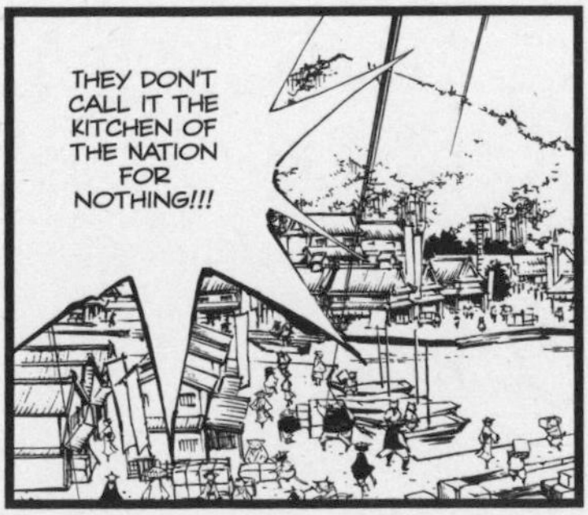
THEY DON'T CALL IT THE KITCHEN OF THE NATION FOR NOTHING!!!

In the real world, this was a nickname for Osaka, as it was the commercial center of Japan. One of its cities, Sakai, has been one of the most important seaports in the country for centuries.

The Black Museum: The Ghost and the Lady

By Kazuhiro Fujita

Deep in Scotland Yard in London sits an evidence room dedicated to the greatest mysteries of British history. In this "Black Museum" sits a misshapen hunk of lead—two bullets fused together—the key to a wartime encounter between Florence Nightingale, the mother of modern nursing, and a supernatural Man in Grey. This story is unknown to most scholars of history, but a special guest of the museum will tell the tale of The Ghost and the Lady...

Praise for Kazuhiro Fujita's *Ushio and Tora*

"A charming revival that combines a classic look with modern depth and pacing... **Essential viewing both for curmudgeons and new fans alike.**" — Anime News Network

"**GREAT!** The first episode of Ushio and Tora captures the essence of '90s anime." — IGN

Japan's most powerful spirit medium delves into the ghost world's greatest mysteries!

Story by Kyo Shirodaira, famed author of mystery fiction and creator of *Spiral*, *Blast of Tempest*, and *The Record of a Fallen Vampire*.

Both touched by spirits called yôkai, Kotoko and Kurô have gained unique superhuman powers. But to gain her powers Kotoko has given up an eye and a leg, and Kurô's personal life is in shambles. So when Kotoko suggests they team up to deal with renegades from the spirit world, Kurô doesn't have many other choices, but Kotoko might just have a few ulterior motives...

IN/SPECTRE

STORY BY KYO SHIRODAIRA
ART BY CHASHIBA KATASE

A Kodansha Comics Trade Paperback Original.

Nekogahara: Stray Cat Samurai volume 4 copyright © 2018 Hiroyuki Takei
English translation copyright © 2018 Hiroyuki Takei

All rights reserved.

Published in the United States by Kodansha Comics,
an imprint of Kodansha USA Publishing, LLC, New York.

Publication rights for this English edition arranged through Kodansha Ltd.,
Tokyo.

First published in Japan in 2018 by Kodansha Ltd., Tokyo, as *Nekogahara*
volume 4.

ISBN 978-1-63236-438-8

Printed in the United States of America.

www.kodanshacomics.com

9 8 7 6 5 4 3 2 1

Translation: Alethea Nibley & Athena Nibley
Lettering: Scott O. Brown
Editing: Ajani Oloye
Kodansha Comics edition cover design: Phil Balsman